# SM 101

## A Realistic Introduction

### Second Edition

## by Jay Wiseman

greenery press

Cover photograph by MichaelAdrienne.

Published in the United States by Greenery Press. Distributed by SCB Distributors, Gardena, CA.

# Table of Contents

## Acknowledgements, first edition

My thanks to Robin Roberts of Backdrop for being my first teacher. Robin has taught many valuable lessons to many people over the years, and he doesn't get the credit he deserves.

My thanks to the late Cynthia Slater, founder of The Society of Janus, for setting such a wonderful example of vision, courage, integrity, and clarity.

My thanks to Bill Burns and the other wonderful folks associated with the Service of Mankind Church for their support and friendship over the years, through both good times and bad.

My thanks to the many, many wonderful people of The Society of Janus who have given and taught me so much over the years. I hope I have given at least a fraction of that back.

My thanks to Mistress Lana White, whom I have been proud to call a close personal friend for nearly twenty years.

My thanks to Mistress Augusta Fury, who "interned" under me with skill, grace, and a wonderfully vital intelligence. Few things please a teacher more than watching a pupil grow and develop so beautifully under their guidance.

Recognizing that "the first rule of friendship is to be there in time of need," my thanks to Bill, Bruce, Charlie, Don, Fran, Frank, Glenn, Joann, Josh, KJ, Lynn, Karen F., Karen M., Marie, Mic, Nicole, Robin S., Ronnie, Sage, Scott, Sherry, Tom, and the many others who, on several occasions, held me, healed me, and helped me get back on my feet after life knocked me over.

And, finally, my thanks to Janet. To love and be loved, absolutely, unconditionally, and wholeheartedly, is one of the most divine joys a human being can experience. Thank you so much for bringing that joy into my life.

## Acknowledgements, second edition

I would like to think that I've learned and grown a great deal in the years since the first edition of this book was published. Listed below are some of the people who helped in this growth. Some I talked with, some I argued with, some I hung out with, some I played with, and some I did all of the above with. (You get to guess which is which.) My thanks to you all.

| | |
|---|---|
| Bert Herrman | Cecelia Tan & Corwin |
| Bill Henkin | Charles Moser |
| Bill Majors | China |
| B.N. Duncan | Constance |
| Brandie | Damien |
| Carol Queen | David & Molly |
| Cat | Deborah Addington |

Derek
Donnie Rice
Dossie Easton
Elizabeth of Differences
Empress Eisanna
Francesca Guido
Glenn Olsen
Gregg Loy
Guy Baldwin
Jaymes Easton
Janette Heartwood
Joel Tucker
John Warren
Joseph Bean
Karen Mendelsohn
Kim M.
Lady Cassandra
Lady Tanith
Laura Goodwin
Laurie O.
Lee Hawaii

Leona Joy
Leonard & Michelle
Manx
Mark & Laura Lee
Michael Decker
Molly Devon
Nadja & Lurker
Oberon & Morning Glory Zell
Philip The Foole
Phillip Miller
Robert Dante
Robert Morgan
Russell Brunelle & Erika
Snow White
Susan S.
Sybil Holiday
THYST-L
Tom B.
Tony DeBlase
Wayne & Margo

Special thanks to Lori Zieran, Maryann B., and The Nymphet.

And finally, once again, my thanks to Janet, for the many years of love, for the adventures and misadventures, and for her utterly superb and outstanding help with this book.

**The publisher's special thanks go to Frites and Chameleon for helping this book become a reality.**

engaged in by millions of people all over the world throughout history.

7.  Opinions vary about SM – especially regarding safety. Some activities I consider safe are regarded as unsafe by others; some activities they consider safe I regard as unsafe. Please try to get different opinions regarding the safety of various activities. Listen carefully to all, and make your own decision.

8.  No widely accepted quality or safety standards exist for most SM equipment. What we know about safe design we mostly learned through painful experience. Many items used in SM, including most in this book, were never designed or intended for such use. Therefore, the risk of using them may be much greater than apparent. Also, possession of some SM equipment is illegal in some states. Check your state's laws, appropriate federal laws, and other regulations. Make sure you are not breaking the law by simply possessing certain items. Consult a knowledgeable attorney if necessary.

9.  *Please do not rely on this book as your sole source of information.* Perspective is essential to understanding SM. While I have done my best to present it realistically, mine is still only one point of view. The Bibliography cites several other excellent books and magazines on this topic.

    If you can, contact an SM club. Attend its functions and talk with its members. Seek out opinions and advice from experienced, knowledgeable people. However, remember that just because somebody has done something for a long time does not itself guarantee they understand it – particularly regarding health and safety. As in other areas, some people who claim "ten years of experience" actually have one year of experience repeated nine times. Listen carefully and politely, but do not automatically and uncritically accept anyone's advice or opinions – including mine.

10. SM compares to conventional sex in ways similar to how flying a small aircraft compares to walking to the corner store. Neither is entirely safe, but the former is much riskier. SM is not so dangerous that everyone should avoid it but, much like flying, mountain climbing, white water rafting, skydiving, bungee jumping, or auto racing, its substantial risks demand that you approach it with a responsible, mature appreciation of the knowledge, judgment, ethics, and skill required to participate in it safely, consensually, and with caring.

*This book is lovingly dedicated
to the memory of Don Miesen
a brilliant SM pioneer
a generous friend to those in need
and a thorough scamp*

# Preface

This book is about passion. While much of it is philosophical, sociological, or technical, underlying it all is passion – erotic, sexual passion. No one really knows from where, or why, this passion arises, but arise it does.

I cannot place this passion within you. It's either there or it's not, and you must, if you so wish, discover that for yourself. Like a whitewater-rafting instructor, I can teach you things that will assist you while you are being carried along by its current, but neither I nor anybody else can implant this passion within you. Dance steps can be taught, but dancing cannot.

## About the Quotes

Throughout this book, in an attempt to convey a taste of what it's like to engage in SM or to be part of the SM community, I have included a number of quips, remarks, and other comments I've heard over the years. None of the people felt, as far as I know, that they were making a "significant" statement at the time they spoke. These are just passing comments, and therefore, more revealing.

# Sonnet 57

Being your slave, what should I do but tend
Upon the hours and times of your desire?
I have no precious time at all to spend,
Nor services to do till you require.
Nor dare I chide the world-without-end hour
Whilst I, my sovereign, watch the clock for you,
Nor think the bitterness of absence sour
When you have bid your servant once adieu.
Nor dare I question with my jealous thought
Where you may be, or your affairs suppose,
But, like a sad slave, stay and think of naught
Save where you are how happy you make those.

So true a fool is love that in your will,
Though you do anything, he thinks no ill.

– *William Shakespeare*

# Preliminaries

## *Introduction* _____

So many of you are out there, wondering. I know some of your questions, and something of the torment these questions often cause.

First, know you are not alone. You may believe you are the only person in the world interested in SM. Let me say to you, quietly but emphatically, that no matter how bizarre, extreme, or "perverted" your fantasies and desires may seem to you, please know that thousands of other people have similar thoughts. Indeed, if one highly credible source can be believed (<u>Sexual Behavior in the Human Female</u>, by Kinsey, Pomeroy, and Martin; published way back in 1953), at least 11% of the population feels attracted to SM.

> Learning how
> to do SM
> is like
> learning how to
> have sex
> all over again.

## *The Purpose of This Book* _____

I am writing this because (1) I believe many people want and need a realistic introduction to SM, (2) I believe I have enough knowledge and experience to provide such an introduction, and (3) I want to make a whole lot of money. Let's look at those reasons one at a time.

1. I believe that by far the greatest reason people fear SM is that they don't understand it. In this book I will clearly explain the basics of what SM is and what it is not.
2. I have been in the SM community for more than 20 years. I have spent time as both a dominant and a submissive, have talked with many other practitioners at length, and have met people from all over the world who enjoy SM.

   I do not claim to be a "World Class Expert" on SM. (I would suggest that you be wary of anyone who does.) Many people understand its fine points, depths, and nuances better than I do, but I believe most of them would agree with me on most points in this book.

3

3. I believe the information in this book will be of far greater value to you than the money you paid for it. (You *did* buy it, didn't you?) Thus we have a fair exchange in which we both come out ahead. That's a great way to make money.

4. Another purpose of this book is to ease the terrible pain and isolation SM people often feel. I want this book to be a resource that enables those people to contact the mainstream community.

My basic goal in writing this book is to provide you with a level of knowledge about equal to that contained in an introductory college class. (Four units. Three hours lecture, two hours lab per week.) In other words, to get you basically oriented and informed. After that, I'll toss you to the experts.

I know of only a few "experts" in the traditional, academic sense. This form of sexuality has traditionally been discovered by individuals and handed down by word-of-mouth, lovers who taught lovers who taught lovers. As far as I know, the first edition of "SM 101" was the most comprehensive discussion of this information at the time of its publication. One of my goals was and is to put SM basics down in tangible form. I wanted to write a "pillow book" about SM – something one lover could give to another.

*Please* seek the advice and opinions of knowledgeable others. Choosing whether or not to participate in SM – and, if so, to what extent – is a terribly important decision. You want to make as informed a choice as possible, and your ability to do that is hampered if your information sources are limited. By all means, get as many "second opinions" as you feel necessary.

Also, I want my fellow community members to regard this book as an explicit invitation to contribute their own thoughts, feelings, and expertise. Please don't conclude that this book tells all that needs to be told. We could have used a dozen or more books on this topic a dozen or more years ago. If you are working on a book, article, video, or other project that portrays SM realistically, please feel free to contact me regarding whatever advice or assistance I can offer.

For too long, the only widely available material on SM concentrated on its extreme, pathological aspects such as sex murders (which I don't consider SM at all), or unrealistic fantasy material that perhaps made interesting reading, but was of little practical value. We in the SM community need to remedy that situation.

I worry somewhat about writing this book, because I know some people, despite how carefully and reasonably I present its contents, will be outraged by its mere existence. They will argue I am advocating, rationalizing, or assisting cruelty, violence against women, immoral behavior, sin, and so forth. They will assert the information I present could be used to nonconsensually torture somebody, even if I never intended that. They will insist this knowledge is dangerous and should be suppressed.

My response is as follows:

1. I am absolutely not advocating cruelty, violence against women, or anything similar. SM is distinctly different, and I believe an informed person will readily grasp those differences. I hope that, after reading this book, my reader will be such an informed person.

2. It's true someone could misuse this information. However, it takes no intelligence to be brutal, and information on techniques is everywhere. Your local library contains abundant information. Indeed, anyone who wanted to learn how to torture somebody could learn all they needed to know by reading the Bible.

I think *much* more harm is caused by misinformed or improperly educated people than by intentional abuse. One of my goals is to educate people so that, if you will pardon the term, "unintentional" injuries do not occur. Another of my goals is to clarify what behavior the SM community considers pathological.

I've occasionally heard of creeps trying to persuade their lovers to accept abuse because it was "part of SM." I hope the exposure provided by this book greatly reduces such incidents. The Bible says, "He who doeth evil hateth the light." I want this book to be a floodlight, exposing evil and cruelty.

As to suppression, that is impossible. The recent emergence of films and books with an SM slant, the popularity of handcuffs and chain-style necklaces as jewelry, and the groundswell of interest in the subject (almost 100 SM clubs now exist in the U.S., with several new ones appearing yearly, and they are swamped with inquiries) make suppression completely unrealistic. What *is* realistic is disseminating accurate information.

*SM relationships are ultimately relationships between equals.*

## Why Am I Writing This?

Hello there, Humankind. My full, legal name is Jay Joseph Wiseman. I'm a heterosexual, Caucasian male and I was born in New Albany, Indiana, on June 16, 1949.

For more than 25 years, I have studied, practiced, and taught the erotic activity most of you know as sadomasochism (SM for short). Before we go on, let me add that you may have a *very* different understanding of that term than I have. Indeed, a large part of the reason I'm writing this book is to make sure we are talking about the same subject before we discuss it at any length.

Since 1975, I have been a "known member" of a loosely organized, highly diverse group of individuals informally known as the Bay Area SM community. (Please understand that this is a term of collective recognition; no organization with that particular name exists.)

Like all communities, we are a varied lot. We have several (self-appointed) "in crowds" and we have "outcasts." We have our stars and our peasants. We have our leaders and our followers. Within this community, people make friends and enemies. Within this community, people start romantic relationships and end them. Within this community, people gossip, flirt, bitch, hug, conspire, invent, backstab, celebrate, and sometimes mourn. For reasons I will explain later, I consider the people of this community, when considered as a whole, to be the finest group of human beings it has ever been my proud privilege to know.

*( from a student in a beginners' SM class )* Are all sadomasochists as friendly and nurturing as you guys?

One of the most noticeable characteristics about the Bay Area SM community is its rate of growth. We are *much* larger now than when I first arrived in 1975, and we're getting bigger all the time. In 1975, only about four organizations existed. All were relatively small and somewhat underground. More than a dozen clubs exist in the area today, along with as many stores, support groups, and similar resources. While exact figures don't exist, the number of Bay Area people who have willingly participated in at least one explicitly SM-oriented event easily runs into the thousands or even tens of thousands. Furthermore, this phenomenon is not by any means confined to this area. SM organizations also exist in New York, Los Angeles, Chicago, and many, many other cities.

And there's more. A recent article in the San Francisco Chronicle mentioned that 25% of all adults in this country have at least experimented with bondage.

SM is the riskiest form of sex (and bondage is one of the riskier aspects of SM). In addition to having all risks of regular sex, SM involves, to put it plainly, such things as one person tying another person up, striking them with various blunt instruments, and otherwise "torturing" them. Under such circumstances, the results of either intentional abuse (rare) or accidental injury (much more common) can be serious, even fatal. Unfortunately, "basic

6

instruction manuals" for this form of sex are nowhere near as widely available as they should be.

So the situation is that literally tens of millions of people are experimenting on their own with the riskiest form of sex with little or no basic instruction in its techniques and safety measures. This is, to put it *very* mildly, unacceptable.

Therefore, I've taken it upon myself to write such a basic instructional manual. I have more than 25 years of experience in SM. I've given presentations on this topic, either by myself or as part of a panel, dozens of times. Furthermore, I'd like to think that I'm good at presenting information in a useful, written form. I'm not an expert in all aspects of SM (nobody is), but I have the knowledge and experience required to write a solid introduction.

Consider this book a starting point. It won't cover everything. It won't deal with advanced philosophies or practices. It won't go into in-depth discussion of SM's fine points. It won't cover any particular subject in exhaustive detail. Those are matters for my knowledgeable fellow practitioners to write about, and some of them have done so.

This book's purpose is to turn a basically uninformed reader into a basically informed reader, and to turn an unknowledgeable, and therefore unsafe, "player" into a knowledgeable, safe "player."

I've included numerous resources for additional learning and growth. Please take advantage of these resources. While my perspective is a valuable one, there are many other valuable perspectives (and, candidly, a few that are not so valuable). Please seek them out. The more of them you become familiar with, the better your understanding will be.

My main priority in writing this book is to help you become a safe player, not turn you into some sort of kinky sex demon. Because the primary goal of this book is to reduce the number of accidental injuries that occur during SM erotic play, I am going to emphasize the safety aspects. If you look through this book for "hot parts," you're going to be disappointed.

## *Sexual Extremes*

"That's too much." "That's going too far."

In my life, I have seen many sexual activities labeled "going too far." When I was a child in an average American neighborhood, sex within marriage was permitted, but pre-marital sex was "going too far." I remember when vaginal intercourse was all right but oral sex was "going too far." Then oral sex became acceptable but anal sex was "going too far." Then came group sex, then bisexuality, then... Where will this end?

I believe almost all of the SM community would agree that the following activities would be "going too far."

1.  Doing anything without informed, freely given consent. (I use the consent definition formulated by therapist and SM author Dossie Easton: "An active collaboration for the benefit, well-being, and pleasure of all persons concerned.")
2.  Doing anything that causes great damage or death, even with consent.
3.  Doing anything with someone incapable of consent – for example, someone too young, too intoxicated, or too mentally unbalanced to give consent.

Society agrees with these limits. Laws exist regarding all three conditions, and I want to encourage my readers to obey all applicable laws.

> I can tell instantly if a man is dominant or submissive: I just tell him to sit on the couch. If he's submissive, he'll obey at once. If he looks at me for a moment, deciding for himself, he's dominant.

I'm serious about that. Obey the laws. Some, like laws regarding age of consent, are highly arbitrary, but I want you to obey them. If you think they're unfair, then work to change them or move to an area where what you want to do isn't against the law, but don't break the law.

As I write this, SM activists around the world are working hard to change unfair laws. SM clubs, publications, and Internet newsgroups can keep you informed about the status of these changes and about how you can help.

## Who Is This Book For?

If you are already a member of the SM community, this book is not aimed primarily at you. While you may find it useful, and while I won't feel at all insulted if you buy it, as a community member you are probably already familiar with at least the basics of such subjects as negotiation, safewords, consent, limits, and so forth. Furthermore, you already have access to that most wonderful of resources: a supportive peer group.

This book is primarily for the person who has not yet contacted our community. This book is for the single person or couple in a small town, hundreds of miles from the nearest SM club. This book is for the person who knows of no other reliable source of basic, realistic information, and who is exploring (and learning the hard way) on their own. This book is for the person whose life circumstances force them to remain deeply "in the closet." This book is for the person experiencing terrible pain and loneliness because they feel certain they are the only person in the world with such "sick, perverted" desires.

**The scope of this book.** An old writing truism goes: it's possible to write about any subject at any length. Another is: it's always possible to improve the grammar, clarity, and power of something you've already written. Given those facts, I had to decide what should, and should not, be covered in this book. I could boil it down to one page or I could expand it to over 1000 pages.

One rational criterion available to a writer is to decide what the work is intended to accomplish, and to evaluate it from that perspective. Will the form it's in accomplish the "mission" of the book? How do I want my readers to be different after they've read it? Will what I've written create the change I desire? If it will, then the book is arguably "done."

**Gender neutrality.** I have made a diligent effort to write this book in as "gender neutral" a style as possible. (It may not be possible to write a completely pansexual SM book, at least partly because too many people judge a book based much more on its author's sexual orientation than on the book's actual content. However, I've done my best.) An interest in SM spans all sexual orientations. SM is popular with gay men, lesbians, bisexuals, transsexuals, and heterosexuals. I therefore tried to write this book in a way that favors no particular gender or sexual orientation.

> Just because you're a slave to your lover in the bedroom doesn't mean you have to be a slave to him in the rest of your life.

**Basic SM vs. advanced SM.** There is no such thing as risk-free SM. Furthermore, opinions regarding which practices are acceptably safe vary between expert practitioners. This book is an introductory text that describes the most basic, safest practices. Please understand that experienced practitioners may play with "advanced" procedures that you, as a beginner, may have been told "never" to do. This does not necessarily make such people unsafe or irresponsible players; it also does not make them "better" than you. Nor should you think it inevitable that you will one day do such things.

Please understand that, as is true in many other fields, highly experienced practitioners may choose to do things that beginners are told to avoid. If you see what appears to be an experienced player doing something that you were told never to do, consider asking them about it afterwards. They may (or may not) know something useful – most of them are skilled, careful practitioners, but some of them are reckless nutcases. As always, listen carefully and come to your own conclusions.

An invitation to knowledgeable others. Many people understand SM more deeply than I understand it. Many people understand some technical aspects of it much better than I do. I want such people to see the publication of this book as an explicit invitation to contribute works of their own. This is an introductory manual, not the last word.

People benefit by hearing from more than one perspective. Furthermore, I'm certain that some of my SM "peers" will disagree with at least a few points I make in this book. All well and good! Let such dissenting opinions (provided they're not *too* nasty) be published as quickly as possible! The good-faith discussion of differences often allows underlying truths, and points of agreement, to emerge. Everyone benefits from that.

Also, please do me (and everyone else involved) a favor. If you are an experienced SM person, I expect you will agree with most points I've made in this book. However, I don't expect you to agree with all of them, and it won't shock me if there are a few assertions in here that you find outrageous. (One of the questions I've learned to ask whenever I publish a book is, "What am I going to get yelled at for writing *this* time?") If you believe there is a factual error in here, or if you believe I'm somehow otherwise off base, please feel free to write me and let me know. It would also be nice to hear what you *do* agree with. Please keep your letters brief (I won't read dissertations) and reasonably polite. Also include how I can contact you. I assure you that I'll carefully consider your comments.

I've been tied up on five continents.

Truth be told, I wish I didn't feel so alone out here on this "stage." I'm just a former ambulance crewman doing his flawed best to keep people from hurting themselves and each other due to a lack of basic information.

Headquarters, this is Medic 35. We are on the scene, and the problem is far bigger and more serious than we believed. Please send additional units at once. Medic needs help!

## *What is SM?*

I define SM as the knowing use of psychological dominance and submission, and/or physical bondage, and/or pain, and/or related practices in a safe, legal, consensual manner in order for the participants to experience erotic arousal and/or personal growth.

A widely accepted upper limit to SM is that the dominant will not do anything to the submissive (and, for that matter, the submissive will not do anything to the dominant) that would require a physician, psychotherapist, or other external resource to heal.

Because SM varies widely in manner and intensity, people use several terms to describe it. "Bondage and Discipline" (B&D) should rationally refer to the dominant restraining the submissive in some fashion, then "training" them to behave in certain ways. However, it more commonly refers to "lighter" SM, and not the more "extreme" sadomasochism. Unfortunately, no uniform opinion exists regarding where the line lies between the two.

Another term sometimes used is "D&S" or "DS," referring to "Domination and Submission." This is more to the point.

"SDS," for "Sexual Domination and Submission," had been proposed and is actually quite good, but "SDS" has unfortunate political implications.

A new overall descriptive term rapidly gaining currency is "BDSM," which incorporates Bondage & Discipline, Domination & Submission, and Sadism & Masochism.

However, tradition has firmly established the slightly alarming and rather easy to misunderstand term "sadomasochism" as the word in general use to describe this area of sexuality. Sadomasochism is long and polysyllabic, so it's more commonly abbreviated to S&M, S/M, or simply SM. I'll use the term SM throughout this book. (It's easier to type.)

'A stiff prick has no conscience' – what a contemptible rationalization!

## Is SM for You?

Statistically speaking, probably not. SM people can be subdivided into "self-motivated" people, who themselves desire to do this, and "other-motivated" people, who have the subject brought up by their lovers. The Kinsey study of 1953 concluded that only about 11% of the population felt self-motivated to try explicit SM-type behavior such as bondage, whipping, and so forth.

My experience has led me to believe that, when other-motivated people (no previous SM desires or fantasies) are offered a safe chance to experience it, their reaction will put them into one of three groups with about equal frequency.

The first group is just not interested in SM, not even in its lightest, least threatening form. They won't try being submissive. They won't try being dominant. They're not interested, period. That's it. No way. Take your whips and go home.

The second group will sample SM but, with time, they'll come to know that it doesn't arouse them. They may continue doing it if that pleases their lover (and may start resenting it if their lover wants SM too often or intensely), but it arouses nothing in them personally. They eventually will drift away.

The third group will try SM, and these people will discover (and I specifically mean discover, as opposed to decide) that SM arouses them. They may go through changes – indeed, this may become a personal sexual odyssey – in terms of interest and taste (for instance, they may start as a dominant and discover they prefer being submissive – or vice versa) but they learn that, in one form or other, at some level of intensity or other, SM moves them.

That final third may actively, even lustily, enjoy SM during that relationship. However, if the relationship should end, only about one-third of them will take the initiative of raising the subject of SM with their next lover. In other words, two out of three probably will *not* suggest SM to their next lover.

This leaves the final group of one-third of one-third, or about 11%, of those who try SM and will try it again with their next lover. That 11% figure equals the Kinsey estimate.

I can remember going to the circus when I was about four years old, and fantasizing about being spanked by the strong man.

In summary, SM does not appeal to most people, but does appeal very strongly to a significant percentage of the population.

**Monday Morning Rebound Syndrome.** I sometimes ran into a curious phenomenon back in the '70s, when I was single and dating "vanilla" women. These ladies would try SM for the first time, usually in the submissive role, and find doing so deeply erotic. They would really get off on it, and have a grand old time. Dating realities being what they are, such sessions usually occurred on a Saturday night.

We would usually spend a hot, erotic night and a friendly, relaxed next day together. I would then return to my home with every reason to believe that all was well. What occasionally happened is that I would call them on Monday night and be told, often in a somewhat angry or frightened voice, "I never want to see you again." As I said, this was rare, but did happen often enough that I came to think of it as the "Monday Morning Rebound Syndrome."

What was going on? As far as I could tell, everything had gone just fine. I was certainly never accused of doing anything nonconsensual or of going too far. Furthermore, there was no question that the erotic response of the lady involved had been strong, positive, and genuine. Yet afterwards she was freaking out, or "bolting," as it's sometimes called. Why?

Unfortunately, I can only speculate as to the reasons. I imagine that by far the most common reason was that these women had seen an aspect of themselves that made them feel very uncomfortable. While I think "Monday Morning Rebound Syndrome" can certainly affect novice men and women of all orientations, I also think that, particularly given the feminist tone of those times, those women's discovery of their erotic submissiveness to men was more than they could handle. (Women submitting to men, no matter how consensually and willingly, is still the "least politically correct" form of SM.) I hope that those women have since been able to integrate their desires and their politics in a fulfilling way.

## You May Already Be "Into SM"

The dividing line between SM sex and "vanilla" sex can sometimes be arbitrary. Obviously, somebody who owns a suitcase full of whips, chains, restraints, and so forth is "into SM." But what about the woman who can reach orgasm by having her nipples bitten? What about the man who really loves it when his girlfriend gets on top of him and fucks him silly? What about the two lovers who really get off on tying each other up with silk scarves? What about the person who loves getting spanked?

We, too, are everywhere.

If you enjoy erotic play that involves one person holding the other down or restraining them in any way, or involves one person giving the other orders, or involves any form of erotic pain such as biting, scratching, spanking, and so forth, then what you do could fall under the broadest definition of SM. You may already be a "pervert." Congratulations!

## Why On Earth Would Anybody Want to Do this Stuff in the First Place?

Why, indeed. That question, perhaps more than any other, has caused many people great emotional pain. I think that anybody who has an "other than conventional" sexual interest must have wondered why they feel that way.

The "why" question is too broad to answer with a single reason. No one right answer exists. However, if we break the question into smaller pieces, and take them one at a time, we can make progress.

It's like asking, "Why do people go to the movies?" Those who go find it rewarding, at least enough so to continue going. Exactly what is rewarding, and how rewarding it is, varies from person to person. SM is like that.

One important aspect of this question is defining conventional sex. Not long ago, many if not most people considered oral sex and anal sex, even among heterosexuals, "sick," "disgusting," "perverted," and "unnatural." Some people still regard them in that way, and laws forbidding these practices – with lengthy prison terms for "violators" – exist in many states.

So as we ponder "why," it helps to remember that there is no universal agreement regarding "natural" and "unnatural" sex practices; people define them in many different ways. (As opposed to robbery, for example, where much more widespread agreement exists.) Many sexual practices considered unspeakable in one culture or period of history are considered normal, even preferable, in another. Indeed, if you think there's such a thing as "natural" sex, consider the variety of sexual expression found among animals.

Still, most men and women, even if they've had a reasonable exposure to SM, feel no attraction to it. Why do others?

The first seemingly reasonable explanation is that people attracted to SM, particularly submissives or masochists, must be mentally disturbed. (Many people believe they can imagine why someone would want to be dominant or sadistic. But why would someone want to be given orders, tied up, or – God help them – whipped? How can *pain*, of all things, be enjoyable? A person who desires to feel pain is clearly crazy.)

*Most couples don't have conversations like this.*

Well, if so, there certainly are a *lot* of "sickies." As I mentioned earlier, at least one person in nine feels attracted to SM. Also about one person in three discovers that they enjoy SM. Can one-third of the population be sexually sick?

Furthermore, these sickies deal with their illness remarkably well. My SM friends hold jobs as well as my non-SM friends. They begin and end relationships, marry and divorce, and make both friends and enemies with a frequency apparently equal to that of non-SM people. They seem to have no greater or lesser frequency of alcoholism, suicide, mental illness, or history of having endured child abuse. In fact, they seem identical to "normal" people.

One study (An Initial Study of Nonclinical Practitioners of Sexual Sadomasochism by Janet P. Miale, 1986, the Professional School of Psychological Studies, San Diego, CA) found no significant differences between a group of SM people and a control group of "normal" people.

So, if we're not crazy, what are we?

I think many people explore SM because, as horny creatures, we feel somewhat curious about all forms of sex. Most heterosexual couples explore sexual intercourse in various positions, locations, and times of day. Many also try oral sex and anal sex. Some try "mate swapping," group sex, and bisexuality. As they work down the sexual menu, these couples come to SM. It's yet another sexual adventure, perhaps made more alluring by being considered too far out by many.

What many of us are, then, is not crazy, but explorative.

**Beyond Curiosity.** Even the most conventional sexual arousal is not "rational." Arousal is deeply emotional, physiological, sensual, even primordial. It involves sights, sounds, touches, tastes, smells. Sexual arousal is ultimately (and "ultimately" arrives quickly) visceral.

Let me add that sexual arousal is also highly individual. If you have no empathy for another person's turn-ons, they will probably appear ridiculous, or even repulsive, to you. Even if you share a particular interest, another person's activity may look overrated. If you have ever directly watched other people having sex, you may understand what I mean.

Why would somebody get aroused by "kinky" stuff? Could it be imprinting? Past trauma? Early childhood experiences? In some cases, undoubtedly so, but not in every case, or even most cases. For many of us, though, this is much more than simple curiosity or a reaction to something in our pasts; it's been a deeply ingrained part of us for as long as we can remember.

Some motivations *are* pathological. Dominants may have "old stuff" going on regarding frustration, sadists regarding anger, submissives regarding dependency, masochists regarding guilt or self-loathing. But I see no evidence that everybody who enjoys SM has these things going on, at least no more so than "normal" people. Also, most people who enjoy SM find it rewarding to switch roles sometimes. They enjoy both dominant and submissive energy.

I think many people find the experience of SM itself rewarding because there is an excitement, an *intensity*, to SM, that many people don't feel with "normal" sex. People don't repeat behavior that is not rewarding, and SM is highly rewarding for many. The nature and degree of that reward seems more than one would expect from the "acting out" of psychological flaws.

**The limbic system.** Not just SM folks, but a great many "normal" people, combine some aspects of domination and submission with their sexuality. (Many is the time, prior to my becoming interested in SM, that a straight woman would cry out "take me" or "I'll do anything you want" to me during the heat of passion.) Clearly, there are elements of domination and submission connected with the sexuality of many people who do not identify as being into SM. What's going on?

I have a very strong hunch that the answer may lie deep within our brains. More specifically, the answer may lie in the part of our brains known as the limbic system. This part of our brain is connected with emotions, instincts, drives, learning, and memory. Stimulating certain parts of the limbic system will result in the person feeling anger, pleasure, fear, or sexual arousal. Furthermore, stimulating certain parts of the limbic system may result in other parts of it also becoming aroused. For example, stimulating the anger part may also cause arousal in the sexual part. This is sometimes called the "fuck/fight syndrome." It sometimes expresses itself when two members of a couple, while having a furious argument, suddenly realizing that they are terribly hot for one another and want to have sex *right then*. It also sometimes expresses itself when, after a period of very satisfying sex, one person will suddenly start an argument with the other, for no apparent reason.

Given that we see these behaviors, given that we know that the brains of men are subtly but definitely different from those of women, and given that there is at least some evidence that the brains of male homosexuals may be subtly different than the brains of male heterosexuals, it's reasonable to wonder if the brains of SM folks are also subtly different from the brains of non-SM folks. Could there be some sort of enhanced connectivity between the sexual arousal section of the limbic system and the anger (domination) and/or the fear (submission) sections of the brain? Could arousal in one section cause above-average arousal in another section? Possibly. Actually, very possibly.

Their
fantasies
always
bring
them back.

If this is so, then a major difference between SM people and non-SM people is that SM people bring these facts out and look at them. They try to figure out how to deal with the urges and desires thus created in a safe and realistic way. They devise rules to control and contain these urges and desires, and thus give them form. In a word, they "ritualize" how these urges will be expressed. Therefore, if I had to describe SM in a very concise manner, I'd describe it as "ritualized sexual aggression and submission."

**Why are so many people against SM?** The major reason I used to be "in the closet" about my interest in SM (other than the normal reluctance to discuss the details of my sex life with anyone other than my lover) was that when I told somebody about my interest in SM, they usually had a radically different image of SM than I had.

I see SM as a caring, consensual, safe form of intense erotic play that causes no significant damage (much less than is caused by participating in many sports). Most uninformed people, on the other hand, conjure up images of rape, wife-beating, mental coercion, kidnapping, and psychopathic torture. They think that stuff turns me on! No wonder they conclude that I'm dangerously crazy.

So let me make a few things clear. I oppose rape. I oppose wife-beating. I oppose mental coercion. I oppose kidnapping. And, yes, prude that I am, I oppose psychopathic torture. I think many people feel repelled by SM because they mistakenly see it as cruelty. SM is *not* cruelty.

Unfortunately the media, especially, I'm sorry to say, the adult, erotic media, frequently and falsely portray nonconsensual, violent, and brutal acts as SM. Stories, photographs, videos, and so forth that depict coercion, kidnapping, rape, and torture as part of SM – and that fail to distinguish between the fantasy of nonconsent and the reality of consensual play – are all too common. Most of this crap is made by "mainstream" adult publishers who don't have the slightest realistic understanding of SM. Thus, they mislead their customers.

We have a direct, effective remedy for this: *Don't buy that garbage!* Better yet, contact the publishers who mislead their customers about what is and is not consensual SM. Tell them that you're not buying their stuff, and tell them why.

The first time I read *The Story of O*, I got so wet that I soaked the chair I was sitting in.

It's time that the SM community organized to oppose the representation of nonconsensual, brutal material as SM. If we see such material in magazines, books, movies, or elsewhere, we should confront it for the damaging fraud it is.

This is absolutely not censorship. I have no opposition *per se* to the artistic depiction of rape, abuse, or other forms of violence. I don't personally enjoy seeing that stuff, but I deeply oppose censoring it. What I *do* oppose is its being falsely labeled as SM. SM is SM. Violence is violence. No connection whatsoever exists between the two!

Also, I believe we should oppose giving the violent abuser "rationalizations" for their behavior, perhaps especially if the victim is a woman. Statements such as "Deep down inside, she really likes it," or "She'll learn to like it," or "She deserves it," are dangerous.

I don't think people oppose SM. I think people oppose cruelty, and rightfully so. We in the SM community need to clarify that no connection exists between SM and cruelty.

**The psychology of masochism.** How could anybody experience pain as erotically arousing? That question stumps many people when they consider SM.

Most of us have been in powerful, dominant positions a few times. We remember how enjoyable that felt (in, perhaps, a slightly dark way), so we believe we feel some empathy for the dominant. Most of us have at least once felt angry with someone and lashed out at them. We remember how satisfying that felt, so we believe we feel some empathy for the sadist. Most of us have felt confused and overburdened at times, and wanted to turn responsibility for running things over to a competent caretaker, so we believe we feel some empathy for the submissive. But the masochist? The person who actively enjoys feeling pain? That creature confounds us.

Frankly, I don't understand masochists all that well myself. I have enjoyed playing submissive, but I almost never enjoy receiving pain. If my dominant wants to whip me, or otherwise give me pain, I'll strive to accept it with grace because I want to please them but, beyond the mildest levels, pain doesn't arouse me.

Masochists, on the other hand, seem to have a different type of nervous system than the rest of us have. Levels of pain that would traumatize other people send them into ecstatic orbit. They love it, and want more.

I must emphasize one point: Masochists feel *very* particular about the pain they enjoy. It must be felt only under controlled, consensual circumstances. They experience the pain of an auto accident, punch in the face, bee sting, or similar treatment exactly like the rest of us, and dislike it just as much. You are not free to walk up to a masochist and slap them. Such behavior is nonconsensual, nonerotic, and *illegal*. A good dominant administers pain as carefully as a surgeon cuts. You act the same.

What's going on inside a masochist's mind? Possibly something important. People who respond deeply to erotic pain have a range of response that needs closer analysis. Reactions occur in them in response to erotic pain that we cannot satisfactorily explain based on simple intensity. Furthermore, these reactions cannot be fully explained by the "jaded" theory: the theory that these people are burned out on regular sex, and thus need this extra-intense stimulation to feel aroused; masochists seem to enjoy conventional sexual sensation as much as anybody else.

Many masochists report entering an altered state of consciousness. If they feel safe and secure about their situation and the people they're with, they relax and surrender to an astonishing degree. They sometimes enter a mental state where the blows no longer feel unpleasant. One reported that the blows from a heavy wooden paddle felt like gentle drops of welcome, warm rain falling on a far-away part of his body. Masochists seem to have states of consciousness in common with yogis, fakirs, and other people who follow altered-consciousness pathways. I've heard talk of the intricacies of the nervous system, of endorphins and enkephalins.

One thing is certain: The old theories "explaining" masochism solely in terms of conventional western psychopathology, while no doubt true for some people, completely fail to answer the questions raised by examining these ecstatic masochists. I have seen people have out-of-body experiences while being whipped or otherwise erotically tortured. Something important is happening here, and if we insist that we already understand it, we will miss a major learning opportunity.

**Should people with SM fantasies seek psychotherapy?** Maybe. Maybe not. Let's explore this further.

First, if someone is either physically or mentally suffering (and I don't mean the special, erotic "suffering" experienced during consensual SM play; I mean real suffering) then they should get help. Many people suffer years of guilt and self-loathing because of their SM desires.

Second, psychotherapy with an SM-interested person should begin with both patient and therapist understanding that SM desires do not automatically indicate pathology. (See the Resource Guide for more information on finding such a therapist.)

Third, both therapist and patient should understand that even if an underlying cause of the SM desires is discovered and cured (and I believe this is both possible and beneficial for some people), the person might still find SM an exciting and intense form of erotic play.

Fourth, both need to understand that sexual arousal is not "rational," at least in terms of how we usually define rationality, and differs from person to person.

Having reached those understandings, how might psychotherapist and patient proceed?

I need to feel really heavy pain about every six weeks or so, or I get really bitchy.

**If you're feeling that you might harm someone.** One of the first things to consider is whether or not the patient is likely to harm or kill another person, or to seek out someone willing to harm or kill them. (I've heard of people who wanted to die but were unwilling to kill themselves seeking out the SM community hoping to find someone who would oblige them.)

I want to speak to the reader who feels it likely they will do something nonconsensual and damaging.

When somebody hurts us, we have a natural urge to hurt back. This urge is built into us and is a good thing. It discourages contemptible bullies (and there are millions of them in this world) from thinking they can hurt us with no fear of negative consequences. Everybody has the right of self-defense. Almost all anger has a rational origin.

However, one person shouldn't be punished for something another person did to you. If you have an angry desire to hurt somebody who has done you no harm, or, especially, to damage them beyond their ability to self-heal, then I believe it's in your own best interests to suspect that "old stuff" is going on regarding someone in your past. The same goes if you find yourself overreacting when somebody harms you or people you care about.

I say to you that it's unlikely you will find peace of mind until you resolve things with the person who originally hurt you. I further say to you that such resolution *is* possible, even if the person who hurt you is dead or otherwise irreversibly gone from your life.

People get raped, abused, molested, battered, neglected, and abandoned, and all too often by those people who should have been kindest to them. This is horrible and tragic, but it's possible, with time and a good therapist, to heal these wounds. For everyone's sake, most especially yours, please get help.

> Some people were put on this earth to be slaves. They're unhappy if they're not a slave, and they'll keep searching until they find someplace where they can be one.

I've spent time in therapy, and sometimes I've felt afraid to let go of thoughts and feelings I've held. But I've learned to trust the "therapeutic fall." You must choose the time, conditions, and therapist carefully or you can be further hurt; but if everything is sound, letting go of old stuff allows better, healthier thoughts and feelings to emerge. Those wonderful results entirely justify taking an intelligently chosen risk.

**If you're feeling that you might harm yourself.** While I'm not a mental health expert, I dealt with many suicidal people during my days as an ambulance crewman. In addition, I spent many hours as a trained volunteer on a suicide hot line. (I've also considered suicide myself during some dark periods of my past life.) So I think I can speak to this issue with some credibility.

I think most people who want to kill themselves feel that way for one basic reason: they're faced with a problem that they don't know how to solve, and that they literally don't feel they can live with. They and the problem can't live together, and they can't see any way to eliminate the problem, so they feel they must eliminate themselves. You aid the suicidal person by helping them find an alternative solution. In many ways, the motto of suicide prevention is, "Can you see any other way?"

I doubt that people who want to die know what they're getting into. For one thing, nobody actually knows what happens when we die. For another, the dying process is irreversible if it proceeds beyond a certain point. If it's not what you wanted, you're stuck anyway. Death is final.

Few people truly want to die. On the other hand, many people want to escape terrible suffering, and they believe – sometimes validly – that dying may offer relief.

I have learned through experience, both personal and professional, that it is almost always possible to find a less traumatic solution to a problem than suicide (or killing someone else, or having someone kill you). I have found alternate solutions for myself – sometimes with help, sometimes alone – and I have helped others find solutions for themselves. And I'll tell you, I'm now delighted that I didn't kill myself. Please try to find another way. Talk to friends, see a shrink, write a journal. Do *something*.

It may help to write down the following questions, one per page.

1. What, exactly, is the greatest problem right now? There may be several, but one is probably greatest.
2. What caused it?
3. What, specifically, can be done about it?

Call a suicide-prevention hotline. The people who work on these lines can often help a great deal. They're mostly trained volunteers. (Quality may vary; if you have a poor experience with one counselor, call back another time and talk to someone else.) They can do much to ease your pain, help you regain your emotional balance, and assist you in finding valid reasons to hope again.

(By the way, if your life is in good shape, consider volunteering yourself. The knowledge and skills I learned there greatly eased things for me and many other people I have since talked to over the years.)

Understand that the pain of the situation has probably caused you to lose your perspective. Further understand that the pain you're feeling is likely to pass after a while. (It's often, and quite validly, said that suicide is a permanent solution to a temporary problem.) If you can regain a realistic perspective, you are well started toward finding a workable solution.

> In SM, things are often happening on several different levels at once. At one level, the dominant is selfish and cruel; at another, the dominant is giving and nurturing.

## A Tough Decision

I wanted to write this book for over a dozen years. Indeed, back in 1980, when I was trying to find a way to raise the money to go to medical school, I wrote an entire book-length manuscript on this subject and was working on finding a publisher. Another method of paying my way emerged, so I dropped the idea (for then, anyhow) and went on my way.

Later, I tackled it again. I worked on the first edition of this book from 1988 till 1992, and yet somehow hadn't finished it. In fact, I "detoured" enough to write and publish three other books. I would work on it and work on it, and yet somehow it wouldn't get finished.

And I knew why: I was scared to publish it. With the publication of this book, I would reveal myself to the world as a practicing sadomasochist. I dreaded the reaction.

The subject of sex makes a lot of people nervous. Many folks out there have strongly negative attitudes toward it. I learned that lesson very clearly with the publication of my first two books. A fair number of retailers and others refused to have anything to do with my books because of "the sex parts." Understand that these were non-fiction books. Any reference to sex was put there with the intent to inform, not to titillate or arouse. That didn't matter to them.

Before he had a chance to say anything about the bruises on my butt, I said, 'Doc, it was consensual,' and that took care of that.

I plan to write a variety of books on ambulance work, humor, martial arts, creative thinking, and so forth. One of my biggest worries is that publishing this highly controversial book will forever stigmatize and pigeonhole me. Writing about sex is "different"; writing about kinky sex is "even more different."

I worry that, no matter what else I write about, I will be known for the rest of my life as "the guy who wrote that SM book." I don't want this book to be the most conspicuous accomplishment of my writing career, perhaps even my entire life, but I must face the definite possibility of exactly that occurring.

Faced with this problem, I considered several options. There was, of course, the choice of simply not writing the book at all. I could do very well by staying with less controversial topics. Yet the truth was that I wanted to write this book. Furthermore, many people out there needed, some desperately, the information it contained. I didn't feel that I could just walk away from those people.

While I pondered whether or not to write this book, I also considered what form it should take. I considered writing it as a novel. I would present SM, and its basics such as consensuality, "disguised" as a novel. If challenged, I could retreat to "It's only fiction." But the truth is: It's *not* fiction. It's very real, and it's all over the place, and it's soon going to be even more all over the place. *Somebody* had to start talking about SM in a straightforward, realistic way. It's not enough, and it makes for terrible fiction, to have the characters talking to each other when the real purpose of the dialogue is to have the reader overhear.

I thought about writing a novel in which a young woman enters a "bondage manor" for training as a professional dominant. My goal would have been to "train" the reader along with my fictional heroine. I couldn't make it work. I may try my hand at SM erotic fiction someday, but I'll wait until my "teaching piece" is complete. For now, I've decided I need to talk directly to my reader, so that's what I'll do. Hello there, Reader.

I thought about writing under a pseudonym, but my writing style is so distinctive that it would take about two days after publication for "the secret" to be found out. Also, I knew I would rather take the heat associated with publishing this book under my own name than have to live in fear of discovery – and eventually take the heat anyway. Finally, I knew there were people who would take evil glee in "outing" me as the author of this book. Giving them such power over me was simply unacceptable.

Finally, I had to look deeply at how I truly felt about SM. Did I, as an SM practitioner, truly believe that I was doing something wrong? I was very clear that I believed no such thing. Well then, why was I afraid to talk about it "on the record"?

The core truth was: I feared being ridiculed. Even ordinary sex is terribly easy to satirize and sensationalize. Something like this, for those already inclined to twist and distort, is just simply too good and too juicy to be true. I felt afraid of those people. I didn't want to have to deal with them.

> A pervert
> is anybody
> kinkier than
> you are.

Furthermore, I have not lived a life free of controversy. I could be made to appear a near-saint, or despicable, by selectively choosing certain aspects of my life and presenting them in a certain way.

Like the rest of you, I'm somewhere in the middle. I have my strengths and my virtues, and I have done things about which I now feel proud. I also have my full human share of faults and weaknesses, and I have done things about which I now feel ashamed. Like the rest of you, I work on improving my strengths and clearing up my weaknesses, and I like to think that I'm making progress.

One thing I'm definitely *not* ashamed of is my participation in SM. I find revealing it somewhat embarrassing, much as anyone might feel embarrassed at revealing what they do in the bedroom – a place where nobody looks dignified – but I'm not ashamed.

Among other things, I have a few friends that I'm not yet "out" to, and I'm sure there will be some chagrin on my face when we next meet, but that's just part of the dues I'll pay for writing this book. Also, I can just imagine the reaction of various people I used to work or go to school with. A few, I'm sure, will view my writing this book as validation of every nasty thought they ever had about me. I'm also sure that others, while they may join in ridiculing me, will secretly feel very glad that I wrote this – and quietly purchase it on their own.

It's time for SM people to stop needing to hide. What could the people I feared actually do to me? Well, some left-wing feminist lunatic or right-wing evangelical nutcase might try to assassinate me, but I thought that extremely unlikely. "The Powers That Be" couldn't fire me; I'm self-employed. They couldn't revoke my professional licenses; I have none. (One of this country's greatest strengths is that you still don't need a license to write.) They couldn't take custody of my children away from me; my kids don't live with me. They couldn't use what I'd done to alienate me from my family; I'm already "out" to them. In short, I'm about as invulnerable in this respect as a person can get.

So, really, the only viable choice was to publish it under my own name and just simply deal with what happened next. I expected that people's reactions would fall into one of three categories: some people would object to this book and give me various degrees of flak about it; others wouldn't care much about it one way or another; and still others would think this book was wonderful, and feel grateful to me for having written it. (That prediction has since proven true.)

> I wouldn't accept your submission if I didn't respect you.

So the question became: Would it be worth putting up with the flak from the first group in order to benefit (and, yes, get the rewards from) the third group? After much reflection, and discussion with trusted others, I decided that the answer was "yes." In fact, the answer was not only "yes," but "hell, yes."

Many, many people needed and wanted the information this book contains, and some needed it desperately. Many people who dealt with requests for information about SM, and knew that I was both a writer and into it myself, repeatedly (and a bit pointedly) mentioned to me that "there's nothing out there" on this subject.

Actually, there's some pretty good stuff out there, and I've included the works I know of in the "References" section of this book. Unfortunately, much of it was either (1) written by gay or lesbian authors, and was thus (unfairly) "dismissable" by the more mainstream aspects of society or (2) written by researchers who only studied it (but who didn't actually *do* it), or (3) written as fiction, usually under a pseudonym, by authors who, again, claimed that they only fantasized about it (but who didn't actually *do* it).

Much supposedly "SM" fiction in fact describes wildly unsafe, unrealistic, nonconsensual acts that no SM practitioner in their right mind would ever attempt. The movie "Blue Velvet," for example, was widely referred to by reviewers as an SM movie, yet the virtually unanimous opinion among my SM friends who saw it was that this movie had essentially nothing to do with the realities of SM. One of the main problems surrounding SM is that the average person, having been exposed to such material, has a wildly inaccurate understanding of what's actually involved.

At the time I wrote the first edition of this book, no "mainstream" (that's code for heterosexual) person had yet stepped forth and, using their full, legal name, written about SM in an accurate, non-sensational, realistic manner from the standpoint of someone who actually *did* it. Since then, several more have, and I'm delighted to see them. If SM is to gain the acceptance it rightfully deserves then, just like being gay, bisexual, or lesbian, it is time to stop keeping it a "dirty little secret" that people need to hide. It is both unjust and morally wrong for people who practice consensual, responsible SM to live in a society where they must fear discovery of that fact.

Regarding the revelation of my participation in SM, I feel some embarrassment, but absolutely no shame. I feel a touch of chagrin, but absolutely no contrition. I feel a bit of reluctance, but absolutely not one bit of remorse.

The time is long overdue for the tens of millions of people in this country who share my interest in this form of responsible, intense, and, yes, caring form of sexuality to no longer have to live with the fear that their interest will be discovered and used to harm them by ignorant or ill-intentioned others.

> When I first got into SM I was convinced that 98 percent of all the people were going to be dominant. Hoo, boy, was I ever wrong.

For more than four years now, I've been about as "out" as you can get, and nothing terrible has happened to me – in fact, many very wonderful things *have* happened. I continue to refuse to hide.

## My Very Own, Official, "Coming Out" Chapter

**First fantasy.** During the midafternoon of a late spring day in 1970, about a month before the Kent State murders, I was sitting out on the balcony of a Northern California house with my feet propped up on the rail, enjoying the sunlight. I was a 20-year-old, long-haired hippie who had moved out of the Haight-Ashbury slightly less than a year before. My "old lady" and I were "crashing" (please excuse the sixties terminology) indefinitely with some friends at a large house in the "notorious hippie haven" of Cotati, California – located about an hour north of San Francisco.

The combination of the warming sunlight and gentle breezes felt luxurious. I leaned back in my chair and let drowsiness sweep over me. My mind began to drift as I lazed in the chair, and a number of images floated through. One image that stopped and focused itself more and more clearly was of me sitting in a chair. My old lady was naked and down on her knees in front of me, and she was energetically sucking my cock. That was definitely an image I could "groove" with, so I focused in on it some more. If memory serves, a grin spread across my face. And it was right about then that I looked at the image closely enough to see, to my utter shock, that her wrists were tied behind her back with a small, black cord.

The rest of the world has absolutely no concept of what a warm, loving, and intimate act this is.

My eyes popped open and my feet came down off the rail. I sat bolt upright and blurted out loud to the only person there, me, "Where the hell did *that* come from?"

I had no idea. I had absolutely no idea. I had never fantasized about anything like that before. The only time I had ever done anything like that was about two years before when I was living in New York's East Village. A lady I met there once asked me to tie her up while we had sex. I did so (as best I could in my then-fumbling manner) and I enjoyed the sex, but the tying-up part aroused nothing at all in me other than vague uneasiness. So this wasn't anything I had a prior interest in.

My old lady and I were going through a rough phase, but things surely hadn't become *that* bad. Or had they? I didn't think so.

I put the image out of my mind as best I could and went on with my life, but it refused to stay away. The image began to appear in virtually every erotic fantasy I had. It got stronger and stronger, clearer and clearer. I found that more and more I wanted to act it out. I once timidly asked my old lady if she would let me tie her up while we had sex. Not only did she turn me down flat, but she also started looking at me with slightly wary eyes. What in the world was going on?

Understand that I was a hippie. I was a Haight-Ashbury-living, marijuana-smoking, LSD-taking hippie. Other than acting as a medic at several demonstrations, I wasn't even political. I was a thoroughgoing peacenik pacifist – to the point of having taken several beatings from bullying groups of "straight" men without lifting a hand to defend myself. *People like me just didn't do things like this.*

**Trouble.** I began to feel seriously concerned. Remember, this was just a year or so after the Manson killings. I wondered and worried – boy, did I worry. Was I was turning into somebody like that?

I looked through the local bookstores and found nothing but discouragement. Even "The Sensuous Woman" thought that the people who wanted to tie or be tied during sex were sick. Oh, great. That was all I needed.

I went to the library of nearby Sonoma State College and looked through its psychology section to see what I could learn. What I found was grim. There were several books that talked about sexual sadism and its often-murderous results. One especially disturbing book contained numerous police photographs of rape/murder victims. The sight of these women's bodies, often horribly mutilated, sickened me and terrified me more than I can say. Was I turning into a person who might someday do something like that?

I decided to keep myself under surveillance. I made up my mind that I was not going to allow myself to hurt anybody. If I thought I was turning into someone that would harm somebody else, then I would either put myself into a mental institution or commit suicide. And thus I lived, waiting and watching to see if I was turning into someone that I needed to shoot. Such a life was, shall we say, not fun.

My old lady and I went our separate ways a few months later. (For the rest of our relationship, I had never had the nerve to raise the issue with her again.) The image, however, stayed in my mind, clearer and stronger than ever. The desire to do it grew stronger, too.

**Despair.** After that relationship ended, I was certain of one thing: no "decent" woman would ever want anything to do with me. As soon as I revealed my "sickness," she would be gone. For the rest of my life, I would have to settle for women too crazy or too desperate to object. Such a conclusion was, to say the least, depressing.

One day I walked into a local variety store and bought a length of rope with no other purpose in mind than to use it to tie a woman up. (Exactly how I was going to do this, I had only the vaguest of ideas. I'd think of something. Or try, anyway.) During this purchase, I felt like slime, complete slime. I was certain the clerk knew why I wanted this rope, and I felt somewhat surprised that he would sell it to me. The utterly bored look on his face as he handed me my change convinced me that I was right. He knew, all right. He just wasn't letting on that he knew.

On my way home I wondered what kind of defective person *he* was. (I knew, to my shame, what kind of "sicko" I was, or might become.) What kind of merchant sells something to a customer so clearly determined to use the purchased item for "immoral purposes"? What was our world coming to?

**Weirdness.** Then a strange thing happened. I started regularly dating a pleasant, utterly normal, lady. She wasn't even a hippie. We had an enjoyable if routine sex life. I, however, wanted more. One night, while we embraced, I pulled together every bit of my courage. It was just barely enough to allow me to stammer out "the" question.

Feeling terrified, I pulled slightly free, then leaned over and removed the rope from a nearby desk drawer. I held it in my hand and, quaking, managed to ask her, "Would you do me a favor?" She looked at me with a distinctly guarded expression and asked what the favor was. I was barely able to stammer out, "Would you please lie down on your stomach and put your hands behind your back?" There couldn't have been any doubt as to what I intended to do to her once she did that.

A *very* long moment of silence passed while she scrutinized my face, then she said, rather cheerfully, "OK." There was absolutely no doubt that, as I tied her up, I was much, much more scared than she was.

*Master, you were always good to me.*

Well, we got through that evening without any major problems. In the morning, she was still there, looking at me with a smile – and perhaps even a bit of a smirk. Rope became a regular part of our sex life after that, and I often thought how fortunate I was to find such a woman, who managed to so completely conceal her craziness or desperation (I never did figure out which it was), on my very first try.

During this time, I discovered that adult magazines devoted to something called "bondage" existed. It took a lot for me to fight down my guilt and fear in order to enter the adult bookstores and look at them, but I did. I had to. Some of these magazines even had "how to" articles in them, and the techniques they described really worked! Furthermore, they recommended consulting military hand-to-hand combat manuals. This was something our government had studied? Unbelievable!

**More weirdness.** That lady and I separated after a few months. What stunned me was that the next woman I dated *also* liked being tied up during sex.

And so did the *next* woman. She, in fact, would ask me to tie her up if it had been a while since I'd last done that. She even went so far as to suggest how I could tie her up better! I took the extraordinary step of letting *her* tie *me* up a few times.

Clearly, I had to do some more thinking about this whole bondage thing. I had now batted three for three in meeting apparently mentally healthy, normal women who enjoyed being tied up during sex. Either this meant that there were a *lot* more "sick" women in the world than I had imagined, or that my thinking was somehow off regarding this matter. Things just weren't adding up, and I still felt worried as hell. It didn't help that the next woman I dated absolutely refused to have anything to do with bondage.

**Relief.** The turning point came in the fall of 1973. <u>Playboy</u> magazine, in its "Advisor" section, had a question to the effect of: Dear Playboy, My boyfriend wants me to tie him up. What should I do about that? I expected that, like "The Sensuous Woman," their answer would be something like "get rid of him, fast."

Instead, to my utter shock, they started talking about what lengths of rope worked best, and giving tips on how to tie him, and suggestions on what to do after he was tied. They went on to mention that more information could be found in a book called "The Joy of Sex" by Dr. Alex Comfort.

Bondage was acceptable to a mainstream resource like <u>Playboy</u>? I could do this, could be interested in this, and still be regarded as a mentally healthy person? I wasn't somebody that I had to keep an eye on? I can't describe the relief that flooded over me when I read that section. I literally felt that I had been re-admitted to the human race.

Remember, one sign of good SM is that after the session is over, both parties would like to do that same session again.

It was still a struggle. I found a copy of "The Joy of Sex" in a nearby mainstream bookstore (of all places!) but I had to come back to the store to look through it a dozen times or so before I actually worked up enough courage to buy it. (If the clerks felt annoyed by my repeated visits, they didn't show it – and I'm grateful for that.) When I got it home, I read the "Bondage" and "Discipline" sections (I wasn't so sure how I felt about that "discipline" part) over and over and over.

**First contact.** About two years went by, and I was involved with yet another lady who enjoyed bondage. (Ye gods! How many of them were out there, anyhow?) One day, for no particular reason, I bought a local adult newspaper. While looking through the ads in the back, I came across one from, of all things, an SM club called Backdrop located in the entirely normal, All-American city of Hayward, California. There were clubs for this sort of thing? I had read about clubs in fiction but, for all sorts of reasons, I didn't think any *really* existed. Apparently I was (yet again) wrong. I sent them a self-addressed, stamped envelope along with a request for information.

The information I requested arrived about a week later, and reading it almost gave me a stroke. Backdrop had events like master/slave dinner parties, bondage demonstrations (that one caught my attention), slave auctions, and many other events. I couldn't believe this! This couldn't be right! And yet there it was: dates, times, addresses, phone numbers, admission fees, and all the rest of it. Could it really be?

There was a "slave auction" happening on a night I was free. Once again, I gathered my courage (I had needed to do that many times in recent years), and called the phone number. A pleasant, quite matter-of-fact lady answered and confirmed that the information I had about the date, time, address and fee were indeed correct. I thanked her and quickly hung up.

And off I went. I traveled to Hayward, found the address, and parked across the street. I sat there for almost an hour while I gathered my courage. After all, I didn't *really* know what waited on the other side of that door. I didn't *really* know what would happen to me once I stepped inside. For all I knew, I would be immediately grabbed, strapped to a table, covered with whipped cream, and tortured to death...or something like that.

It was an ironic moment. I was an ambulance crewman at the time. I wasn't unduly scared about responding to unstable crime scenes, or of going out to the always-dangerous sites of freeway crashes, or of confronting violent crazies, yet the idea of crossing that street and knocking on that door made me, shall we say, very, very nervous.

Well, I finally went over and knocked. I don't remember who let me in, but I wasn't grabbed. Instead I was shown into a large, normal-looking living room and offered a seat. I was in a nervousness-induced haze at this point, and most of my memories are a bit unclear, but I remember being introduced to Mr. Robin Roberts, who ran Backdrop.

I eventually managed to calm down somewhat, and found myself able to look around the room and make a bit of conversation with the other guests. Which ones, I wondered intently, were the submissives? I had never met a "real" submissive. (In my mind, the women I had talked into letting me tie them up didn't count.) I was dying to meet one. What would they be like? Of one thing I was sure: 95% or more of the people into SM were going to be dominants, like me. Submissives had to be rare. After all, what kind of pathetic wretch would actually volunteer to be bound, whipped, or worse?

About 30 of us sat around the spacious room in a rough circle. At the appointed time, Robin came out and made one of the strangest announcements I had ever heard. "Will all of you who are submissive," he asked, "please come with me?" I wondered if *anybody* would stand up. Maybe we were *all* dominants here? What kind of an evening would *that* lead to?

The only word that can be reasonably used to describe what happened next is "stampede." While I sat shocked and wide-eyed in my chair, a long line of men and women streamed into the next room. When the dust had settled, only *four* of us remained behind. The room suddenly seemed as big and empty as a basketball gymnasium two hours after the big game.

I remember the auction only hazily. Various "slaves" were brought out by Robin for us to bid on. I didn't bid on any of the men, but I clearly remember the old, healed whip-scars one giant of a submissive man had on his back. The sight of them sent my vision swimming to the point where I feared I'd pass out. (You might think that very little in the way of what could happen to a human body would make a veteran ambulance crewman feel faint – and, actually, you'd be right – but, trust me, this was a different type of situation, and I wasn't any sort of veteran around this place. I was the rawest of novices.) I also learned one of the most fundamental lessons of the SM world: submissive heterosexual males can all too often be bought cheap.

**Basic training.** Thus began an association with Backdrop that lasted about two years. I went to as many of their events as I could, and even moved so I could be closer to the organization.

Backdrop had two major facets to its structure: During the day, ladies worked there as professional dominants and submissives. During most nights and on weekends, club activities took place. I hung around the place as much as I could. My presence undoubtedly got on Robin's nerves at times, but he was usually gracious and friendly to me.

> I don't do things at the expense of my submissive.

And I learned. Ye Gods, did I learn! I spent hours talking with dominants, submissives, and "switch-hitters" (as they were called in those days) of both genders. I interacted with raw novices and with people who had been doing this for years. I had many "play sessions" (as they were called at the time) and I watched many more. I talked and I listened and I read and I watched. I taught the few things I knew, and had many, many things taught to me. I dominated women and I submitted to women. I tied up and got tied up. I spanked and whipped, and I got spanked and whipped. I played at parties and I played privately.

I met masters and mistresses, submissives and slaves of both genders, novices and veterans, light players and heavy players, people who did this only occasionally and people who were "in role" with their partners 24 hours a day. (These people, I learned, were sometimes called "lifestylers.") Many people I met at Backdrop became my friends. We shared hopes and confidences, good times and bad times, erotic play and mundane tasks.

At Backdrop events, male-dominant/female-submissive energy rarely mixed with female-dominant/male-submissive energy. As the parties progressed, the male-dominant folks usually went to one part of the house and the female-dominant folks to another. In fact, one night during a party I went over into "female-dominant" territory to get a piece of equipment and, while I got the item I wanted, it was made much more than clear to me that male dominants weren't welcome around there just then.

Unfortunately, while Robin and the Backdrop staff didn't regard their professional sessions as prostitution, some local cops disagreed. Backdrop got busted and put out of business (although charges were later dropped).

**Abhorring the vacuum.** Backdrop's demise put the rest of us at, so to speak, loose ends. What were we to do? Where were we to go? Eventually, other people started holding events.

Bill Burns, a man I had met at Backdrop, started a legally recognized, female-dominant organization he carefully named the Service of Mankind Church. Bill is erotically submissive to women in his private play, but he's something of a dominant and an organizer out there in real life. A male-dominant couple started an organization called Roissy (named after the town mentioned in "The Story of O"), but they broke up shortly after that, and the club dissolved.

So Bill was doing a pretty good job of organizing the female-dominant folks, but us male-dominant folks had nowhere to go. Months went by, and nothing happened. I still considered myself a beginner, and didn't even have a girlfriend at the time, so I didn't feel it was my place to do anything about the situation. I kept waiting for the senior members of our community to do something.

Finally, as I am wont to do, I ran out of patience regarding the situation and decided to start a club on my own. I named it "Gemini" because of the "double life" I and many of my friends were forced to live regarding our SM interest. (Gemini is also my astrological sign, but that fact was purely secondary.) I placed ads in a local adult newspaper and spread the news through word of mouth. On my way to the Hooker's Ball of 1978, I mailed the invitations to the first Gemini event.

And, boy, did we ever start out small. Our first event was a discussion-only meeting held on a Sunday afternoon at some picnic tables in a secluded part of a Berkeley park. (I wasn't about to invite people I didn't know to anyone's private home.) Seven people showed up — five men and two women, if I remember correctly.

The discussion went well enough, and I decided to hold an SM dinner party at which the submissives would prepare and serve dinner to the dominants. That event drew around a dozen people, including both a "lifestyle" couple and a master who brought both of his female slaves.

Gemini grew from there. The parties got more organized, I got better at running things, and we slowly grew. Many people in the community understandably felt dubious about Gemini at first (I mean, who was this guy and what gave him the right to take on a job this big?), but they learned that I was committed to this task and that the organization was here to stay.

**Continuing education.** During this time, I also attended my first meetings of the Society of Janus. I met its founder, Cynthia Slater, and many other people who were also doing pioneering work in SM sexuality. Janus was almost exclusively composed of gay men in those days, and platoons of black-leather-clad guys filled our meeting areas. Several SM lesbians also attended, along with a few professional dominants and a sprinkling of bisexuals and heterosexuals.

The level of knowledge and skill these folks possessed was incredibly advanced. I was clearly back "in school" here. Other than once being asked to give a lecture on rope bondage techniques (a subject that remained dear to my heart) I listened a *lot* more than I talked.

I gained many insights while discussing SM with people who were other than heterosexual. Listening to men talk about what it was like to erotically dominate or submit to another man, and listening to women talk about what it was like to erotically dominate or submit to another woman, proved fascinating. I also talked with bisexuals, some of whom would only dominate one gender and only submit to the other. Again, hearing about that led to priceless knowledge.

> Whenever I'm in bottom space I become sort of non-verbal. It becomes hard for me to remember how to talk.

I took a certain amount of kidding about being a "token het" in Janus. One day a leather-clad man came up to me and said, " You know, Jay, I have so much in common with you and yet I still can't figure you out. We're both in Mensa, we're both est graduates, we're both into SM, and we're both dominants, and yet you're straight and I'm gay." When I nodded, he continued, "To this day, I'm still trying to figure out where you went wrong."

**Raising and letting go of my "child."** Gemini was tough to build from scratch. It could have folded at several different points, and many people expected it to do exactly that. But the Gemini Society kept on existing, sometimes for absolutely no other reason than because I kept on insisting that it exist, kept on recruiting new members, kept on putting on parties, and just generally kept on.

Gemini eventually made it "over the hump" and was accepted as part of the Bay Area SM community. I was its sole officer for about the first three years of its existence. When I finally stepped down because I was leaving the Bay Area to attend medical school, I must admit that I was much more than willing to turn over the job.

Let me add that I had become terribly proud of Gemini. It was a tolerant, inclusive organization that had helped many people resolve often-thorny issues around their sexuality. I felt especially proud of the work Gemini and I had done helping women realistically integrate this aspect of their sexuality into the rest of their lives. Male-dominant/female-submissive play is the "least politically correct" form of SM, and many women I met felt terribly guilty and ambivalent about doing this. They were clear that they liked it, and found erotically submitting to a man deeply reward-ing, but weren't at all sure that doing so was all right.

I felt you enjoyed my submission, but didn't exploit it. That felt really good.

I remember in particular the time I told a novice submissive woman who was having trouble setting limits with her far-too-pushy boyfriend, "Look, just because you're a slave to your lover in the bedroom doesn't mean you have to be a slave to him in the rest of your life."

She looked at me with astonishment.

"I don't?" she asked incredulously.

"No," I answered, "you don't. Not unless you want to, anyway."

A very thoughtful look appeared on her face.

Hearing that statement from the head of a male-dominant SM club clearly had an effect on her. That relationship didn't last much longer.

During those days, I once wrote something to the effect of "Nowadays, a woman is free to do anything she wants except sometimes give up her freedom." I heard from many, many erotically submissive women who agreed with that statement, and had experienced considerable emotional pain at how confining their new "freedom" was in this respect. Even though their sisters told them that they were completely free to make any choices they wanted, they weren't *really* free to make some of the choices they were "free" to make. Thus is the human condition.

**My return.** I was away at medical school for about two years. During that time, I heard occasional bits of gossip, and occasionally got to read a copy of the Society of Janus newsletter "Growing Pains," but, by and large, I was out of touch. When I returned late in 1984, the situation had changed quite a bit.

**Digression.** I've mentioned to you that I started medical school, yet you may have noticed that I'm not an M.D. Because I raised the issue, I believe I owe it to you to complete it.

Shortly after I returned to the Bay Area, I had to quit medical school, even though I was doing quite well. I was in the top third of my class, and passed the internship qualifying examination in about two years. I also helped teach classes in advanced cardiac life support to physicians, nurses, and paramedics.

Why, then, did I have to quit? This period, as I look back on it, was one of the darkest and most frustrating episodes in my life. I went to a Caribbean medical school somewhat like the one on Grenada. My money ran out, my family was no longer willing to help me, and the American medical establishment was trying its damnedest to limit the number of Americans studying medicine abroad by, among other things, denying us student loans. In this and many other ways, the treatment my fellow students and I received exposed me to the dark realities of the political and, especially, economic underbelly of how medicine is practiced in the United States. Despite the fact that many people wish it were otherwise, health care in this country today is, before anything else, a for-profit business; that brutal, basic fact is pervasive and decisive. Profit is to medicine what blood is to tissue.

It may seem contradictory to regard SM as life-affirming, but I assure you that it's true.

Anyway, by that point it was also becoming increasingly clear to me that, while I was well-suited to being a doctor, I was even better suited to being a writer, and it was making less and less sense to spend my working life not using my strongest talents. I therefore, very sadly and reluctantly, let go of my dream of becoming a doctor and concentrated on my writing career.

**Now back to our story.** Backdrop had re-emerged, and changed somewhat. I'm sure I had also changed. Robin Roberts and I were still on friendly terms, but the place just didn't seem like "home" anymore.

Gemini had become more couples-oriented and bureaucratic. It was now also quite isolated from the rest of the SM community, and preferred it that way. (Among other things, my suggestion that Gemini donate money in support of a local, highly respected woman who had been badly injured in an auto accident was bluntly refused on the grounds that she was a dominant.)

They also now prided themselves on having "a better class of people." Once again, thus is the human condition.

Gemini and I went our separate ways not too much later, under very bitter circumstances. Frankly, I'm glad I played no part in what it had become. (Let me add that it is now under different management.)

On the other hand, Janus now had many more heterosexual members than before. It also now gave parties and socials in addition to its educational programs. Janus offered a flexible, tolerant option, and many of my friends were already members. I re-joined and started hanging out there again.

The final change was the grim and forceful emergence of AIDS. Several people I knew were now sick. A few were no longer with us. (More would follow, including Cynthia Slater.)

I've basically been hanging around Janus since then. I've found and lost lovers here, made many friends and a few enemies, been put on some "in crowd" mailing lists for private SM parties and taken off others, made contributions and created disturbances, helped edit the newsletter, taught "all pervert" CPR classes (I'll never really stop being a medic), and otherwise continued as a "known member" of this community.

And what a wonderful community it is! The people I have met here have a sense of honesty and a level of personal responsibility for their lives that I have never found in any other group. They are caring people, excellent communicators, and top-notch negotiators. (I've long said that when two people are alone together, and one of them is naked and tied up, and the other is standing over them holding whips and other "torture" implements, this is *not* the time to have a serious mismatch of expectations.)

I have here found my friends, my peer group, my tribe, and my lovers. While they all, of course, have their flaws, these people, these "damnedest, finest perverts," with their honesty, their honor, their high sense of personal responsibility and ethics, their strong communication skills, their caring for one another, and their playfulness make them the finest group of human beings it has ever been my proud privilege to know. That they have accepted me "warts and all" into their community is one of the highest compliments I have ever received.

## *The Sociology, Politics, and Economics of SM*

In the 1970s, we saw a fascinating phenomenon: the "Gay Liberation" movement. Rejected by society, these people joined together, pooled their resources, and became a potent economic, social, and political force.

The gay community's support is now important, sometimes essential, for election in many cities. County, state, and even national candidates often take stands on gay-rights issues. If the Kinsey estimates can be believed, a group that forms about five percent of the population has become a major political force.

That being so, what are the implications for a group more than double that size? New York, San Francisco, Los Angeles, and Washington are only a few of the cities that have had a self-aware SM community emerge. Such communities are also emerging in many other cities. Also, efforts are under way to link the SM groups in various areas into a national organization.

Gay-related parades, rallies, and demonstrations now often include an SM group. Organizations that refuse to include such a group are asked detailed, repeated questions regarding the refusal's basis. The leather-clad people asking these questions do not feel inclined to take "no" for an answer.

Again, we see the beginnings of the emergence of a self-aware, organized group of people banded together based on their sexual preference. This movement is growing and getting stronger. Its implications are at least as strong as the gay movement.

Laws banning discrimination based on sexual orientation or sexual preference do not currently explicitly include SM people, and they should. I would have no problem with an SM person teaching in an elementary school, performing surgery, or serving in the military. Indeed, I happen to know that SM people have been doing all of those things, and many more, for quite some time.

You would never have gotten me to believe that I would enjoy that.

I'm told that the National Organization for Women's official position is that SM is inherently incompatible with women's interests. Given that most of the SM women I know identify as feminists, this may be the next area in which we need to raise consciousness.

Five years ago, I would have considered the idea of an SM Freedom Day Parade absurd. Today, I'm not so sure. In five more years, I may help organize it.

Make no mistake about it. We feel tired of apologizing for and covering up our interest in SM. We feel tired of being considered sick. We feel tired of being considered unacceptable. We are coming out. If you're not ready for that, too bad! Your unreadiness is not our problem.

This form of sexuality has unusually strong economic implications. SM has been a cottage industry for some time. Women work as dominants, submissives, and switches. (So do a handful of men, who have an almost entirely gay clientele.) Those who do phone sex take dominant and submissive roles. People earn money by making, distributing, and selling SM equipment and clothing such as restraints, whips, clamps, corsets, boots and so on. (And books!)

Besides the costs of regular sex (for lotions, birth control measures, and so forth), SM-interested people purchase ropes, clamps, whips, leather gear, and many other items. It is common for a player to spend several hundred dollars on SM equipment. Outlays of several thousand dollars are not at all rare, especially if elaborate leather or rubber items are purchased. SM-oriented books, magazines, audiotapes, videotapes, and similar materials sell briskly.

In short, a large and growing demand for SM-related goods and services exists. Many adult bookstores now carry SM supplies, and stores exist in several cities that sell little else. Let's put it this way: This is an area that about 10% to 30% of the population seems interested in, and each interested person may spend a few hundred dollars on equipment. The emergence of suppliers to meet such an enormous demand is inevitable.

As the SM community becomes larger and more organized, its political and economic power mounts. Pay attention, politicians and businesspeople!

*By their fantasies ye shall know them.*

## Should You "Come Out" As Being Into SM?

This is a *big* decision, so think about it at length, then mull it over some, and then think about it a little longer. I have come out, but more for professional reasons than personal ones – and even then it was a decision that took me years to make.

Remember, we live in a time when SM is still widely misunderstood and unaccepted. Coming out to the wrong people, at the wrong time, or in the wrong way could cost you your job, your marriage, and much more.

I think that, as general rule, it's best to keep your SM interest on a "need to know" basis. While you should certainly tell a new lover about it before your relationship with them gets too deep, I see no major reason to mention it to anybody else. Indeed, talking about it with someone you don't usually talk about other aspects of your sex life with raises consensuality issues. Your lovers need to know, and it shouldn't be something you need to keep a dark secret from your closest friends, but I see no reason to mention this (in great detail, anyway) with your parents, children, co-workers, casual friends, and so forth. In fact, doing so could cause serious real-world problems.

Also, regarding your kids, be sure to keep your SM gear, videos, magazines, and all other "adult" material out of their reach. *This usually means keeping these items under lock and key*, just as you should with insecticides, caustic chemicals, medications, and firearms. (And be sure to buy good quality locks. Kids have nimble fingers and nimble minds.) Many SM people who are also parents keep footlockers, locking cabinets, and similar items in their solidly locked bedrooms.

Be sure to keep your adult materials away from your kids, especially if you leave the older kids in the house without your supervision. I know of a case in which a woman nearly lost custody of her son because he played an adult video (that she had accidentally left out) for a friend while she was away. When her son's friend told his parents about it, a "shitstorm" of major proportions erupted, with the local newspapers gleefully reporting every detail.

Regarding who you should tell, a few exceptions exist. You might need to alert your neighbors that "certain sounds" may occasionally come from your home. As one submissive lady told her new downstairs neighbors, "It may sometimes sound like I'm being murdered up here, but unless you hear this (three hard, sharp thumps on the floor, perhaps repeated after a short pause), don't worry about it. I'm all right."

Vanilla people can do their best to accommodate your desires, but it never quite works - they just don't get it.

If you have a non-kinky roommate, you should certainly tell them to be concerned but not freaked out if they come home unexpectedly and find you naked and hog-tied on the living room floor. Ask them to check in with you briefly before they start yelling for the cops (or, worse yet, attacking your partner).

Be careful about telling physicians, psycho-therapists, police officers, social workers, and other health care or legal professionals about your interest in SM. Again, it's far from widely understood. They may conclude that you are either being abused or are a dangerous person, and there may be mandatory reporting laws involved here, particularly if you are a parent. Unless you're certain that your healers are "SM-positive," keep quiet and find other healers. (By the way, the SM community is saturated with health care professionals, so this shouldn't be all that difficult. Author/educator Race Bannon maintains a list of "Kink-Aware Professionals"; contact information can be found in the back of this book. Your local SM club may also be able to help.)

The basic principle here is that SM is still widely misunderstood. I usually didn't tell anyone about this aspect of myself unless (1) there was some particular reason that they needed to know about it and, (2) I was prepared to spend some time with them (usually at least an hour) explaining what I meant.

It's helpful to have some credible printed material to help explain. This book may help.

Keep in mind that once you've told them, then whatever is going to happen will happen, so think about it carefully. Remember this fundamental truth: *You can't untell.*

## Definitions

The following section is, necessarily, a bit "academic," so please bear with me.

**SM defined in one sentence.** SM is the use of psychological dominance and submission, and/or physical bondage, and/or pain, and/or related practices in a safe, legal, consensual manner in order for the participants to experience erotic arousal and/or personal growth.

**SM defined in one page.** The first thing to understand is that SM is entirely *consensual*. Either party, but especially the submissive, always has the absolute right to slow down, change, or completely stop the activity *for any reason whatsoever.*

I'm highly eroticized to being in charge.

The second thing to understand is that SM has *limits*. The basic limit is that, even with consent, the "dominant" will not intentionally do anything beyond the ability of the submissive's body (and mind) to self-heal. Also, even with consent – or, indeed, the desire for it – the submissive should not and legally may not be killed, severely damaged, or recklessly endangered.

The third thing to understand is that SM is done with *safety*. The dominant should always give the submissive a special word, commonly called a "safeword," or some readily communicable non-verbal signal, to use when the submissive *really* needs the activity slowed, changed, or stopped. The dominant must, by law, always respect and abide by this signal.

Other basic safety considerations include never engaging in SM when any participant is markedly tired, emotionally upset, or intoxicated, not introducing too many new things in a single session, never tying any body part so tightly that it begins to tingle or lose feeling, never (unless both of you are very experienced) striking so hard that you draw blood or leave large marks, and always staying as close to a bound person as you would to an infant left in your care. The primary responsibility for knowing what can be done safely in a session rests with the dominant.

Participation in an SM session should be *negotiated* beforehand. People should only participate in SM with those they know well, trust a great deal, and with whom they have a very good relationship. Engaging in SM with strangers, especially in private, can be disastrous. Also, the people involved should spend "straight time" together after the SM encounter to discuss what went on and their feelings about it. One sign of a good session is that afterward the people involved would like to do it again.

Remember, SM is about consensuality, limits, safety, negotiation – and fun!

People strongly interested in SM should contact an SM club. The knowledge, understanding, perspective, and skill that result from discussing, observing, and participating in SM with knowledgeable practitioners is invaluable.

## SM vs. Abuse

SM play differs from abuse in many of the same ways that a judo match differs from a mugging. Consider the differences:

1. SM play is always consensual (according to the definition of consent on Page 8). Abuse is not.

    Can you help me move this whipping post?

2. SM players plan their activities to minimize the risks to one another's physical and emotional well-being. Abusers do not.
3. SM play is negotiated and agreed to ahead of time. Abuse is not.
4. SM play can enhance the relationship between the players. Abuse cannot.
5. SM play can be done in the presence of supportive others – even at parties given for this purpose. Abuse needs isolation and secrecy.
6. SM play has responsible, agreed-upon rules. Abuse lacks such rules.
7. SM play may be requested, and even eagerly desired, by the submissive. Nobody overtly asks for abuse – although self-destructive people may sometimes attempt to provoke it.
8. SM is done for the consensual erotic pleasure and/or personal growth of both or all participants. Abuse is not.
9. SM play can be stopped in an instant, at any time, and for any reason when the submissive uses a safeword. The victim cannot stop their abuser in that way.

10. In SM play, the dominant always keeps their emotions under control. An abuser's emotions are out of control.
11. After SM play, the submissive often feels grateful toward the dominant. A victim never feels grateful for abuse.
12. SM players do not feel that they have the intrinsic right, by virtue of their gender, income, or other external factors, to control the behavior of their partners. Abusers often do.

**Warning signals.** The more of the following that are present in your relationship, the more likely that it will become, or is already, abusive:

- Excessive alcohol or drug usage.
- Isolation, decreased contact with friends or family members. For many years I have had a saying: "If it (the relationship) is going to go bad, it usually goes bad in isolation." Beware especially of the person who will not read books, attend workshops, or go to club meetings, and/or does not want you to do those things. (Some people may need to avoid events because of privacy concerns; this is a different matter.) They may know that such resources discuss safety, consensuality, negotiation, ethics, and limits – and your hearing that would reveal their abusiveness.
- Unemployment and/or severe money problems.
- Strong feelings of jealousy or possessiveness. Unwarranted suspicions of flirting or arranging secret meetings.
- A history of violent confrontations with friends, family members, co-workers, or others.
- A family history of being battered or other violence. (Abuse is, to a large degree, learned behavior. They had to learn it somewhere.)
- Dealing with relationship problems by issuing threats or ultimatums about what will happen if a perceived problem arises again. (Playful "punishments" that have been negotiated as part of the relationship would be an exception.)
- Non-negotiated, hurtful verbal abuse taking place on an uncomfortably frequent basis – especially if it's not balanced by a lot of affection and support. Examples may include sarcasm, pointed "interrogation" of motives or behavior, belittling in front of others, frequent "teasing," or "playful" insults.
- Furniture violence. This is a major red flag. If objects are being damaged during a blow-up, people may be damaged during the next one.

**The cycle of violence.** A basic truth of abusive relationships is that the abuse usually escalates in what authorities call "the cycle of violence."

Emotions reach the boiling point and abuse happens.

Following the abuse, the abuser often feels genuinely sorry and asks for forgiveness. This request is often accompanied by promises to change. Unfortunately, the abuser is not usually able to change without outside help.

Abusive incidents are often followed by a "honeymoon period" of relative happiness. Unfortunately, the stresses that led to the original abuse are usually still present, and tensions again slowly build. Before too long, abuse occurs again.

A major point is that abusive incidents usually become more severe, and the time between the incidents usually becomes shorter. Eventually major destruction, even the death of the abused and/or the abuser, will take place.

The cycle of violence must be broken as early as possible. The key to breaking the cycle is simple: Get outside help! A third party must become involved, and both parties must know that.

This third party should be someone with professional training in dealing with abuse, such as a physician, psychotherapist, or religious counselor. (Note: Some professionals are better than others at dealing with abuse, so finding effective help may involve contacting more than one person.)

He looks so beautiful down there.

Involving well-meaning friends or family members may make the situation much worse. For example, threats by the victim's friends to the abuser about what will happen "if you ever do this again" are likely to do little except raise tensions, and perhaps even provoke a fatal confrontation.

The people involved must not fool themselves into thinking that a pattern of abusive behavior is something they can solve between themselves. In particular, victims and abusers must not kid themselves that "better behavior" on the victim's part will prevent further abuse.

If more than one abusive incident has occurred, it's time to get outside help. If even one incident occurs involving *any* physical injury, it's time to call the police.

One positive note: Abuse is learned behavior much more than most people think it is. An abuser is not necessarily evil or weak, but they need to see that their abusive behavior is harming their relationships and driving people away. It helps to view the abuser as someone who needs to learn alternative ways of effectively dealing with frustration and anger.

All communities have resources available to help both abusers and their victims. Your telephone book, particularly the front section of the white pages, lists local resources.

For additional help contact the National Domestic Violence Hotline at (800) 799-SAFE (799-7233).

## SM and Censorship

SM is a negotiated form of safe, consensual, erotic interaction between adults. By definition, it is not abusive, exploitative, violent, demeaning, or otherwise harmful to its participants. If an activity is somehow abusive, exploitative, violent, demeaning, or otherwise harmful then, also by definition, it is not SM.

*Submissives should be a renewable resource.*

There's an interesting anti-SM book out there called "Against Sadomasochism: A Radical Feminist Perspective." I've read it, and, frankly, I was disappointed. In a way, I was looking forward to reading some skilled criticism. One often learns a lot that way. Unfortunately, most of the arguments seemed to boil down to, "Well, I just think that stuff is gross." Only one essay came close to scaring me. A fairly sharp lady presented an argument against SM that consisted of five interrelated points, and I agreed with four of them! It was the only time anybody has ever come close to talking me out of this on a purely intellectual, reasoned basis.

One specific point they repeatedly raise is that our society is so patriarchal that women cannot validly consent to participate in SM. In other words, they specifically reject the "consensuality defense." Of course, I don't suppose these authors would say that our society is so patriarchal that a woman cannot validly consent to have an abortion. After all, a woman's right to decide what she does with her own body is one of their most fundamental principles – almost an article of religious faith.

So, if I get this straight, their argument is that our society is not so patriarchal that a woman is not competent to decide what to do with her body *after* she has had sex (i.e., have an abortion if she deems that necessary), but it is so patriarchal that a woman is not competent to decide what to do with her body *while* she is having sex. I'm reminded of the only-semi-joking saying that the only "truly politically correct" form of sex is celibate lesbianism, including no masturbation.

(I imagine that now I'll be the recipient of that current withering phrase, "You just don't get it." That has become the current feminist argument-winning statement. You don't have to prove that your opponent is wrong and you are right, you don't have to present evidence that supports your case, and you don't even have to respond to your opponent's assertions or present a case of your own. You simply look witheringly at them and scornfully say, "You just don't get it, do you?" Then you leave the stage, pausing briefly to acknowledge the wildly cheering audience.)

From time to time, various laws are proposed, often by a rather uneasy coalition of "feminists" and right-wing fundamentalists, to outlaw the production and distribution of "all that weird sex stuff." Sociologists often refer to flurries of such activity as "sex panics." (We seem to be going through such a panic right now.) This is often allegedly done to, among other things, protect our children. (There's a saying that dates back to ancient times, and it loosely translates as, "When all else fails, accuse them of corrupting our youth." Furthermore, this argument is often effective regardless of the facts, as Socrates learned.)

Nowadays, we see diligent actions to prevent the publication and distribution of "violent pornography" (that's code for SM), "patently offensive acts," and similar material. A catch-phrase that often appears is something to the effect of "including depictions of bestiality, pedophilia, and sadomasochism." In other words, we folks who enjoy SM-type videos, no matter how mild and consensual, get lumped in with those who enjoy watching videos of people having sex with children or sex with animals. And that is wrong.

I left my
toy bag
on the bus!

SM is about consensual, negotiated erotic interaction between mentally competent, consenting, *adult human beings*. Bestiality and pedophilia are distinctly different, and that distinction deserves more recognition than it gets.

Because I am neither a bestiality fan nor a pedophile, I wouldn't dream of attempting to plead their case for them, but I will ask that legislators and judges realize the distinctions, and not victimize SM folks with overly broad, unfair laws. I will also ask my readers to stay alert regarding new "anti-obscenity" laws. Such proposed laws are often horribly unfair and unjust, but they will get on the books unless we act. Among other things, make sure you're registered to vote. The gay community has learned that it is large enough to wield political power if it organizes. We in the SM community are at least as large, and should pay attention to the lessons the gay community has taught us.

For more information, see the "Censorship" section in the "Finding Help with Problems" chapter.

By the way, remember that "erotica" is material that arouses me and people I like, and "pornography" is what arouses people I don't like.

## Basic Terms

A certain amount of jargon exists within the SM community. I've included a more complete glossary at the end of this book, but I thought I would briefly define the more commonly used words here. They'll be showing up throughout the book, so a short introduction (in logical order, not alphabetical order) of twelve commonly used terms should be useful. (Note: There is widespread, but not universal, agreement within the community regarding these definitions.)

- Dominant: One who gives orders during SM play.
- Sadist: A person who specifically enjoys giving pain.
- Top: A generic term for someone who enjoys being dominant and/or sadistic. Many people use the word "top" to mean someone who enjoys giving sensation, as opposed to a "dominant," who enjoys being in control of others.
- Submissive: One who obeys orders during SM play.
- Masochist: A person who specifically enjoys receiving pain.
- Bottom: A generic term for someone who enjoys being submissive and/or masochistic. Many people use the word "bottom" to mean specifically someone who enjoys being given various sensations, as opposed to a "submissive," who enjoys being controlled.
- Switch: A person who enjoys both the top and bottom roles.
- Play: SM erotic activity involving bondage, pain, domination, and so forth.
- Scene: A meeting between two (or more) people for the purpose of SM play. Also known as a "session."
- Toy: A piece of SM equipment such as a whip, collar, length of rope, and so forth. One "plays" with "toys" during "scenes."
- In the scene: A member of the SM community. A person might say "I've been in the scene for five years." One person might ask another, "Is so-and-so in the scene?"
- Pervert: A term of affectionate recognition with the SM community. "Hey, Pervert" is sometimes called out on the street if only the other person is within earshot.

# Basic Basics

## *Consent*

Consent is one of the most important issues, perhaps *the* most important issue, in SM. Before you can do something to another person, they must agree. Touching another person, or even their clothing, without their consent, regardless of the degree of force used – even if it's minimal – is a crime. Don't do it.

People below the age of consent (which varies widely from state to state) cannot legally agree to participate in sex – and SM is definitely a form of sex. This could include tying someone or being tied by them. Avoid playing with those too young to consent, even if they request it. Say no.

Also, intoxicated or unconscious persons cannot consent. If you give somebody drugs or alcohol to "short-circuit" their objections, you could face rape charges.

Finally, a person too feeble-minded or senile to understand what is happening cannot meaningfully consent. Again, having sex with them is rape.

> I don't enjoy the pain. I want it as a counterbalance to the pleasure, but I don't like it. Masochists, on the other hand, actively enjoy it.

You might find it enlightening to go to the library and get a copy of your state's penal code. Look over the sections dealing with rape, assault, child abuse, reckless endangerment, false imprisonment, lewd and lascivious behavior, and related matters. You are expected to know what acts are illegal. Remember, "ignorance of the law is no excuse."

Don't extort or manipulate consent. Don't use unfair pressure to get it. Only accept freely given consent. Examples of unfairly obtained consent include the threat of withdrawing any type of support – such as shelter – if the other person is not willing.

I know of one "dominant" who told his submissives they could refuse to obey, but if they did that ended their relationship. They had to pack and immediately leave. How contemptible! (This guy had a hard time keeping submissives. I can imagine why.)

Also, the approach of "If you really loved me, you'd do SM with me" is reprehensible, perhaps especially if you're trying to persuade the other person to be submissive. If *you* really loved *them* you wouldn't treat them in such an unfair way, and I hope they're smart enough to realize that.

Informed consent includes an understanding about limits, how much or how little experience both parties have, how long the session will last, safety measures, and what specific acts will or won't occur.

A submissive has an ethical duty to offer themselves to the dominant in a good-faith way. They should not try to control the session (or "top from below," as it's called – more about that later) by placing unnecessary limits. A submissive should genuinely try to accept their dominant's desires, unless they have a specific problem or concern. (While the dominant must always honor any refusal, even an "unjustified" one, they can also decide whether to play with an overly troublesome submissive again.)

A dominant always has an ethical duty to act with concern for the submissive's well-being. They should never ask or demand anything from the submissive that would, in any way, seriously damage them. A dominant may wish to take a submissive further than that submissive has previously gone. (This is sometimes called "pushing limits.") However, they must always do so with an understanding of how difficult that may be for the submissive. They also must understand that going *too* far may cause lasting damage to both the submissive and their relationship with them.

### No SM on the first date.

For many people (not all, not most, but many) SM offers a chance to experience some of the most intense sexuality that exists. Also, SM can and frequently does have spiritual, therapeutic, and other aspects. However, those who would try it must approach SM with caution, knowledge, skill, and an unwavering, absolute respect for their partner and their partner's well-being.

## The Silent Alarm

Private play is considerably riskier than public play. I suggest you assume there is a 99 percent probability that any potential partner is at least basically safe and ethical. That still leaves a very dangerous one percent. How do you protect yourself against that one percent without becoming so armored that you scare off *too* many of the others?

A silent alarm is a safety device used when two people who don't know each other well meet for private play. You set up a silent alarm by telling someone you trust where you will be and with whom you will be playing. If you don't send an "I'm safe" message by an agreed-upon time, your "silent alarm partner" should understand that means your life is in danger.

A silent alarm's main purpose is deterrence. Therefore, diplomatically tell your prospective play partner, preferably *very* early in your negotiations, that you always have a silent alarm in place while playing with someone new. It's also good etiquette to encourage them to set up their own alarm.

Since the publication of the first edition of this book, I've heard many horror stories about highly nonconsensual – in some cases even life-threatening – private play. I've made a point of asking the victims if a silent alarm would have prevented these incidents. In every single case, they have answered, unhesitatingly, "Yes."

By the way, silent alarms are not only for people who have just met. People in long-term relationships who are new to SM play also might need such an alarm. I read about a husband who murdered his wife by first convincing her to let him tie her up as part of supposed SM play. Silent alarms are not just for new people. They can also be for veteran players – no matter how long the people involved have known each other. Always use a silent alarm if you feel even the *slightest* need for one.

Plainly tell a potential partner that you will use a silent alarm when the two of you play. An ethical, experienced person will understand, and will *not* question you about its details. An inexperienced person might ask questions, but should stop when you tell them such questions are inappropriate. Anyone who continues asking about your silent alarm after you tell them such questions are improper sends a strong message that they are unsafe.

A silent alarm's use is absolutely non-negotiable. If a potential partner objects, consider immediately ending contact with them. Playing SM in private with someone new, especially if you don't know them well and nobody else knows about it, can be dangerous – even fatal. In a worst-case situation, this lunatic could slowly torture you to death! This being so, SM people should understand a new partner's need for trustworthy reassurance that they will be treated well. *Accountability* creates this reassurance.

By the way, silent alarms are not only for submissives. Dominants also should use one the first few times they play privately with a new partner.

Get verifiable information about a potential partner before you play with them privately. Find out such things as their home phone number, home address, real name, e-mail address, auto type, license number – the more the better. Anyone who will not provide you with at least their (verifiable) home phone number is someone you probably should not play with privately. (You should be willing to provide a comparable amount of information to your partners as well.) A highly considerate player will offer some of this information even if you don't request it. I've even heard of dominants who *order* their submissives to set up silent alarms. I think this is an excellent idea – and I think the submissives should obey this order.

Tell your silent alarm partner the phone number and address of the play location. It's also wise to call them immediately *before* you enter the house to confirm the address (a cellular phone can be useful here). Have them call you shortly *after* you enter to confirm the phone number. This call-in is especially valuable as it makes clear to your new partner that someone knows your location. (This is sometimes summarized by the saying, "I'll call out. You call in.") It's also not out of line to have your silent alarm partner speak briefly to your play partner "to wish them a good time."

If your silent alarm partner doesn't hear from you by more than 15 minutes past the agreed-upon deadline, they should attempt to contact you by phone (or pager, if you have one). It's wise to agree ahead of time on a "silent alarm word" to signal "I'm in trouble," and another to indicate "I'm OK." These words

*Begging is not a safe word.*

shouldn't be unusual, so including them in a conversation won't provoke undue notice. For example, "hi" could mean "I'm fine," and "hi there" could mean "help!!!" "Robert" could be a green light and "Bobby" a red alert (assuming, of course, that their name is Bob).

If they hear the "in trouble" word, or fail to hear the "OK" word, or can't reach you at all, they are to assume you are in mortal danger and they are to *call the police.* They are to give your name, and theirs, and your play partner's. They should tell the police that you are being held against your will at that address, perhaps hidden in the house. They might meet the police at your location, but your silent alarm partner should *never* go to where you are without the police. This is true even if they bring friends and/or weapons with them. They are *not* to play hostage rescue team. They are to call the police.

Because of the seriousness of what will happen if you don't check in by the deadline, you have a *major* responsibility to remember to call. One way to help you remember is to set the alarm on your wristwatch if you're going to their house. If the session is at your house, you can use an alarm clock or other timer. (And if you cancel the session, remember to cancel the silent alarm!)

Also, please deactivate the alarm as soon as it's no longer needed, usually shortly after you and your play partner have parted company. If something were to happen to you later – say, for example, you were in an auto accident while driving home – you wouldn't want the cops descending on your innocent partner! Stop at a nearby pay phone, or use your cellular phone, and call your silent alarm partner. During this conversation, include a previously agreed-upon "all clear" phrase – an unusual phrase which should never be used in the presence of your play partner. Examples would be the name of a dinosaur, planet, astrological sign, or color.

By the way, if your play partner returns to your house after you have deactivated your alarm (perhaps claiming that they forgot something), reactivate it *before* you let them back into your house. A trustworthy, courteous person will call before they reappear. An untrustworthy person will simply show up and want in. Make them wait outside! *Never open the door, not even to hand them something they left, without reactivating the alarm.*

If you can't do that, tell them you're sorry but you can't let them in right now. Ask them to return at a more convenient time. If they won't leave, call the police! This may sound harsh, but coming back unannounced and uninvited is serious misbehavior.

Silent alarm deadlines are usually set for one of two times: either shortly after the session should have ended, or much later. The latter is useful if you think you might be spending the night with your play partner. For overnight sessions, noon the next day is a good deadline.

Two advantages of a longer silent alarm deadline are that it allows for longer sessions and reduces the chance you will forget to call. One disadvantage is that if a session does go bad, it could be a long time before anyone got worried. (By the way, there's no reason you can't use *two* silent alarm deadlines – one for the night in question and another for the next morning.)

Use a silent alarm as often as you feel necessary. I have used one up to four times with a given partner.

By the way, you are not obligated to tell a partner when you have decided to stop using one while playing with them. Again, if they ask, that's a bad sign.

If you don't have someone in your life who can act as your silent alarm partner, leave the information on your kitchen table or call it in to your telephone answering machine. You can talk into your answering machine as follows, "Hi, this is Debbie. It's 7:05 p.m. on June 19 and I'm calling from Tom's house at 1301 Reage Street. His number is 555-1369. We're about to do some private play."

Dominants often make excellent submissives. They know the rules of the game.

Alternatively, mail the information to yourself, mail or e-mail it to a friend, or take some similar action. (Some SM clubs provide "silent alarm service" to their members.) It may be a good idea to carry a printed copy of this note in your pocket or purse. If your partner starts to behave nonconsensually, tell them about it and tell them a trusted friend has another copy.

Silent alarms may sound scary and cumbersome, but using them becomes routine with practice. For example, when Janet or I is playing with a new partner, the other knows the address, phone number, and identity of that partner. The "all clear" call comes in on or before the pre-arranged time, and that's about it.

If you follow basic precautions and negotiate properly, your chances of needing a silent alarm are slim. I've personally never needed one, although I once had a close call, but now and then somebody does – and when they do, they need it desperately.

Remember, the main purpose of a silent alarm is *deterrence*. Most of a silent alarm's effectiveness comes from letting the other person know, the sooner the better, that it's in operation.

Mistress, I'm really deep.

## Safewords

One unique aspect of SM is the creation of an agreement between dominant and submissive that the submissive will use a specific signal, usually a particular word, to signal that the play is becoming too intense for them and that serious distress and/or damage is possible. SM folks usually call this a "safeword." It's also occasionally called a "key word" or a "stop word."

By using a safeword, the submissive may yelp, wince, cry, plead for mercy, scream for the cops, threaten revenge, and so forth, and such behaviors need not overly concern the dominant. They are "part of the game." But if the submissive utters their safeword, the dominant must respond, usually by stopping, decreasing, or changing the activity.

The basic safeword is one used to end the session completely. If the submissive (or dominant) calls this word, they completely end the session. A player should take such action only for serious cause.

Safewords are usually chosen from words not likely to come up in a session. Commonly used safewords include: "red," "mercy," "peace," "key," "safe," "enough," and "easy." Sometimes the dominant's name is used. A generic safeword, often used at SM parties to indicate that the people involved want others outside the scene to come to their assistance, is "safeword" itself. (Words like "harder" and "more" are poor choices for safewords.)

The one-word system, while suitable as an absolute safety measure, is clumsy. It's an all-or-nothing device, and submissives often don't want to go that far. Many players thus use a second safeword to signal, "The play is getting too intense for me. Let's lighten up or rest for a while." Players often use the word "yellow" for this purpose.

Sometimes people use an additional safeword to signal, "Please, no more of *that*." This signals that they want to continue the session, but they have a serious problem with a specific activity. "Blue" is sometimes used as this signal.

Note: Some SM players use the term "911" as an "emergency/stop immediately" safeword and the term "411" as an "information/we need to talk" safeword. (Do they know that "611" is the repair service number?)

I cannot overemphasize the importance of *always* having a safeword system in effect when you play. Some experienced players consider themselves so skilled, perceptive, and advanced that they don't need such a "basic" safety measure. This is dangerous folly. Understand clearly: playing without a safeword will *inevitably* lead to serious problems. You may get away with playing without a safeword for a while, perhaps even a long while, but eventually some disaster *will* occur that a safeword would have prevented. (It's also my experience that submissives who have a safeword are noticeably more likely to accept intense play than those who lack one.)

A wise dominant remembers that submissives sometimes forget their safewords. A wise dominant also remembers that submissives may feel too embarrassed to confess this. Therefore, they make sure a submissive remembers their safewords before beginning another session with them. It's also smart for the dominant to make sure the submissive remembers their safewords before significantly increasing a session's intensity – especially regarding pain. (For these reasons, particularly when playing with somebody new, it may be a good idea to ask the submissive what safeword they're used to using, and to choose that one for the session.)

Also, a submissive sometimes becomes so accepting of the dominant's wishes or so "endorphined-out" by the session that calling their safeword will not occur to them. I know submissives who "go under" so deeply that they seem to leave their body. In such a case, an unperceptive dominant could unknowingly cause severe damage because the submissive wouldn't be "home" to object.

One characteristic of a good dominant is that – while they always give their submissives safewords – the submissives rarely need to use them, especially a scene-stopper like "red." As a submissive approaches their limits, a skilled dominant watches them closely. The submissive will typically become increasingly tense. Their breathing will become tighter and more labored.

Their muscles will grow more rigid. A good dominant backs off before the submissive calls their safeword.

## The Ethics of Safewords

Ethical and practical considerations exist regarding safewords. They are our number-one safety measure. Treat them with proper respect. A dominant absolutely must honor a safeword. This is true even if they believe the circumstances do not warrant the submissive's calling it. This is true even if the submissive calls the safeword in an unethical attempt to manipulate the session. A dominant must *always* honor a safeword – whatever the submissive's motives. Understand that continuing to whip or otherwise inflict pain on a submissive, or to keep them restrained after they've called a safeword, is a *crime*.

Failure to honor a safeword is serious misconduct – perhaps the most serious misconduct an SM player can commit. It would justify never playing with that person again, and might justify ending your relationship with them altogether. Failure to honor a safeword also might be grounds for expulsion from an SM organization. The offending player would have to show why they should not be expelled, and they would face an uphill fight.

Sometimes I want you to do things to me that I hate.

Another serious breach of ethics on the dominant's part is to say or imply to a submissive, especially to a bound submissive, that maybe they don't feel like honoring the safeword. This may destroy the submissive's trust, and is grounds for the submissive to end the session immediately.

Don't joke about safewords. Don't imply that you won't honor them. Even one such remark may permanently destroy the trust a submissive considers essential to play with you. If the submissive thinks you might not honor the safewords, they may quietly conclude they are in danger of being tortured to death. They might then, particularly if they don't know you well, decide not to test you on this point and end the session in the way that will most reliably remove them from danger – possibly by attacking you.

I heard of a dominant woman who bound a novice submissive man and then told him that maybe she wouldn't honor their safewords. When the session became too intense for him, he simply slipped out of his restraints (she wasn't as good at bondage as she thought) and left. When she tried to stop him, he doubled her over with a kick to her stomach and almost smashed in her face with a pair of heavy leg irons.

Get clear and stay clear about this: a dominant who "jokes" about not honoring safewords can get themselves killed.

Also, dominants should remember that some submissives want to be badly hurt. A few even want to be killed. And it's not unusual for an endorphined-out submissive to decide that they want an activity that they would definitely regret later – and be very angry at you for doing. (Thus giving rise to the community saying, "Tops need safewords too.") Remember that just because a submissive does not appear close to calling their safeword is *not* enough grounds to inflict more pain. Even with consent, you must not (and legally cannot) cause severe injury.

Safewords carry responsibilities for submissives, too. The submissive must never call a safeword, especially "red," for frivolous or unethical reasons. On the other hand, a submissive shouldn't wait until they are seconds away from a nervous breakdown before they call a safeword, particularly when playing with somebody new. Remember that it will take time to remove clamps, untie ropes, and so forth. The submissive might be carried beyond their limits and into trauma during that time. Don't wait until the last instant to "bail out." No heroics!

On the other hand, it's common for a submissive to "test" a safeword during a session to make sure that the dominant will honor it in the future. This is particularly likely during their first few sessions with a new partner. Don't worry, they'll get over it.

Also, when being submissive, don't use your safeword to "top from below." It's not enough that you'd simply rather be doing something else. Safewords exist to protect you from serious damage. Never use them frivolously.

> You haven't tied me up in over three weeks. Is something wrong?

## *Non-Verbal Safewords*

Players who use gags or similar devices obviously need non-verbal signals. Some such signals include vigorous nodding of the head "yes," waving the foot in a particular pattern, snapping the fingers, grunting a certain way, or dropping something held in the hand. People who play in darkened rooms need *audible* signals – some players give the submissive a squeaky toy to hold.

One good non-verbal safeword is snapping the fingers. (This may not work if the submissive is on their back with their hands tied behind them.) Loud grunts are also possible for a gagged submissive. These work well, but a dominant might confuse them with a submissive's moans. One workable pattern is that two grunts equal yellow and three grunts equal red.

A few clever submissives learn how to finger-spell the deaf-mute alphabet. If the dominant learns to read it (the basics are easy), much communication becomes possible between the silenced submissive and the dominant.

## Checking In

One problem with safewords is that they require initiative on the part of the submissive. From time to time, I hear about a scene in which the submissive had a bad experience and afterwards is feeling reproachful, and the poor dominant is bewilderedly saying "But they didn't safeword!" I think the fact that the submissive did not safeword is a partial, but not a complete, defense. However, it's certainly no excuse for not knowing what's going on with your submissive.

She had that expectant glow about her. You know, the kind that masochists get?

For this reason, dominants need some way that *they* can ascertain what I call "affirmative consent," preferably without asking a somewhat-mood-disturbing question like "Are you OK?" (After all, they're "tormenting" the submissive.)

Some verbal "check-ins" that work well are "Are you still with me?" and "Do you remember your safeword?" (By the way, "Yes" is not an adequate answer to this second question; "Yes, master or mistress, it's 'gorgonzola'" is much better.)

**Two squeezes means I'm OK.** I invented the "two squeezes" technique, and I've found it works well. To use this technique, the dominant places their hand on the submissive's body and gives two firm and noticeable (but *not* painful) squeezes. The dominant usually does this by grasping the submissive's hand, but also can use other places such as the wrist, shoulder, or thigh. (I suggest avoiding the breasts and genitals.) The two squeezes ask "are you OK?"

The submissive replies that they are OK by giving two squeezes in return. Note: The dominant can learn a lot about the submissive's state of mind by noting *how* the submissive returns the squeezes. Two quick, brisk squeezes show that the submissive is alert and "in the room with you." Two long, slow squeezes show that the submissive is OK but "deep under."

If the submissive is in a position that makes it difficult for them to squeeze in return, they could answer by opening and closing their fist twice. They also could answer by nodding their head twice, by pointing their foot twice, or by sending another non-verbal signal.

(By the way, an experienced submissive who is "teaching from below" can also use this technique to check in with a novice dominant.)

What if you squeeze and *don't* get two squeezes in return? The first action you should take, particularly if the preceding play has been intense, is *wait*. (In particular, don't give any more pain.) Remember that it sometimes takes a submissive a while to "swim back up" far enough to answer. It also sometimes takes a while for them to realize that their dominant asked them a question and they must reply. (Remember, sometimes submissives go so deeply under that they experience themselves as having melted or dissolved.)

If you've waited about thirty seconds and haven't received "return squeezes," give two more, slightly stronger, squeezes. If the submissive doesn't respond to these new squeezes after about thirty seconds, check in with them in a more verbal, direct manner. Ask them a question like, "how are you doing?" or "what's going on?" Make sure of their condition before you proceed.

The "two squeezes" technique usually works extremely well. It provides a simple, workable way for both parties to communicate that they are all right without either having to break the mood verbally.

**Degree of spread equals degree of distress.** I once did a session in which I bottomed to a very experienced and well-known mistress who specializes in flogging. She instructed me that if my hands were somewhat relaxed and curled, she would interpret that as meaning I was OK. I was to spread my fingers to show my degree of distress – the wider-spread my hand was, the more trouble I was having receiving the flogging. I found that this signal worked very well for me, and have since used it in my own dominant sessions to good effect.

> The first time I talked my wife into tying me up, I was trembling like a leaf – not with fear, with excitement.

## Negotiation

There's an old SM saying (which I invented) that goes, "When two people are alone together, and one of them is naked and tied up, and the other is standing over them holding whips and other torture implements, this is *not* the time to have a serious mismatch of expectations."

I regard negotiation as the single most important SM skill. Before two (or more) people play, they must agree who will do what, within what limits, and for how long.

*Failure to negotiate well is the single most common cause of a bad SM session.*

Three reasons account for most poor pre-session negotiations. First, the people involved may have little idea of how to negotiate properly. Second, they may know how, but feel so aroused by the prospect of imminent play that they let their hormones carry them further than they should. Third, they may do so many negotiations that they become bored or careless. Professional dominants and submissives often suffer from this last flaw.

Some players try to negotiate as they go along. This is dangerous. First, people may agree in the excitement of the scene to activities they shouldn't, which they will regret later, and which they'll probably blame on you. Second, the submissive may not feel free to refuse. They often find it difficult to come temporarily out of "bottom space" for negotiations on equal terms and then resume their role.

The best time to negotiate is at the beginning, preferably while both players are still dressed and neither is in role.

The primary responsibility for complete, ethical negotiations rests with the dominant. A good dominant shows their skill and control by insisting on high-quality negotiations. A poor dominant, and therefore one of doubtful trustworthiness, proceeds recklessly.

If one player has much more experience, that person also has a strong responsibility to make sure negotiations are handled properly.

Basic negotiations between experienced players can often take only five to ten minutes, but these are the most important minutes of the session.

The following matters commonly arise during SM, and thus players should negotiate them before playing. If a specific matter is not agreed upon, the players, especially the dominant, should not introduce or propose it during that session. Wait till next time. Agreement changes once the session begins, especially if proposed by the dominant, begin to stink of nonconsensuality. Instead, think "next time." Dominants must master resisting temptation; they must become experts at self-denial.

A good, basic SM negotiation should cover 16 points.

1. **The people involved.** Who will take part? How much experience do they have with the activities proposed? Who, if anybody, will watch?

2. **Roles.** Who will be dominant? Who will be submissive? Any chance of switching roles? Will the participants be acting out a particular fantasy such as teacher/schoolchild, pirate/captive, or owner/dog?

   Is there clear agreement by the submissive to obey, within limits, the dominant's orders? Can the dominant "overpower" the submissive? "Force" them to do something? What about verbal resistance? Physical resistance? May the submissive try to "turn the tables" on the dominant? Will the submissive agree to wear a collar? Will they agree to address the dominant as "Master," "Mistress," or some similar term?

*Warning:* Physical resistance can easily be misinterpreted. I therefore strongly recommend that, particularly for the first few sessions, the dominant allow *any* physical resistance by the submissive to "succeed" immediately. A dominant should tell the submissive, *in so many words*, that they will consider any physical resistance on the submissive's part, no matter how slight, a "strong yellow" and will not even begin to try to overcome it. Major physical resistance will be considered a "red" and will result in the session instantly ending.

3. **Place.** Where will the session occur? Who will ensure privacy? (Usually the dominant.)

4. **Time.** When will the session begin? How long will it last? How will its beginning and end be signaled? Who will keep track of time? (Again, usually the dominant.)

    Note: Unless deliberately built into the play, a clock visible to the submissive often detracts from the scene's energy.

I enjoy the contrast – a sweet, feminine, innocent-looking lady who enjoys the heck out of torturing me unmercifully.

5. **Oops!** SM play is always somewhat unpredictable. No matter how carefully you negotiate and plan, accidents, misperceptions, miscommunications, and sometimes unintentional injuries will occasionally happen. Therefore, it's a good idea to talk about these matters ahead of time, discussing how you will handle them and how you will treat each other if they do occur. It's important to agree that both parties are negotiating and playing in good faith, and that any mishaps will be discussed in a constructive, non-blaming way.

6. **Limits.** This mainly involves the submissive's physical and emotional limits. Do they have any relevant health problems such as a heart condition, high blood pressure, or epilepsy? Are they wearing glasses or, especially, contact lenses? How well do they see without them? Do they have any physical limitations? I would hesitate, for example, to tie someone with their arms stretched tightly overhead if they have a history of a dislocated shoulder. Any history of plastic surgery? (You don't want to deliver strong whip strokes to breasts that contain implants.)

Any history of back surgery, joint surgery, sprained ankles, neck injury, joint disorders, arthritis, etc.?  Any other range-of-motion limits?

The submissive *must* be completely honest with their dominant about limits.  Some submissives conceal information because they may feel embarrassed or fear that revealing it may cause the dominant to decide not to play with them.  This is stupid.  While revealing the information may indeed cause a dominant to cancel a session, withholding it may cause a disaster.

Emotional limits:  Any known phobias or other emotional hotspots?  Any "real life" incidents in their past that might come up?  Note:  Both players should understand that SM play has a small but distinct chance of touching an unknown emotional hot spot in either player.

7.  **Sex.**  It's crucial to agree clearly and specifically, *before* beginning the session, about exactly what kind of conventional sexual contact, if any, is mutually acceptable.  What about masturbation?  Cunnilingus?  Fellatio?  Swallowing semen?  Analingus?  Vaginal intercourse?  Anal intercourse?  Condoms?  Birth control precautions?  Does either person have herpes?  Has either tested positive for the AIDS virus?  Keep in mind that not everybody agrees on the definition of "safer sex practices"; before you begin your session, make sure you are in agreement regarding which activities will involve a barrier and which will not.

Don't act shy or squeamish on this point.  The negotiations on conventional sex absolutely *must* be clear and agreed upon before going further.  Failure to make sure of this point, or going into the session "hoping for the best," can set the stage for a very frustrating session – as I have learned from experience.

8.  **Intoxicants.**  Don't play if either of you is seriously drunk or stoned.  Particularly avoid drugs that make the submissive insensitive to pain or that impair the dominant's judgment or coordination.  (SM often has a potent, drug-like effect on many people.  It needs little outside help.)

As of this writing, I know of no serious accidents during SM play where the players used only small amounts of beer, wine, or marijuana.  I suggest avoiding SM play if either person is under the strong influence of liquor, heroin, cocaine, amphetamines, tranquilizers, barbiturates, or potent psychedelics. Many injuries and nonconsensual incidents can be traced directly to players using strong intoxicants, especially alcohol!

Note: Introducing any intoxicant not previously agreed upon is serious misbehavior. If the dominant pulls out hard liquor, cocaine, or something similar, the submissive should immediately call "red," get dressed, and leave.

9. **Bondage.** Who will be tied up? To what extent? (Some submissives allow a new dominant to bind them, but don't allow the dominant to tie them *to* something such as a bed or chair.) What about blindfolds? Gags? Hoods? (Wise players avoid blindfolds, gags, and hoods during the first few sessions.) Does the submissive have a history of claustrophobia? Have they been bound, gagged, blindfolded, or hooded before? How did they react?

10. **Pain.** How does the submissive feel about receiving pain? Can they be spanked? Paddled? Whipped? Slapped? What about nipple clamps? Genital clamps? Clamps elsewhere? How about hot creams? Ice? Anything else painful? Some submissives cheerfully admit they are "pain sluts." Others hate receiving pain, but will endure it if doing so pleases their dominant.

We talk a lot about the vulnerability of the submissive to the dominant. What we don't talk about as much is the vulnerability of the dominant to the submissive.

11. **Marks.** Will it cause the submissive problems if the session leaves marks? (Whipping is likely to mark.) Do they know from experience how easily they mark? Do they understand it might be difficult to tell whether a given activity is marking them? Do they care if an activity draws small amounts of blood? If it's crucial that the submissive not be marked, then it's probably best to avoid spanking, whipping, clamping, pinching, and so forth.

(Note: Sometimes marks not normally visible can be "brought to the surface" by a hot shower. This can happen up to several days after the session.)

12. **Humiliation.** This can include "verbal abuse," forced exhibitionism, water sports (peeing on the submissive), enemas, slapping the face, spitting, and scat (feces) games. Does the submissive have any experience in these areas? What was their reaction? Are they curious? Are these areas definite turn-offs?

Playing with humiliation is playing with emotional dynamite. This area, therefore, is exceptionally important to negotiate.

Never "surprise" a submissive with a golden shower or something similar. Their reaction could be immediate and extreme – panic, intense shame, violent rage.

Remember, the less well you know someone, and the less experience you have with them, the more carefully you must proceed. This is especially true about humiliation.

13. **Safewords.** I recommend using at least two safewords: one for "lighten up," and one for "stop completely." These are usually enough for a basic session. I also strongly recommend including the "two squeezes" technique.

If the players will use a gag or hood, they *must* agree upon non-verbal "safe signals." Again, gagging a submissive without previously setting up a non-verbal safeword and getting their consent is asking for trouble.

14. **Opportunities.** Is there anything either person has wanted to try but not had a reasonable opportunity to experience? Is there anything they feel curious about? Does either have unique talents or skills to offer?

Don't try to do it all in one night.

15. **Follow-up.** What arrangements can be made for the two people to spend "straight time" together immediately after the session? What about follow up contact the next day? A week later? If a crisis occurs?

16. **Anything Else?** Is there anything else to discuss or negotiate about before beginning?

Sixteen points seem like a lot, yet with practice experienced players can cover them in only five to ten minutes – if they closely agree. On the other hand, negotiations may take *much* longer. As a rule of thumb, if it takes over an hour to agree on all points, you may not be compatible enough to play together then. Stop for the time being and schedule another meeting.

Caution: Negotiate only when both of you are alert and in good spirits. If one or both of you feels tired, sleepy, sad, angry, fearful, or otherwise upset, negotiate (and play) later.

I have used this 16-point checklist with many new partners, and for more than eight years. In all of that time, I have never had a bad session after reaching clear agreement on all 16 points prior to play.

## *To Help You Remember*

The sixteen points are: people, roles, place, time, oops, limits, sex, intoxicants, bondage, pain, marks, humiliation, safewords, opportunities, follow-up, and "anything else?" The first letters of these words, respectively, are: P, R, P, T, O, L, S, I, B, P, M, H, S, O, F, A. I've devised a saying to help you remember. The first letter of each word matches the first letter of a negotiation point.

"*Placing Ropes Properly Tight Only Lets Sex Intensify. Binding Penises May Hurt, So Only Fuck Animals.*"

Its delightful nonsense-ness helps you remember it. (Please don't fuck any animals. I only put that word in because its vividness will help you remember the saying. I oppose bestiality.)

To review:

| | | |
|---|---|---|
| *Placing* | *People* | |
| *Ropes* | *Roles* | |
| *Properly* | *Place* | |
| *Tight* | *Time* | |
| *Only* | *Oops* | |
| *Lets* | *Limits* | |
| *Sex* | *Sex* | |
| *Intensify* | *Intoxicants* | Please slap my face. |
| *Binding* | *Bondage* | |
| *Penises* | *Pain* | |
| *May* | *Marks* | |
| *Hurt* | *Humiliation* | |
| *So* | *Safewords* | |
| *Only* | *Opportunities* | |
| *Fuck* | *Follow-up* | |
| *Animals* | *Anything else?* | |

Say this aloud a few times. Write it down. Post it somewhere. With only a little repetition, it's easy to remember and use.

It helps to prepare a negotiation form and fill in the blanks as you negotiate. This helps both players stay clear about what they agreed upon (and what they didn't).

Finally, remember that neither player, especially the submissive, *must* do anything they previously agreed they would do. While they should make a good-faith effort to obey, they may call their safeword if the session becomes too intense for them.

The dominant has *no* right to "really" force the submissive to do anything, even if the submissive previously agreed to do it. Also, the submissive has no right to insist the dominant do anything to them that the dominant feels uncomfortable about doing or incompetent to do. Dominants, too, have the right to use safewords.

### *"Pre" Pre-Session Negotiations*

Few experiences feel more frustrating than sitting in the playroom, negotiating an imminent session, and discovering your potential partner won't agree to something you consider essential.

Running into a "deal-breaker" in this situation is awful. Your basic options are (1) cancel the session, (2) proceed anyway, hoping "it'll work itself out" (it almost never does), or (3) begin prolonged negotiations to try to resolve the situation. (Not likely.)

I have learned that by far the best way to deal with this situation is to avoid it. You do that by negotiating your deal-breakers well ahead of the time when you and your new partner might meet to play. If you know that something likely to come up is beyond your limits, let your prospective partners know this (diplomatically, please) early.

Basic Point: The earlier you discuss deal-breakers, the better. Also, make a point of asking about your potential partner's deal-breakers. Find out early – as soon as possible after it looks like the two of you might want to play together.

In my experience, the most common deal-breaker is sex. A surprisingly large number of players are willing to get together for bondage, whipping, and so forth only if nothing likely to produce an orgasm will occur. If you know you strongly want (or strongly don't want) masturbation, oral sex, intercourse, or something similar to occur during the session, mention that early in your pre-session negotiations.

### *Group Negotiations*

When play involves more than two people, everyone should participate in the main negotiations. Afterward, the dominants can send the submissives away and negotiate who will do what. (Among other things, making the submissives wait while you decide their "fate" is itself a delicious torture.)

### *Post-Session Negotiations and Feedback*

Post-session negotiations and other feedback are usually done at one of three times: (1) Immediately after the session. (2) The next day. (3) About a week later.

Immediately after the session, it's good for the people involved to spend some "straight time" out of role with each other. Spending this time in a place other than the one in which the actual play took place is an excellent idea. Going to a nearby restaurant or coffee house often works very well.

This time allows the people to reestablish a "genuine" relationship with each other. It also allows them time to decompress and relax after sharing an intense experience.

I have found that this time is not an especially good one for detailed analysis of what happened and the participants' reactions to it. Instead, just relax and get to know the other person again as a person, not as their role of dominant or submissive. If this is not your regular partner, then this is probably not the best time to ask about getting together to play again. The experience is often still too fresh, and too raw, for them to know how they feel about that.

Caution: It's not uncommon for the dominant to experience some feelings of depression and/or guilt after a session (a phenomenon known as "top drop"). Hitting another person, or otherwise "torturing" them, no matter how consensually it was done or how much the other person enjoyed it, is taboo. The dominant has just broken that taboo, and may be paying the emotional price for doing that. A good submissive, therefore, makes sure to thank the dominant for their time and attention, and reassures them (to the extent they truthfully can) that they liked what happened. Submissives don't have to lie about this, and don't have to claim that they liked something that they didn't like. They do, however, need to make sure that the dominant feels thanked for their gifts of time, skill, and attention.

Let me show you where I hide my extra handcuff key.

The negotiations that take place the next day are often the "real" post-session negotiations. By this time, the people have had a chance to think about what went on and react to it. One retired professional dominant used to question her submissives by using the following formula: What was the best thing about the session? What was the worst thing about the session? What was the most memorable thing about the session? After her submissive had answered those questions, she would then answer them herself from her point of view. After these questions were answered, general discussion followed as appropriate.

I have used a similar approach successfully on many occasions. I ask, on a scale of one to ten, with ten the top, what is your overall feeling about the session? I then ask what was the best thing about the session, and on a scale of one to ten how good was it – and what was the worst thing, and on a scale of one to ten how bad was it? The additional information is valuable. Among its other benefits, it often reveals that the good things were very good and (hopefully) that the bad things were not all that bad. We then go on to discuss other aspects of the session as needed.

Asking about getting together for future sessions at this time is usually acceptable. Your partner has usually had enough time to work through their reactions and can give you a realistic answer.

One-week-later negotiations and feedback are mainly to check for complications. Monday Morning Rebound Syndrome, top drop, and any injuries not readily apparent have usually emerged by this time, and can be dealt with. It's certainly all right to ask about getting together again at this point.

## *Second-Session Negotiations*

If the first session goes well, negotiations usually take much less time for a second session. Again, make sure you agree on the 16 basic points. Be sure you cover limits, sex, bondage, and safewords. Incorporate feedback from the first session. Still, negotiating the second session usually takes much less time. Additional sessions usually take even less.

## *Conclusion*

The minutes spent negotiating are usually the most important minutes of the entire session. Rushed or sloppy negotiations open the door to disaster. Good, complete negotiations open the door to a future containing many pleasurable sessions. I have never met a good negotiator who turned out to be a bad player.

## *Negotiation Forms*

To help clarify matters as you negotiate, and to help you remember what your agreements were once the play begins, I've included two "negotiation forms" in this section. They proved to be among the most popular parts of the first edition.

As with your income tax, you can use either the "short form" or the "long form" as appropriate. Among other things, looking over these forms, particularly the long form, helps people realize how many different aspects of SM play can come up during a session. That in itself can be highly educational and clarifying.

Notice: Permission is hereby given to photocopy (only) the negotiation forms in this book.

## *Negotiation Short Form* _____

Note: Please use the back of the form if additional space is needed.

1. People _____

2. Roles _____

3. Place _____

4. Time _____

5. Oops _____

6. Limits _____

7. Sex_____

8. Intoxicants_____

9. Bondage _____

10. Pain_____

11. Marks _____

12. Humiliation_____

13. Safewords_____

14. Opportunities _____

15. Follow-Up _____

16. Anything Else?_____

## *Negotiation Long Form* _____

Note: Please use the back of the form if additional space is needed.

1. **People**

   Who will take part? _____

   Who will watch? _____
   Note: The session will involve *only* those people specifically named above.

   Will any permanent record be made of the session (photographs, audio-tapes or videotapes)?  ☐ Yes  ☐ No

   Explanation _____

2. **Roles**

   Who will be dominant? _____ Who will be submissive? ____

   Type of scene:

   master/slave   mistress/slave   captive   servant/butler/Etc.

   cross-dressing/gender play   age play   animal play   other _____

   _____

   Any chance of switching roles?  ☐ Yes  ☐ No

   Explanation: _____

   Will the submissive promptly obey?  ☐ Yes  ☐ No

   Explanation: _____

   May the dominant "overpower" or "force" the submissive?

   ☐ Yes ☐ No

   Explanation: _____

   May the submissive verbally resist?  ☐ Yes  ☐ No

   Explanation: _____

May the submissive physically resist? ☐ Yes ☐ No

Explanation: _____

Does resistance equal a "strong yellow"? ☐ Yes ☐ No

Explanation: _____

May the submissive try to "turn the tables"? ☐ Yes ☐ No

Explanation: _____

Does the submissive agree to wear a collar? ☐ Yes ☐ No

Explanation: _____

The submissive agrees to address the dominant by the following title(s):

_____

## 3. Place

Location: _____

Who will ensure privacy? _____

## 4. Time

Begin at: _____ Length: _____

Beginning signal: _____ Ending signal: _____

Who will keep track of time? _____

## 5. Oops

Does everybody involved understand that there is some risk of accident, miscommunication, misperception and/or unintentional injury?
☐ Yes ☐ No

Does everybody involved agree to discuss any mishaps in a constructive and non-blaming manner? ☐ Yes ☐ No

## 6. Limits

### Submissive's limits

Submissive's physical/emotional/SM activity limits:

Any problems with the submissive's...

heart ☐ Yes ☐ No     lungs ☐ Yes ☐ No

neck/back/bones/joints ☐ Yes ☐ No     kidneys ☐ Yes ☐ No

liver ☐ Yes ☐ No     nervous system/mental ☐ Yes ☐ No

Explanation: _____

Is the submissive wearing contact lenses? ☐ Yes ☐ No

Does the submissive suffer from carpal tunnel syndrome or related problems? ☐ Yes ☐ No

Does the submissive have a history of...

seizures: ☐ Yes ☐ No     dizzy spells: ☐ Yes ☐ No

diabetes: ☐ Yes ☐ No   high or low blood pressure: ☐ Yes ☐ No

fainting: ☐ Yes ☐ No     asthma: ☐ Yes ☐ No

hyperventilation attacks: ☐ Yes ☐ No

Describe any phobias: _____

Submissive's other medical conditions: _____

Any surgical implants (breast, face, etc.)? ☐ Yes ☐ No

Explanation: _____

Is the submissive taking aspirin? ☐ Yes ☐ No

Is the submissive taking ibuprofen, Aleve, or other non-steroidal, anti-inflammatory drugs? ☐ Yes ☐ No

Is the submissive taking antihistamines? ☐ Yes ☐ No

Other medications submissive is taking: _____

Allergic to:

bandage tape: ☐ Yes ☐ No    nonoxynol-9: ☐ Yes ☐ No

Other allergies: _____

In case of emergency notify: _____

## Dominant's Limits

Dominant's physical/emotional/SM activity limits:

Any problems with the dominant's...

heart ☐ Yes ☐ No    lungs ☐ Yes ☐ No

neck/back/bones/joints ☐ Yes ☐ No    kidneys ☐ Yes ☐ No

liver ☐ Yes ☐ No    nervous system/mental ☐ Yes ☐ No

Explanation _____

Dominant's other medical conditions: _____

Medications dominant is taking: _____

In case of emergency notify: _____

Is the dominant currently certified in First Aid/CPR?    ☐ Yes ☐ No

Safety gear on hand:

paramedic scissors: ☐ Yes ☐ No    flashlight: ☐ Yes ☐ No

first aid kit: ☐ Yes ☐ No    blackout light: ☐ Yes ☐ No

fire extinguisher: ☐ Yes ☐ No

Will the play be in an isolated area such as a farmhouse?    ☐ Yes ☐ No

If yes, what will ensure the submissive's safety if the dominant becomes unconscious?

no bondage to chair, bed, etc.: ☐ Yes ☐ No  no gag: ☐ Yes ☐ No

silent alarm: ☐ Yes ☐ No    third person present: ☐ Yes ☐ No

telephone/radio/panic button within submissive's reach: ☐ Yes ☐ No

Other_____

7. **Sex**

Does any participant believe they might have a sexually transmitted disease? ☐ Yes ☐ No

Explanation: _____

Does any participant believe they might have herpes? ☐ Yes ☐ No

Explanation: _____

Have participants been tested for HIV? ☐ Yes ☐ No

Has any participant tested positive? ☐ Yes ☐ No

Explanation: _____

Circle which of the following sexual acts are acceptable:

Masturbation        dominant to submissive    submissive to dominant

    self-masturbation by submissive    self-masturbation by dominant

Fellatio            dominant to submissive    submissive to dominant

Cunnilingus         dominant to submissive    submissive to dominant

Analingus           dominant to submissive    submissive to dominant

Anal fisting        dominant to submissive    submissive to dominant

Vaginal fisting     dominant to submissive    submissive to dominant

Vaginal intercourse dominant to submissive    submissive to dominant

Anal intercourse    dominant to submissive    submissive to dominant

Is swallowing semen acceptable? ☐ Yes ☐ No

Is any participant menstruating? ☐ Yes ☐ No

Will sex toys such as vibrators, dildoes, butt plugs, etc. be used?
☐ Yes ☐ No

Describe: _____

Which of the above activities will involve birth control pills, diaphragms, spermicidal suppositories, lubricants containing nonoxynol-9, or contraceptive foam/suppositories/gel? _____

Which of the above activities will involve condoms, gloves, dental dams, and/or other barriers? _____

## 8. Intoxicants

The dominant can use (only) the following intoxicants during the session: _____

Acceptable quantity: _____

The submissive can use (only) the following intoxicants during the session: _____

Acceptable quantity: _____

## 9. Bondage

The submissive agrees to allow (only) the following types of bondage:

hands in front: ☐ Yes ☐ No     hands behind back: ☐ Yes ☐ No

ankles: ☐ Yes ☐ No          knees: ☐ Yes ☐ No

elbows: ☐ Yes ☐ No    wrists to ankles (hog-tie): ☐ Yes ☐ No

spreader bars: ☐ Yes ☐ No          tied to chair: ☐ Yes ☐ No

tied to bed: ☐ Yes ☐ No        use of blindfold: ☐ Yes ☐ No

use of gag: ☐ Yes ☐ No      use of hood: ☐ Yes ☐ No

use of rope: ☐ Yes ☐ No      use of tape: ☐ Yes ☐ No

use of handcuffs/metal restraints: ☐ Yes ☐ No

use of leather cuffs: ☐ Yes ☐ No    suspension: ☐ Yes ☐ No

mummification with plastic wrap, body bag, or similar techniques:
☐ Yes ☐ No

Any past bad experiences by either person with bondage, gags, blind folds, and/or hoods?:  ☐ Yes   ☐ No

Explanation _____

## 11. Pain

Submissive's general attitude about receiving pain:
☐ likes   ☐ accepts   ☐ neutral   ☐ dislikes   ☐ will not accept

Quantity of pain submissive wants to receive:
☐ none   ☐ small   ☐ average   ☐ large

Explanation _____

Dominant's general attitude about giving pain:
☐ likes   ☐ will give   ☐ neutral   ☐ dislikes   ☐ will not give

Quantity of pain dominant wants to give:
☐ none   ☐ small   ☐ average   ☐ large

Explanation _____

Will the "now" technique be used?  ☐ Yes   ☐ No

Explanation: _____

Will the "nod" technique be used?  ☐ Yes   ☐ No

Explanation: _____

Will the "one to ten" technique be used?  ☐ Yes   ☐ No

Explanation: _____

The following types of pain are acceptable:

spanking:  ☐ Yes   ☐ No        paddling:  ☐ Yes   ☐ No

whipping:  ☐ Yes   ☐ No        caning:  ☐ Yes   ☐ No

face slaps:  ☐ Yes   ☐ No        biting:  ☐ Yes   ☐ No

nipple clamps:  ☐ Yes   ☐ No        genital clamps:  ☐ Yes   ☐ No

clamps elsewhere:  ☐ Yes   ☐ No    locations: _____

hot creams: ☐ Yes ☐ No     ice: ☐ Yes ☐ No

hot wax: ☐ Yes ☐ No     tickling: ☐ Yes ☐ No

Other types/methods of pain: _____

Additional remarks: _____

## 12. Marks

Is it acceptable to the submissive if the play leaves marks?
☐ Yes ☐ No

Visible while wearing street clothes? ☐ Yes ☐ No

Visible while wearing a bathing suit? ☐ Yes ☐ No

Other: _____

Is it acceptable to the submissive if the play draws small amounts of blood? ☐ Yes ☐ No

Explanation: _____

How easy or difficult has it been to mark the submissive in the past?

_____

## 13. Erotic Humiliation

The submissive agrees to accept being referred to by the following terms:

_____

The submissive agrees to the following forms of erotic humiliation:

"verbal abuse": ☐ Yes ☐ No     enemas: ☐ Yes ☐ No

forced exhibitionism: ☐ Yes ☐ No     spitting: ☐ Yes ☐ No

water sports: ☐ Yes ☐ No     scat games: ☐ Yes ☐ No

other: _____

Any prior really good or really bad experiences in these areas? _____

### 13. Safewords

Safeword #1 and its meaning: _____

Safeword #2 and its meaning: _____

Safeword #3 and its meaning: _____

Non-verbal safewords and their meaning: _____

Will "two squeezes" be used?  ☐ Yes   ☐ No

Will the "extended hand" technique be used?  ☐ Yes   ☐ No

### 14. Opportunities/Special Skills

Anything in particular either party would like to try or explore? _____

_____

### 15. Follow-Up

(Please include a note about who will initiate contacts.)

After the session: _____

The next day: _____

A week later: _____

In case of a crisis: _____

### 16. Anything Else?_____

What will become of this form after the session? _____

## Post-session notes

### Dominant

Overall feeling: _____     one to ten scale (ten tops)

Best part: _____     one to ten scale

Worst part: _____     one to ten scale

Other comments _____

### Submissive

Overall feeling: _____     one to ten scale

Best part: _____     one to ten scale

Worst part: _____     one to ten scale

Other comments: _____

## Variability

One of the most basic principles of SM is that people vary in how they react to it.

First, people vary *tremendously* from person to person in what arouses them. It's common in this community for one person to feel deeply aroused by something another person would find highly unpleasant, or even traumatic.

Second, and not so obviously, a given person varies over time in how they respond to something and in what aspect of SM interests them. This is particularly true during their first year. It's not at all rare to meet someone who insists that they could never be interested in bondage, spanking, piercing, and so forth – and yet, eight months later, you see them at a party happily engaging in exactly what they said they would never do.

I need to make the sub-point here that this is not a matter of escalation. People are most definitely *not* inevitably drawn to giving or receiving ever-increasing levels of pain, humiliation, and so forth. The usual pattern is that the levels they feel comfortable about tend to increase for a while, but level off with time and experience. Also, most of these activities cannot be done beyond a certain intensity without causing harm, and SM people have no interest in causing genuine harm. Therefore, their interest stabilizes. If anything, people usually come to enjoy *more varieties* of SM play rather than *higher intensities* of SM play.

> I can't imagine dominating a man.

Firmly asserting that you would never be interested in some particular SM activity often comes under the type of behavior sometimes known as "tempting the gods."

**Nobody is 100% dominant or submissive.** I have met thousands of SM practitioners over the years. Some have insisted that they are completely dominant or submissive. I'm willing to believe that usually the statement was an honest one *at the time it was made*. However, in practice, it just doesn't seem the case. What they tell you in the presence of others at 9 p.m. is one thing. What they tell you in private at 3 a.m. is often another. They may or may not choose to act upon their "taboo" desires, but I've yet to meet anyone who didn't have at least some fantasies about taking the opposite role.

Among other things, always playing in one role runs a very high risk of eventually getting *boring*. This can be particularly true of being dominant – a role that usually involves relatively few surprises.

Also, I think that if you always play in one role, eventually you will become very curious about what it's like "on the other side."

Finally, and I've used this argument effectively on several dominants, if you take the opposite role, you'll learn when the other side is getting away with something. Taking the other role at least occasionally gives you an empathy, perspective, and understanding that you just can't acquire any other way.

Having said the above, I must add that most people do come to prefer one role or the other. This preference usually takes at least a year of substantial exploration to find, but it's usually there. Just as essentially nobody is 100% dominant or submissive, very few people are equally comfortable with both roles. Most have a preference. I, for example, usually prefer the dominant role, but I do have a submissive side. I have learned (through the wrong type of painful experience) that I must be careful about who I let have access to it, but I have had many of my most profound SM moments while playing in my not-usual role.

## Learn How It Feels

Another basic and important SM teaching is that you should learn how a new toy feels on your own body before using it on anybody else. This is particularly true of whips, paddles, clamps, and other items that cause pain.

I like big penises. There's more to torture!

You can either use the item on yourself or have somebody else use it on you. It's very common to see people, especially dominants, whapping themselves on the forearm, thigh, back, or other location and then pausing to feel the sensation. The sight often reminds me of wine connoisseurs at a tasting. Indeed, highly experienced practitioners can often take up a new whip, tap themselves very lightly with it a few times, and exchange knowing glances (and often wicked smiles) with each other.

This principle also applies to experiences. For example, a wise dominant will not ask a submissive to kneel for 30 minutes on a hard floor unless they have done that themselves. Also, because empathy is important, dominants will do it again if it's been a while since they last did that.

Such experiences help you grow. Provided you pick the who, what, where, and when *very* carefully, you will learn a great deal about giving a spanking by getting a spanking, you will learn a great deal about giving a skillful whipping by getting a skillful whipping, and you will learn a great deal about being a dominant by spending some time as a submissive.

There is one caution that I need to include here. This matter always has *two* components: (1) the experience itself, and (2) how the person involved reacts to the experience. The same whipping might feel joyous to one person but awful to another (also, some submissives are "into" feeling awful). Still, it's always valuable to have a good idea of what the experience feels like from the other side.

**The goal of a first session.** The first time you play with a new partner is the time things are most likely to go wrong. Also, it's the time your (and their) hormones are likeliest to be at their highest pitch – and clouding judgment.

That being so, the first session is often the one that needs the most structure, negotiation, and limits. *In many ways, it's much more important that the first session not end badly than that it end really, really well.*

Don't try to do too many different things in your first session with a new person. If you try *two* new activities, that's plenty. Go easy on the bondage and go easy on the pain. *In particular, don't mix types of pain.* The classic mistake is to mix the pain of nipple clamps with the pain of a whipping on a partner new to both. This approach can almost guarantee that the submissive will reach their "emotional overload" point and cause a terrible end to the session. A much safer approach is to play with only one type of pain in a session. Spanking or clamps is often about right.

Come over here and kneel in front of me.

If you're not already in a long-term relationship with this person, don't try to start one now. Remember, this is much more about getting to know each other than it is about trying new and strange forms of erotic play, yet there's a tendency to try to do "everything" the first time you play together. The dominant, as "captain of the ship," must especially understand the considerable danger of this approach and resist the temptation.

*A highly useful rule is that the best possible ending of a first session is with both parties feeling slightly frustrated and thinking that they could have gone further than they did.* A little bit of such frustration can actually be fun. And, of course, if the first session did end in this happy way, you can usually arrange a second session quickly.

## Setting the Scene

In a word: orderliness. SM, like mountain climbing, scuba diving, or skydiving, involves substantial risk. An orderly approach to both its psychological and physical aspects greatly reduces this risk. Such an approach also reassures the submissive and/or the novice.

Key point: *Sloppiness in a dominant is ominous.* Orderliness need not stifle spontaneity or creativity; rather, it often enhances them.

Orderliness has eight basic parts: time, cleanliness, equipment preparation, privacy, lighting, temperature, music, and other matters.

**Time.** An "SM quickie" is almost a contradiction in terms. While experienced players can do them enjoyably, quickies can be dangerous if anything or anyone is unfamiliar. Most SM takes considerable time.

How much time? If this is a new partner, allow about three hours. Figure half an hour for negotiations, general discussion, and "getting in the mood," two hours for the session itself, and at least another half-hour for post-session straight time.

Note: Don't wait until late in the evening to play with somebody new. You don't want sleepiness to intrude. Nobody can feel too erotic, or conduct a proper negotiation, if they're dozing off. Also, emotional upsets and physical errors are *much* more likely if either person is tired. Caution: This is true even if the players don't feel tired.

I only let adorable people beat me.

Understand that any play that takes place after your normal bedtime is likely to be much riskier, even if it doesn't feel that way. My primary inclination is dominant, and it is not easy for me to "go under" for somebody else. I, and my play partners, have learned through painful experience that a session in which I am submissive is much more likely to end badly if it takes place late in the evening.

**Cleanliness.** Dusty bedside tables, dirty sheets, unvacuumed rugs, and so forth kill erotic arousal. Clean up the place before the session, especially if playing with someone new.

**Equipment preparation.** You'll want your toys clean, neat, handy, and in good repair. Running into the bathroom, rummaging through a drawer, or otherwise unnecessarily fussing and fumbling to get something, drains the erotic energy. Get everything ready and in position beforehand. One caution: Don't spook a novice by having too many toys in view. Keep them discreetly out of sight in a handy drawer, case, or closet.

**Privacy.** Play in private. This means play only in the presence of people who feel comfortable about what's happening. The dominant has the primary duty of ensuring privacy. The more experienced player also has a strong duty, as does the person whose place is used.

Privacy usually has two major parts and one minor part. These are sight privacy, sound privacy, and smell privacy.

What can an outsider see? Have you actually gone outside your bedroom/dungeon/playroom and looked in the supposedly draped windows? What about at night? The angle of the blinds can make a major difference regarding what an outsider can see.

What can an outsider hear? Sounds carry much farther at night (when it's quieter) than during the day. High-pitched sounds, such as a woman's screams, carry farther than low-pitched sounds. It's quite sensible to "test out" your new playroom by inviting a few friends and/or lovers over and deliberately making those "special sounds." Don't forget to include whispered, spoken, and shouted speech. (I've been part of such testings, and they're wonderful fun.)

If it's your place, make sure you personally go outside and listen to both the sound level and identifiability of what you hear.

Keep in mind that several incidents have occurred in which the sounds coming from an SM play session prompted "vanilla" neighbors and/or passers-by to call the cops. Also keep in mind that cops responding to "woman screaming for help" type of calls tend to be, shall we say, a tiny bit more aggressive than normal – and trying to explain matters like consensuality and safewords while looking down gun barrels can be such a bore.

*Sometimes my nipples feel hungry for clamps.*

Footnote: There is also the very real concern that many states now have "mandatory arrest" laws cops must follow regarding domestic disputes that involve *any* violence, no matter how slight. An SM scene that involves restraints, whips, bruises, welts, and so forth could easily be mistaken for an extreme form of ritualized domestic violence by an uninformed police officer. This can result (even if the submissive strongly objects) in the dominant being taken away in handcuffs, seizure of their toys, criminal charges, and names appearing in newspapers.

To help prevent such misunderstandings, some SM club members have helped educate local police officers, prosecutors, defense attorneys, health professionals, and relevant others about the differences between consensual SM and nonconsensual abuse. I wish more clubs would get involved in this. Feel free to contact me if you want my help.

Another footnote: Music does mask the sounds of SM play, but not as much as many players believe it does. Don't rely overmuch on music to "cover your tracks."

82

Finally, there's "smell privacy." This is normally not much of a problem, but remember that odors from menthol-containing creams, incense, cigarette smoke, perfumes, and bodies can linger in rooms, on clothing and bedding, and on both your hair and body for up to several days after a session. It might also be worth keeping in mind that women, as a rule, tend to have a sharper sense of smell than men have. (I've known several who must have been part bloodhound.)

By the way, O Great and Mighty Dominant, you *did* remember to lock the household's exterior doors before beginning the session, didn't you?

Some people like to play SM more publicly, but this is generally frowned upon both within the SM community and by "straight" people. Among other things, making an obvious, non-private display of SM raises a serious consensuality issue. You might fantasize that it would be fun to shock your relatives by having your slave-husband kiss your boots during the family Thanksgiving dinner, but doing so would be an assault on the other people present.

Similarly, be careful about playing in "publicly private" areas, such as woodlands. Let's say you take your girlfriend into the woods, bind her hands behind her back, tear open her blouse, and force her onto her knees to suck your cock while you have one hand jammed into her hair and another holding a doubled-over, heavy belt. (All this is done, of course, only after getting her hearty consent well in advance.) How would this look to a passer-by? A well-meaning "rescuer" might break your neck before either of you could explain.

Some people who own private farms and similar places make them available to couples and clubs for outdoor play. That should be somewhat safe, but remember that screams and other sounds may carry a "country mile." This is especially true of high-pitched sounds such as a woman's screams, and of sounds made at night.

When playing at home, consider that your non-SM apartment mate, to whom you are not out of the closet, might walk in and find you and your lover deeply involved in a session. Again, a violent misunderstanding could occur. Warn your roommate. Tell them your new lover is a bit kinky, and you're thinking of exploring it with them. If they walk in and find one or the other of you tied up and getting whipped, ask them please not to overreact.

Also, think twice about doing things like leading your handcuffed lover down the street on a leash, except perhaps during Halloween – particularly if either of you is female. Such behavior, regardless of whether it's female-dominant or female-submissive, often provokes a strong negative reaction, particularly among excruciatingly politically correct, "feminist" women.

(I should point out that many younger feminists are much more supportive of SM than their older "sisters" are – and may even be somewhat "in your face" about flaunting their support. SM is a bitterly controversial matter within the feminist community, but gradually gaining acceptance.)

About as far as you might go in public would be to wear SM symbols. Collars and handcuffs are becoming common items of jewelry and decoration, as are handcuff keys, leather wrist bands, and, to a lesser degree, leather rings. I suggest you avoid carrying whips. Among other things, there's a chance that an unamused or unenlightened cop might arrest you for carrying a weapon.

One note: avoid "practicing" bondage or using your whip in public, especially in places like city parks. While not (usually) technically illegal, such activities often provoke strong emotional reactions. In particular, teenage males will undoubtedly come over and aggressively insist upon watching, commenting, and eventually participating. This invites catastrophe.

**Lighting.** Lighting enhances mood. People feel turned on by SM-associated sights: ropes, whips, leather clothing, boots. Allow enough light to see them.

*At certain times, I really like pain – the more the better.*

Play with the lighting. Experiment with colored light bulbs (red, golden, blue), black lights, candles, strobe lights, and dimmer switches. Shine a floodlight on your submissive as you whip them. Examine intimate areas of their body with a small flashlight, and make comments.

Candlelight arouses intimacy and passion. Just don't create a fire hazard. (Remember about flammable materials and liquids – and your extinguisher.)

Light offers wonderful opportunities. Explore them.

**Temperature.** Submissives tend to spend a lot of time naked. They often wear only a collar. Cold kills eroticism and prevents relaxation. Keep the room warm enough for comfortable nudity – 75 degrees or warmer. Smart players often keep a thermometer discreetly available to measure playroom temperature.

An old sex-party trick is heating the house until it's distinctly warm, 80 degrees or so, thus creating an urge in the guests to cool off by disrobing.

Of course, don't get the room *too* hot. Non-passionate sweating isn't erotic. (Remember, some submissives start sweating as they reach their pain-acceptance limit.) I know of one session that ended because the temperature was so high that the dominant, who had been giving an intense whipping, began to suffer heat exhaustion.

**Music.** If the other basics are handled, music can provide a rich atmosphere. While tastes in music vary widely, certain preference patterns emerge. You'll want your partner to concentrate on what's going on between the two of you, not the music. Songs that contain considerable amounts of lyrics, such as top forty music, are often avoided. (Although I do know one sadist who likes to tie his victims up very securely and then play "Feelings" over and over and over.)

Classical music, jazz, and rock music with long instrumental passages are popular. If nothing else is available, tune your radio to an all-classical station.

Music helps block out the sounds of mundane life around you, creating a unique world for just the two of you. Music also somewhat covers the sound of a whipping and other SM-related sounds.

Many people like rhythmic music for whippings. (Be careful not to get so caught up in the rhythm of the music that you stop paying attention to what's going on with your submissive.) Others – devious sadists that they are – prefer more erratic music.

*If I have to listen to that damn Hallelujah Chorus at one more play party, I'll scream.*

## Other Matters

As you can see, SM play involves all the senses. Pay attention to sights, sounds, smells, textures, and tastes.

**Smell.** Smells reach deep into the brain, touching us on a primitive level. If we like, or dislike, the way someone smells, everything else we think and feel about them is subtly and powerfully shifted. Repellent body odor and bad breath usually kill arousal (although a few dedicated perverts find them especially attractive) – as will excesses of any fragrance.

The smells associated with SM – leather, latex, rubber, and so forth - are a deep part of its eroticism for many people.

Incense adds a lot to a session. Again, experiment.

**Taste.** Consider the sensual aspects. Fresh fruit, fruit juice, candy, anything sensual, can add to the scene. (Also remember that playing SM, in either role, can create a real thirst, so keeping something non-alcoholic to drink in the room can help preserve the energy of the session.)

Mirrors. Many players want to see the activity. Men, especially, often have a high visual aspect to their arousal. Some women do, too. A bound man may have his experience deeply intensified if he can see what is happening to him, especially to his genitals. (An old prostitute's trick is to position themselves so the man can see his cock in their hand or mouth.)

Also, people often have intense reactions to the sight of themselves in bondage, and you can use a mirror to good effect here. It's also sometimes hot to position a mirror in front of the submissive as you whip them, so they can watch. On the other hand, a submissive who is unhappy with their own body may be turned off by their image in a mirror.

Bound submissives often can't see what's going on, and would like to. A considerate dominant's use of a mirror can help.

Safety Note: Because mirrors can break at the most unfortunate moments, many playrooms are replacing glass mirrors with unbreakable mylar mirrors. This is especially true of mirrors mounted directly over beds – particularly in earthquake country!

Clocks and watches. A large part of SM's energy and power comes from its ability to allow the players to create "their own special world." This world can be compromised by the intrusion of "mundane" items.

Time can be such an item, particularly for the submissive. It's often necessary for someone to keep track of the time, and that duty usually falls to the dominant. Therefore, unless you deliberately build it into your scene, it's generally a good idea to position timepieces out of the submissive's view.

Urinal. If your play involves extensive, immobilizing bondage, a portable urinal can save having to undo everything while the submissive runs to the bathroom. A plastic urinal with a lid that snaps into place usually works nicely. Use only unbreakable items for urinal duty. A mixture of broken glass, bondage, and exposed genitals is not a recipe for serenity.

The telephone. A ringing phone intrudes. Turn off your telephone's ringer, and turn down your answering machine's volume, before playing. Make this step as routine a part of your play preparations as you make light, heat, music, and other matters. Play time is a special time set aside for just you and your partner. Leave the phone out of it.

One tip: Many people forget to turn their phone's ringer back on after playing. To prevent this, attach a reminder note or something similar to the phone.

## Don't Do This If Anyone Involved Is Drunk or Stoned _____

As I've said before, will say now, and will say again later: SM is the riskiest form of sex. You know better than to ride in a car with someone who is drunk or stoned. You should also know better than to play SM with somebody who is drunk or stoned.

This form of erotic play requires coordination, empathy, attention to detail, and the ability to react quickly and correctly to unexpected developments, including emergencies. Anybody who would deliberately impair themselves and then do this is grossly unsafe and irresponsible. If somebody is too intoxicated to drive, they are too intoxicated to play. Play with them anyway and you can die after screaming for hours. End of discussion.

# Finding Partners

Once someone decides to explore SM, the question arises: "Where can I find a partner?" Partner-seeking strategies vary depending on your interests, whether you're looking for play partners or long-term relationships, your geographic location, and, especially, your sexual orientation – gay male partner-seeking strategies are very different from lesbian strategies, which are different from heterosexual strategies. Still, to a significant degree, we're all in this together – looking for responsible, exciting people with whom to do SM.

Some people seem to fixate on the activity and not on the person. The billion-times-asked questions are, "Where can I meet a submissive man or woman?" and "Where can I meet a dominant man or woman?" This is self-defeating, "cart-before-the-horse" reasoning. The trick is to concentrate on meeting someone you really like who also happens to be sexually compatible with you.

One of the most awful dating experiences (as I learned at great and painful cost a few years ago) is meeting someone whose interest in SM is deeply compatible with yours, yet with whom you have little emotional rapport. If you are not "in tune" with each other (Janet and I, I'm happy to say, are almost telepathic), and all you have in common is a compatible interest in SM, you are in for a painful, frustrating, and probably short time together. This is the great double-edge to meeting someone through any specifically sexual venue, including an SM club, professional studio, or personal ad.

I'll start with some general observations about partner-seeking that will apply to most readers, then add some ideas that will apply specifically to various genders and orientations. However, everyone should benefit from reading all the sections. Note: My personal experience with female/female and male/male partner-seeking is essentially nonexistent, so I don't consider myself qualified to go beyond the basics on these topics. Still, the strategies outlined in this chapter have worked well for many of my gay and lesbian friends, and are well established in those circles.

All the men who want to dominate me can't, and all the men who can dominate me don't want to.

89

**Personal ads.** I continue to feel that the best partner-seeking option for most people – the strategy that offers the best results for the least effort – is the strategically placed, intelligently worded personal ad.

In the usual "personal ad courtship," one person places the ad and the other answers it, usually including their first name and telephone number. The two people talk on the phone a time or two, and if some "chemistry" seems present, they meet. This meeting is usually a brief, inexpensive meeting in a public place, such as meeting for coffee in a restaurant. If that meeting goes well, they arrange a "real" date. Common etiquette is to mention any possible "flaws" early, including obesity, smoking, herpes, HIV-positive status, age, children, marital status, and financial condition.

I'll let you know this: though you may meet many partners through ads, remember you cannot predict physical attraction or chemistry. Figure there'll be about a four percent chance that after the first meeting both of you will want to see the other again. Thus, if you average one date a week, and that's a realistic expectation if you run a polished ad in an urban-area magazine, then within six months you'll likely meet a partner with whom you feel significant mutual attraction. In the dating world, that's doing fairly well.

If your ad contains an easily-understood reference to SM, you'll probably get many fewer responses, but you'll likely get some. An occasional "letter freak" or sex worker will write, but most letters will be genuine.

I have to surrender sometimes or I go nuts.

**Writing and placing an ad.** Regardless of where you advertise, it's a good idea to remember the following points:

1. Include a few basics such as your race, sex, age, and sexual orientation.
2. Avoid being crude about what physical type of partner you're seeking, especially if you're seeking a long-term partner. If you're looking for a male partner, you can bend this rule a bit, but it's still a bit tacky to get too specific. If you're looking for a woman, it may be very wise to eliminate all references to appearance. (Such references offend many women, including the attractive ones.)
3. Don't focus your ad exclusively on sexual activities. Include a few references to your interests and hobbies – again, especially if you're in search of a long-term partner. (One woman I know who

works for a mostly heterosexual sex publication wryly describes the typical, terrible personal ad she handles as "Dick, Man Attached, Personality Optional." She also handles the replies, and knows from experience that such ads typically get almost no response.)

4. Try for a light touch or slightly clever wording.
5. Talk about what you have to offer, as well as what you're looking for.

Most papers now have voice mail that allows callers to leave a message (for a fee, of course) at a specified phone number. Some charge *you* to call in to check your messages. Some charge both them and you. Comparison shopping is essential.

Some publications will receive and forward letters for you – for an extra fee. Sometimes you pay, sometimes the responder pays: try to set your ad up so repliers pay nothing except regular postage. If you use this option, you'll need a private mailing address (do you want to be "out" to your mail carrier?). A post office box provides almost ideal privacy at little cost. Private "P.O. boxes" are also good, but cost much more.

One other point: I strongly advise you not to list your telephone number, even if the publication will permit it. (Many won't.) If you list your number in a sex publication or swingers' magazine, "phone freaks" will call, repeatedly, around the clock. I know people whose telephone became so swamped by such callers that they had to get a new number. It was impossible to use their phone for anything else. If you must list a phone number, have a second line installed for this sole purpose and buy an answering machine for it, or get voice mail.

From now on, the last word out of your mouth when you speak to me is 'Mistress.' Do you understand?

**Answering personal ads.** In general, you'll probably do better by placing your own ad instead of responding to other people's ads. After all, placing your own ad allows you to send out a very specific signal about who you are and what you're looking for. However, sometimes you will see an ad that will definitely interest you. I do suggest that you be selective in answering only those ads which genuinely sound like a good fit – calling every person of the gender that attracts you is a waste of your time and money and theirs. In particular, I've heard many women bitterly complain about men who seem to answer every single ad from a woman in a periodical, no matter what the ads actually said (and sometimes including explicitly lesbian ads).

Keep an eye on your phone bill. If you're not careful, you can run up a tab of several hundred dollars responding to voice mail ads without getting any sort of satisfactory response. One thing to keep in mind is that not all these ads may be from "real" people. While the publishers of these publications heatedly deny this, it is all too easy for them to place false ads in order to reap the per-call charges. Serious money is involved here, and there is essentially no way that you can verify an ad's validity. Watch your wallet. If you don't get some concrete results fairly early in your voice mail adventures, take your business to another publication.

**Personal ads in cyberspace.** This is an exciting new option for people of all genders and orientations, and its potential grows daily. Two Internet newsgroups are of particular interest: alt.personals.bondage and alt.personals.spanking. (Do a search on the word "personal" to discover other regional and specialized options.) Several World Wide Web sites accept SM-related personal ads. Also, large Internet service providers such as America OnLine and CompuServe have sections where SM-type personal ads can be posted. Finally, many local and regional SM computer bulletin boards have sections devoted to personal ads.

My girlfriend is quite the gleeful little flagellant.

One advantage to advertising in cyberspace is that it costs nothing beyond your regular subscription cost, and you usually have as much space as you want to describe yourself and your interests. One disadvantage is that cyberspace personal ads tend to reach a *very* large audience, so you may have to deal with the frustration of being contacted by a like-minded person who happens to live on the other side of the planet.

**SM clubs.** People often hope to find partners at an SM club. This strategy has much to recommend it for heterosexual women and for gay men, lesbians and bisexuals; it doesn't work so well for heterosexual men. The major advantage is that a person you meet at an SM club's functions probably likes SM. It's not like meeting a vanilla person and trying to decide when to bring up "the big subject." (Although in larger cities, many vanilla people now know something about SM fundamentals. While they may not know techniques, many people now know about basics such as consensuality and safewords.)

The major disadvantage to meeting this way, and it's formidable, is that most clubs open to both men and women must deal with large numbers of inquiries from men. SM seems to interest men and women with equal frequency, but men are *much* more likely to contact a club. The male/female ratio of requests for information can be as high as ten to one, and sometimes higher.

Blunt observation: Because there are usually many more single men than single women at mixed-gender SM functions (some years ago Janet and I went to an SM party attended by twelve couples, twelve single men, and zero single women), and because these men are almost invariably looking for female play partners, some men absolutely will not bring their new girlfriend to an SM event until their own relationship with her, particularly the matter of playing outside the relationship, is entirely clear, agreed-upon, and secure.

One man told me that when he brought an attractive young woman he was just getting to know to a lecture given by an SM club, a small mob of single men (and a few couples, and a few women) was "circling like sharks" around her. She (rather innocently) exchanged phone numbers with various people there, and was slightly shocked at the volume of calls she immediately received from people wanting play dates. "I thought they were just being friendly," she later, somewhat ruefully, re-marked.

Many clubs "solve" this problem by limiting either membership or attendance to couples only. I'm not happy with this "solution," but I understand it. I've attended functions where the gender imbalance was severe (greater than five to one). Few people, male or female, had a good time. If you are a heterosexual man seeking a partner, your chances of finding one at an SM club are distinctly dim.

*I just love a man who can take heavy pain.*

To make it worse, single men do sometimes meet partners at SM clubs. It's rare, but it does occasionally happen. So that means many single men persist because each believes he will overcome uphill odds and find the mistress or slavegirl of his dreams.

The only men for whom this is not true are those who have been in the SM community for years. These men have slowly come to know people in the community. Their personal contacts and years of experience give them opportunities closed to other men, but even these guys have long dry spells. Don't think you can overcome the male/female imbalance by spending "time in grade." If you are an inexperienced, single, heterosexual male, it's simply not practical. You could "patiently wait" for years.

One valid reason to join a club is to learn SM's techniques and safety measures. Many clubs offer excellent educational programs at little cost. You may not go home with the partner of your dreams, but you will go home with useful information.

**An additional benefit.** Most SM clubs also offer personal ads in their (usually monthly or quarterly) newsletters. A personal ad placed in your local SM club's newsletter has substantial potential to work well. I've placed several, and I've never failed to get at least one serious response.

**Leather bars and dance clubs.** This is an area that has changed a great deal since the first edition of this book. At that time, there were a fair number of gay male leather bars, a few lesbian ones, and no heterosexual ones. Since then, we have seen the emergence of dance clubs and night clubs that allow or encourage SM people and, in some cases, SM play. The most typical pattern seems to be for such clubs to have some nights that are for men only, some for women only, and others that are open to players of all genders. Some, however, are entirely pansexual.

Leather bars have been a vital link in the growth of the gay male and lesbian SM communities for several decades, and have proven themselves as a place to find partners. The pansexual variants can be interesting to attend, but all-in-all, I'm not too wild about them as a place to meet partners, particularly if you're over 30. The music is often loud, and the cigarette smoke thick. The play is sometimes clumsy or even dangerous, and monitors are not always present. Scenes are also often surrounded by a clueless crowd of vanilla spectators.

While I'd be delighted to be proven wrong on this assertion – I'd love for there to be more places for SM people to meet like-minded others – most of the clubs I've seen haven't impressed me much. Still, a growing number of them exist, and with time and experience I expect them to be a more important venue for players of all orientations.

## Signs and Signals

Gay men, lesbians, bisexuals, and a small but growing number of heterosexuals interested in SM sometimes wear particular items of clothing in certain ways.

**Keys.** Keys worn on the right hip indicate that the wearer is submissive; keys worn on the left hip indicate that the wearer is a dominant. Keys worn on both hips indicate that the wearer is a janitor.

**Handkerchiefs.** Handkerchiefs signal an interest in a particular "sub-specialty" of SM. A black handkerchief, for example, usually shows an interest in "heavy" SM, particularly whipping. A red handkerchief suggests an interest in fisting. Checkered handkerchiefs signal a desire for safer sex.

A handkerchief worn in the right hip pocket, or tied around the right boot, indicates an interest in the submissive or receptive aspect of the subject. A handkerchief worn on the left suggests an interest in the dominant or active role. These signals are usually accompanied by leather clothing, boots, and similar regalia, and apply primarily to the gay and lesbian community.

The handkerchief code varies from place to place, although red and black are fairly constant. Check the code in your area before you do too much "advertising." You can often get a card outlining the local code from a leather store that sells handkerchiefs to gay customers.

Be cautious about drawing similar conclusions from apparently heterosexual people. Of course, nowadays it's not entirely inappropriate to ask someone (politely and discreetly, please) if the keys or handkerchief they're wearing have any "unique" significance.

One other point: nowadays members of some subcultures delight in wearing collars, handcuffs, and black leather clothing. From what I can gather, they wear most of these items only for their decorative value. (Although the idea of SM is far more acceptable to many young people than ever before.)

**A proposal.** It's time heterosexuals had a discreet, but definite, way to signal their interest in SM. I propose the wearing of a simple, black leather ring, held together by a single rivet. Such a ring would be inexpensive, and could be discreetly removed as the situation permitted.

Can I be
your pet?

I suggest, in keeping with tradition, that dominants wear such rings on their left hand and submissives wear them on their right.

## *Men Looking for Women*

While the situation is not as bad as it was, there are still many more men seeking women within the SM community than there are women to accommodate them. For this reason, the heterosexual male seeking a play partner or a life partner faces some special challenges. I've seen many such men waste huge amounts of time, money, and effort on ineffective partner-finding strategies. Fortunately, there is hope – I found a partner, most of my men friends have found partners, and you probably can too.

Basic fact: The odds strongly favor finding a woman you like and getting her interested in SM, not finding a woman into SM and hoping you'll like each other.

Let's look at some basic partner-finding tactics.

**Personal ads in sex magazines.** Many men advertise in sex magazines and newspapers. This usually wastes their time and money. Very few women, other than sex workers, read such publications. Even fewer answer their ads. If you advertise in a sex publication, you probably will get a few responses, but almost all will be from...

1.  "Professional" women wanting you to buy photos, panties, or similar items, or wanting you to pay to see them.
2.  Other men, some of whom will be gay and proposition you, and some who get off by sending dirty letters.
3.  Men impersonating women. These pathetic wretches are "letter freaks." They will represent themselves as a woman whose interest in SM is compatible to yours. "She" may even include a photo of "herself." Be careful here. These assholes know you might doubt their truthfulness, so they can go to incredible, even insane, lengths to convince. (One friend of mine spent several months, and several hundred dollars, writing to the dominant woman of his dreams – and then found out that "her" letters were originating from the state men's penitentiary.)

> No woman has ever been able to tie me up so that I can't get loose.

**Recognizing and dealing with letter freaks.** These classic warnings suggest you may be dealing with a letter freak:

1.  A typed letter. These guys know their handwriting is unfeminine, so they type their letters.
2.  The letter will not include a telephone number. This is a bit tricky, as a cautious woman quite sensibly might not want to send her number to a stranger, at least with her first letter. But if "her" second or third letter lacks a telephone number, beware.
3.  They will describe their appearance in graphic, visual terms. Most real women won't do that, especially regarding specific parts of their body or clothing they like to wear. Also, most women would never send a nude picture to a stranger. If you receive such a photo, particularly if you didn't ask for one, you can almost conclude on that basis alone that you're dealing with a fraud.
4.  Especially, especially, especially, they will want you to reveal as much as possible about yourself in your return letter. Be suspicious of requests for your full name, your street address, home telephone number, and photographs (especially nude photographs).

96

5.  Another key sign: extended exchanging of letters with no contact either on the phone or in person. Remember, a letter freak's goals are to prolong the correspondence as long as possible, and to get you to reveal as much as possible.  Get *very* suspicious if "she" wants more than two rounds of correspondence before more personal contact.

Note: Letter freaks rarely place or answer ads in singles' publications.

Another note: One way to counter-attack a letter freak, especially if he (and it's almost always a "he") is using a private mail drop, would be to show the letters he has sent you to the staff.  If you convince them this guy is defrauding others, they might drop him.  Also, also consider sending copies to the other local mail drops so the letter freak will have trouble renting another box.

If the letter freak is using a U.S. post office box, you might consider staking out the box and confronting him.  Prepare to meet an extremely pathetic individual – often sloppily dressed, ugly, and with no friends. You also might consider sending the material to the local postmaster (after, of course, cutting away – don't just cross out – your address).  Sending obscene material through the mail is a crime, so the letter freak could land in jail.

Remember this:  The letter freak knows that eventually each victim will "wise up."  But they also know most will do nothing other than send one final, angry letter. If you get letter-freaked, by all means, in some way, counter-attack.

In summary, the number of sincere replies to a man's sex-publication ad will be very small.  They do sometimes happen.  A strongly motivated woman will buy such a paper, and from time to time I have heard of someone playing "matchmaker" by showing a man's ad to an SM-interested woman they know, but these women are rare and quickly find partners.  If you advertised in a sex paper and got two sincere replies in a full year, I would consider you fortunate.

**Personal ads in swingers' magazines.** These work somewhat better. Although most readers will still (of course) be men, women sometimes read them.  Unfortunately, almost all will already be solidly coupled, and most others will be sex workers, but a few (a very, very few) will be single.

You may hear from married couples who feel curious about SM and want to try it.  If so, remember that when meeting a single man, the usual practice is to meet both her and him.  Her husband or boyfriend will often insist on being present. (She also will often insist on this. After all, who knows what kind of lunatic *you* are?)

Some men will only want to remain in the house or apartment while you and she go into the bedroom.  Some will want to watch.  Many are voyeurs who get off by seeing their lady have sex with another guy. Others want to learn by observing. Some are impotent. Some are not. (It's often unwise to ask the guy questions about these points. If they wish to volunteer some information, fine. Otherwise, don't pry.)

Some guys will want to photograph, tape-record, or videotape the session. It's up to you. Ethical swingers understand the need for discretion. They therefore discuss and agree upon in advance any arrangements for making permanent records. Pulling out a camera without prior agreement is serious misconduct (and may start a brawl).

Some guys will want to both observe and participate. You might want to discuss specifics. Please note that although bisexual women are common in the swing community, bisexual men are rare.

Also, the swing community seems widely split regarding AIDS precautions. One group has adopted safer sex, the other group seems to believe "there is nothing to worry about" and is continuing as before. I'd suggest you avoid doing anything you'll worry about the next morning.

> Being a woman and into SM is like getting to be prom queen when you're a grownup.

One note: Sometimes people swing even though they dislike it (or even hate it) in order to please their lover. This is usually the woman doing it to please her man. If you feel she is doing this only to please her lover, and that she personally hates it, please stop the session. Stop it as politely as possible – maybe even lie a little, fake an upset stomach – but stop. Remember, it's wrong to cause or aid in causing genuine suffering, even if the other party consents.

Advertising in swingers' magazines has a better chance of finding you a real partner (a genuine female, with no money involved) than the sex magazines, but she probably will already be happily, solidly coupled.

**Personal ads in singles' papers.** Ads in these types of publications have a fair chance of working well. Just remember that most people who place and answer ads in these papers don't want sex partners. They want a relationship.

Many singles' publications prohibit explicit sexual references. They also prohibit graphic references to SM, so you must express yourself discreetly. A few "code phrases" that sometimes appear include "yielding fantasies," "sinister," "amazon," "erotic power," "Roissy," and "9 1/2 Weeks."

Very few SM-experienced women read these ads when seeking a new partner. Most such women find their new partners through the clubs they belong to and through their SM friends.  However, if you aim your ad at the woman who has little or no experience, but has SM *fantasies*, you may get lucky. Many, many women have SM fantasies but no idea of where to find a suitable partner.   If you present yourself as a safe, considerate fantasy exploration partner, the odds are reasonable that you will receive a small but adequate number of responses.

There are a few conventions to finding and meeting people through singles' ads:

First, there are typically many more ads from men than women – usually about two to three times as many. (If there are more than three times as many ads from men as women, I doubt many women read the publication.) Don't despair about this if you are a man. Key point: Many more women are willing to answer ads than they are to place them.

If you advertise in a singles' magazine, the women who write will typically send you a brief note along with their telephone number.  They only rarely send photos, but may send a photocopy of one.

If you get one sincere inquiry a month from a woman who understands the ad's reference to SM, with a five percent chance of compatibility, then you should find someone within two years.  In the "SM dating" world, meeting someone suitable every two years is batting fairly well.

*I want to be the best slave you ever had.*

**Finding a partner on your own.**  Let's go over a few other options about how to meet people.

First, understand that *anything* which promotes social interaction is likely to succeed eventually.  Some people are lucky in this respect because their work brings them into contact with new people.

In many respects, finding someone is largely a numbers game.  It's all a matter of probabilities.  If you just keep on meeting new people, it's almost inevitable that eventually you will meet someone with whom you spark.

You may worry about your attractiveness. I think that everybody, and I mean *everybody*, has a built-in degree of attractiveness.  No matter how good-looking or how ugly you consider yourself, keep in mind that whether you're attractive is something largely decided by others.  There will always be people who consider you attractive, and always people who consider you unattractive. Still, you can stack the odds in your favor.

Look in the mirror.  Any obvious, correctable flaws?  How's your fitness level? Teeth? Clothing? How's the haircut? You get the idea.  How about your social skills?  Have trouble talking with someone at a party?

Consider taking a class in conversational skills. In general, shape yourself up. Making yourself basically presentable takes little time or money.

OK, so you're spruced up. Where do you go? The single most important thing to keep is mind is to go *somewhere*. You are *not* going to meet someone if you stay at home. Get out of that house! Go somewhere at least once a week.

**Singles' events.** Advantages: Those who attend will be single – and interested in a relationship. Everybody knows why people attend.

Disadvantages: The atmosphere at these events is sometimes self-conscious and strained. However, the people in charge of these events are often experts at "breaking the ice." I've attended such events. Some were dull, others lively. Another disadvantage: Again, more men than women attend. It's usually not completely lopsided, but a two-to-one, or three-to-one, ratio is not unknown.

Comment: The people who attend are not usually looking for someone to take home and to bed that night. (Let alone an SM partner!) The evening's basic goal is to exchange phone numbers. Those who make these initial contacts then get in touch later to schedule a more conventional date.

I want to be kidnapped.

(Keep in mind, chum, that even in this liberated era, many women are still just simply *not* going to call a man, even though they have his number and are free to do so. A few will but, if you wait for her to call you, the overwhelming probability is that you will never hear from her again. Call her.)

Another convention of these singles rituals is that refusals for further contact are accepted nicely and never protested. That sometimes means having to accept an occasional "unreasonable" refusal, but that's the way it is. If she doesn't want you to see or call her again, that's it. Case closed. Throw away her number and all other traces of her. The best you can do is to tell her that if she changes her mind she is welcome to call you in the future (which may greatly impress her and motivate her to, someday, do just that).

All in all, I'm not too great a fan of singles' events. They have worked well for some people, but I, in general, will only attend one if I see no better opportunities.

**An exception.** There is one type of singles event that I recommend. Events that cover such things as where and how to meet people, communications skills such as assertiveness and body language, and relationship skills tend to be

100

worthwhile. While you may or may not meet someone at these events, you will learn how to meet someone, establish communication, and build a relationship. I have attended such events, and always felt doing so was worthwhile. These singles events are worth going out of your way to attend.

Essential point: Nothing nothing nothing is more important in starting or maintaining a relationship (romantic or otherwise) than good communication skills. If attending an event improves your communication skill as little as one percent, it was time and money well spent.

**Singles' bars.** Bars are the generic singles scene in many areas. Again, more men than women attend. Also, women usually attend in groups, making it difficult to approach them. Additionally, these places tend to be frequented by yuppie-types. If you're a supermarket stock clerk and drive a pickup, you probably won't feel comfortable here.

Note: some guys specialize in prowling bars. These "bar sharks" dress and act in a way calculated to fit in at such a bar. It's hard to compete directly with them, but their "hard core" style is obvious and turns off many women. You may have a chance with a woman who doesn't like bar sharks.

Women who come to these bars often feel defensive. They fear the men only want to take them home, screw them, and never again have anything to do with them. Their fear is often 100% justified, so be nice.

Be careful about how much you drink. You don't want to get arrested for drunken driving (or killed in a crash) on the way home. Keep in mind that getting a woman so drunk or stoned that she's incapable of consent and then being sexual with her is rape. Also keep in mind that taking home an intoxicated woman you just met for SM-type sex equals begging for a disaster to happen.

I took one look
at him and
I knew
he was
my Master.

The most you should expect from an evening in a bar is getting a phone number. Call her to set up a more "respectable" date. Among other things, each of you will get to see the other without soft lighting, background music, and "social lubricant."

I'm not too fond of or hopeful about going to bars, but it may be reasonable, especially if there's nothing better going on, including a singles' event.

**Dating services.** These might help, but they can be expensive and (as you probably guessed) have more male than female clients. Slender women under 40 are particularly rare.

One comment: most dating services won't let you make any kind of overt reference to SM.

**So where are all the women?** By now you probably feel discouraged. It seems that at every turn the number of men always exceeds the number of women. What's going on? The number of women in this country is slightly greater than the number of men. Therefore, there are more single women than there are single men. Where *are* they?

The simple answer is that most women are just simply never going to go anywhere near a sexual event or singles' event. Most are never going to place or answer a personal ad. Most are not going to have anything to do with a dating service, etc., etc., etc.

Okay, okay, you answer. So what *do* they do? Where *do* they go?

Well, like most of us, they either work or go to school. They spend time with their family. They have a circle of friends. They meet new people through the natural turnover in their lives. Therefore, the best place for you to meet new people is in the natural turnover in your life. Be open to striking up a conversation with a woman you feel attracted to. This can be at work, on a bus, at the supermarket, wherever.

Mistress,
I'll do
anything
you want.

Some good events might include: parties, discussions, communications skills workshops (usually more women than men attend), political work, adult education classes, and so forth. Church groups often offer these. (*Big* hint here, many women who would never attend any other sort of "singles" event will attend an "entirely respectable" church social.) Also check resources such as Parents Without Partners, the PTA, softball leagues, and similar opportunities.

## *Women Looking For Men*

In a way, the advice for women seeking men is almost the opposite of that for men seeking women. Due to the heavy imbalance of men making inquiries, a woman is *much* more likely to succeed in finding a compatible man than a man is in finding a woman at an SM club.

However, keep in mind that women have the same basic problem men have: The fact that a man's interest in SM harmonizes with yours is no guarantee you will otherwise be compatible.

To put this in perspective, compare SM to other interests. You and another person may both like bowling, dancing, or going to museums, but those shared interests don't guarantee personal compatibility. True, it's a start, and a good one, but that's all.

We all know that a relationship based only on sex is unlikely to last. SM is an even narrower base, and thus even less likely to endure.

If you contact an SM club, take a few precautions.

1. Get a P.O. box or private, confidential mailing address and have your mail sent there.

   Most clubs stringently protect their members' identities (many do not require them to use their true name), but unethical breaches sometimes occur. You don't want some moron showing up at your front door. Get a P.O. box.

   I want to take a moment to tell you that most clubs go out of their way to be considerate and helpful to prospective women members. Also, because of the oversupply of male members, you are more likely to find men interested in you despite your age, weight, or other "flaws." I have very mixed emotions about the implications of that last sentence, but it is true.

   I will also point out, somewhat against my better judgment, that there are many men out there willing to marry a woman amenable to playing SM. Some of these men are wealthy and considerate.

   I feel I must also note the old saying, "Marrying money is the hardest way to earn it." I think marriage should be based on mutual love, attraction, caring, and respect. Don't marry the guy if you don't both love and like him. It almost never works out, and both people are left hurt and unhappy.

   *I'm totally enjoying being owned.*

2. Be *very* careful about revealing your telephone number.

   Remember, every now and then (very rarely), some jerk just won't know when to quit. Generally, you should be willing to accept a man's home number, but be very conservative about giving him yours. Ordinary social etiquette doesn't apply here. Explain to the man that you don't give your number to someone you don't know well. He should understand and graciously accept that. If he doesn't, you should probably write him off right there (and return his number, again right there).

Seriously consider having a second line installed. Particularly with new Caller-ID and "star-69" technologies, you don't want to answer SM-oriented calls on your regular line. You can give out this unlisted "sex phone" number more freely. Of course, you'll want an answering machine, with call-screening, for this line. Another alternative is getting a private voice mail number for callers to leave messages.

If you're on-line, trading e-mail addresses offers a good alternative way that you and he can get to know each other better without taking the risk of sharing home addresses or phone numbers.

Also, if a man gives you his number, but you don't give him yours, and you decide you want to see him again, you'll have to overcome your ladylike inhibition against calling a man. This is only painful at first. Remember, he probably will be delighted to hear from you. (On the other hand, he may not feel delighted. If he doesn't wish to pursue the contact, you must accept his turn-down every bit as graciously and pleasantly as you would want him to accept yours.)

3. As you come into the club, take your time, look around, and talk to many different members.

Don't get deeply involved with the first man you meet. Check out the field. Remember, particularly in this, the time of AIDS, you may not want to do a lot of partner-changing. Be picky, and choose a man you feel you could spend some time with.

**Running a personal ad**. If you are somewhat isolated, you might consider running an ad. If you do, keep in mind that you will probably get a flood of responses. Some will be somewhat bizarre or obscene. Some will be (unintentionally) hysterically funny. But many will be from reasonable men.

I suggest the following safety precautions: if you get an obscene, obsessive, or generally bizarre letter (or package, or audiotape, or whatever) the best action is throw it away. Above all, *don't answer it*. Not even to give this jerk the "drop dead" reply he obviously deserves. Understand that *any* response, no matter how hostile, will encourage him. Just forget it. If he sends several letters, do the same. Don't even open them.

If he tries to send a letter by certified or registered mail (which you have to sign for to accept), just refuse it. The post office will leave a notice in your box that they are holding a certified or registered letter for you and that they will send it back if you don't pick it up (and sign for it) within a certain time. Let them send it back.

If would be a good idea, therefore, to refuse *any* registered or certified mail that comes to your P.O. box. This guy may put his latest letter in an "innocent" or "official" envelope to trick you into signing for it, so simply refuse everything.

Subpoint: Make sure you rent your P.O. box as a private citizen. If you rent as a commercial firm, the post office is required by law to disclose your name and address under certain circumstances.

If you use a commercial "maildrop," instruct them to refuse to sign for registered or certified mail that comes for you.

When going over your responses, remember that these men have revealed one of the most private, intimate parts of their lives to you. Unfortunately, some are terribly indiscreet. They will list their home address, full legal name, home and work phone numbers, and send photographs of themselves – sometimes full-frontal, erect-penis nudes. Some will include obscene letters, sometimes written on their company's letterhead stationery.

Basic Answering Rules:
1. Unsolicited nude photos = no reply.
2. "Obscene" letters = no reply.
3. Letters on "letterhead" = no reply.

A considerate man will send you a brief letter initially – usually no more than two pages long. The letter will briefly describe his race, sex, age, weight, and height. He will discuss his interests and hobbies other than SM or any other aspect of sexuality. If he has herpes, is HIV-positive, smokes, or has custody of his children, he should mention that.

Leather's OK, but what really turns me on is a guy in denim.

He might include a portrait-type photograph of himself (although the absence of a photo is not necessarily a bad sign; men, too, need to be discreet) and maybe a self-addressed, stamped envelope for your reply.

He may also include his home phone number. Be suspicious of a man who only sends his work number, or his answering service number, or any other number besides his home phone number. It's almost 100% certain that a man unwilling to give you his home number, but willing to give you another, is married.

His initial letter may not include any number, and that may show cautious discretion. (After all, he has no way of knowing what type of clinging, obsessive lunatic *you* might be. You could, for all he knows, start calling him 50 times a day.)

In any event, promptly throw away any letters from men who don't interest you. *Don't* keep them. You don't want those letters to fall into indiscreet hands.

## Women Looking For Women

Many lesbians are more open to experimenting with SM than they were in the past. It's still not "politically correct" and so you may have to be discreet, but you should be able to find someone. (I've heard a semi-joke that the only politically correct sex for women is celibate lesbianism – including no masturbation.)

A few large cities have lesbian bars. They also have many lesbian organizations. Women-only SM organizations are often listed in local weekly or monthly "alternative" or "feminist" newspapers. SM-positive magazines aimed at lesbians are listed in the "Resources" chapter. Note: Some women's bookstores refuse to carry such magazines. They apparently feel that "a woman's right to choose" does not extend to reading matter. Boycott such stores, and make sure they know that you're doing so, and why.

> I never had an
> SM fantasy
> until my girlfriend
> gave me a spanking
> for my
> 40th birthday.

Bright note: once you contact the lesbian SM community, you should quickly meet many "kindred spirits."

Final note: Many members of the "vanilla" lesbian community despise the "straight" world because it discriminates against them on the basis of their sexual orientation. I hope these women will soon quit discriminating against their SM sisters on exactly the same basis.

Anyone who opposes a woman's right to engage in whatever consensual, responsible form of sexual behavior that she feels is best for her needs a refresher course on the full meaning of "a woman's right to choose."

## Men Looking For Men

SM has long been a matter of intense interest among gay men. Most of the stores that sell SM-type leather gear are oriented mainly toward a gay male clientele. (Although they are getting an ever-increasing number of lesbian, bisexual, and heterosexual customers.)

In any event, finding partners is almost too easy for gay men, especially in major cities. Most such cities have leather bars where gay men interested in SM can meet partners. Men commonly attend dressed in a "full leather drag" of boots, chaps, jacket, and cap all made of black leather. Black leather bracelets, vests, collars, arm bands, and other accessories abound. Handcuffs and whips hang from belts.

There aren't as many bars as there used to be. The AIDS crisis has devastated the leather subculture of the gay community as much as any other part of it, but some bars survive.

Many magazines and newspapers aimed toward gay men also carry many commercial and personal SM ads.

So gay men have it easy in one respect because, more so than any other group, they can readily find potential partners. In another respect, they have a problem. Having sex with a stranger always carries risks (including, nowadays, the obvious risk of AIDS), but having SM sex with a stranger almost invites disaster.

Most of the murders I have heard of in the SM community have involved gay men playing with someone they just met. Let me add that these murders are rare, but they happen.

In many respects, gay men deserve most of the credit for being the pioneers of safe, consensual SM. They founded (and continue to found) SM clubs where interested people can meet others who are oriented, educated, and screened. Incidents of unsafe or non-consensual behavior are almost unknown at these clubs. I strongly suggest that any interested gay man contact a local SM club.

Please
let me
obey you.

## Introducing SM Into an Existing Relationship

It's great to meet a new partner at an SM event or through a kinky personal ad. You both know, from the beginning, what's likely to happen during sex. Nobody is likely to panic at the sight of a whip, set of cuffs, or other toys. Unfortunately, most people – especially heterosexual, single men – must still find their partners in the "straight" world.

The situation in that world is better than it was. SM is not nearly as taboo and underground as it was even ten years ago. Many people, for example, now have some idea that SM is a negotiated activity. They've heard something about safewords and so forth, but they've never played.

How, when, and where should you bring up SM play with a new partner? This is perhaps *the* key question, especially if you believe they are an "SM virgin" with no fantasies or experience.

The basic answer is: gradually, but relatively early.

One tip: *Don't* "intellectually" discuss SM with someone you feel attracted to, but haven't yet played with – especially if they're an SM virgin. Their understanding of SM is probably wildly inaccurate. While you are thinking of whips, passionate moans, and orgasms, they may be thinking torture, rape, and chainsaws. No wonder they aren't interested! (Intellectual discussions are best held after playing, preferably after playing several times. Many questions answer themselves during play.)

Remember, as good salespeople know, once the customer has said "no," it's hard to change their minds. In my experience, "intellectually" discussing SM with an inexperienced person almost inevitably leads to them saying, "I'm not at all interested in that stuff." If you try to persuade them to play once they've said that, they'll usually refuse.

"Springing" SM on a potential partner is a terrible idea. A "surprise attack" may relieve some of your anxiety about how to bring it up, but it will almost always radically *increase* their resistance. If you try to tie them up or whip them without prior negotiation, you risk a bloody nose or worse – perhaps *much* worse. Remember, in most cases, the person you propose playing SM with will feel considerable anxiety and resistance. Never force the situation.

All a woman has to do is pinch my nipples and bang, that's it, I'll come.

First establish a mutually satisfying "vanilla" (conventional) sexual relationship with your new partner. Remember that "a strange person with even stranger desires" will usually be rejected. You want your potential play partner to get to know you; you also want to get to know them. A woman thinking "Tom wants to tie me up" is much more likely to consent than a woman thinking "This guy wants to tie me up."

I'm often asked how to tell if a person is likely to want to be dominant or submissive. My basic answer is: "You can't." I have tried. Believe me, I have tried. After years of trying, I gave up. You just can't reliably tell. You just have to get them in the playroom and see how they react.

One *possible* indicator is their attitude toward oral sex. (Which you find out in bed, not by asking.) I personally have never met a good submissive who didn't love giving head.

Once you know how sexually compatible the two of you are, and how they feel about performing oral sex, you might proceed. One note: Many people don't like receptive anal sex because it hurts them. Don't make sweeping conclusions if they refuse it on those grounds.

How they feel about conventional sex toys such as dildoes, vibrators, lotions, and feathers also can be a hint. If they like them, that's a good sign. The outlook is bleak if you get a frosty reaction like, "I don't need any artificial help."

Raise the topic of SM play before the relationship gets too deep. I have met many people who spent years in unhappy relationships because one person wanted SM play and the other couldn't stand the idea. An end to the relationship was the most common outcome. Please don't get seriously involved with someone unless you are sexually compatible.

No two people match exactly, but if one of you strongly wants something the other cannot stand, find that out early. Certainly find out before you move in together. (Interestingly enough, I have also met couples in which both people were interested in SM, but neither one dared to raise the subject with their partner.)

On the other hand, you don't want to bring SM play up too early or you'll likely frighten them away. A good rule is, "No SM on the first date" (meaning the first time you go to bed).

I think the method most likely to succeed in introducing SM is to do it, without discussion, during the heat of passion. Try mild "mainstream" activities such as biting, scratching, and pinching. Erotically "order" them to do something. Notice how your lover reacts. Remember to avoid heavy intensity, and to avoid doing too many different things. (Be extra-sensitive to their reactions and remember that the regular rules regarding consent still apply here. "Stop" still means stop. "No" still means no.)

My Mistress couldn't be here today. She's home pruning the roses.

For example, a man having intercourse with a woman in the missionary position might try holding her hands on the bed over her head. A heterosexual woman wanting to be dominant might sit on top of her partner and holds his hands above his head. You also might see how they respond to having their nipples lightly but firmly pinched, or having their toes licked. If you are the active partner while doing it "dog style," you might pull their hands behind their back and hold them there. Perhaps give their buttocks a few light, but noticeable, spanks.

Don't do anything suddenly or with great force. This is not formally negotiated play, so keep it mild and somewhat mainstream. Go slowly. Don't do anything too long or too intensely. You don't want your partner to object – or, really, even to notice.

Also, stop if they're accepting it but not clearly enjoying it. They may be tolerating it only to please you. Acceptance does *not* equal enjoyment. Play SM only with those who enjoy it.

If you're looking for a dominant, you can also ask your partner to do things to you. Notice their reaction (and yours). Perhaps ask them to sit on the edge of the bed while you kneel at their feet and use your mouth on their feet and genitals. You might say, "Just tell me what you'd like me to do. I want to please you." You also might place their hands on your head, especially your face.

Avoid ropes, whips, and other toys during this time. It helps preserve "deniability" if your partner has a strong negative reaction.

When discussing more formal play, remember that more people are willing to try being dominant than are willing to try being submissive. They are more likely to consent if you offer to be the one who gets tied up, spanked, and so forth. (Remember to use all safety precautions. A well-meaning novice can be dangerous, and they are always unpredictable.)

> I wish he wouldn't be so fucking nice to me all the time. He's really considerate when we play, always asking me if it hurts too much or if I'd like more, and I just hate that!

Many people are more willing to experiment with SM than they used to be, but many others (two out of three) still find it unattractive. Take your time, go slowly — especially at first, and find out how they react before you become deeply involved.

**Limited submissive roles.** If your partner wants you to be submissive, but you feel doubtful, you might try the following "limited submissive" roles.

Note: Play that is this formal definitely needs to be negotiated beforehand.

**Role #1: Light dominance, no bondage, no pain.** In this role, you assume a submissive attitude. You obey orders, perform tasks for your dominant, and generally make yourself available and subservient, especially sexually.

You would kneel on command, kiss and lick your dominant's feet if ordered, and stay in a desired position until given permission to move. You might agree to go naked or to wear a costume your dominant wanted you to wear, and perhaps wear a collar. You also would agree to call your dominant "Master," "Mistress," or some similar term, and you might be called "slave" or something comparable. With adequate pre-session negotiations and your silent alarm in place, this could be a good first session.

110

**Role #2: Light dominance, light pain, no bondage.** In this role you would agree, besides assuming a submissive role, to experiment with light pain. Although the definition of "light pain" varies, a bare-hand spanking or clothespins on your nipples would be where many dominants would start.

I probably would start with the spanking. Spanking's skin-to-skin contact makes it more personal than clothespins are. Also, spanking can be done softly at first, with the pain spaced out over time and mixed with pleasure.

However, nipple clamps also may work well. Clamping a submissive's nipples and giving them head until they come is a time-honored method of introducing SM.

**Role #3: Light dominance, light bondage, no pain.** This might be a good way to try SM with someone you already know well. Again, the definition of "light bondage" is somewhat arbitrary. You might begin by allowing your partner to tie your hands behind your back, but nothing more. (Note: there is nothing "only" about allowing your hands to be tied behind your back if you doubt the other person's trustworthiness.) This degree of bondage leaves your legs free, avoids a blindfold or gag, and, especially, avoids tying you *to* something such as a bed or chair.

> People dominate in the way that they would like to submit.

Many players think bondage should begin by tying the submissive staked out to the four corners of the bed. I strongly disagree. This is *much* too vulnerable a position during the first sessions, especially for a novice or when playing with a new partner. Let your partner tie only your hands at first. If that goes well, there's always next time.

If these sessions (and their pre-session negotiations, and their post-session feedback) go well, further sessions can usually mix and expand on the bondage, pain, and domination experienced so far. Once I've had three good sessions with someone, the probability of more good sessions with them is high. On the other hand, serious problems usually surface during the first three sessions, *particularly* the first session.

This is a slower "schedule" than many people want, but it's considerate from the novice's perspective – especially the novice submissive. If you have SM fantasies or experience, you may feel impatient with this pace and want to "get right into it." Please remember that if your partner is an "SM virgin," this is new, strange, and probably frightening (even if they're the dominant).

At this point, they're probably doing this to please you, not to please themselves. Appreciate their considerateness, and be grateful. Remember, you almost never get in trouble by going too slowly.

Also, it's smart to give them time to get used to this. You are *much* more likely to cultivate a compatible, enthusiastic partner if you take your time. Many promising partners get scared off by being pressed for too much, too soon. On the other hand, I have never lost a promising partner, or gotten in trouble, by taking a slow pace. Give it time. Doing so is far better for both them and you.

# Bondage 1A

Bondage is a general term for physical restraint. It refers to restricting the submissive's movements by applying rope, leather cuffs, tape, handcuffs, and similar materials.

"Psychological bondage" refers to stringent obedience by the submissive, usually holding a specific position even if doing that becomes difficult. Locking a submissive in a cage, or using armlocks to restrain them, is not usually considered bondage.

Because of the bound person's extreme vulnerability, players must establish trust and understanding beforehand.

If you are considering taking the submissive role, understand that SM (just like kitchen knives and the family car) has strong abuse potential. Also understand that the person with the greatest ability to prevent your being abused, perhaps even – God forbid! – murdered, is *you*. One major way you prevent this horror is by being *very* cautious about who ties you up, and under what circumstances, and how.

Once you're bound, you're at that other person's mercy. If they're crazy, drunk, stoned, a psychopath, or enraged, your life is in danger. Never let yourself be tied up if you don't feel absolutely safe. *Never make exceptions.*

Conversely, as a dominant, you should accept a submissive's refusal to allow you to bind them – at least for that session. Do not overly coax, argue, persuade, or otherwise try to change their mind. Instead, reassure the submissive that you accept their decision, and move on to something else. Perhaps offer to let them tie you up. (Tactical tip: If you let them bind you, they are more likely to let you bind them during your next session.)

Attention, submissives: Get suspicious if a dominant strongly continues trying to persuade you to accept being bound after you have clearly refused. If this person acts so disrespectfully now, how will they treat you once you're bound?

I'm completely
at home being
blindfolded
and bound.

113

To be gracious, try to avoid giving the dominant a flat refusal. Propose an alternative. You might, for example, offer to stay in any position they order, or you might offer to submit to what they planned to do after they bound you. Accommodate them if you can, but if a little voice inside you is saying don't let this person tie you up, *listen to that voice.*

Just because you know someone well, and are even perhaps married to them, does not mean you should allow them to bind you. I know married couples whose relationship deteriorated to where it became unsafe for them to play SM with each other.

Even if you have let your lover tie you up dozens, even hundreds, of times before, and that has always gone well, it does not automatically mean you should let them bind you again. Each decision to permit or not to permit them to tie you up (and thus put yourself at their mercy) is a separate one. Consider it carefully.

If you're not sure, you might want to proceed after setting up a silent alarm. You might also want to wait until another person is around – preferably a trustworthy, discreet person who cares about both of you and feels positive about SM. This person may or may not, depending on what you negotiate ahead of time, participate in the session. A fourth possibility is playing at an SM party. A fifth is renting dungeon space from an SM professional.

*She was in no particular hurry to untie me.*

## *Some Basic Bondage Principles*

1. It is never necessary to tie any body part so tightly that it begins to tingle or "goes to sleep."

2. No bondage involving the front of the neck.

3. Never (and never means never) tie somebody up and then leave them alone. Always stay as close to a bound person as you would to an infant in your care. If you gag them, stay even closer. Be especially careful about any doors between you and the submissive – I know of at least two cases in which a dominant carelessly allowed a door to lock behind them, making it very difficult for them to get back to their submissive quickly.

4. Bondage should be secure. Neither the submissive nor the dominant should doubt that the submissive would find it impossible, or at least extremely difficult and time-consuming, to escape without help. Keep in mind that rope bondage often loosens slightly with time.

5. Both parties should make sure that some emergency "quick release" method is available. This release should take less than 60 seconds, and preferably less than 30. Usually, this will mean that a pair of paramedic scissors is immediately available and that emergency lighting (both flashlights and blackout lights) are also immediately available.

6. Watch out for dragging. Avoid dragging rope across skin during tying or untying. Such dragging hurts in a very unerotic way. Don't do it unless you specifically want your submissive to experience that particular sensation. If you must do something like that (say you're passing one rope under another), put your finger between the rope and the submissive's skin. Note: Some dominants use very smooth rope and make a point of dragging this rope slowly across the submissive's skin as a sensual experience.

Some dominants consider it slightly impertinent for a submissive to examine their bondage closely, but other dominants encourage it. This latter group wants their submissive to understand how securely they're bound.

## Types of Rope

Good bondage rope tends to be soft and flexible, with a slight outer roughness to hold knots. It's neither too thick nor too thin, neither too rough nor too smooth. Rope that's too thin cuts into flesh. Rope that's too thick is cumbersome and difficult to knot. Rope that's too rough abrades skin. Rope that's too smooth often won't hold a knot.

Recommended thickness for general use: $^3/_{16}$".

Very smooth rope, particularly nylon rope, is flexible and soft but holds a knot poorly. (Braided nylon may work well.)

Rough rope, such as sisal rope, chafes the submissive's skin. I know one professional Mistress who uses it for exactly that reason, but she only uses it on experienced masochists who don't mind (or even like) abrasions or other marks. She stocks smoother rope for her other clients.

For ordinary bondage, I recommend standard pure cotton clothesline. (100% pure cotton only; no plastic or wire cores.) It's the right size, the right texture, readily available, easily cleaned, and cheap.

Some bondage fans like the "tubular webbing" popular with backpackers, campers, and climbers. Such material works well, lasts forever, and is very strong. It's easily cleanable and comes in a delightful variety of colors. It also can be applied flat on the skin, and that reduces rope marks. Tubular webbing is excellent bondage rope. It's also, however, harder to find and much more expensive than ordinary clothesline.

Some players like the rope magicians use in their acts. This pure cotton "magician's rope" is soft, flexible, holds knots well, and is an excellent rope for general bondage use. It's more expensive than standard clothesline but less expensive than tubular webbing. It's also somewhat hard to find. Try a magician's supply house.

Marine supply stores, and stores that stock supplies for rock climbers, often have a wide array of ropes in numerous widths, colors, strengths and degrees of stretchability. Some of these ropes are excellent for bondage. One advantage is that they're usually clearly labeled as to strength and stretch. I suggest that you try buying a small amount of several kinds, experiment, then come back and buy larger amounts of the kinds you like.

Note: Rope can often be bought in bulk at a substantial discount, and SM folks sometimes pool their money to do just that. I once watched a sweet-faced woman walk into a magician's supply house and buy 300 yards of magician's rope – their entire stock. When the surprised clerk asked her if she had a big show that night, she smiled prettily and replied, "something like that."

I want to be helplessly bound at your feet.

Safety warning: Ordinary clothesline, magician's rope, and similar materials work well for ordinary bondage but may be a poor choice for bondage that might have to bear the submissive's weight. These materials stretch, and may break, under heavy loads. Be sure you know the "breaking strength" of any rope you use for such bondage. Tubular webbing, yachting rope, and similar materials are often good choices. A game hoist is also a possibility. *If you don't know a rope's breaking strength, don't use it for weight-bearing bondage, period.*

**Washing the rope.** After you buy your rope, wash it with fabric softener. Wash and dry the entire rope *before* you cut it into the desired lengths. It should come out soft and flexible. Repeat the washing and drying if it doesn't.

Note: This refers only to cotton rope, not to rope made with a wire core, plastic fibers, and so forth.

Short lengths of rope can jam washing machines. They also often form a tangled mess while being washed. For these reasons, many SM folks use a "lingerie bag," or put the ropes into a pillowcase and knot it, when washing such short lengths.

**Securing the ends.** With time and use, the strands of cotton clothesline, magician's rope, and similar material will unravel, sometimes more than an inch. Such unraveled ends look ugly (and may subtly signal sloppiness on the dominant's part). Therefore, the ends of each rope should be treated to prevent this. Most people do so by simply placing small stitches with a thread and needle near the end of the rope. This is called whip-stitching.

Whip-stitching the rope's ends (along with cutting it, washing it, and marking its midpoint) can be an appropriate task for the submissive. They can be given the long, uncut rope and ordered to return it cut, stitched, washed, and marked. This assignment is particularly delicious if the submissive knows the ropes thus prepared are for use on them.

The ends of nylon rope, tubular webbing, and similar materials often cannot be secured by whip-stitching. Applying heat melts the ends together. This works well, but may leave an end with rough or sharp edges – a safety hazard. File off any rough or sharp places.

**Marking the ends.** Determining a rope's length can be difficult, especially if there's not much light (common during SM play). One way to deal with this is to "color-code" the ends. For example, the ends of a six-foot length might be whip-stitched with blue thread, the ends of a 12-foot length with red thread, and so forth.

Put your hands behind your back!

Alternatively, a laundry marking pen can be used to draw circles around the rope at both ends. One circle for a six-foot length, two for a 12-foot, and so forth.

A third way is to color-code the ropes by length. All blue ropes would be six feet, all yellow ropes twelve feet, and so forth. (Cotton ropes can easily be dyed.) Again, remember that much SM play takes place under low light, so make sure the color difference is apparent under these conditions.

**Marking the midpoint.** Much, perhaps most, bondage starts at the middle of the rope instead of the ends. The middle must therefore be located, and it's both awkward and time-consuming to grab a piece of rope, match the ends, and find its midpoint. This is particularly annoying if you must do it several times during a session.

You can solve this problem by placing a visible mark at the rope's midpoint. This mark can be a piece of thread whip-stitched into the rope or a ring made by a laundry marker. Anything will work, provided its color sharply contrasts the rope's color. Remember, much SM play takes place under low-light conditions, so good contrast helps.

One hint: Cotton rope shrinks when washed, particularly the first time. Therefore place the midpoint mark *after* washing the rope. Otherwise, it may be slightly off-center.

**Lengths.** Many people like to cut their rope into six-foot lengths. Shorter lengths, unless intended for a special purpose such as genital bondage, are often inconvenient. Other useful lengths tend to come in multiples of six feet, such as 12 feet, 18 feet, and 24 feet. The longest length in everyday use is about 24 feet.

Buy a 100-foot rope for your basic bondage kit. Wash it with fabric softener, then cut it into four 12-foot lengths and eight 6-foot lengths. (Include the extra two feet in your cuts for "rounding off" purposes.) Whip-stitch the ends, then use thread or a laundry marker to mark each length's midpoint and ends. This project only takes about one evening, and you will probably use these ropes often during the rest of your bondage days. (Remember that preparing the rope that will be used on them is an excellent task to assign a submissive.)

Some people use longer lengths of rope, 50 feet, 100 feet, or more, to apply elaborate bondage – sometimes called body harnesses. This type of bondage takes considerable time to apply. (Some people like that. They enjoy the process of tying someone, or of being tied, and want it to last.) It also takes considerable practice to get right. In addition, if part of the harness is applied improperly, the dominant may have to be loosen or remove almost all of it to make the needed adjustments. For these reasons, I suggest you use several short lengths instead of one long length for routine play.

> I learned how to do bondage by tying up my slaves and ordering them to try to escape. I'd see how they got loose, and tie to prevent that next time.

**Storing rope.** Uncoiled ropes dropped into a toy bag look careless, are difficult to use and, again, signal a sloppy player. Rope can be stored in many ways. One simple way is to match up the two ends and fold the rope in half back upon itself. Fold those halves, and continue the process until the rope is about 12 to 18 inches long. Finish by knotting the folds in an overhand knot. A six-foot length will probably take two folds. 12, 18, and 24 foot lengths will take three.

*stitched, marked & stored rope*

Another way to store a rope is to coil it around your hand, then run the free end back inside the coil. Finish by knotting in an overhand knot.

## Knots

One common misconception about bondage is that it involves fancy knots. This is not so. True, some dominants "into" knots learn many (I once learned more than 30), but you can quite effectively bind your submissive with only a few easy-to-learn knots.

One point: A bondage knot doesn't need to be fancy or pulled tight to work. What it does need to be is *inaccessible*. Any knot (or non-locked buckle or snap) a submissive can reach with their fingers, toes, or teeth will eventually be worked loose.

By the way, your handy dictionary and/or encyclopedia probably illustrates several knots, and you may have an old scout manual somewhere around the house.

Let's look at a few knots.

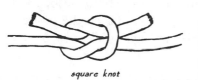
square knot

**The square knot.** The square knot is easy to learn, reasonably secure, and looks nice. The classic description of this knot is, "the more you pull on it, the tighter it gets." This could make it a *terrible* bondage knot. You may need to release a submissive quickly. A "frozen" square knot could lead to disaster. Another unique aspect of the square knot that can sometimes cause problems is that it is possible to "capsize" a square knot by grabbing one of the free ends and pulling sharply upwards. This converts the square knot into a slip knot that can be pulled loose fairly easily. (For this reason, many rescue squads specifically ban the use of the square knot.)

That's the thing I like about rope: One size fits all.

The square knot may cause serious problems. You need not avoid it altogether, but think twice before using it. Make certain you have a "plan B" for loosening ropes tied with one – such as a pair of paramedic scissors.

**The surgeon's knot.** The surgeon's knot is a good first choice. It's easy to learn and less likely than a square knot to jam. It also maintains the tension on the binding ropes during the knotting process. I like and recommend this knot.

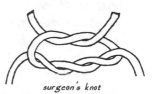
surgeon's knot

**The bow.** The ordinary bow's combination of security and quickness of release makes it an excellent bondage knot. (Keep the ends away from the submissive.) Also, some submissives find being bound with bows a bit humiliating, and that's not necessarily a bad thing. (Don't tie a "granny bow.")

*running loop*

You also might tie a "half-bow" by making a loop with only one of the strands.

Also, a "surgical bow," combining the good points of both a surgeon's knot and a bow, works well.

**The running loop.** The running loop is a good way to start a tie that uses a single long length of rope. To tie this loop, fold the end of a rope back against the rest so the two strands lay side-by-side for about six inches. Treat these parallel strands as one rope and tie them together in an overhand knot. To complete the knot, run the other end through the loop or, if the rope is very long, start about a foot away from the loop and push some rope through, then pull on the pushed-through part until the knot "flips over" and you have your loop.

It never fails: As soon as your hands are tied behind your back, your nose will start to itch.

**Tying off the end.** To finish tying off a single long length of rope, circle it around the final bound part two or three times, then place your finger against the rope and run the rope back *over* your finger and the rest of the rope until it reaches the opposite side of the bound body part, thus creating two opposing ends. Tie these ends in a surgeon's knot or similar knot.

*end tie-off*

This process is well-illustrated in the bandaging video of the first aid class. Some first aid books also show it, but I suggest you see the film.

**The lark's head.** You may also have to secure a rope after passing it through an eyebolt or around a post. One way is to pass the two ends through (or over) side-by-side, then separate the ends and pass one on either side back over the parallel ends. Knot the two ends together. You can also use the midpoint to start a tie here, as shown in the illustration on the next page.

The lark's head is a handy, versatile knot with many bondage applications, some of which I'll discuss later. It's well worth your time to learn it well. (This knot is also sometimes called a cow hitch or a lanyard hitch. It's a simpler version of the cat's paw knot.)

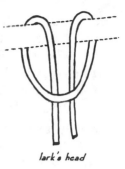

lark's head

**Obi knot.** To my delight, I discovered that the knot I'd learned for tying my *obi*, or martial arts belt, worked beautifully as a comfortable bondage knot for limbs. It enables the dominant to place several loops around the limb for maximum comfort, and unlike most bondage, distributes any pull over all the loops.

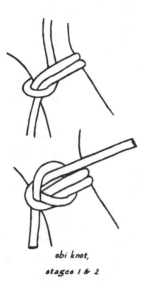

obi knot,
stages 1 & 2

Place two to four loops around the limb. Run one end of the rope under all the other strands of rope. Bring it back over, and finish it with an overhand knot.

He kept bugging me to tie him up, so I did – just to shut him up. Then, while I was tying him, I got this incredible rush, and I thought, "Hey, this is really neat!"

**Cinch loops.** As a dominant, you must carefully regulate tightness. If you apply bondage too loosely, the submissive may escape. If you apply it too tightly, you may harm them.

Cinch loops offer a wonderful way to make tightness "just right." These are coils that run between the bound parts, taking up slack.

Imagine that you have two six-foot ropes and that a pair of hands is being offered to you, palms facing each other. Take one rope and, leaving about a finger-width of space between the wrists, wrap it repeatedly around the wrists and tie its ends together. Then take the second rope and wind it between the wrists over the first rope. The second rope provides cinch loops.

Cinch loops can be used whenever two body parts are bound together, such as ankles, knees, or elbows. They are especially useful when tying wrists. They can also be useful when tying body parts to bedposts, rods, and so forth.

## Basic Bondage Techniques

**Tying the wrists.** A dominant will usually tie the submissive's wrists behind their back. This is the most restrictive position, and thus usually the position of choice. Wrists tied together in front of a submissive's body, unless the arms are otherwise restrained, hardly qualify as bondage.

When tying the hands behind the back, consider how to arrange them. The best way to decide this (and many other bondage questions) is to plan what you will do to the submissive after you've bound them.

Note: Many people who do keyboard work such as typing or programming suffer from carpal tunnel syndrome and/or related physiological problems in their hands, wrists, and arms. Such people may need to wear wrist braces under their bondage. Some of them may not be able to assume certain wrist bondage positions at all, particularly those that require twisting or bending the wrists. It is important to discuss such issues before playing, and to maintain ongoing communication about any pain, numbness, or tingling in the wrists or hands while playing. If you are a submissive who suffers from such problems, consider having a custom set of restraints made for you that will protect your hands and arms.

One classic position for hands-behind-the-back bondage is crossing the wrists at right angles to each other with the submissive's palms facing to the rear. A second position is placing the backs of the hands together. These positions are used for simple wrist bondage. They can work well, particularly as part of a hogtie (discussed later), but have a major drawback: a bound submissive usually has difficulty lying on their back if their wrists are bound either of these ways – and it's common for submissives to be placed on their backs. Their body weight will put their hands to sleep and, as you know, that's a bad idea.

A third hand position involves placing the palms together and tying the wrists. This often precedes tying the elbows together. This position often makes it even harder for the submissive to lie on their back. (Although some light, flexible submissives have no problem lying on their back while tied in any of these ways).

Note: Binding slender, flexible submissives is both a joy and a challenge. Their bendability makes it possible to put them in positions impossible for heavier submissives, even physically fit ones. On the other hand, these "rubber band people" can arch, bend, twist, and reach in ways the less flexible cannot, and that makes tying them a challenge. For example, I knew one woman who could, even with both her wrists and elbows lashed together behind her back, casually reach around and pluck the clamps off her nipples. She would then stand there and beam at her master with that sweet, mischievous grin somehow unique to the female submissive.

All the hands-behind-the-back positions I have presented so far have another drawback. They also bring the hands down over the upper buttocks. This may interfere with spanking and similar activities. Even masochists and well-trained submissives may instinctively reach back to shield their buttocks with their hands during spankings, canings, and so forth. This might cause serious hand injury. Bondage that holds the hands away from the area therefore increases safety.

The position I like best for general hands-behind-the-back bondage is to place the submissive's arms so the backs of their hands are against their back, one above the other, just above their waist. This position keeps the hands away from the buttocks, especially if you secure them in place (more about that later). This is usually also a comfortable arm position if you place the submissive on their back.

Still, a submissive on their back with their wrists tied behind them is at risk of having their hands go to sleep. One excellent way to prevent this is to place a thick pillow, or something similar, under their buttocks. This often solves the problem by creating a space between their lower back and the bed for their hands. (To date, I have heard no reports of pain or back problems from anybody who has used this technique.)

The narrow point of the wrist seems a natural place to apply ropes, but is actually somewhat insecure. Nimble submissives can often easily slip a hand free. A more secure alternative is to apply the bondage to the lower forearm instead of the wrist. The forearm bones flare slightly at their ends. You can see this most readily by noting the knob on the back of your forearm at the little-finger side. Wrist bondage will be considerably more secure if you apply it above this knob.

*I love seeing you all tied up like this.*

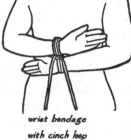

*wrist bondage
with cinch loop*

**Tying the ankles.** After tying the wrists, it's natural to turn your attention to the submissive's ankles. Binding someone's ankles considerably increases their vulnerability. Unbound feet can run, kick, and generally cause a ruckus.

Remember, for a first bondage session, it's a good idea to tie only the submissive's wrists. Don't tie them to anything such as a bed or chair, and don't tie their legs or ankles.

Once you decide it's appropriate to bind the submissive's ankles, how should you go about it? Well, as with all bondage, you should have some idea of what you want to do with them after they're tied.

The most basic way to tie the ankles is simply to place the submissive's feet together, wrap the rope around their ankles, and tie off it in a knot. Cinch loops are good, but not necessary. The spur-like heel usually holds the ropes in place. Note: Some submissives may need a slight amount of padding, such as a small, soft towel, placed between their ankles to prevent the inner ankle bones from pushing painfully against each other.

While missionary position vaginal intercourse is essentially impossible with the ankles tied this way, rear-entry vaginal intercourse, or anal intercourse, is usually possible. (Some submissives are fond of being taken from the rear. For them, it feels more impersonal and/or more like they're being "used." That feeling/fantasy arouses them.)

When I first realized that I had you tied up so that you really couldn't get loose, I got this really big rush down in my cunt.

Another advantage of this position is that it's difficult (not impossible, but difficult) to tie the ankles so tightly that they go to sleep.

In most people, if the ankles are tied side-by-side and then crossed, the bondage will loosen somewhat. Conversely, if the ankles are crossed and tied, and then uncrossed, the bondage will tighten.

Safety tip: Remember that a person standing unsupported with their feet tied together is unstable and at great risk for being injured by falling. This can be remedied somewhat by tying their knees instead of their ankles.

Another excellent way to bind the ankles is to order the submissive to cross their ankles and spread their knees apart, then circle the ankles in a "vertical" direction (along the same axis as the submissive's spine) without using cinch loops. A submissive whose ankles are bound this way will find it nearly impossible to stand or bring their knees together. It also allows good access to their genitals.

A woman bound this way may be able to have missionary-position intercourse. The man ties her ankles, then raises her legs, and climbs between them – either from above or below. His body weight thus pins her down and holds her legs apart. The vulnerability of her vagina to his penis in this position makes it popular with many male-

*ankle bondage*

dominant couples. If the woman's hands are tied behind her back and a pillow placed under her buttocks, this can be a psychologically powerful position for male-dominant intercourse.

The ankles also can be tied apart and held there by eyebolts, a spreader bar, or something similar. Again, this provides excellent access.

One drawback (or is it?): a man whose legs have been tied apart often has a much harder time reaching orgasm than a man whose legs have been tied together.

Finally, the ankles can be pulled up toward the buttocks in the classic "hogtie" position (discussed later in this section).

**Tying the knees.** Tying the knees in addition to the ankles makes the legs more secure and the bondage more complete. The knees can also be tied without tying the ankles.

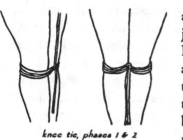

knee tie, phases 1 & 2

The best place to apply the ropes is usually just below the kneecaps. Bondage applied at or above the kneecaps tends to fall to the area below the kneecaps until stopped by the widening calf muscles, often becoming very loose in the process. Placing the ropes there to begin with solves this problem.

I love looking down at you and seeing rope everywhere.

One advantage to binding the knees is that a submissive whose knees, but not ankles, are bound is usually much more stable when standing. While still somewhat dangerous, this position is usually less risky than standing with bound ankles. Keep this in mind if you are going to tie their hands over their head in preparation for a whipping.

A person whose knees are bound but whose ankles are free can often walk surprisingly well (but will have difficulty going up or down stairs).

Binding the knees is an excellent way of "shackling" the submissive. Cinch loops can be used to good effect here, especially if you finish with the knot at the front of the legs, where the submissive can see it.

One excellent form of knee bondage is to tie the submissive's wrists to their knees. You may or may not also choose to tie their knees together. This can be a good position for spanking and/or anal play. Another advantage of wrist-to-knee bondage is that it is fairly immobilizing and yet probably still allows missionary-position intercourse. Indeed, it can even be applied while such intercourse is "in progress."

**Tying the elbows.** Tying someone's elbows together behind their back greatly increases the inescapability of their bondage. They are obviously not going to reach this with their fingers, toes, or teeth, and it holds their wrists together in a way that makes most wrist bondage much more secure. As an extra benefit, elbow bondage makes the breasts and nipples stand out.

Alas, not many people can have their elbows tied together this way. Most of us can't get our elbows anywhere near together behind our back even with someone pushing to help. Also, many find that bringing the elbows together pinches off the main artery and/or the nerves in their arms, thus immediately beginning to put their arms to sleep. Finally, even if their elbows do touch, and the position doesn't put their arms to sleep, the pressure on the submissive's shoulder joints frequently becomes very painful, usually after just a few minutes.

A submissive whose elbows are tied together behind their back usually cannot lie on their back at all (although some very slender, flexible submissives can).

In general, only slim, flexible submissives can tolerate significant elbow bondage. Rats.

*Bondage helps keep the game honest.*

Some people can tolerate partial elbow bondage by placing a rod between the elbows and binding them to that. Others run several loops of rope around both elbows and secure them with many cinch loops. The finished tie looks something like a double-headed hangman's noose.

**Shoulder pain in a bound submissive.** The human body was not designed to have its hands tied behind its back for long lengths of time. Many people, particularly if they are not both young and thin, develop pain in their shoulders – usually the front of their shoulders – if their hands are bound behind them for long. This pain may develop within minutes for some people. It's often due to the unusual strain the position causes the muscles, ligaments, and tendons of the shoulder joint.

Bondage stretching exercise: it's the tricep and anterior part of the deltoid muscle that are the source of most pain. The deltoid is stretched when the wrists are tied behind the back, and the tricep when the arms are stretched overhead. This pain may suddenly, briefly worsen when the submissive's arms are moved suddenly when released. An extreme case can even strain the muscles.

You may be able to prevent or minimize this by trying to touch your elbows together behind your back and by bringing your elbows back as far as

126

you can over your head. Remember to take your time about it. Avoid bouncing motions and fast movements into and out of the stretched position. Take it easy and avoid heroics. The shoulder joint is very prone to dislocation, so don't go to extremes. Exercise books and yoga instruction can give you additional pointers on how to do stretching exercises.

Sadly, if shoulder pain does appear, little can be done to relieve it and yet keep the submissive tied in that position. About the only thing that can be done is to tie the hands in another position entirely, or to increase the distance between the wrists. This is hard to do using only rope, but people have been successful using rope in combination with rods or spreader bars. Handcuffs and leather cuffs also may be useful here.

**Lark's head bondage.** Besides being a good "anchor point" for other types of bondage, the lark's head itself can be used very effectively.

One effective use is to apply the loop of the lark's head around the two parts to be bound such as wrists, ankles, knees, elbows, and so forth. For this example, let's say that you are tying the submissive's ankles together, side-by-side. Make sure you position the top of the loop at the space between their

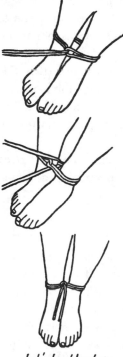

ankles and draw the rope tight. Remember to leave about a finger-width of space between the ankles. Don't press "flesh to flesh." Now take one free end in each of your hands, split them apart, and run them in opposite directions between the submissive's ankles and back to you, thus creating cinch loops. Check for the right amount of tightness, tie off, and you're done. This is a very useful, versatile bondage procedure with many applications. I strongly suggest that you spend some time learning it; one good way is to practice tying your own knees together.

**The restraint knot.** A second use of the lark's head is also excellent. I call it the "restraint knot." This knot is often used with wide gauze in the "real world" to restrain mental patients. It is most useful when you have a limb "out there alone," such as when tying a submissive spread-eagle to a bed. The restraint knot is very secure, almost cannot jam, and generally does not tighten to any dangerous degree during use. If you're into bondage at all, this knot is well worth your time to learn.

*lark's head bondage*

One hint: This knot works best when using slightly rough bondage material such as magician's rope or cotton clothesline. Of course, you also can use actual gauze. I recommend using gauze that's at least four inches wide. A brand of extra-thick gauze called Kerlix has been used for years to restrain mental patients. It's a bit expensive, and you'll probably need to go to a medical supply store to buy some, but it's reusable.

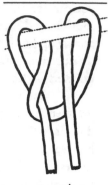

restraint knot

To create this knot, first make a lark's head knot that is big enough to hold in your fist with the midpoint of the rope on the little finger edge of your left hand. The free ends should be of about equal length, dangle straight down, and not cross. Open your fist and grasp one coil in each hand. You should now be holding one coil in each hand with your thumbs pointing away from you. Turn the coil in your right hand inward, so that your right thumb first points at your left hand and then at your abdomen. The palms of both of your hands now face to your right with the thumbs pointing in opposite directions.

Open your left fist and ease the fingers of your left hand under your right fist, then ease out your right fist so that both coils rest on your left palm, and you're done. You use your free hand to adjust this loop to the desired tightness. (This knot is *much* simpler to tie than to describe. People pick up on how to do this with very little practice.) To try it out, slide the loop over one of your wrists, tighten it down, and hold the free ends in your other hand. Try pulling against the loop and you'll see what it does.

This knot is particularly comfortable if it's tied with a double length of rope, thus placing an additional loop around the limb.

*I'm really into being tied up.*

## Breast Bondage

Breast bondage – in this book we'll refer to binding the female breasts – is fun to fantasize about but difficult to do. The breasts, unlike the wrists or ankles, have little "flare" at the end, so ropes often slip off. Still, many bondage fans feel it's worth a try.

Most breast bondage involves encircling each breast where it joins the chest wall. Large breasts are *much* easier to bind than small breasts. You might start by winding a six-foot length of rope fairly tightly around the breast at its base. Having the woman bend forward at this point may help. Capture as much tissue as possible "beyond" the ropes, tie off, and see how that feels. Is it secure? Does it feel good?

You might supplement this with another six-foot length. Place its midpoint at the back of her neck, then bring each free end down onto her chest. Loop one end under each breast a few times – preferably in the in-to-out direction – then bring the rope back up and tie it behind her neck, thus creating a "bondage bra."

Bound breasts may swell and turn pinkish-red after a few minutes. This is not particularly dangerous if it doesn't last more than about an hour or so, but the breasts will have less "give" in them than usual. The breast veins and capillaries are fuller, and thus more likely to bruise if slapped, whipped, or clamped. Such activities may also be considerably more painful than they are on unbound breasts.

Many breast bondage fans experiment with using a long rope to create an elaborate bondage bra. Such a bra is made by wrapping the rope around the breasts, around the torso, over the shoulders, behind the neck, and so forth. Sideways figure-eight patterns are often employed. It can be fun to experiment with this, using your imagination.

Some breast bondage fans place heavy rubber bands around the base of the breasts as a basic form of breast bondage. I have heard of no problems resulting from this if done in moderation and, on the right woman, it looks hot.

You mean that you really can't get out of that?

## Genital Bondage

Bondage is about physical control. The idea of controlling someone else's genitals, or of having your genitals under someone else's control, is powerfully attractive to many people. When you add that the genitals can be bound in ways to enhance sexual pleasure, you have definite interest.

Many dominants believe that once they have bound their submissive male's arms and legs, they should immediately turn their attention to his genitals. Some dominants begin their bondage there.

Binding the genitals can have a powerful effect on both dominant and the submissive. Besides the sense of control thus established, the submissive has the benefit of the sensations created by having their genitals bound. The physical sensations associated with this may be intensely pleasurable. (In some men these sensations may be enough to either cause or bring them very close to orgasm.)

The psychological effects of having your genitals controlled by another person can be profound. Our genitals are perhaps the most intimate, private parts of our bodies. Having them under another's control puts us in an extremely submissive, vulnerable position.

**Binding the female genitals.** Binding the female genitals usually covers them or exposes them. One simple method involves taking a 24-foot rope and placing its midpoint on her belly just above her hipbones. Wind the ends around her waist (a total of two coils) and tie in a surgeon's knot. Make sure the coils can't slip down over her hipbones by pulling on the rope until you've made them narrower. This leaves two free ends, each about six feet long. Order her to spread her legs (not too far, you don't want her to lose her balance), then run the ends up between her legs and cheeks.

Run the ropes between her labia so they pass over her clitoris. Pass the free ends together under her waist coils in back, then again run them between her legs and up the front of her body. If you wish, you can run these ropes outside her labia, thus pinching them slightly between the ropes. (Be careful the ropes don't pull on her pubic hair.)

Bring the two free ends up to the front of her waist, pass them up under the waist coil – one end on either side of the surgeon's knot. Then run the ends under the first two coils, bring them out the opposite side, and knot them together. She can look down and see the knots.

Obviously, this seals her vagina and rectum. Intercourse would be essentially impossible, so this is a "bondage chastity belt." On the other hand, anything *already* inside her vagina and/or rectum – vibrators, dildoes, butt plugs, ben-wa balls, and so forth – will be held fairly securely. One experienced lady noted that a vibrator could be externally applied to these ropes to good effect.

*Remember, you're going to have to untie them sooner or later.*

A second method of binding the female genitals, sometimes found arousing by the wearer, is to loop one end of a 24-foot rope around her waist and then position the end of the loop (where the knot is) above one hip. Run the rope down between her legs and out the other side, bringing it back up and across the crest of her hip bone and back down again. You can run the rope back up to the hip on the same side, or run it across to the opposite-side hip. Continue in a figure-eight pattern until you run out of rope, then knot it. This tie has the same advantages and disadvantages as the first.

A third, extremely interesting, method of tying the female genitals is to fold a 12-foot rope in half. Place the midpoint on her lower belly, just above

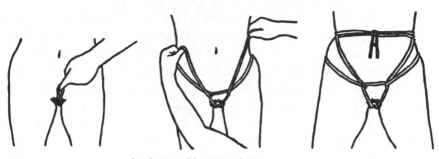

*female genital bondage, phases 1, 2, & 3*

her pubic hair. (She may have to help hold this loop in place.) Run the free ends back between her cheeks, then run one end over the top of each hipbone and back to the loop. Thread the two free ends through the loop, preferably in the inside-to-outside direction.

Here's the interesting part: Pull the free ends back up to her hipbones. This pull (be careful not to catch her pubic hair) spreads her outer labia up and away from each other, thus exposing her clitoris. As the woman who taught me this technique said, "That gets her attention." Finish the tie by bringing the free ends back up to her waist, around to her front, and tying them together there. With this tie, intercourse is difficult (but not impossible), and inserted objects are not secure, but the exposed clitoris raises exciting possibilities.

> I want to see you naked and tied up.

**Binding the male genitals.** A submissive male's genitals cry out for bondage. I mean, come on, they're just hanging out there, undisciplined, out of control, a menace to navigation. Clearly something must be done at once.

Many dominants, especially dominant women, find the sight of unbound male genitals offensive. On the other hand, they delight in the sight of a securely bound cock and tightly wrapped balls.

As with most bondage, before you tie a submissive male's genitals you should have some idea of what you want to do after they're bound.

Basic questions: Do you still want him capable of erection? Intercourse? Ejaculation? If you want him "functional," here are some approaches.

Standard-sized rope usually works adequately. It's cumbersome for some aspects, but can do the job. As an alternative, many people use thinner material.

Black leather bootlaces have a big following. The sight of a cock and balls securely bound in a black leather bootlace arouses many people. Such laces are cheap, readily available, and can be "innocently" bought at local stores.

Plastic wrap can also be used very effectively for genital bondage.

If you simply want decoration, wind and knot off a few coils between his cock and his balls, thus slightly constricting his upper scrotum.

If you want him to feel more sensation, wind additional coils until the rope lightly squeezes his testicles within his scrotum.

Another way to add sensation is to wrap a few coils around the top of his scrotum, then join the free ends and run them from back to front, thus separating his testicles. One way to join the free ends is to twist them together at the back of his scrotum, and continue winding as you bring them to the front. At the front, separate the ends and wind them in opposite directions around the top of the scrotum, then knot them together (usually at the top-front of the scrotum, just under his penis).

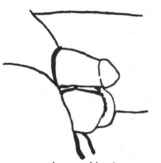

*male genital bondage*

The above ties are decorative and add sensation, but don't involve his cock. It's still capable of erection and ejaculation.

**Binding his cock.** Most cock bondage is a variant on the cock ring, so let me explain that device. A cock ring is a metal ring about $1^1/_2$ " in diameter. To apply it, first slip one testicle, then the other, then the (limp) penis through the ring so it encircles all of his genitals.

When his penis becomes erect, blood flows into it. A cock ring somewhat constricts the veins that allow blood to drain from the penis, thus keeping it erect more firmly and longer that it otherwise would. Also, and perhaps even more important from the dominant's view, applying a cock ring, or similar material, usually locks the skin along the shaft of the penis in place. This prevents it from moving as it usually does during intercourse, masturbation, or fellatio. Therefore, simulating such movements – such as by using a well-lubricated hand – produces a unique, very pleasurable, and almost unbearably intense sensation.

One drawback is that this ring will constrict, to a degree, the tube his sperm must pass through (his urethra) as he ejaculates. This may make his orgasm somewhat painful.

If you bind his cock so tightly that his urethra completely shuts, and he is brought to orgasm, he probably will have a "retrograde ejaculation." Such an orgasm diverts his semen back into his bladder. This is usually not damaging if only done occasionally, but I wouldn't make a steady practice of it.

A quick, easy way to apply male genital bondage is to use a leather "cock strap." This is a strip of leather about ¹/₄" wide by 6" long. It usually has two or three snaps on its inside and sometimes has studs on its outside. Such a strap is often worn as a bracelet, especially by gay men and both male and female "punk rockers."

The cock strap can be quickly snapped into place above a man's cock and balls. The different snaps allow tightness adjustment. (Some strap fans carry a second one to apply between the penis and testicles.)

Coils of rope, leather, or chain can be attached to a leash, thus providing a convenient, persuasive method of leading a male slave. This leash is even more persuasive if applied only around the top of the scrotum.

Safety note: Be careful about tying the genitals to any heavy or immovable object. For example, I once read an article that recommended keeping a male sub-missive stationary by tying rope around his scrotum, then attaching it to a doorknob, leaving only about a foot of slack. Obviously, if this submissive stumbles or falls he almost certainly will suffer severe, permanent injury to his testicles. This technique, therefore, is unacceptably dangerous.

*I know they may not look like it, but this collar and these ropes are implements of love.*

An excellent method of basic male genital bond-age is as follows: You will need two ropes, each six feet long. Place the midpoint of the first rope on his belly just above his hips, then wind both ends around his waist. Pull until the coils are narrower than his hipbones, then tie off.

Place the second rope's midpoint on top of his penis at its base. Wind two loops around his cock and balls, being careful to keep the coils side-by-side, not overlapping. That finished, run the free ends down between his legs, through his cheeks, and up to the rear of the waist rope. Separate the two ends and run them in opposite directions under the rope running from his genitals. This will give you two free, opposing ends. Knot them together, and you're done.

This genital bondage produces an intense cock-ring effect. Combin-ing it with scrotal bondage can be powerful. The rope will hold the skin covering his cock firmly in place, making it exquisitely sensitive to touch.

Breast and genital bondage are some of the most intense aspects of SM. Responsible players recognize both the dangers and the opportunities.

## *The Hogtie Position*

Ye Gods, is "hogtie" ever an inelegant word! I prefer, as do many others, the more genteel french term of "craupadine." (I've seen buttons that read "I'd rather be in craupadine." These can be fun to wear in public.) Variations on this position are seen fairly frequently during SM play, so I'm going to discuss some of them.

**The basic hogtie.** The basic position is simple: The submissive is made to lie face down, then their wrists are tied behind their back and their ankles are tied together. The ankles are then pulled up toward their wrists and a rope is run from the wrists to the ankles, lashing them together. This is a highly restraining position (probably too much so for first bondage) and provides good access to the front of the submissive's body.

I can't relax unless I'm really tied up.

One important safety consideration is that tying someone in this position may increase the amount of work they must do in order to breathe. In a worst-case situation, this extra work could exhaust them and they could die of respiratory failure. (This is one cause of what's known as "positional asphyxia.") Breathing difficulty may become apparent almost immediately, or may develop slowly over time.

The hogtie usually causes no problems, particularly if the dominant closely monitors the submissive. However, it can be dangerous if the submissive is significantly overweight or inflexible, and/or if the surface they are lying on is exceptionally hard or soft. The submissive can usually ease the work of breathing by rolling onto their side for a while, with their dominant's help if needed.

How far back should you pull the ankles? That depends on how immobilized you want your submissive to be. The farther back you pull the ankles, the more you immobilize the submissive. A submissive whose ankles are pulled "all the way back," for example, cannot do much except lie on their stomach. On the other hand, a submissive whose ankles are only pulled

*basic hogtie*

134

back about halfway (forming a 90-degree angle with the ground) can – with assistance – lie on their back or stomach, roll onto their side, kneel, and sit cross-legged. This is especially true if the ankles were bound using cinch loops.

Beware of sneaky submissives. If the ankles are tied side-by-side, the submissive may be able to defeat the tie by crossing their ankles. This allows their ankles to be brought closer to their fingers. One way to defeat this is to tie the submissive's knees together, thus preventing them from spreading their knees apart. Another way is to order the submissive to spread their knees apart before you tie their ankles.

**The "military" hogtie.** A hogtie variant widely taught in military and martial arts circles involves using one long rope or several short ropes to tie the captive's hands behind them, then pushing their hands high up on their back and wrapping the rope around their neck to hold their arms in place. The rope is then run back down to their wrists and wrapped a few times. The submissive is then told to bend their feet back up toward their buttocks and the last of the rope ties their ankles together.

The basic argument in favor of this tie is that it is escape-proof because the captive's struggles to free themselves produce very uncomfortable pressure on their neck. If they struggle too hard, they could choke themselves unconscious. In extreme cases, they could even choke themselves to death. They therefore don't struggle and lie still. Obviously and unfortunately, this tie can kill if the pressure around the submissive's neck becomes too great.

Complete
immobility really
turns me on.

I have been on both ends of this tie several times. After much experience, thought, and debate, I have concluded the risks of this bondage technique outweigh its advantages to the point where it should not be used. (I noticed that the rope running from wrists to ankles seems the source of most neck tightness, and therefore most danger.) It is most certainly not a technique for beginners.

Footnote: Any form of neck bondage is considered too dangerous by most practitioners. About as far as most will go would be a leash attached to a collar and held in the dominant's hand.

**Hogtie alternatives.** Alternative approaches exist that are as secure, and avoid such severe risks.

The first alternative works well when using a single 20 to 24 foot rope. Secure the wrists with one end of the rope, then run it under an armpit, up and over the submissive's collarbone, and across the back of their neck. Then run the rope across the opposite collarbone, back through the opposite armpit, and back to the wrists. Loop the rope once or twice between the wrists, then go to the ankles.

The second alternative approach calls for a 12-foot rope. Have the submissive position their wrists as you order. Starting with the middle of the rope, wrap and cinch-loop their wrists, perhaps finishing in a surgeon's knot. Then run the two ends under the submissive's armpits and up across their collarbones to the back of their neck. Knot the ends together there with a surgeon's knot. Dominants need to be careful that a nimble submissive doesn't work their fingers up to the knot at the back of their neck, and thus defeat at least that much of the tie. Other than that, this is a secure, safe, and effective tie.

*hogtie alternative 1*

A third, even more secure, approach calls for an 18-foot rope. Use the rope's middle to tie the submissive's wrists behind their back. Then run the two ends over the submissive's back near the base of their neck, cross the ends in front of their neck and run the ends under their armpits. Pull the ends through, cross them over their back, and again run them through the armpits toward the front of the body. Finish the tie by bringing the two ends together in front of the submissive high on their chest. Tie the ends with a surgeon's knot. (I have never had any reports of uncomfortable or unsafe neck pressure from the use of this tie.) In this position, the submissive can see the knot that holds them but cannot reach it – always a nice touch.

A fourth approach: tie the wrists together using the middle of the rope, then run the two ends around the submissive's waist. Pull the ends tight enough to make the waist loop narrower than the submissive's hipbones, and knot in front. This is simple, safe, and secure.

**Hogtie leg variations.** Sometimes the wrists are tied behind the back and the ankles are drawn up toward the buttocks but not actually tied to the wrists. Such a "split-level" hogtie maintains much of the inescapability while allowing the submissive a bit more flexibility.

One way of hogtying the submissive's legs is to order them to kneel back on their heels with their toes drawn in. Tell them to spread their knees about 45 degrees apart.

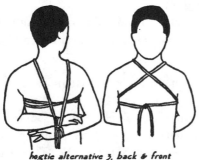

*hogtie alternative 3, back & front*

Wrap a 12-foot length of rope around both the ankle and thigh then, if you wish, cinch-loop it. Repeat this with the other leg.

With their legs tied this way, the submissive can lie on their back, or lie on their stomach, or kneel. The legs can be placed together, or separated. The position allows excellent access to the genitals. Depending on the submissive's body (and yours), anal or vaginal intercourse may be possible.

An alternative method is to use the middle of a 24-foot length of rope to tie the ankles, then have the submissive kneel with their knees together and wrap the rope around both thighs. Finish by cinch-looping between the legs.

It's a nice touch to place the knot on the front of the ankles – away from the submissive's hands. Some nimble submissives can reach their ankles, and this position keeps the knot as far as possible from their fingers.

Footnote: When turning a hogtied submissive over, you may find that it works best to start with their ankles. A little experimentation here will help.

In summary, the hogtie, if properly and safely applied, is a powerful bondage technique with much potential. Just make sure you understand the risks and benefits of each variant and, as always, keep your paramedic scissors handy.

## Using a Bar as Bondage Implement

Using a rigid bar, usually made of metal or wood, to reinforce the submissive's immobility is a measure about halfway between permitting them the relative freedom of only binding them with rope or similar materials and the more complete immobility of binding them to a fixed object such as a chair or bed.

> I'd like to do a scene where I tie a loop of sewing thread around his thumbs, attach it to a thumbtack in the wall, and that's the bondage and he'd better not break it.

Because bars are popular devices for holding ankles or knees apart, they are often called "spreader bars."

Bars can be of many lengths. I have seen them as short as six inches – usually as an adjunct for elbow bondage. I've also seen them as long as ten feet – serving as a "portable rack." Commercially available bars that can be adjusted in length are popular.

Bars may be flared at the ends to help prevent ropes from slipping off. They also may have eyebolts placed into them or holes drilled through them for ropes to pass through.

Bars need not necessarily be round. I've seen them with flat rectangle shapes. (The edges and corners of such bars were sanded smooth as a safety measure.)

A bar (or bars – combinations can be created) should be avoided for first bondage sessions. Again, too much immobility is involved.

**How to lash wrists to a bar.** Place the wrist (usually its back) on the bar with the wrist bones extending slightly beyond it. Place the midpoint of a six-foot rope on part of the wrist opposite the bar on the side closest to the shoulder. Run the ends behind the bar and in opposite directions over the wrist. Make sure the ropes pass each other and do not overlap. Pull the ends back around the bar. Cross the rope on the little-finger side over the wrist and bring the ends together on the back of the wrist at the thumb side.

*wrist lashed to bar*

Cross the ends and run them between the back of the wrist and the bar, creating a cinch-loop. Finish by bringing the two ends back together and knotting them on the back of the hand, away from the fingers. The resultant lashing is secure, very difficult to escape, and eye-pleasing. It can easily be loosened slightly if necessary.

A similar procedure can be used to bind ankles, knees, and elbows to a bar. A very short bar can be placed between the submissive's elbows. A very long bar – ten feet or so – can be used as a portable rack with the submissive's feet lashed to one end of it and their wrists lashed toward its other end.

A bar can also be lashed under a submissive's hips to prevent them from rotating from side to side. In this position it can also be tied to a submissive man's genitals.

Did you remember to buy more rope?

Safety note: Be sure any rod or bar placed under a submissive is strong and not likely to break. This is particularly important if they are on a bed or other noticeably soft, giving surface.

## Tying A Submissive to the Bed

In many ways, this is a classic SM image. I've seen it in movies, cartoons, and many other areas. Many beginners and non-SM people have told me of tying someone or of being tied in this way.

As I've mentioned several times earlier, this a *very* unfortunate situation. Such bondage is far too restrictive for beginners or people who don't know each other well. (I know of a case in which a woman was nonconsensually tied to a bed for over three days.)

I usually don't let a dominant tie me to anything immovable, such as a bed or chair, until at least the third time we play together. Also, I would definitely have a silent alarm in place and make sure that my dominant knew about it.

Having said all the above, let me add that this form of bondage has great potential. Many bondage fans explore it in depth.

**Tying wrists to bedposts.** Eventually, once you know someone well, you may want to tie them to a bed in the classic "spread-eagle" position. This position combines high security with high accessibility.

The restraint knot and the gi knot described earlier in this chapter are first-rate knots to use in this situation, particularly when used with a 12-foot length of rope for each limb. After tying the knot at the midpoint of the rope, take the two free ends up to the bedpost, and wrap them around the post once or twice. Then, drop the two ends down to the bed's legs, wrap them around the lower part of the leg, and tie them in a bow. (This will keep the final knot well out of the submissive's reach, but, if necessary, allows you to release it instantly.)

Is that too tight?
Is that too loose?

Submissives often want to grab their ropes to "brace" themselves when tied this way, so if you are feeling benevolent that night, you might run the rope across your partner's palm. Doing so allows them to grab the rope. On the other hand, if you're not feeling particularly nice right then, tie the knot at the back of their wrist. You might even order them to keep their hands off the ropes.

**A few thoughts on tying submissives to beds.** The classic, face-up, spread-eagle bed bondage position has, of course, many advantages: the breasts, genitals, and insides of the thighs are well-exposed, and the position is not unduly uncomfortable and can be held by some people for hours. A woman tied in this position is often capable of sexual intercourse, but it may be easier if you free her legs or tie them to either an overhead bar or eyebolts in the ceiling. If she has to keep her legs parallel to the floor, entry may be difficult.

Caution: If you do tie her legs to overhead eyebolts, make sure you use many coils of rope around her ankles. This is especially true if you get on top of her for intercourse. Otherwise, the tension of this position can cause the ropes around her ankles to cut more deeply into her flesh than either of you want. In an extreme case, the pressure could be so severe as to leave permanent marks. You can also reduce this risk by using wider-than-average rope or leather cuffs.

This position also has a few disadvantages: the submissive's back and buttocks are almost inaccessible, and their anus difficult to reach. Also, because his legs are tied apart, it is often somewhat difficult for a woman to mount a man for intercourse if he is tied this way. Also, as with most positions where a man is tied with his legs apart, it is likely to be difficult for him to reach orgasm. (A fact used to good effect by some mischievous dominants.)

Also, it is difficult for a submissive tied this way to perform oral sex on a penis. (The testicles and anus, however, can be well-reached.) Cunnilingus is possible, but the dominant must have some self-control. Finally, it's difficult to turn the submissive over, and thus gain access to their backside, without removing most of the bondage.

Accordingly, you might try some of these other positions:

1. Tie the submissive face-up, hands tied apart to the corners, feet tied together at the bottom center of the bed. This is a particularly good position for a dominant woman to use on a man. It allows you to mount him, and it's easier for him to reach orgasm. (Don't make this *too* easy.)

2. The submissive is tied face-up, hands together at the upper center of the bed, legs apart. This position makes it easier to turn them. Untie one leg's securing rope (leave the coils in place around the ankle), bring it over to the other leg and tie it in place there. (Tie it to the bed, not the other leg.) Then free the other leg and bring it back to where the first one was tied, thus turning the submissive. This is a fairly good position for binding a woman. It has one drawback: in this position, it's hard for the submissive to perform oral sex.

3. The submissive lies face-up, the hands tied together at the head of the bed, and the feet tied together at the foot. This is a good position for a submissive male. He can be turned readily, and thus most of both the front and back of his body is available. About the only drawback is that it makes it difficult for him to perform oral sex.

4. The submissive is tied face-up, the legs are tied together at the foot of the bed, and the wrists are tied behind the back. A pillow is placed under his buttocks and a strap is run across his chest and under his armpits to the top center of the bed. This is perhaps the best overall position for tying a man to a bed.

To apply this tie, order him to him lie face-down on the bed about one-third of the way from the side. Tell him to put his feet together and his hands behind his back. Tie his wrists with a 12-foot rope. Finish this tie by bringing the ends around his sides to his abdomen, and tie them firmly together. Take a second 12-foot length of rope and place its midpoint on his upper back, level with his armpits. Run either end under his armpits to the front of his body, then bring the two ends back over his collarbones to the rear of his neck at its base and tie them together using a surgeon's knot.

Order him to roll toward the center of the bed until he is on his back. *Place a pillow under his hips to elevate them.* (He may be lying on his back for a long time.) Run the free ends of the "shoulder harness" up to the middle of the top of the bed and tie them there. Tie them loosely – he'll need some slack so he can turn from face-up to face-down positions. Finish the tie by using a third 12-foot length of rope to tie his ankles together and then to the bottom center of the bed.

This position gives you almost complete access and excellent security. Female-superior intercourse and cunnilingus are very possible, and almost his entire body is accessible.

I'm working on getting my elbows to touch behind my back.

**The psychology of applying the spread-eagle tie.** Two schools of thought exist regarding how you should tie a submissive spread-eagled onto a bed. The first schools says to go for immediate, maximum vulnerability. For instance, if your submissive is right-handed, begin by tying their right wrist. Then tie their left wrist, then right ankle, then left ankle. The other school is a bit more teasing. These scamps tie in reverse order, thus letting both people savor the approaching moment of inescapability. Personally, I prefer the second approach.

A similar approach can be taken with most other bondage. For example, because a person whose wrists are bound is much more helpless than a person whose feet are bound, the dominant begins the bondage by tying the feet.

Note: because many people consider this approach less threatening, you might use it when tying someone new to the experience.

## *Notes and Hints*

Face-up bondage: One prime principle of tying someone's hands behind their back and then having them lie on their back is to put a thick pillow under their buttocks. (Make sure this doesn't make their back feel strained.) Doing so lifts most of their body weight off their hands and helps prevent the hands from going to sleep.

Face-down bondage: It's usually difficult and painful for a submissive to be bound face-down for any length of time. People weren't built to lie face down. They must either turn their head to the side or arch their head back somewhat, and either is painful after a while. If you like face-down positions, consider getting a special device from a massage supply company that can be placed on a bed and allows people to lie face-down.

A massage table, by the way, is easily converted into a bondage table. A few eyebolts or holes are all you need. (Be careful where you place them. Don't weaken the table!)

One caution: Think twice about getting onto such a table with the submissive. Most tables aren't built to take that much weight, and are too narrow (and thus unstable) for erotic thrashing about. You don't want to collapse or topple the table! An alternative is to lay the table on the floor with its legs folded away and the ropes passed under it. The submissive's own body weight holds them in place, and joining them on the table would be much safer.

*Now, how did you tie that again?*

If you must loosen the submissive's bondage, try to do so as little as possible. For example, when moving a submissive who is in a spread-eagle tie, move only one bound limb at a time. (Or, if necessary, two.) Don't take off the whole thing.

A submissive may be tied to a bed for a very long time. Thus, having something for them to drink will help preserve the session's energy. Furthermore, because it's difficult for them to drink from a cup or glass (they can't hold it) a straw can come in very handy. Those "sport bottles" with the built-in straw also work well.

Also, following the principle of "what goes in must come out," having a urinal handy can do a lot to preserve the mood. A male urinal, with a lid that snaps in place, usually works acceptably well for both sexes.

## First Bondage

Binding someone for the first time is a special moment. This is particularly true if they have never before been bound in an erotic context. (Most people played "cowboys and indians" games during childhood.) A wise dominant recognizes this opportunity. They "imprint" their play partner in a positive way. This may open the door to years, even a lifetime, of enjoying erotic bondage.

Some people have "really" been arrested, kidnapped, captured during wartime, or otherwise held captive. Show extra consideration and patience to them. Among other things, if erotic bondage is done appropriately, it may hold significant healing potential.

**First bondage safety tip.** As a safety measure, a submissive should avoid letting themselves be tied *to* anything, such as a bed or chair, during their first bondage session. Understand and agree upon this in pre-session negotiations.

A first bondage session should probably involve tying only the submissive's wrists. Your agreement to let your hands be bound does not in any way give your dominant the right to bind your ankles or any other part of you. Giving someone you don't know extremely well permission to tie you up without first negotiating what parts of you will be tied, with what material, for how long, and under what conditions is a *terrible* idea. Be content with only tied wrists the first time. Additional sessions, involving more extensive bondage, can be arranged afterward if the first session goes well.

*(Answering machine message):*
I can't come to the phone right now, I'm all tied up. Leave a message and I'll get back to you just as soon as I'm untied.

**First bondage equipment.** I suggest avoiding formal equipment, such as leather cuffs, for first bondage. Instead, use "improvised," soft materials such as bathrobe sashes, scarves, and soft belts. "First bondage" materials should be soft and wide, and it won't detract from the session a bit if they're colorful.

## Precautions When Playing in Isolated Areas

A few years ago, novelist Stephen King published a book in which a man takes a woman to a cabin deep in the woods, handcuffs her securely to a bed, then suddenly and unexpectedly dies of a heart attack.

While such incidents are extraordinarily rare, it is not out of the question that they could happen. A dominant could tie a submissive into a totally inescapable position and then suffer a heart attack, stroke, seizure, accident, or another situation, thus leaving the submissive helpless and both of them in a truly terrible situation.

OK, so what to do about it? Several precautions come to mind. The first and most important precaution is to recognize that this situation could occur and needs to be planned for. This includes recognizing that cabins deep in the woods are not the only risky locations. Farmhouses, boats, isolated campsites and other "natural" locations, suburban homes, and even some city apartments may be highly risky. Above all, the possibility that this might happen must *not* be ignored or denied. "Listen, honey, I'm just not going to have a heart attack," is an explanation you should simply not (ever, ever, ever) accept.

A few specific precautions include (1) as with first bondage sessions, not tying the submissive *to* anything immovable such as a bed or heavy chair, (2) setting up a silent alarm, (3) playing with bondage but not gags, (4) having a third person present, (5) avoiding the use of relatively inescapable bondage equipment such as handcuffs, (6) making sure that the submissive can reach a telephone "if they *really* have to" (phones equipped with both a speakerphone and one-touch speed dialers are especially useful), (7) placing a citizen's band walkie-talkie or similar two-way radio within the submissive's "really have to" reach, and (8) setting up an alarm system equipped with a "panic button" (a device similar to a garage door opener; you push the button and the alarm sounds). Electronic stores often stock simple but very effective alarm systems that include panic buttons. Please note that it's entirely reasonable to have a "dress rehearsal" on these matters.

Prevention measures include (1) limiting such play if the dominant has a heart condition, seizure disorder, or other condition that puts them at risk for sudden unconsciousness, (2) extra caution on the dominant's part to make sure they aren't injured (because falling is probably the main risk, keep the play area floor clean, well-lit, and otherwise safe), and (3) making sure that the dominant stays well-fed, sober, and neither too hot nor too cold. Low blood sugar, intoxication, and even heat exhaustion can cause unconsciousness.

Caution: A dominant should keep in mind that if they should become unconscious while playing in isolation with a stringently bound submissive, then that submissive will probably be unable to come to their aid in time to do any good – a cardiac arrest being a worst-case example. That being so, they might want to think twice about how extensively and inescapably they want the submissive tied.

The main question to consider is: can the bound person either free themselves or summon help if the dominant suddenly becomes unconscious? If they cannot, it's essential that the bondage be modified.

## *Self-Bondage*

Many people have bondage fantasies but no partner, so they bind themselves. Many, many people interested in SM have partially tied themselves up while they masturbated.

The person interested in self-bondage faces a problem. They want to bind themselves so they can't escape, yet, obviously, eventually they will want release. What to do?

Self-bondage can obviously be extremely dangerous. As you know, I recommend staying as close to a bound person as you would to an infant left in your care, and even closer if you've gagged them. Clearly, a self-bound person has deprived themselves of this very basic safety measure. Problems such as positional asphyxia, or outside-world problems such as fires and earthquakes, can be life-threatening without a "lifeguard" standing by.

I have heard of several deaths resulting from self-bondage that went wrong. I've even heard of the death of a couple that took place when both of them were tied up and the house caught fire. Many of these deaths involved "highly experienced" players who "knew what they were doing" yet died anyway. Most such fatalities involved gags, hoods, ropes around the neck, or some other device that had the potential to restrict breathing.

I'd be happy to tie you up.

I've also heard of people having panic attacks, accidentally knocking over heaters, and other mishaps.

Most self-bondage involves locking devices, especially around the wrists. The person works out some plan by which the keys again come within their grasp. Unfortunately, failure-proof mechanisms simply do not exist. If the device fails to work (and, eventually, it will) the self-bound person often has no other way to get free or summon help.

Also, bondage not tight enough to immediately put the bound area to sleep may still be tight enough to do that gradually. The self-bound person's hands may go numb after an hour. If the keys fall within reach after that – trouble.

I have experimented with self-bondage and found it somewhat interesting, but – besides its dangers – it has other drawbacks.

First, if you bind yourself so that you can't get loose you may rapidly discover that being alone and in bondage is *boring*. Without a "sweet tormentor" for company, this situation can get very stale very fast. The vibrators, clamps, dildoes, and other gear that aroused you when you first put yourself in bondage may feel awful after your arousal fades – even if it doesn't malfunction or go out of adjustment. If, genius that you are, you set the situation up so you can't get loose for three hours, you may find that the last two hours and 50 minutes go on for a very, very long time.

Seriously, be careful with self-bondage. It's something that often seems like a good idea in fantasy, and offers plausible exploration, as long as *absolutely nothing* goes wrong. Remember that even a minor malfunction or unexpected development can cause you to die a slow, agonizing death. Many "experts" died exactly this way.

You might try binding your breasts and genitals, but be very conservative about using anything that would restrict your breathing (gags, hoods, neck ropes), make you vulnerable to a fall (blindfolds), or restrict your limbs – especially your arms.

Many people have died of self-bondage gone wrong. Some "experts" who wrote about how to do this are now dead due to a self-bondage accident.

## On Being Untied

As part of their basic training, submissives should be ordered to "hold position" while being untied. They must remain still until their dominant has removed their bondage and given them permission to move. Many submissives wriggle and escape as their bondage comes off. Such movements can sometimes cause a knot to jam, or otherwise interfere with the untying. The movements can also be a safety hazard. Train your submissives to remain still while you are untying them until you give them your permission to move.

Another principle: let them move their own body. Muscles become sore and joints become stiff when they haven't moved in a while. If a well-meaning dominant "helps" by moving the body part for the submissive, they may cause a strain or similar injury. Let the submissive regain their ability to move at their own pace.

Also, don't massage or otherwise rub freshly released limbs, especially if indentations remain in their flesh from the restraints. Such rubbing may be painful and cause tissue damage. Let freshly released tissue re-expand at its own pace. If you want to be nice to the submissive, rub them later.

# Bondage 1B

## *Gags*

Using a gag *substantially* increases the risk involved in SM. Many people think a bound person should "automatically" be gagged. This is absolutely not so.

Just as there is nothing "automatic" about allowing yourself to be bound, there is also nothing automatic about allowing yourself to be gagged. It's an entirely separate decision. Many professional submissives, for example, will allow a new client to bind them tightly and severely, but will not allow themselves to be gagged.

That's a heavy moment, when the lock snaps shut.

One good rule is to avoid using a gag the first few times you play with someone. As a dominant, you need ongoing feedback from a new submissive. You'll lose much of that if you gag them. So, even if they'd let you, don't gag a submissive the first few times you play with them.

Second point: Obviously, a gagged submissive is going to have trouble calling their safewords. You therefore have to give them a non-verbal set of signals.

Some various approaches to this include:

1. Having the submissive hold a ball, scarf, or similar item in their hand. If they drop it, that means the session has become too intense.
2. Having the submissive snap their fingers.
3. Having the submissive vigorously nod their head in an up-and-down direction. (Many people twist their head from side-to-side when they're feeling passionate, especially when they're lying on their back. Almost nobody nods their head up and down.)
4. Having the submissive "grunt" in a recognizable pattern, such as two short grunts, then a pause, then two more grunts, repeated as needed. (A gagged person can still grunt rather loudly.)

5. Having the submissive strongly and audibly tap two times on themselves, their partner, or some object. The tap can be delivered with a hand, foot, or any other body part. This is very similar to the "tap for release" safety signal taught to martial artists.

I like the "grunt" and "tap" signals. SM is often done under dark conditions, so an audible signal (as opposed to a visual signal) is a good thing. People who are lying on a bed with their hands tied behind their back would have trouble snapping their fingers or dropping a scarf.

Note: some submissives learn how to finger-spell the deaf alphabet, and can thus, even though gagged, have detailed conversations with their dominant if the dominant also knows it (and it's not that difficult to learn).

Obviously, one major danger of a gag is that it could interfere with the submissive's breathing. You would obviously want to limit or eliminate gag use when the submissive has a cold or anything else that interferes with their ability to breathe through their nose. If your submissive is at all prone to allergies, a couple of shots of decongestant spray in each nostril, and/or an oral decongestant, is a good idea before gag play.

You do your best SM with someone you love.

A basic gag consists of something placed in the submissive's mouth to limit their ability to make sound – the "mouth stuffing" – and something placed over the mouth to hold it in place – the strap.

Many deaths have occurred – usually during criminal activity, not SM – when the mouth stuffing worked its way into the back of the victim's throat and blocked their airway, thus killing them. This usually happened when the victim was bound and gagged by robbers who then left them alone. These robbers thus ended up going to prison for a murder they never meant to happen.

Two safety points:

First, if you gag a submissive, you obviously have to stay with them and watch them even more closely than you ordinarily would. This usually means staying in the room with them. If you do leave the room, it's *very* wise to assume that the gag slipped and completely blocked their breathing the moment you left. Keep how long you stay away accordingly short.

Some dominants give their gagged submissive a noisemaker such as a bell to use if they "really" get in trouble while the dominant is out of the room. Alternatively, they may order the submissive to use it every minute or so. The dominant may go so far as to tape it into the palm of the submissive's hand so it can't be accidentally dropped.

Second, for safety's sake, you should attach the mouth-stuffing to the strap so that it cannot work its way into the back of the submissive's throat. Again, failure to do that has resulted in many accidental deaths.

Another danger associated with gags is vomiting. If a gagged submissive were to throw up, the vomit would plug their nose and be sucked into their lungs. This is often fatal. You need to use a gag that can be removed within seconds in case of emergency.

Also, you would not want to gag somebody who felt nauseated, and you would remove the gag if they became nauseated during the session. Dominants should instruct their submissives to let them know when they first become nauseated. It's important to react to the early warning signs on this matter. Don't wait until the last instant. One lesson I learned during my ambulance days: when a patient says that they're going to throw up, they don't mean in 30 seconds. They mean *now*.

As a safety measure, you might want to avoid gagging someone who has recently eaten (say, roughly, within the last three hours) and/or who has taken anything, such as alcohol, in sufficient quantity to make them nauseated.

A submissive who has had their jaws forced apart either too far or for too long by a gag may develop problems. These problems include pain and/or spasm of the jaw muscles, aggravation of temporomandibular joint syndrome, or even, in an extreme case, dislocation of the jaw itself.

I always ask to be blindfolded when I bottom at parties – because if someone I don't like is watching, I don't want to know it.

**Types of gags.** Okay, let's assume that this is your third session with a submissive, that the non-verbal safewords have been agreed upon and verified, that the submissive feels fine (they are not at all nauseated), hasn't eaten for three hours, and has not been drinking.

How do you gag them?

Many people use a gag that consists of a leather strap and a rubber ball – the so-called "ball gag." The ball is inserted between the submissive's teeth, then strapped in place behind their head. (No locking buckles!)

This type of gag usually works fairly well. The strap is often black leather, and the ball is often bright red. Many people think it looks sexy. Such a gag muffles sound fairly well.

One drawback with gags, or with something else placed in a submissive's mouth, is that anything placed in someone's mouth causes them to salivate.

A gag forces the submissive's jaws apart, and thus makes saliva harder to swallow (stick two fingers between your own teeth and try it). Usually, the saliva tends to run either down the back of their throat or out their mouth and down their chin. (That adds a humiliating touch that some dominants, and some submissives, like.) Occasionally a submissive will be unable to swallow with a ball gag in place; you should probably use a different style of gag.

One solution is using foam rubber instead of a ball. A fist-sized piece of foam rubber fills the submissive's mouth nicely (as they open and shut their jaws, it expands and contracts in response), is cheap, and absorbs saliva. That last feature is one many submissives like.

One drawback of foam rubber is that some sharp-toothed submissives can bite through it; but, as I said, it's easy and cheap to replace. (There's a hypothetical possibility that a submissive could bite a piece off the gag and choke on it, but I've never heard of this happening.) I would like to see this material used much more widely than it currently is used.

One type of gag you sometimes see is called the pump gag. This gag has an inflatable balloon on the inside of the strap. It's attached to a squeeze bulb, inserted and secured, then inflated – thus filling the mouth. Unfortunately, some submissives have died because the gag was over-inflated and blocked off the back of their throat. Most of these gags are made in England, and I understand that Customs agents now seize them as they come into the country. The use of such gags in connection with a hood is especially dangerous because such a hood prevents the dominant from receiving the feedback allowed by seeing the submissive's face.

Don't use pump gags! Some have "quick-deflate" valves that allow the air inside them to be released in an instant, and that's a good thing, but it won't prevent death due to initial over-inflation.

**Tape.** Tape, widely used in the movies and on TV as a gag, has several dangers. For one, it cannot be attached to the mouth stuffing. For another, it cannot be removed quickly and reliably from the submissive's mouth if an emergency occurs – at least not without risking serious pain and damage. Tape is also hard to use as a gag if the submissive has a beard or mustache. Avoid using tape as a gag.

**Panty gags.** Many submissives (not all, but many) love it when a dominant lady ties them up and then takes off her panties to use as mouth stuffing. The panties should be attached to some sort of strap – some dominant women like to stuff them into a nylon stocking and tie the stocking around the submissive's head. Negotiate such usage ahead of time, of course, but keep it in mind.

**Using a rod or bar as part of a gag.** The mouth-stuffing is sometimes attached to a metal or wooden stick, thus allowing a stronger pull on the stuffing, keeping it more firmly in the mouth.

**Using an elastic bandage as a gag.** Some people attach the mouth stuffing to flexible material, such as an elastic bandage, to keep it firmly in the mouth. This usually works fairly well. An elastic bandage also can be used as mouth stuffing by wrapping it around the strap.

In summary, gags can add quite a bit if used in the right way, at the right time, and with the right person. Just understand that using one will noticeably increase the session's risk level.

## Blindfolds

A blindfolded person is more vulnerable than an unblindfolded person. Also, when you can't see, you pay closer attention to your other senses. Hearing and touch seem to become more acute.

If the submissive is already extensively bound, adding a blindfold actually does very little to increase their vulnerability – they already can't do much about what's going to happen – but it often increases their *feeling* of vulnerability.

*If you want to find out what they're really into, watch their eyes. They can't fake the eyes.*

I think blindfolds are especially frustrating for men to wear. Many men have a particular fondness for seeing what's going on, and can't if they're blindfolded. Some dominants use this to good effect. For example, one professional dominant had an effective way of dealing with requests by her submissive that she undress. She would tie them up and blindfold them, and only then would she take off her clothes. She would arrange touching and being touched so that her submissives knew she was indeed naked in their presence, but they would never actually *see* her naked. It drove them nuts.

Wearing a blindfold significantly increases the degree of surrender involved in a scene.

**When to use a blindfold.** I recommend that you wait until at least your second or third SM session with someone before using a blindfold. Like gags, they increase the degree of vulnerability, and you want to increase the vulnerability involved slowly and gradually. (I should note that a blindfolded submissive will have a much harder time maintaining their physical balance, and thus are at greater risk for falling.)

Many professional SM studios, for example, forbid customers to blindfold a submissive staff member unless another staff member is also in the room. The reason for this is that most of these institutions also have a "no gag" rule – unless, again, another staff member is present – because if a submissive allows themselves to be blindfolded, then "you can't see a gag coming."

Another reason to limit using blindfolds early on is that a person's eyes are often the most expressive part of their face. If you cover their eyes, you shut yourself off from an important source of feedback. You'll want to know how they're reacting. Their eyes will often tell you.

**Notes on using blindfolds.** It doesn't hurt to mention to a blindfolded submissive that the emergency scissors are handy, and that other safety precautions have been taken.

Blindfolds may cause a loss of perspective. The submissive can "drift away" into their own world. Continuing to speak to them, even if they can only nod in reply, helps keep the two of you "in tune" with each other. If you drift seriously apart, the potential for misunderstanding increases.

> I'm not interested in doing anything that diminishes my submissives.

As the dominant, you have a special choice when the time comes to remove the blindfold. If you're feeling kind, let them take it off themselves – which they'll usually do slowly. If you're feeling mean, take if off yourself – rapidly.

Safety note: blindfolding someone de-personalizes them to a significant degree, and you may be more likely to go too far with a whipping or something similar if you can't see their face.

**Blindfold material.** Completely blindfolding someone is difficult. The eyes are somewhat set back in the skull, and thus hard to cover entirely. Often small "peek holes" remain in the blindfold, usually to the side of the nose.

To prevent this, most blindfolds use some sort of "eye-padding" to cover the eyes completely, and some sort of strap to hold the eye padding in place. The eye padding is usually leather, fur, or foam rubber, and the strap is often leather or elastic bandage.

You can buy "sleep masks" in drugstores that cover the eyes without pressing on them the way most blindfolds do. These are comfortable enough to wear for several hours, even overnight. They are also relatively inexpensive.

Note: The eye muscles relax somewhat when blindfolded, so when the blindfold comes off it may take a few minutes for the submissive's vision to come back into focus.

Safety note: Obviously, a blindfolded submissive is forced into rather "passive" submission, and can't move very much, especially if they're also bound. If you want to move them somewhere, "escort" them closely. Be ready to steady them if they lose their balance.

**Using gags and blindfolds together.** Don't use them together on a new partner early in your play. You might try using just a blindfold in your second or third session, then next time use both a blindfold and gag.

## Ear Plugs

Sooner or later, you probably will want to limit your submissive's ability to hear.

It's almost impossible to deafen somebody completely. You can completely shut off their vision, but not their hearing. This is because sound reaches the ears through bone conduction as well as through the ear canal. You could completely plug the canal, and they could still hear to a limited extent.

Still, you can reduce their hearing to a significant degree, and that can be fun. However, you may want to think twice about doing that. Submissives usually pay close attention to sounds, especially if blindfolded. The clink of a chain, the snap of a lock, or the whistle of a whip through the air – not to mention the sound of your voice – are often highly exciting sounds.

> I want you
> to keep me in
> the leather hood
> a lot.

Many earplugs come with a Noise Reduction Rating (NRR) marked on the package. I personally recommend soft foam earplugs that have a flare at the base for easy insertion and removal and an NRR of at least 30. Drugstores usually carry different types. You can also buy them at gun shops – maybe the same place you buy your handcuffs.

You also can buy wax earplugs that soften after being held in your hand for a minute or two. These soft plugs are then inserted into the submissive's ears, where they "custom fit" themselves to their ear canals.

You can also deafen a submissive by substituting noise. Use headphones to pipe in music you want, or simply set it on static "white noise."

One word of caution: You won't be able to hear directly what the submissive is hearing, so try this on yourself first. Listen for about an hour.

One good safety measure is to mark the volume dial on the equipment you'll be using so you don't accidentally turn it up too far.

If you use a combination of earplugs and music headphones, you should effectively deafen your submissive. The earplugs will also provide some protection if the noise inadvertently becomes too loud.

Remember, the submissive can use their safeword if the noise becomes too loud. They should do this early. Hearing loss is hard to repair, so no heroics.

## *Hoods*

Many people in the scene use hoods of one sort or another. These hoods are also called "discipline helmets." They are usually made of black leather. Some are made of rubber, latex, or spandex.

A hood is a very powerful SM device. It strongly increases the sense of helplessness, confinement, and vulnerability the submissive feels, and their reactions may be correspondingly intense. Many people find a hood too intense to bear. For example, some submissives who have no problem at all being both blindfolded and gagged become claustrophobic when hooded.

On the other hand, some submissives absolutely *love* being hooded. They get inside and drift off into their own world. It's common for them to not want it removed.

Hoods, because they are so confining, often increase the degree of isolation felt in the scene. They also depersonalize the submissive to a significant degree. Dominants need to beware of this depersonalization. When the human being in front of you is transformed into a faceless torso, you may find it easier to be crueler than usual, and that can be dangerous. Police hostage negotiators know that a terrorist will have an easier time killing hooded people than people whose faces, especially eyes, are visible. Firing squads also use this fact.

Because they cover both the nose and mouth, hoods can be *much* more dangerous than gags. I have heard of several deaths from over-confining hoods.

You want to be able to remove a hood in seconds during an emergency, therefore you want a hood that zips on and off. Many hoods use leather laces to be tightened down, and that's fine, but laces are too slow for emergency release. Get a zippered hood.

You also will want a pair of paramedic shears immediately handy to cut off the hood if the zipper jams. Probably the safest places to cut off a hood are along the laces or upwards along the back of the head, between the ears.

All hoods should have permanent holes near the submissive's nose. Don't buy or use a hood that lacks "nose holes."

Hoods often come with snap-on blindfold and gag attachments, and I think that's a good idea. A hood without such options, especially for the mouth, lacks versatility.

One caution: one type of hood especially associated with deaths has a pump gag on the inside. Apparently, it's difficult to tell how much gag inflation is "too much" if the submissive is hooded. I understand this type of hood has been withdrawn from the market, but many are still out there. Don't use it. Cut it in two and throw it away.

Hoods often come with D-rings and other attachment points. These are fine for light bondage, but nothing more. Don't, for example, run a strap from a D-ring on the top of a hood to an eyebolt in the ceiling and expect it to hold the submissive's weight.

An ordinary cotton pillowcase makes a good improvised hood. Put it over the submissive's head and tie it in place, perhaps by placing it under their collar. Most people can breathe adequately through the single layer of cotton.

In general, hoods are advanced pieces of equipment, with strong implications for psychology and technique. They are not for novices or people inexperienced with each other. They should probably not be used before your fifth session together, and only after you have had at least one successful session in which the submissive was both blindfolded and gagged.

*I like it when you take over.*

Remember, "hoods are heavy."

## Handcuffs

Many people think immediately of handcuffs when they want to restrain somebody. Handcuffs have advantages, but they also have disadvantages.

Note: unless otherwise noted, the advantages and disadvantages also apply to thumbcuffs and shackles (leg irons).

Advantages:
1. Handcuffs are easy to apply.
2. Properly applied handcuffs are almost inescapable.
3. Handcuffs have their own unique sights, sounds, and feels that often add to the erotic energy of the session.
4. Handcuff tightness can be closely adjusted.
5. Heavy-set or muscular people may be unable to cross their wrists behind their back for bondage. Handcuffs (or leather cuffs) offer an effective way to deal with this.

6. Handcuffs can (and should) be "double locked" to prevent their becoming dangerously tight. Cuffs that aren't double-locked can go on ratcheting tighter and tighter until they have done serious damage to your submissive. The instructions that come with the handcuffs should show you how to double-lock them. Make *sure* you understand how to apply and remove double-locked cuffs before playing with them.

Disadvantages:

1. Handcuffs are somewhat expensive. Shop around and compare prices. Some mail-order outfits (which advertise in gun and survival magazines) may offer a much better price.

2. Handcuffs must be bought at special stores, usually at police supply stores. The employees at the "cop shop" are sometimes reluctant to sell handcuffs to civilians, especially if they think they will be used for "kinky" things. (Ironically, many cops love being erotically submissive.)

   If you live in a large, cosmopolitan city, such as Los Angeles, San Francisco, or New York, you can go to a "toy store" and freely buy your cuffs there. Only friendly questions will be asked. If you can, I recommend buying your cuffs at such a store.

The submissive
doesn't need to know
what time it is.

3. Handcuffs need a key to be opened. Obviously, if you have no key, you have a problem. Most cuffs operate off a standard handcuff key that opens handcuffs, thumbcuffs, and leg irons. I would not buy cuffs that needed a "nonstandard" key. You usually get two keys when you buy a pair of cuffs. Keep one with the cuffs and the other nearby. I keep my spare key on my personal keychain. Some professional dominants keep their main handcuff key on a light chain or leather thong around their neck, with the key tucked into their bra. They also may have a few hidden away that nobody but they know about.

The store where you buy the cuffs can usually sell you extra keys. If you are part of a couple, for example, it might be a good idea for each of you to have a spare key. If the store doesn't have any extra, most locksmiths do. Spare keys usually sell for one to two dollars. Of course, if you buy more than one pair of cuffs, and they all use standard keys, that solves your key problem.

Handcuff keys are excellent, discreet little "signals." Some people wear them to good effect on neckties, earrings, bracelets, and so forth.

4.  Handcuffs are hard and narrow. Handcuffs exert their force over a narrow area, so they can create a great deal of pressure. (Remember that handcuffs which have not been double-locked are especially hazardous in this regard). Unlike coils of rope or leather cuffs, that can distribute the cuffs over a wider area, handcuffs concentrate it. Among other things, this means it's not wise to use handcuffs in a way that might increase the force by which they're pressing against the skin. For example, it's usually a bad idea to secure someone's hands vertically overhead by using handcuffs. The weight of their arms will pull the hard, narrow cuff into their wrists and this could quickly cause serious injury.

    One way of relieving the excess pressure problem that steel handcuffs present is the use of special leather bracelets around the submissive's wrists and ankles. These bracelets snap on, and consist of two rows of pyramid studs with about one-half inch of space between the rows. The cuffs are applied between the rows. This seems to allow for both security and safety, and might be worth a try. Another tactic is to slip some tubing over the cuffs. I've seen this done with plastic tubing that had a special cutout for the hinge and, while there was some range of motion loss, it looked and felt excellent.

> Being a dominant is like being a combination of tormentor and nursemaid.

**A note about handcuff quality.** Don't buy cheap handcuffs! You can spot some brands of these instantly because they have a three-link chain between the cuffs instead of the more common two-link chain.

These "toy" cuffs are made of poor material, work sloppily, use a non-standard key, and are easy to break. You can probably break such a cuff if you lock it shut, grip it with both hands, and apply about a 25-pound pull. They also have a borderline safety locking system, bent metal links instead of welded links, and are just generally junk. Nobody who uses cuffs "for real" uses this design. They are the mark of an amateur. I immediately lose a great deal of respect for a "dominant" who displays a pair of these cuffs.

157

Another poorer-than-average brand of handcuffs has cuffs that are identical. These cannot be applied evenly, and that can cause problems. In a proper pair of handcuffs, the cuffs themselves are "mirror images" of each other, not "identical twins." This is also true of leg irons. Inspect cuffs closely on this point before you buy them. "Identical twin" designs are a hassle.

Foreign-made handcuffs, often from Spain, are significantly better. They have a reliable double-lock, the correct type of chain, use a standard key, and generally work like normal cuffs. However, they don't seem to last long before wearing out.

If you're going to buy handcuffs, I strongly recommend that you spend the extra money and purchase yourself top-quality, American-made handcuffs. The two best-regarded brands are Peerless and Smith and Wesson. Of the two, I personally prefer the Peerless brand. Both brands are excellently constructed, use a standard key, work beautifully, look great, and last practically forever.

In summary, many people buy handcuffs, but in actual practice they end up using rope and leather cuffs much more often.

**Thumbcuffs.** These can be used alone or in combination with handcuffs. They can be applied to thumbs or big toes. Some dominants apply them to the submissive's penis. (Just be careful about how tightly you crank the cuff.) Some thumbcuffs use a non-standard key, and you know by now how I feel about non-standard keys.

**Leg irons.** These can be great fun. They naturally complement handcuffs. A person wearing leg irons can have intercourse, walk fairly well, and even negotiate stairs.

To apply them, have the submissive kneel, and apply the shackles to their ankles with the keyhole facing toward their feet. Some cuffs are made so this cannot be done without an asymmetrical presentation. I suggest you avoid these cuffs.

Leg irons are expensive, but you might want to buy two pairs – or even four pairs – if you wish to chain somebody to a bed.

Note: Leg irons cannot be narrowly locked, so if you attempt to use them on a person who has slender wrists, they may be able to slip out even with the cuffs set at their narrowest setting.

Caution: The locking mechanism on handcuffs and similar devices will not last forever. While good quality cuffs will last a dozen years or more, eventually the locking mechanism will fail and you won't be able to lock or, more importantly, unlock them with a key. Therefore, buy a hacksaw and at least six top-quality blades (the more teeth to the inch, the better) on the same day that you buy your metal restraints. It's also very wise to buy a pair of bolt cutters capable of cutting hardened steel. A metal file, a small amount of oil or other lubricant, and a pair of vise-grips or a vise will make the "rescue" much easier.

## Leather Cuffs

Like handcuffs, leather cuffs have many pluses and minuses.

One of their major advantages is that they are simple to operate. Many people have trouble learning basic bondage (although a surprisingly little amount of practice goes a long way) but almost anyone can figure out how to apply leather cuffs. A second advantage is that they are fast to apply.

The major disadvantage of cuffs is that they are expensive. As with any purchase, it's important to comparison shop regarding both quality and price before you buy.

The second disadvantage of leather cuffs is that they are not as precisely adjustable as rope or handcuffs. With most cuffs, you have to choose between one-half to one-inch intervals, as with an ordinary belt. Unfortunately, wrists and ankles are usually only about five to ten inches in circumference, unlike 24-inch or wider waists. A half-inch can therefore make a great difference in determining whether the cuff is too tight or too loose.

Some players prevent this problem by having a set of wrist and ankle cuffs custom-made to a specific submissive's measurements. These can be presented to the submissive as a special gift if they have been especially pleasing, or as a token of celebration regarding their relationship. Some couples who switch roles have the cuffs designed to fit both of them. These cuffs are sometimes dyed a unique color and monogrammed.

The relatively thick, stiff leather used for cuffs can abrade the underlying skin, so cuffs usually have a lining of softer leather, wool, or fur. (Be careful that this lining isn't too thick, or you might not be able to get the cuffs on securely enough.)

> Sometimes it's easier to learn how to do this with someone who is not your regular partner. It's a cleaner slate, and allows a purer experience. There's not all that past history there.

*fur-lined leather cuffs*

Hospital-type leather cuffs and other restraints are some of the best and most reliable you can buy. (Unfortunately, they're only available in a rather bland institutional brown color.) Some vendors are hostile to SM folks, but others are quite friendly. These restraints are of excellent quality and adjustability. They are expensive, but should last nearly forever. They also use a special key that is long and thin, so be sure you get a few extras.

Obviously, the cuffs need to be attached to something to be effective, so they usually have one or two metal D-rings attached to them. For safety's sake, these loops should be welded-link, not bent metal.

Simlilarly styled restraints are also available in nylon and nylon/velcro combinations. These are less expensive than leather cuffs but not usually as hot-looking.

## Suspension

I like to scare them just a little bit.

Helplessness is the name of the game for many bondage fans. A submissive suspended off the ground is obviously more helpless than one who is not. (We've all seen cartoons that show "missionaries" tied by the wrists and ankles to a pole being carried by two "cannibals.") The basic problem, however, is this: the human body was not designed to support its full weight being suspended from its wrists and ankles. This is particularly true of being suspended off the ground by the wrists alone. Those joints, and/or the elbow and shoulder joints, can be dislocated in fairly short order if this is done to a submissive.

Many serious suspension fans use leather slings especially designed for this purpose, or "erotic" swings, or special body harnesses that resemble the ones skydivers wear.

In a few cases, we find people who like to be suspended from their ankles alone. Those folks use special "gravity boots" and related equipment bought at health and fitness stores. The important point here is that this equipment is specifically designed and intended for this purpose, and comes with an instruction manual.

Suspension is an advanced bondage practice that obviously has great potential and great danger. It offers a delicious, entirely new dimension of helplessness and control. Many submissives enter a dreamy, trancelike state while in suspension bondage; they are literally "off the planet."

It also offers entirely new dangers. Submissives may develop dizziness and nausea while being suspended. Adding a blindfold makes this complication more likely, and placing a blindfolded submissive in a head-down position makes it still more likely. In addition, eyebolts can pull loose, straps – or even chains – can break, and restraints can cut too deeply into flesh. I have heard of many injuries that resulted from suspension bondage accidents.

Safety note: I do not recommend suspending a submissive in any type of head-down position if they have a history of stroke or high blood pressure. Also, some submissives rapidly become nauseated while being placed head-down, and they could vomit. Therefore, it's a good idea to avoid mixing a gag with head-down suspension, particularly at first.

Also, much suspension bondage requires the submissive's active cooperation to get into – and, more importantly, to get out of. Dominants who play with suspension much always have a clear, workable plan about how they will free an unconscious (and therefore dead weight) submissive.

two types of panic snap

Special suspension precautions include incorporating a "panic snap." This is a special release mechanism that allows two chains (or straps, or whatever) to be released even if they are still under tension. Panic snaps can be bought at many leather stores. You can also find them in boating supply stores (several different models exist for nautical use) and riding equipment stores, sometimes labeled "snap shackles."

Unfortunately, the panic snap is an all-or-nothing device. If you release it, you may still have to cope with the submissive's unconscious weight. I handled many unconscious people during my ambulance days and (trust me on this) they can be extremely difficult to manage. They're heavy, "floppy," move in ways and directions you don't expect, and are otherwise just damn difficult to control. If you're trying to get them down on the ground, you have to be careful or they can take you down with them – sometimes even under them! Among other things, this can result in injury to *you* at a time when you especially don't want to be injured. Having a panic snap is a lot better than having nothing, but you should consider them the first word, not the last word, on the subject.

A winch can be an excellent alternative. The better ones for this purpose allow you to keep control without assuming the load's weight when

When she was stretched out like that in front of me her skin looked like an artist's canvas.

both raising *and* lowering. I once saw a fairly bad accident occur when the handle on a less-than-ideal winch slipped from the dominant's hand while lowering a submissive. This winch required the dominant to "control" the handle during lowering. When it slipped from their hand, the submissive plummeted down. The submissive was hurt by the fall. The dominant was hurt when they tried (unsuccessfully) to grab the winch's whirling handle.

I have seen several block-and-tackle arrangements that I like. These allow gradual raising and lowering with excellent control. The ones sold in hunting stores look especially good. (Just make sure the load-securing line can't unexpectedly come loose!)

Suspension can be one of the most intense forms of bondage, but its much-greater-than-average riskiness requires knowledgeable instruction and close attention to detail.

## *Chains, Locks, Etc.*

It's difficult to bind someone using only chain. I suppose some people can do it, but it's not a generally useful bondage practice.

In general, you should use welded-link chain. Light chain is strong enough for most ordinary bondage. Very heavy chain tends to be more trouble than it's worth.

> I want to know that you will if I want you to.

Chains tend to clank a lot. One way to deal with this is to coat them with a velvet or rubber sleeve. Some people pull their chain into a length of light plastic tubing.

Before you buy chain, you should have some special idea of what you wish to use it for, and have it cut to that length in the hardware store. Many people use two-foot and three-foot lengths. The links allow for a wide and very fine range of adjustments.

Some dominants reward their submissives by allowing them an extra link's worth of freedom if they do something pleasing.

**Chain safety measures.** Chains are unforgiving and unreasonable. Unlike rope and leather, in an emergency you cannot simply cut them off with the nearest sharp instrument. Furthermore, locks sometimes break or simply wear out. For this reason, you need to have the following safety equipment handy if you play with chains.

1.  A hacksaw and at least six blades hard enough to cut through the type of chain you have. Ask the hardware store clerk if you aren't

sure. Using your new saw and blades to saw through an expendable link "for practice" is an excellent idea.

2. A pair of bolt cutters. Get a little extra chain and practice cutting.
3. A pair of vise-grips or a vise. These can help steady the chain while you cut through it, speeding up the cutting process.
4. A metal file. You can use this to make a shallow cut as a guide for the hacksaw blade.
5. Quick-release "panic snaps" that allow the chain to be instantly loosened.

**Padlocks.** Padlocks are used to lock chains and cuffs securely together. They are generally either combination-operated or key-operated. Key-operated locks are faster to remove – always helpful in an emergency. (How well do you think you could accurately dial in a combination if your submissive were chained to the bed with combination-operated padlocks, especially if each lock had a different combination? If a fire or medical emergency occurred, you – not to mention they – would be in major trouble.)

Some dominants, as a mind game, leave their submissives alone in chains with the combination lock within reach. The submissive has a certain time to free themselves, or they get "punished."

Combination padlocks are fun, but they have a sharply limited range of safe use. Most people use key-operated locks.

**How to deal with the different key needed for each lock.** Some people use colored dots to match keys to locks, but that's cumbersome, time-consuming, and potentially dangerous. A much safer, more efficient practice is to buy locks that are "keyed alike" and can be operated with the same key. You can either do this at the time of purchase or have a locksmith do it for you. Again, you'll want lots of spare keys.

**Special links.** One excellent way to attach a chain to either a cuff or an eye-bolt is to use a "quick link." These links have a side that screws open and shut, thus allowing the chain to be attached. The link is twisted tight then, if the dominant wishes, further tightened by a small wrench. This tightens the link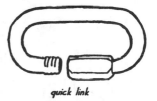

*quick link*

enough that a bare-fingered submissive will never be able to twist it loose even if they can reach it – a nice touch. A good safety aspect of this is that such a mechanism is much less likely to break or wear out than a padlock mechanism. (Oil them lightly once in a while to help prevent jamming.)

These links are an excellent combination of simplicity, security, and safety. I would like to see them much more widely used. Also, I think the sight of a small wrench hanging off somebody's left hip could come to have an interesting significance. The quick links can also, of course, be used alone to link two leather cuffs together, or to link a cuff to an eye-bolt.

**Carabiners.** A carabiner is a device used for mountain climbing and similar sports. It is a large oval, D-shaped, or pear-shaped metal device, with a spring-loaded side that snaps into place. Some types "lock" with a rotating latch that prevents them from opening accidentally.

carabiner (shown open)

The advantage of carabiners is that they are designed to bear large amounts of weight (such as people), and are very easy to use. One disadvantage is that if chains are attached to a carabiner, and then the whole thing is twisted by a wriggly submissive, the carabiner may eventually twist sideways and be forced open. (For this reason, it's not a good idea to attach one carabiner to another.) You can avoid this problem by using a locking carabiner.

The other disadvantage to carabiners is that they're easy for the submissive to open. If you want to use carabiners, place them out of the submissive's reach.

**Double snaps.**
Many people use double snaps to lock cuffs into place. Double snaps are

double snap

quick and simple to operate but, obviously, very insecure. If a submissive can reach a double snap with their fingers, they can be free of it in an instant. Wise dominants therefore secure "reachable" cuffs with padlocks or quick links. Wrist cuffs joined by a double snap are a farce. Double snaps do work well, however, on ankles – provided the submissive's toes aren't too nimble. Double snaps may not be safe for heavy load-bearing such as suspension.

I love being in extreme bondage.

eyebolt

**Eyebolts.** Eyebolts are a very common item. You find them attached to beds, chairs, massage tables, walls, and ceilings. I've even seen one set into a fireplace hearth. Some screw into wood, others have bolts and nuts at the end for going through a wall, ceiling, or board.

If you use eyebolts, make sure they're securely attached. I remember once having an attractive lady tied naked and spread-eagled to eyebolts in my bed. I told her that if she could get loose in ten minutes, I would be submissive to her. Otherwise, she was mine for the night. I figured I couldn't lose. This session took place during my "bondage days" and I felt certain those ropes were on very securely.

And I was indeed quite correct. She squirmed and struggled for a while (a quite pleasant sight, by the way) and glared at the ropes around her wrists. All this got her, as I expected, absolutely nowhere. She continued to glare at her ropes, and then a small smile spread across her face. She stretched out one hand, grabbed an eyebolt and, grinning evilly in triumph, began unscrewing it from the bed! More than 20 years have since passed, and I still remember that very, very long night.

Be sure to "load-test" any weight-bearing eyebolts you install in a ceiling or wall. Because I'm taller and heavier than average, a professional dominant once asked me to help her do such testing on 12 hooks that had been installed in her dungeon's ceiling by a submissive carpenter. I was to teach a somewhat formal first aid class later in the day, so when I stopped by I was wearing my instructor's uniform.

We went into the dungeon and I looped some rope through one of the eyebolts. I grabbed an end in both hands, and was just about to pull myself up when the thought crossed my mind: what if that bolt *does* pull out? It'll smack me with entirely too much force right on the top of my head.

Obviously, I needed to pad my head with something. We looked around, and the only thing handy that would work was a small, lacy, pink pillow. So, all right. We got another length of rope and I tied the pillow onto the top of my head as padding.

Have you bought those new wrist cuffs yet?

And thus I found myself, dressed in my instructor's uniform and with a pretty, pink pillow tied to the top of my head, dangling from the ceiling in the dungeon of a Mistress in order to test the load-bearing capacity of her new eyebolts. The things I do for my friends!

And a good thing, too! For eyebolt number three pulled loose, dumping me on the floor and showering us both with plaster. (I felt a light tap on the top of my prettily padded head.) Eyebolt number nine pulled loose, too, as did eyebolt number ten.

Well, she graciously thanked me, we brushed off the plaster, chatted a bit more, and drank some refreshments. After a while, I left to teach my class. The fate of that submissive carpenter remains unknown.

**Ribbon.** Ribbon can be a very deceptive bondage device, and one female dominant I know uses this to good effect. This lady has a particular interest in the psychology of dominant/submissive encounters and mind games. She therefore asks new male partners if she can tie them up with "these pretty ribbons." She says that they'll look real cute that way, and that would really turn her on. The ribbon itself appears harmless enough.

"What they don't know," she gleefully confided to me at an SM party, "is that stuff is made of braided nylon. It's strong as hell, and no way are they going to break out of it."

"I just love the look on their face," she continued, "as it slowly dawns on them that they really can't get loose." She then emitted a cackle worthy of a wicked witch.

Play with ribbon if you wish. Because it narrows under pressure, I recommend that you stick with relatively wide material. Also, knots in ribbon pull so tight that nobody can get them loose again, so be prepared to cut the ribbon off.

**Tape.** Sometimes people use tape for bondage purposes. They usually use adhesive tape or duct tape.

Tape is highly secure. There are no knots and, obviously, no slack, so it's difficult to escape.

*I was thinking about going swimming today, but I decided to get tied up instead.*

Its disadvantages are that, because it's a use-only-once item, there's an ongoing expense if you want to play with it frequently. It's also not highly adjustable once you've applied it, either in tightness or position. Therefore make sure you put your submissive in a position you'll want them to remain in for some time before you tape them down.

Also, tape works best when it has something to press against, so the wrist or ankle usually has to be pressed against a bar, rod, or other body part to be effectively taped.

Some people are sensitive to various kinds of tape and may develop a skin inflammation if it's applied. You could try a different brand the next time, or, if that doesn't work, consider first applying a layer of plastic wrap or some other barrier between the skin and the tape.

Other people simply find that the tape hurts too much when removed. (Of course, a few perverts get off on the pain associated with tape removal. This can allow the applying and removing of tape, sometimes several times, to be used as part of the session.) For these folks, you can use the plastic wrap trick, or try applying talcum powder to the skin before putting on the tape.

I do not recommend using tape to blindfold or gag a submissive. It often pulls mustache, eyebrow, and eyelash hair as it's being removed, and it cannot be rapidly and safely removed in an emergency. I know tape blindfolds and gags get a lot of play in the crime movies, and – regrettably – in some "bondage" magazines, but in practice they just don't work all that well.

Tape can be a lot of fun and, in some respects, is easy for novices to use. There is a kind of "spinning the web" energy associated with it that many dominants, particularly female dominants, enjoy.

**Plastic wrap.** Plastic wrap has a lot going for it. It's readily available, inexpensive, disposable, "deniable," can be very useful in safe-sex situations, and can be a very effective bondage tool.

Plastic wrap can be used in one of two ways for bondage. First, you can peel off a length from the roll and run it through a narrow hole created by your thumb and forefinger. This creates a very usable rope for limb or genital bondage. Second, you can use sheets of it to "mummify" your submissive. As with tape, there is a "spinning the web" energy associated with such mummification that many female dominants enjoy. (This practice is also popular in the gay male SM world.)

Plastic wrap can also be used as a partial or full blindfold. In addition, it also deafens hearing somewhat. These qualities make it possible to use plastic wrap to create an intense "hood." Just make *extra* sure that you leave an opening for the nose. (See the above section on hoods.)

The ends of a length of plastic wrap can be knotted together effectively, but such knots may pull very tight and be all but impossible to loosen. Therefore, always keep a pair of scissors handy when playing with plastic wrap. Paramedic scissors zap right through this stuff.

Discovering the erotic possibilities of plastic wrap has made me glad.

# Giving and Receiving Erotic Pain

## *What Is Pain?*

Clinically speaking, pain is the name given to the sensation perceived by a person when certain specialized free nerve endings called "nociceptors" in the skin and other parts of the body are stimulated. This sensation can be caused by mechanical stimulation, by extreme heat or cold, and by stimulation from certain types of chemicals such as acidic substances. It occurs anytime a tissue is being damaged or overstressed. Once the damage ceases, the pain usually quickly subsides.

One of the great fallacies is that people vary in their pain threshold. Medical research has proven that all persons begin to feel pain at almost exactly the same degree of stimulation. What *is* true is that people vary a great deal in how they react to painful stimuli, and to some extent can learn different ways of reacting to those stimuli.

I like to be spanked.
I like to be slapped.
I like to have
my hair pulled.

The body can secrete its own natural morphine-like pain-inhibiting substances called "enkephalins" and "endorphins." Serotonin plays a role in this process.

One unique characteristic of the sensation of pain is that the perception of pain does not diminish as you get accustomed to it. Unlike other sensations like pressure and light touch, which your consciousness tends to screen out (do you feel your shoes on your feet most of the time?), pain stays in your awareness.

Pain is probably the strongest sensation you can feel. Being able to turn some kinds of pain into erotic sensation is a remarkable accomplishment.

## *Giving Pain*

I chose "giving pain" as a deliberate contrast to the more common "inflicting pain." "Inflicted" pain is delivered in anger, to punish or to hurt. "Given" pain, by contrast, is carefully measured, thoughtfully considered, and done to create a specific effect, usually the erotic arousal of both giver and receiver.

I'm entirely certain that "erotic" suffering differs vastly from "real" suffering. Erotic suffering usually, at some level or other, sexually arouses the submissive. Real suffering never does. If you're involved with someone who causes you real suffering, get help or get out. Genuine abuse is completely unrelated to SM.

When introducing your lover to erotic pain, it's often wise to begin by using parts of your body. Lightly bite, pinch, or spank. Notice how your lover reacts. Go down on them and, while you're giving them head, reach up and lightly pinch one or both nipples.

Take your time. Don't rush. Don't do anything sudden or sharp. Watch how they breathe. Pinch their nipples lightly. Slowly increase the pressure until they gasp, then ease off. Was their breath deep, slow, and gasping – a good sign – or high, fast, and tight, suggesting displeasure? Remember, mix this with a *lot* of pleasure. Don't even think about giving them a pinch, spank, or bite until they're strongly aroused.

Who's the boss –
you or the pain?
C'mon, show me
who's the boss.

It often helps if the submissive has an orgasm occur during their first erotic pain experience. If a woman is multi-orgasmic, try to get her to have several. You want to build a connection between erotic pain and sexual pleasure; an orgasm can contribute much toward achieving that.

Key point: The more erotically aroused somebody is, the more likely they are to be receptive to erotic pain – and the more they can accept.

Stop the pain immediately if their arousal level falls. Remember that nobody likes non-erotic pain. Heavy-duty masochists find falling off a horse or getting stung by a bee just as unpleasant as the rest of us find such things.

Also, keep in mind that some people find certain types of erotic pain a turn-on, yet find other types a distinct turn-off. It's not uncommon for a submissive to enjoy a spanking or whipping, even to orgasm, yet absolutely hate any sort of nipple play. Others love having their nipples erotically tortured, but can't stand spankings or whippings.

Everyone responsive to erotic pain has their own unique pattern of likes and dislikes. A wise dominant will learn a particular submissive's pattern well.

One important point about giving erotic pain: When working with a novice, give only one type of pain at a time. Especially avoid combining a whipping with clamps. People often react differently to the pain of a whipping and the pain of clamps, and mixing them may be disorienting. They are just beginning to explore how they react to the different types of pain. Don't overwhelm them. Stay with one type of pain at a time.

**"Nod."** How is the dominant to know they are not "going too far"? One excellent way is to have the submissive indicate when they are ready to receive the next "bit" of pain. This can be the next spank, whipstroke, clamp, or whatever.

One great strength of this technique is that it allows the submissive to recover their emotional balance between strokes. A spank can cause a strong reaction, and repeated spanks can overwhelm, and therefore frighten, the submissive. This method prevents that.

Of course, for this approach to work the dominant must abide by its terms and not deliver any unsignaled-for strokes (or anything else painful).

Let us say that a dominant is spanking a novice submissive. The dominant might say to them, "I'm going to spank you now. Each spank will be of about the same intensity. I'll give you one spank at a time, and I want you to nod when you're ready to receive the next stroke. Do you understand?" When the submissive indicated that they did, the dominant would then place their hand on the submissive's buttocks and hold it there, then tell the submissive, "Nod when you're ready to receive the first stroke."

> Accept the unacceptable. Endure the unendurable. Bear the unbearable.

This "measured" method of giving pain works very well with novice submissives and with submissives unfamiliar to the dominant. Because the submissive gives a definite signal before receiving each stroke, the chances of "going too far" are greatly reduced. Also, as with a safeword, because the submissive has some control over how much pain they receive, a novice submissive is less likely to feel overly frightened at the idea of receiving pain. This is a very powerful, useful technique. I strongly recommend it.

**"Now."** Another approach is for the submissive to say the word "now" when they're ready to receive the next bit. To paraphrase a drug-education slogan, "Just say now."

Footnote: One interesting aspect of whippings is how some people react very differently to different instruments. For example, I know one submissive who absolutely loves to get whippings from a riding crop or cane, but absolutely hates getting whippings from a cat-o-nine-tails, even when the cat's whipping is considerably milder. If you change implements, such as substituting a riding crop for a paddle, advise the submissive that you've done that (and therefore the sensation they feel will be different) before striking them with the new instrument.

**How hard should I hit?** The upper limit, of course, is that you should never hit hard enough to cause an injury unlikely to heal completely without professional help. A cut large enough to need sutures is a good example.

The lower limit: very gently.

When playing with somebody new, start your blows, no matter what you're using, very gently. Remember the saying: "Start lighter than light. Build slower than slow."

You might begin with the implement resting on the submissive's body, then perhaps lightly stroking them with it. The first blow should be the lightest and softest of pats, especially if the submissive is a novice or unfamiliar to you. Starting with a hard, slashing blow on a novice or unfamiliar submissive almost guarantees an immediate, angry end to the session.

**"One-to-ten."** A good way to decide how hard to hit the submissive is to let them decide. Tell them, "I want you to tell me how strong a stroke you think you are ready for. We'll do this on a scale of one to ten. A one will be very light. A two will be twice as strong as a one. A three will be three times as strong as a one, and so forth. If you reach ten, we'll start with a new one instead of an eleven. You choose the strength, and I won't deliver the stroke until you call out the number. Also, don't feel that you must always increase the number. If fours are a little too intense, we can go back down to threes, or even lower if that's what you need. We can also do something else or stop altogether.

"We're doing it this way, this time, so you can explore this and see what it does for you.

"One other thing, I'm going to start with your bottom. I won't deliver the strokes onto any other part of your body without telling you first, and I won't change what I'm using without telling you first. If I do change either the body area or what I'm using, we'll immediately go back to 'one' again. Is that clear?" (As with all instructions, you should have the submissive repeat this back to you to make sure that they understand. This is especially important with a new partner.)

"Are you ready to begin? All right, I'll wait until I hear your number. Please start with a one. We'll do this for about ten minutes and see how it goes. Ready? Take a moment to collect yourself, then give me a number."

Note: The "nod," "now" or "one-to-ten" techniques can also be used for groups of strokes. In other words, the submissive nods, or gives a number, and the dominant gives an agreed-upon number of strokes of that intensity.

Obviously, this is an extremely considerate approach, but I firmly believe such an approach is proper with a novice or unfamiliar submissive.

**Feeling benevolent?** If you want to stop and do something pleasurable, tell the submissive, "Let's stop the pain for a while," then rub, stroke, or lick them. Doing this for a minute or so usually feels about right. When you're ready to resume, tell the submissive, "Okay, let's resume. Nod when you're ready." A few breaks of this type help the submissive accept what's going on.

After the session, it's important for you as the dominant to tell the submissive that you are happy with the efforts they made to please you. Keep in mind that this person went through a lot for you. Let them know that you appreciate it.

A person's first experiences with erotic pain are terribly important. Lasting impressions are formed and basic decisions made. A wise dominant understands this, and lets the novice set the pace. After the first few sessions, the dominant can resume control.

## *Receiving Pain*

Open up to the pain.

Submissives have different reactions to different types of pain. These reactions can run the entire spectrum (and intensity) of human emotion from disgust and fear to arousal and joy – or even spiritual revelation. Also, the type and extent of their reaction to the same stimuli may change considerably over time – often in ways they could not have predicted. Additionally, the submissive's relationship with the person who is giving them these stimuli can also affect their reaction. For those who "get into it," exploring how they react to receiving erotic pain can be a profound, deep, personal journey.

One reaction that needs a special mention is anger. In general, any feelings of genuine anger that come up, either for the dominant or the submissive, are a very strong indicator that things need to be immediately changed or halted. SM is not about genuine anger. If something is going on to cause you to feel angry, stop what is going on. This is especially true for novices and players who don't know each other well.

As part of their training, dominants should specifically instruct a new submissive, "If anything that's going on causes you to feel genuine anger, tell me immediately. Don't hold it in and let it build up. Tell me immediately. Understand?"

I think that when somebody hurts us in a non-erotic way we have a natural tendency to want to hurt them back. If the hurt exceeds a certain level, we will try to hurt back. If genuine anger starts to come up, immediately call for a rest. Stop the particular activity and regroup for a few moments.

Remember: don't try to push through anger, especially with beginners. Expert dominants playing with submissives they are already very familiar with might try this, but the techniques involved are explosively risky, and most certainly beyond the scope of this book.

Anger can explode into deadly violence. Respect it, and keep it out of your scenes.

## *Straight Time and Checking In Later*

It's very important for the psychological balance of both people, perhaps especially for the submissive or the less experienced of the two people involved, to spend "straight time" together after the session. This time is spent together out of role, as ordinary people. A good way to do this is to dress in ordinary clothes and leave the premises where the session took place. Going to a restaurant or out for coffee is a good approach.

Professional dominants, of course, usually cannot leave their place of business, but they can share coffee, tea, or juice (anything non-alcoholic) with their clients, preferably away from the playroom.

Let the novice talk, but don't aggressively question them too much about what they're now thinking and feeling. They may still be sorting that out, and thus unable to give you a clear answer.

One professional dominant asks her clients three post-session questions: (1) What was best about the session? (2) What was worst about it? (3) What was most memorable about it? She may have her clients answer in a follow-up letter instead of immediately after the session.

If you have just done a session with someone who is not your steady partner, check back with each other, if possible, the next day. Also check about a week later to make sure both of you are all right. This check-in may be done in person, by phone, or by e-mail, but be sure to choose a time when you're not rushed and have privacy.

# Flagellation

"Start lighter than light. Build slower than slow."

In this chapter, I'm including all techniques that involve striking motions. Topics I'll discuss include spanking, slapping, paddling, strapping, whipping, flogging, and caning. I'll describe other methods of giving pain in the "Erotic Torture" and "Clamps" chapters.

## Where to Whip

The basic principle is that you want to whip body areas where the stroke will cause pain but no significant damage, especially to anything underneath the skin. "No significant damage" is defined as anything that will heal on its own; welts and bruises are not generally considered significant damage.

The heavier the stroke, the more carefully it must be placed. Almost anyplace on the body, except earholes and exposed eyeballs, can be *very* lightly whipped. Strong, heavy strokes, on the other hand, must be confined to the buttocks and backs of the thighs, and perhaps the upper back. In general, the more fat and/or muscle on a given body area, the stronger stroke it can tolerate.

Do you have a riding crop that I can borrow for tonight?

Again, if you want to get some idea of how hard is too hard, try it on yourself before doing it to anyone else. Also, play "one-to-ten" with your partner.

The following parts of the body can take only the lightest strokes: the head, face, neck, arms, wrists, hands, fingers, collarbones, sides of the chest, anywhere along the spinal column, tailbone, front and sides of the abdomen, middle and lower back, testicles, knees, shins, ankles, tops of the feet, and toes. Until you are very experienced and have received much more instruction than I can give you in this book, *I strongly suggest that you avoid the above-mentioned areas entirely.*

The following body areas can usually take light to moderate strokes: upper chest (stay above the xiphoid process and below the collarbones), backs of the lower legs (calves), bottoms of the feet, vaginal area, shaft of the penis, insides of the thighs, and upper buttocks.

Note: The xiphoid process is found at the notch on the front/center portion of the chest where the ribs meet. Among other things, learning how to find this notch is an important part of CPR training. Take a moment to locate it on your own body.

The following can usually accept moderate to heavy strokes: upper back (especially inner part), buttocks (especially lower half), fronts, outsides, and backs of thighs.

The buttocks themselves have different areas. Imagine either the left or right buttock divided into four quadrants: upper outer, upper inner, lower outer, and lower inner. The two upper quadrants are usually the less desirable for receiving a spanking or whipping. In particular, when the submissive's body is vertical, gravity often pulls the overlying muscle and fat down, leaving the underlying bone relatively exposed.

the author locates a tailbone

The upper inner quadrant is particularly vulnerable in this regard. Before you administer any strokes in that area, feel the upper and middle parts of the crack between the cheeks with your fingers to locate their tailbone; hitting the tailbone can be extremely painful in a non-erotic way, and can even dislocate or fracture the bone.

*I want to be whipped until I cry, then made to please someone with my mouth.*

The lower quadrants are more desirable. In particular, strokes to the lower inner quadrant are most likely to feel erotic, thus causing that area to be called the "sweet spot." (For you medical types, this spot corresponds almost exactly with the posterior S3 dermatome.)

Minor digression: The inner half of the lower half of the upper third of the back (yes, that does make sense) is often a second "sweet spot."

Another aspect of spanking or whipping the buttocks to consider is the submissive's body position. A straight body position, such as when standing or lying face down, allows the underlying tissue to relax. A bent-at-the-waist position pulls the underlying tissue tighter and often makes the sensation sharper and more painful. How people feel about that situation varies.

One particularly important part of the body to avoid giving heavy strokes to is the abdominal area. The area between the hip crests and the xiphoid process, going completely around the body, is particularly dangerous because the liver, spleen, and kidneys are in this area, and in most individuals these are only partly covered by the ribcage. A strong stroke to this area could damage them – perhaps even causing life-threatening internal bleeding. I therefore call this area "the forbidden zone."

**What about whipping her breasts?** If a dominant is about to play with a submissive woman, it often takes about ten seconds for them to begin considering how to torment her breasts. Erotic "torture" tends to concentrate on the sexual parts of the submissive's body, so the question of what to do to her breasts receives early consideration.

The basic question is, can the dominant whip her breasts and, if so, how hard? The jury is still out on this question. Looked at on a short-term basis, the answer is yes, her breasts can be whipped – often very intensely and with deep arousal for both the dominant and the submissive. Her breasts can't take nearly as much as the upper back or buttocks, but they can often take a lot, and they usually heal without incident. (An exception is breasts which have implants; these should be whipped very lightly if at all.) Furthermore, whipped breasts are often left with prominent welts and bruises. If you are into this sort of thing, such a sight can be deeply moving.

*(from a professional dominant): I see a lot of engineers. A heavy whipping is the only thing that brings them out of their heads and into their bodies – out of their thoughts and into the here and now.*

The down side of this matter is that such whippings sometimes leave lumps of scar tissue behind. These are supposed to be benign and not the type of mass that could lead to breast cancer, but anxieties remain. As of now, the thinking within the SM community is gradually moving away from heavy breast flagellation, just to be sure.

On the other hand, there are numerous non-flagellation means of tormenting her nipples – and, for that matter, the rest of her breasts – and, as an SM-positive physician friend of mine recently remarked, "the nipples are built to take it."

## *Whipping Positions*

Most whippings are given with the submissive in one of three basic positions: standing, bent at the waist, or lying prone (flat on their stomach). Each position has advantages and disadvantages.

**The standing position.** The standing position, usually with the submissive's hands secured over their head, offers excellent access to almost all of their body. If you secure their legs apart, their vulnerability increases even more. (A kneeling version of this can also be used to good effect, and puts their mouth at about the same height as your genitals.)

Note: If you tie the submissive in this position with their legs together, they will usually be more stable if you tie their knees together instead of their ankles. (You may want to put their ankles in short shackles to prevent their feet from moving too much.)

One disadvantage is the pressure of the restraints against the submissive's wrists. This can be reduced somewhat by allowing them to grab something such as their ropes. A second disadvantage is that gravity will pull the "padding" of the submissive's buttocks down somewhat, and the dominant needs to be alert for that. A third, somewhat more serious, disadvantage is that a submissive in a standing position with their hands over their head is at noticeably increased risk for fainting. (Most faintings involve a submissive in a standing position.)

**The bent-at-the-waist position.** The submissive can be bent over in either a standing or kneeling position, with the kneeling "all fours" position being more stable. (Indeed, some bondage devices hold the submissive in this position.) This all-fours position, particularly with the submissive's knees spread, has much to recommend it. The dominant has excellent access to the submissive's back, buttocks, thighs, calves, and soles of the feet. (If the submissive is male, some protection for his testicles is a good idea; many male submissives wear a leather g-string for this purpose.) The dominant also has fairly good access to the submissive's mouth, breasts, nipples, anus, and genitals. Oral sex, anal sex, and vaginal intercourse are often possible. The position can often be maintained in relative comfort by the submissive for quite some time, and fainting is rare.

One disadvantage (it's more of a caution) is that this position pulls the buttocks muscles somewhat tight, so blows hurt more. Another caution is that gravity will pull the buttocks' padding down somewhat, so if the dominant is not alert they can deliver blows to areas less padded than they normally are.

**The prone position.** In this position, you often find the submissive tied face-down on a bed. The position offers fairly good access to the back of the body. Anal intercourse and other types of anal play are often possible. (Think twice about how you tie the submissive if you also intend to play with the front of their body.) Submissives can relax a great deal in this position, and can usually maintain it for a very long time. Please note that they can also often take heavier whippings in this position than they can take in any other position, and fainting is very rare.

The major disadvantage is that it may be both uncomfortable and somewhat restrictive of breathing for the submissive to lie face-down on such a surface. They must turn their head to one side to keep their face clear, and this can put a definitely unerotic strain on their neck. This can often be eliminated by placing pillows or something similar under their chest. Another alternative is to purchase one of those massage devices that allow lying face-down on a bed.

**Beware of "neck snap."** Submissives may, when struck any type of strong blow on the back or buttocks, reflexively snap their neck back. (Yes, punsters. It is literally a form of "whiplash.") This itself can be a source of unintentional and highly undesirable injury – particularly if the submissive, as I do, has an already-weakened neck due to something like an old injury or arthritis.

Dominants, stay alert for this. Among other things, the submissive may be too endorphined out to notice or care about this during the session itself, but it could reveal itself with awful effects the morning after. Remember to ask about joint weakness during your pre-session negotiations. Perhaps specifically ask about neck conditions. Stay alert for neck snap when spanking or whipping the submissive. If you notice it, do what you can to reduce or eliminate it.

I'm an artist
with my
cat-o-nine-tails.

Possible methods for dealing with neck snap including ordering the submissive to keep their neck still, having them lace their fingers behind their neck, and placing one of your own hands on the back of their neck or head (experimentation and feedback will tell you which works best) while you spank or whip with the other.

**Watch for internal injury.** While it happens very rarely, it is possible to damage someone's internal organs with a whipstroke to the wrong place, usually the "forbidden zone" of the abdomen or back. Signs of such internal bleeding include abdominal pain, nausea, vomiting, blood in the urine or feces, an abdomen that feels painful, "doughy," or board-like to the touch, and no bowel sounds. (You can't hear any gurgling when you press your ear to the abdomen just beside the belly button, not even if you listen for a full minute. Try listening a few times before you play and you'll understand.) The submissive may become pale and sweaty. They also may develop a rapid pulse – greater than 100 beats per minute. (By the way, it's not at all out of line to take the submissive's pulse occasionally as you play. It's easily found in their wrist and their neck, and a little practice helps considerably in developing this ability. You might either want to make it obvious to the submissive that you are doing this or do it discreetly. Again, practice helps.)

If your submissive develops any of these signs and symptoms after a whipping, take them to a hospital – preferably a trauma center, if you can reach one within an hour. (One part of being a responsible dominant is to make sure you know where your local trauma center is and how to get there.) Call an ambulance or, if they are conscious, take them in yourself, whichever is faster. Caution: If you do take them in yourself, don't speed on the way to the hospital.

One way to tell if the whipping damaged the kidneys is to test the submissive's urine for traces of blood both before and afterward. You can buy dipsticks to test urine for blood at your local medical supply store. About an hour after the whipping, dip the stick in a sample of the submissive's urine. If blood is present, a colored patch on the stick will turn a different color. If the test does come back positive, you don't necessarily need to race for the trauma center, but it's worth calling an SM-positive physician for a consultation.

I *hate* being whipped, but afterwards it's fun to look at the marks.

**Take care of your own body, too.** Administering any type of flagellation can tire your arm. Administering heavy, prolonged, or too-frequent flagellation can cause damage to the nerves and muscles of the arm, shoulder and upper back. (Professional dominants and people who do keyboard work seem particularly vulnerable.) If you're a dominant who enjoys flagellation, it's therefore an excellent idea to take care of these vulnerable parts.

I suggest that you develop at least basic competence in using your non-dominant arm to spank or whip. Also, get good at several different styles of whipping, as different types of strokes use different muscle groups.

Dominants who enjoy heavy flagellation often develop a set of warm-up exercises to stretch their arms, shoulders and back, thus helping to prevent muscle strain and injury. I've seen submissives help their dominants with stretching exercises before a whipping scene.

**The pillowcase.** An ordinary, plain pillowcase can be made into an excellent "beginner's whip." Remove the pillow, lay the pillowcase flat, and fold its short side in half three or four times. Grasp the open end in your hand, and you're ready.

This device offers novices a wonderful toy for experimenting and exploring. Pillowcase whippings offer the look and feel of a flagellation scene's atmosphere, mood, and psychology while involving only very mild amounts of pain. (A pillowcase is almost all "thud" and very little "sting" in the sensations it creates.) Novices can use a pillowcase to explore how they react to whipping or being whipped (which itself can be a very intense experience) without going too far into the pain issue.

Furthermore, it is almost impossible to cause serious damage with a pillowcase unless you land a strong blow directly over the submissive's ears or eyes. (Be somewhat careful around the testicles.) Even strong blows are likely to leave little in the way of lasting marks other than light welts.

For close-in work, grasp the end of the pillow case in your non-dominant hand (if you are right-handed, that means your left hand) and hold the middle of the case in your dominant hand.

If you want a slight increase in intensity, "glove" a second pillowcase over the first one.

As a final point, a pillowcase makes an excellent training tool. If you learn how to use a pillowcase skillfully, then your chances of being skillful with a riding crop or other device, particularly a flogger, are much better.

## *Hands-On Flagellation*

When it comes time to start giving "real" erotic pain, I think you should begin with your hand. Your hand is an intimate, personal part of you, and pain that comes from you personally, as opposed to coming from a more impersonal object such as a whip or paddle, often has more intimacy and often is easier for the submissive to accept. The body-to-body contact, the touching, adds intimacy.

I want to find out what it feels like to be whipped by you.

**Spanking.** I think spanking is one of the best ways of introducing erotic pain into a relationship. (The other is lightly pinching their nipples during sex.) Spanking can be done spontaneously, and involves no threatening-looking whips, clamps, or other equipment. Furthermore, you can start lightly and build or ease up as appropriate. In addition to the buttocks, breasts, and genitals, most other parts of the body can be spanked (although these are the three most popular areas).

You might begin the spanking by running your fingers lightly over the submissive's buttocks. (Some submissives find this ticklish, so you might need firmer strokes). One good way to begin a first erotic spanking is by placing your dominant hand – your right hand, if you're right-handed – on the submissive's buttocks and your other hand on their genitals.

Remember to establish and verify safewords before beginning to give pain. Also, to increase their sense of safety, you probably should not bind your submissive before their first spanking. Remember, this whole idea frightens many people. A bound submissive may have a harder time relaxing and opening up to the experience. I also suggest avoiding blindfolds and gags.

It's wise to remove any rings on your hand, and any loose-fitting bracelets, before delivering a spanking, especially if the jewelry is elaborate or expensive. You don't want your jewelry to injure the submissive's skin. You also don't want any gems to go flying across the room – where they will inevitably land in the world's hardest-to-find location.

*(Screamed while receiving a heavy whipping):*
Yes!
Yes!!
YES!!!

Submissives should be able to relax completely when receiving a spanking, so position them accordingly. You might have them lie across your lap with your non-dominant hand on their genitals. (Seating yourself on the bed, and allowing them to stretch out with their hips across your lap while resting their upper body and legs on the bed, can work well – especially if there's a wall or headboard to support your back.) Another approach is to order them to kneel beside a bed with their chest and head resting on it.

To give the spanking, get close to the submissive and maintain skin-to-skin contact. (This is a good time to locate their tailbone.) Perhaps caress their genitals and wait until they're aroused before giving the first spank.

Start with the cheek closest to you. Cup your hand slightly and keep your fingers together. Make your first spank little more than a firm, brief touch that makes little, if any, sound. After the spank, lightly but firmly massage the spot for a few seconds. (This brief massage will take a lot of the sting out of heavier spanks.) Still your spanking hand, maybe fondle their genitals for a few seconds, and deliver another stroke in the same way.

Give another two dozen spanks in this way. Each should arrive at least five seconds after the last. Cover both cheeks. Remember that gravity will pull the submissive's buttock muscles down, so the spanks should land only on the lower half of the submissive's buttocks.

If this goes well, you might slightly increase the spanking's force for 12 more strokes. Repeat twice more if all seems well.

A first spanking should end while still light. Hit no harder than one-fourth of your hardest sustained strokes, and less if the submissive shows distress. Remember, a first spanking – like all good vices, to quote Oscar Wilde loosely – should leave you both wanting more.

If you accomplish nothing except to reduce how threatening a novice submissive finds the idea of being spanked (and perhaps how threatening you find the idea of giving one), you've done a lot. If the submissive responds well to their first spanking, or at least is not severely repelled, subsequent spankings may be longer and harder – if both parties wish.

The dominant might have the submissive lie face down on the bed or floor and dispense with genital stimulation for the spanking's duration. This prone position presents the buttocks in a more rounded fashion, with better protection for the tailbone and other bones. It also allows better spanking of all four quadrants, plus the outsides, backs, and (if the legs are spread) insides of the thighs.

The dominant can keep the force of the spanks constant for long periods of time, perhaps using a steady rhythm, or they can vary the force. A sudden, sharp climb in the force should usually be followed by an easing off and pleasuring, then moving on to something else.

Wanna see my marks?

One good safety measure is for the dominant to use only their bare hand. The pain of the spank goes both ways, and if it's so intense that it hurts the dominant's hand, there's a good chance it's also too intense for the submissive.

A few spanking tips:

1.  When spanking the buttocks, cup your hand and spank in a slightly upward motion. This has a distinctly different feel, and is usually more pleasurable, than a downward stroke. Try to experience the difference yourself.

2.  Experiment with how rigid or loose you want your wrist to be. A slightly flexible wrist is most common, but you can try anything from complete rigidity to using your hand as a flail. Stay alert for feedback from your submissive; each style feels different.

3.  To provide a warm, pleasurable contrast to the pain of a spank, first land the stroke, then keep your hand stationary on the skin for about one second, then slowly rub the freshly spanked area with slightly firm pressure for two or three seconds before giving another spank. This rub usually causes a pleasantly warm feeling. Again, try to experience it yourself.

4. As with every other part of SM, the more you experience the opposite role, the better, more complete understanding you'll have. You'll learn a lot from experiencing a skillfully administered spanking, even if being spanked doesn't (as far as you know) turn you on.

Once the bare-hand spanking has gone well, a dominant might wish to wear a glove. Mistresses, especially, seem to like wearing thin black leather gloves. The gloves lessen the pain she feels, and the feel of smooth black leather on freshly spanked buttocks drives some submissives wild.

Dominants also spank while wearing gloves of various smooth or rough materials, including fur, latex, and rubber.

**Spanking the genitals.** Most genital spanking is done with a flicking wrist motion, snapping the upper parts of the fingers against the skin.

The shaft of a man's penis can usually take a good spanking. (The tip is too tender on many men, the poor dears.) The typical method is to hold its tip against his belly with your free hand and spank the underside. As always, have fun but don't go crazy. A too-intense spanking can cause damage.

Testicles can usually tolerate only the lightest of spankings.

A woman's vulva can be spanked fairly firmly. Again, start light and gradually build. Some women (not all, not most, but some) get very turned on, and may even reach orgasm, through a skillfully administered "pussy spanking."

**Slapping.** Our face is one of the most intimate parts of our bodies. We are very choosy about who we let touch us there. That being so, a slap in the face is a powerful act of domination and can evoke a powerful emotional reaction. A slap in the face can be painful, disorienting, and/or humiliating.

It's therefore a good idea for a dominant to get specific permission to slap a submissive before doing so. This can be covered in pre-session negotiations, and it's a very good idea to re-verify that the submissive will accept a face slap just before the first time you give them one. Afterward, watch their reaction carefully. It is likely, for better or worse, to be a strong one.

Obviously, it's not a good idea to slap someone who is wearing glasses. Not so obviously, it's also not a good idea to slap someone who is wearing contact lenses. Some folks have had cosmetic surgery on their cheekbones or jaws, and should be slapped carefully if at all. (You did, O Mighty King-Hell Dominant, remember to ask about this during pre-scene negotiations, didn't you?)

A slap may cause a sudden, sharp rotation of the submissive's head, and this could sprain their neck. It can also knock their jaw out of alignment. To prevent these problems, place your free hand on the opposite side of their face to cushion it. Be careful to slap only the "meaty" part of the cheek; keep your slap away from the cheekbone, jawbone and, especially, the ear.

**Flicking.** Believe it or not, bending the tip of a finger under your thumb, building up tension, and then releasing it so that it "snaps" against the submissive's skin can create a more than slightly impressive effect. The breasts, nipples, clitoris, labia, and penis shaft all make good targets. The testicles and the head of the penis make targets that are almost too good. (Don't use full force at the beginning.)

One, two, three, or all four fingers can be used, and the thumb itself can be flicked. You can use one hand or both.

This technique, when used with skill, is much more powerful than it appears.

## Paddling

*one style of paddle*

I define a paddle as a relatively broad, relatively rigid instrument used primarily to strike the buttocks. I think many dominants like paddles because they allow spanking the submissive's buttocks without hurting their own hand.

I just love doing that to him.

Paddles used in the "straight" world are usually made of smooth, varnished wood. SM paddles are sometimes wood or a similar material, or sometimes made of thick leather. The leather ones often have a rigid spine of fiberglass, metal, or something similar, which prevents the leather paddle from being too floppy. Sometimes holes are drilled into the leather. This reduces wind resistance when the paddle is swung, allowing it to gain speed and thus land with more force. (It also increases the likelihood that the paddle will abrade or blister skin.)

Hairbrushes, ping-pong paddles, spatulas, and other relatively rigid, broad objects are also sometimes used as paddles.

Paddles have their drawbacks:

1.  Paddles cause a sharper, more intense pain than a spanking hand causes. A stroke of the same force causes greater pain.
2.  Because there is less feedback from the spanking hand, the dominant might not realize how much pain their strokes are causing.

3. Paddles, especially paddles with holes or uneven surfaces, are much more likely to leave bruises and welts than hand spankings are.

4. Sharp edges, sharp corners, or rough areas on the paddle may cause wounds.

5. It's harder to rub and caress the buttocks after spanking, unless you use your other hand.

Still, for all these disadvantages, paddles have a wide following. Many people have past associations between being paddled and authority. You probably should buy at least one paddle.

Footnote: As a rule of thumb, the broader the striking surface, the more noise it makes and the less likely it is to leave marks. The narrower the striking surface, the less noise it makes and the more likely it is to leave marks.

**The slapper.** A subset of paddles is an item called a "slapper," consisting of two fairly stiff pieces of leather sewn together at the handle and left separate at the striking end. These are called "slappers" because when you land a blow, the two loose pieces of leather slap together, making a loud smacking sound. Slappers tend to be only moderately strong in sensation, so they work well for people who want the sound effects of a heavy paddling without a great deal of pain. Slappers are available in stores that sell riding gear, usually at a very reasonable price.

*slapper*

> Nobody wants to submit to a sloppy dominant.

## *The Riding Crop*

A riding crop makes an excellent whipping toy. You can use it to administer the entire spectrum of strokes, from the lightest to the heaviest, and you can use it almost anywhere on the body. A riding crop costs little, lasts for years, looks sexy, and can localize or spread out the stroke's force.

Crops emit a sinister "whoosh" as they cut through the air and make a distinctive snapping sound when they strike the submissive's flesh. These features form part of their appeal.

The most generally useful riding crops measure about two to $2^1/2$ feet long. You cannot use shorter "jockey bats" for much but paddling – they are little more than clubs. Riding crops longer than $2^1/2$ feet tend to be very flexible, and thus hard to control.

*crop*

The best crops are moderately flexible. A too-rigid crop is little more than a thin club. A too-flexible crop borders on being an out-of-control flail.

The riding crop's tip is important. Thin tips (about finger-width) are likely to mark. Broad, square tips are less likely to mark, but may flop around in a clumsy way. Triangular tips make a nice compromise.

Most riding crops are made of fiberglass covered with leather. Fiberglass is flexible, but don't overdo testing this. For instance, it's not necessary when shopping for one to bend your proposed riding crop end-to-end. If it touches, it's probably too flexible, and if it breaks (a distinct possibility), the clerk will look at you with a very special expression. Bendability of about 45 degrees is all you need.

Pay attention to the cord or wire that is wrapped around the end of the crop to attach the tip to the shaft. If it seems harsh or hard, it may be more painful and/or cause more marking than you want.

Whip the back or front of your own forearm to determine a crop's intensity. Go for bare skin contact.

Some riding crops come with a leather loop at the junction of the handle and shaft. This loop is for riders to slip their hands through when riding a horse so they don't drop the whip onto the ground. The loop will do little but get in your way. You can ignore it, tape it to the crop's handle, or cut it off, but don't slip your hand through it. It will interfere. I suggest you purchase a riding crop with no wrist loop.

> I love it when I'm honestly begging for it to stop, and she looks in my eyes and smiles and keeps right on going.

The riding crop is a very versatile whipping toy. Buy one.

**How to use a riding crop.** After the general rules and mood of the scene have been established, you can begin to use your riding crop.

Training tip: One time-honored method of practicing with any of your whipping implements before you use them on a real person is to practice using them on an inanimate object. A relatively firm pillow is an excellent choice. Large stuffed animals can also be used.

Remember, I recommend that a submissive receive their first erotic pain from your own body: spanking, slapping, squeezing, pinching, hair pulling, and so forth. If your submissive reacts well to a hand spanking, then it may be time to introduce the crop. Remember that you should probably defer combining bondage and using instruments to give pain until your third or fourth session together. It is not essential that the submissive be bound.

Avoid blindfolds and gags for the first use of a crop. You want maximum feedback from and communication with the submissive.

Pick up the crop and stand holding it, perhaps with both hands, where the submissive can see it. Smack its tip into your palm a few times, letting the submissive hear the distinctive sound – and letting them imagine the sound the crop will make when it strikes *them*.

Slowly reach out the tip of the crop and lightly trace it along their body, perhaps first touching it to their upper chest, above and between their breasts. Rub the flat surface of the riding crop's tip (not the tip's edge), and the crop's shaft, lightly across their body, perhaps first stroking their breasts, then work up across their shoulders. Using the crop's shaft, lightly caress the sides of their neck and their cheeks. Maybe brush the tip across their forehead and under their eyes, then slowly bring the tip to their lips. If they don't instinctively understand they are to (lightly) kiss and lick the crop, order them to do that. (Submissives should, as ordered, kiss and lick their dominant's equipment.)

After they've kissed and licked the crop for a few moments (15 seconds is about right), slowly trace the crop's tip down their throat, chest, and belly to their genitals. Caress their genitals and the insides of their thighs with the crop for one to two minutes, then slowly move the crop around to their buttocks. The actual whipping is about to begin.

I admit it.
I'm a pain slut.

If you are right-handed, stand on the submissive's left side and steady them by resting your left hand on the front of their left hip. Place the tip of your crop slightly beyond the center of their right buttock and rest the shaft of the crop on their skin. Slowly run the crop up to the top of their buttocks, then down to just above the backs of their knees, thus defining and claiming the area to be whipped. Gradually narrow the area of this stroking until you are stroking only the lower half of their buttocks. Reduce this stroking still further until your crop is completely still.

Hold that stillness for a moment, then say to your submissive, "I'm going to start out very lightly and build very slowly. I'll stop every now and then to give you some pleasure and let you rest. We won't go further than you can handle. Tell me your safewords."

Once your submissive has recited their safewords, ask them, "Are you willing to go on?" If they nod or say yes, begin the whipping.

Strike the first stroke heartbeat soft. Strike the second, about two seconds later, the same way. Continue the once-every-two-seconds rate at the same light touch. Cover their entire buttocks. Then return to the center of their buttocks and double the force – still keeping to a light pat – and increase the rate to once a second. Again, cover their buttocks, then cover their thighs. Stop the whipping. Use your hands and mouth to pleasure the submissive. Caress and soothe them. Hug them. Lightly kiss their neck. (Don't bite. Stick to giving only one type of pain for now.) Tell them they're doing well. Ask if they're all right. Ask if they're up to continuing.

If they say yes, slowly return to your whipping position. Begin softly tapping again, this time at a twice-a-second rate. Cover their buttocks and rear thighs, then move up onto their back. Slowly and softly work your way up to their shoulder blades and back down, and give them two sudden, sharper strokes on their buttocks. Immediately resume the quick tapping and caress their body with your other hand.

Move the patting around to their chest and lightly cover it. Give each nipple a dozen or so direct strokes with the crop's tip. Lightly tap their penis or vulva. *Very* lightly tap their testicles.

Move behind them and work up the backs of their thighs to their buttocks. Finish with three moderately sharp strokes against the lower half of their buttocks.

Stop the whipping. Press the front of your body against theirs and hug them. Let them rest their head on your shoulder. Hold them. Give them "two squeezes" and notice their reaction. Let there be a long moment of silence as you soothe their body with lightly firm caresses.

Understand that being whipped, even if done utterly painlessly, often deeply touches the submissive's mind. They may tremble. Hold them. Soothe them. Tell them they did well and that you're pleased with them.

If appropriate, kiss them and erotically caress their breasts and genitals. They've earned a little pleasure, if only for being so brave.

This might be enough for a very first whipping. Remember, even if it was ludicrously light in terms of the physical pain involved, it may have been a deep emotional experience for them. (And maybe for you, too.)

Also understand that they might not appear, or even feel, deeply moved at the time. After receiving one of my own first whippings, I felt relaxed and calm. I looked forward to being whipped again. A few hours later, however, I began to feel shaken – not upset or angry or sad, just sort of like I was somehow coming apart. The feeling eventually passed, but it was rocky for a while.

Remember how important it is (for both of you) to spend "straight time" with the submissive after the session, to talk with them the next day, and to check in with them about a week later.

During subsequent sessions you can explore, within safety limits, the limitless varieties of rate, rhythm, force, and location of riding crop strokes. Sometimes it works to use a regular rhythm, sometimes it works to use erratically timed strokes. Music and whippings blend well, especially long, instrumental passages.

If you can, arrange for someone highly skilled to whip you. You should, at many different levels, learn much from the experience. Repeat it with others, and watch others.

## *Whips and Floggers*

Whipping can be broadly defined as striking a submissive's body with a flexible instrument. Whips come in two basic categories: single-tailed and multi-tailed.

> When we finish a session, my submissive is all relaxed and loose and happy — and I'm about half dead.

**Single-tailed whips.** When many people think of a whip, they think of a single-tailed whip such as a bullwhip. Other types of single-tailed whips include blacksnakes, stock whips, buggy whips, and signal whips. (The pistol-shot-like "crack" these whips make when popped in the air is believed to be the noise of the sound barrier being broken.)

Because they concentrate the energy of the whipstroke into a single, very fast-moving, narrow area, single-tailed whips produce an intense cutting or burning sensation that some masochists absolutely love. However, these whips can be extremely dangerous to both the submissive and the dominant. Lacerations, eye injuries, ear injuries, and even fractures have been reported. (I'm also told that the marks made by these whips may take an unusually long time to heal.) Thus, if you want to use a single-tailed whip, accuracy is crucial. This level of expertise typically takes months of solo practice on inanimate objects, and I strongly recommend that you receive personal instruction from an expert as well.

Such experts strongly recommend that dominants protect themselves by wearing heavy clothing. Areas of particular concern are the face, ears, neck and forearms. They also recommend that the submissive wear appropriate clothing or padding to protect those areas that are not being whipped. Eye protection is a very good idea for both partners.

Single-tailed whips are a challenge to use properly. But for dominants and submissives who are attuned to their unique energy, they are worth the effort to master.

flat-tailed flogger

**Multi-tailed whips.** Whips with many tails are generally divided into two categories: floggers and cats. A flogger is a whip made of many long, flat tails of leather or other material, typically with a fairly short handle. A cat, or cat-o-nine-tails, has braided tails; its handle is often a bit longer when compared to its total length. (Some people believe that longer-handled whips are easier to control.) Many other kinds of multi-tailed whips, such as horsehair whisks, two-tailed quirts, and whips of manmade materials, also exist. Most multi-tailed whips are between two and three feet long. In this section, for simplicity's sake, I'll refer to all multi-tailed whips as floggers.

Floggers have no "redeeming social importance" or real-world use. They were created for no other purpose than to strike human flesh.

Floggers are extremely versatile. Like the crop, they can deliver all strengths of strokes and can be used almost anywhere on the body. Many people, even those who may not handle other forms of pain well, enjoy the sensation of a skillful, slow-building flogging.

*Just don't mark me, and you can do anything you want.*

"Flogger technology" has improved tremendously in the last decade or so. The best implements, created by a handful of craftspeople across the country, are beautifully balanced and controllable, a wonderful combination of science and art. I suggest you try several, getting a sense for what you like in terms of weight, length, and balance, before you purchase one; the good ones are a big investment. If you can get a friend to let you try some of theirs, that's a good way to explore. Many SM people own at least one flogger, and some, perverts that they are, own dozens.

I recommend you buy at least one flogger whose tails are made of very light, soft leather, such as deerskin or cabretta. This type of flogger can be used with little danger of causing damage or leaving marks. You might

round braided cat

buy two floggers: one of very light leather and one of medium-weight leather.

On the other hand, you often see floggers for sale in poorer quality adult bookstores that are made of heavy leather, with tails that have sharp corners and sharp edges. These floggers are dangerous. They are often made by people who have no idea of how to use one.

Let's look at this type of flogger point by point:

1. The handle: These floggers are usually badly balanced, with tails much heavier than the handle or vice versa. Such a flogger will tire you out quickly and may even strain the muscles in your arm or hand. One friend of mine used to own a whip he called "Top-Killer," because its tails were so heavy in relationship to its handle that it frequently left the dominant's arm sorer than it left his butt!

2. The weight of the leather: A lot of these floggers are made of such heavy leather, and weigh so much, that even a mild swing generates a too-intense stroke – sometimes even strong enough to knock the wind out of the submissive. Very heavy implements also tire the dominant who uses them. And remember: the lighter the leather, the harder you can hit without causing damage or leaving marks.

3. The edges and corners of the tails: This is the fatal flaw. The poor balance and general heaviness of the flogger could conceivably be coped with – sharp edges and/or corners cannot.

   In general, no striking instrument should have any sharp edges, ends, or corners. The sides should be beveled and the tips rounded. If you see a sharp-edged flogger for sale, don't buy it – and tell the store manager why you won't. That last point is important. We need to (diplomatically) educate vendors about the difference between safe and unsafe toys.

Some floggers have a small loop at the base of the handle. This is useful for hanging the flogger on a hook or belt when it's not in use, but for little else.

Braided tails look sexy, but increase the weight of the stroke. Braided tails are often more abrasive than regular tails are. Strokes from such an implement often leave the submissive's skin rawer than strokes from an unbraided flogger leave it.

Some people place large knots in the leather at the end of the whip's tails, or attach beads, or other small weights, there. These changes make the strokes much more painful in a sharp, localized way (very small knots usually cause no such problems). Some submissives who like the relatively spread-out sensation of a flogger's stroke may feel distinctly turned off by the fine points of pain such knots produce. (I know of a case in which a submissive woman who absolutely loved to have a flogger used on her, and had wonderful ways of expressing her gratitude, stopped playing with a dominant man because he insisted upon using a knotted-end whip on her.) If you and/or your partner is a novice, I suggest you leave the ends of your flogger plain.

bootlace mini-flogger

**How to make a "mini-flogger" from two bootlaces.** You can make a very inexpensive, highly versatile mini-flogger from two ordinary bootlaces. Blows from such a flogger are relatively light (and quiet), thus making it a good type for beginners to use. (Strong mini-flogger blows, however, can be of quite respectable strength, and leave welts and/or bruises.) Due to its light weight, strokes from a mini-flogger create more of a "sting" than "thud" sensation.

This flogger is also shorter than most others, thus making it good for close-in work on breasts and genitals. Furthermore, for even more "detailed" play, you can grasp it in the middle while you hold its base in your free hand.

Take two soft bootlaces, each six feet long and $1/8$ inch wide, and cut both in half. (The laces will probably have square edges. That's a problem with heavier items, but usually not with something this small, soft, and light.) This yields four lengths, each three feet long.

Use scissors, preferably small, sharp scissors such as fingernail scissors, to round off the tips of the corners. (Pay attention here, or rounding off can turn into sharpening.) You can also use a fingernail file and/ or an emery board to round off the tips.

I'm really into
screaming.

Place the three-foot lengths alongside each other and fold them at their midpoint. Use an ordinary rubber band to join the midpoints together, and you're done.

A mini-flogger can see a lot of use. It's very inexpensive, easily made, usually doesn't mark much, makes little noise, is highly portable, very versatile, and can deliver strokes that range from light to strong. I've had one for years and it's one of my favorite toys. I suggest that you play for some time with a mini-flogger before graduating to a heavier, more formidable model.

**How to use the flogger.** You'll need room. Unlike a crop or paddle, when you use a full-sized flogger you usually can't stand close enough to your submissive to touch them with one hand while you strike them with the other. For this reason, you probably should use a riding crop (or maybe a mini-flogger) for your first few whippings with a new submissive.

Let's assume that, for this first flogger whipping, your submissive is standing with their hands overhead and their legs apart. Let's also assume that you are right-handed.

Stand about an arm's length away from their left side, with the whip in your right hand. (This is the setup for a basic forehand stroke.) All necessary groundwork and preliminaries have been handled.

As with all whippings, especially if the person or the experience is new, the first stroke should be soft. Strike the lower half of their buttocks. Bring the whip back, wait about three seconds, and strike again. Aim your stroke so that the tips of the flogger's tails strike the lower middle of the buttock farther away from you. Give their buttocks about half a dozen more strokes, then strike their upper back. The tips should land in the lower middle of their upper back – and over muscle, not shoulder blade or spine. Watch their reaction to this stroke. (People often have "strikingly" different reactions to having different parts of their body whipped.) If their reaction is other than total turn-off, strike their back one or two more times, then return to their buttocks.

*Never put your dominant in a position where they feel they have to prove a point.*

You want to avoid "wrapping" the ends of the flogger. Pick the spot where you want the flogger to land, and aim the tips of your flogger there. The important point to remember is that as the lashes land on a curved body surface, such as the flanks, they gain speed (and thus force) as they wrap around the side of the body. This will often cause that section of the flogger to leave marks. Wrapping is considered amateurish unless done intentionally, and most people don't intentionally wrap.

Safety precaution: Even the best dominants sometimes have a flogger's tail go astray during a whipping. To help guard against a stray tail causing injury, dominants sometimes use their free hand to protect highly vulnerable areas. For example, if they are whipping the submissive's back, they may shield the submissive's neck with their free hand. If they are whipping the submissive's buttocks, they will use their free hand to shield the submissive's genitals. (For some strange reason, most submissives don't seem to mind.)

If you're using a long flogger, you may not be able to get in close enough to your submissive to protect them in this way; many dominants therefore place a towel around their submissive's neck, and/or have them protect their genitals with their own hands. A g-string or other thong-style undergarment may offer at least some extra protection for their genitals and tailbone.

Relatively broad, flat places on the human body, such as the buttocks, upper back, and the large muscles of the chest, are good targets for the full lash. Other body parts may be whipped, but take care to strike with just the tip. Don't wrap.

During and after the whipping, check the sides of the submissive's hips and trunk for wrap marks. If you see some, be more careful next time.

A few safety pointers:

1. Sometimes the flogger's tails tangle. You may have to straighten them periodically.
2. Avoid accidentally striking the submissive with the whip's handle. (This can happen if you get too close.) Such a hard, club-like stroke is distinctly unerotic.

Unlike the crop, the flogger can also be used in a variety of other motions.

**Backhand.** This can be useful for reaching both the left and right sides of a submissive's body (it's considered bad form to whip only one side, unless you're being purposefully nasty). If you're right-handed, stand on the right side and slightly behind the submissive's body, facing them. Gather the tails of the whip in your left hand. With a smooth, straight motion from your shoulder, lay the tails flat across the submissive's back or buttocks, with the tips landing on the area you want to feel the strongest sensation.

> Being into SM
> now is like being gay
> 25 years ago.

**Twirling.** The flogger can be spun in a circle. This circle can be vertical in an overhand or underhand motion, or horizontal in a forehand or backhand motion. Overhand and underhand motions are the more commonly used. The tips strike the submissive's body, and the whipping motion is often used to cover large areas of skin.

**Sideways figure eight.** The flogger is swung in exactly the motion named, the tips striking on the downstroke. This motion is often used on the upper back. Careful, though – since it's a downward stroke, it can have a tendency to land on the bony part of shoulderblades and on the upper half of buttocks; aim for the fleshier areas.

**Underhand.** The underhanded vertical swing can be used to whip the genitals. As always, be very careful about how much force you use.

**From in front.** The forehand and backhand motions are also sometimes used to whip the submissive's back and buttocks, while you stand in front of them. This involves *intentionally* wrapping the tails so their ends (usually about the last third) land on the flat areas of the submissive's buttocks or back. This arrangement allows considerably more face-to-face contact than most other positions allow. While this technique takes time and practice to master, it can be *very* powerful and effective.

**Overhand.** The overhand motion is often used to whip a lying-down submissive. It can also be used to strike the back and breasts of a standing submissive. Watch your distance and your aim here. A badly aimed downward stroke to the front of the submissive's body can catch their head or face on the way down. (I have sometimes seen submissives made to wear industrial goggles to help guard their eyes.) A badly aimed downward stroke to the rear of their body can catch the top of their head, their ears, or the tops of their shoulders.

How about if you come over Tuesday and I do terrible things to you?

**Snapping.** Like we used to do in gym, snap the whip onto the submissive's body. You can use underhand, overhand, forehand, or backhand motions. These are usually sudden, relatively sharp, strokes. They can be done in a rhythmic way, or abruptly. They work well as a sudden change of tempo. Because they can be somewhat disorienting, I recommend you begin your whipping with a different stroke.

**Holding the tails.** You can hold the handle in one hand and all but about three to six inches of the lash in the other. This creates a flogger used for close-in work. Such a flogger can be used on the breasts and genitals. (Some people buy a small flogger, about a foot long, for just this purpose.) It's especially useful when the submissive is tied face-up onto a bed. Try it on yourself.

The combination of type of swing, degree of force, rhythm, and location make using a flogger a fascinating thing to explore. In summary, the flogger, in the hands of a skilled user, is a tremendously powerful erotic device.

## Straps

Straps are long, relatively narrow, flexible striking implements. Straps are usually made of leather, although you sometimes see straps of rubber or other materials. Straps sometimes come with a stiff handle, but the most typical strap is flexible along its entire length.

The classic strap, of course, is the dominant's belt. Submissives who enjoy being strapped get a very special shiver from the sound of a belt being drawn out of its beltloops. If you use a belt, you will probably want to either wrap the buckle end around your hand a time or two, or double the belt up and hold both ends in your hand, striking with the folded part. Striking with the buckle is very likely to cause an unacceptable level of damage.

Other kinds of straps include razor strops (which can sometimes be found in antique stores) and all kinds of straps from riding gear shops.

Because of their flexibility, straps are very likely to wrap if not aimed carefully, and the tip of a strap landing on the hip is very non-erotic for most people. Aim your strap carefully.

Note: Many people were punished with straps as children or in abusive adult relationships. Before you use a strap on someone, find out if they have any history of having been nonconsensually beaten with one; negotiate and adjust your play accordingly.

## *Canes*

Whipping canes are very different from the stout, walking-assist devices you see used on the street.

Whipping canes are much thinner – usually about the diameter of a pen – and much more flexible. They are usually made of rattan; bamboo can split and cause deep lacerations. You also see canes made of manmade materials such as fiberglass and Delrin. A cane's flexibility is one of its greatest assets; therefore, many people soak rattan canes in water overnight, then coat them with varnish or a similar finish to retain the absorbed moisture.

Look at my new flogger!

Canes tend to be long – usually about three to $3^{1}/_{2}$ feet. Their tip should always be either rounded off or padded.

*cane*

Some canes have curved handles, although the curve contributes nothing and sometimes gets in the way. Straight canes are usually held by the thicker end. Straight canes sometimes have the handle end finished with leather, rubber, or fabric.

Note this well: Because of the thinness of the striking area, the light weight of the cane, and its flexibility, strokes from a cane can be extremely

197

painful and often leave marks. Strong strokes can be given only to the buttocks, thighs, and *maybe* the upper back. The rest of the body must be treated much more lightly.

For these reasons, accuracy is extremely important when using a cane. Most strokes are therefore given with a flick of the wrist. (Beginners are often advised to keep their elbow tucked against their side.) Cane strokes delivered with both the wrist and elbow are likelier to go astray. Cane strokes delivered with the wrist, elbow, and shoulder are extremely difficult to land accurately.

The sensation from a cane, more than any other implement, has a unique "two-wave" sensation. There is a rush of pain when the cane strikes, and then a second wave a second or two behind that. Try this yourself if you can, and you'll see what I mean.

Striking your submissive again while they're still trying to cope with that second wave of pain can be far too intense for many submissives. Particularly if you and your partner aren't experienced with canes, it's best to leave some "breathing room" between cane strokes. The "nod" and "one-to-ten" techniques can be useful here.

Be careful with canes. They have tremendous potential, and they look relatively harmless, yet they are probably the most dangerous flagellation instrument in common use.

**A few words about the lowly coat hanger.** Most whips make considerable noise, and the sound of a whip striking flesh is fairly distinctive. For people who need a "quiet" whip, a coat hanger may provide an answer.

It's quickly made: take an ordinary, unpainted wire coat hanger, hold it by the hook and the middle of the crossbar, and pull to straighten it. Fold down or twist off the hooked part of the handle, and it's ready to use.

Caution: The striking surface is obviously very narrow. Therefore this whip produces a very sharp, intense pain – comparable to a cane, and more than you might expect. By all means, swat your own thighs a few times before using it on somebody else.

Also, again because of the narrow striking surface, a coat hanger is much more likely than a riding crop or flogger to leave bruises and welts, even with relatively light strokes.

A coat hanger makes little sound and is hard to hear even a short distance away. If background music is being played at normal volume, the sound of the whipping could be almost completely masked.

Coat hanger whips are a favorite discipline instrument of pimps and abusive parents. The idea of being whipped with one may arouse unexpectedly strong emotions in people. Therefore, be extra careful about obtaining consent before using it.

We may have Joan Crawford ("No wire hangers!") to thank for many people's belief that the very idea of using a coat hanger on a submissive is out of the question. However, I'd like to speak up in the defense of this simple and affordable toy. Used with care and attention, they are no more or less dangerous than any other flagellation instrument. I've used them quite successfully, and had them used on me, on many occasions with no untoward effects. A professional dominant I know lives in a thin-walled apartment building and has therefore been using them on her clients quite regularly for several years with no particular problems. Janet and I used one on a vacation cruise (we were traveling light and didn't have room in our luggage for many toys), enjoyed it tremendously, and noticed with pleasure that our steward had carefully put it away in a drawer when he cleaned our cabin afterwards.

## *The Pounder*

*kabonger*

The pounder (which I've nick-named the "kabonger") is a massage implement that consists of a small ball mounted on a flexible strip of metal with a handle on the other end. In addition to being carried by some SM stores, they can be found in massage supply stores and are used in various types of Japanese massage. (Stores that sell various types of Japanese goods often stock pounders.) It's used to strike various parts of the body in a steady, rhythmic manner during massage. (Sometimes two are used – one in each hand.) It's good for relaxing tense muscles and can feel wonderful.

I used to love movies with whipping scenes.

The kabonger can be an excellent SM toy. It's simple to use, inexpensive, durable, strikes lightly enough to be difficult to get into trouble with, is highly "deniable," makes very little noise, and can be used on most parts of the body.

Good kabonger targets include the breasts, back, buttocks, inner thighs, and penis, but there's one target that the kabonger seems designed for: the vaginal area. I'm not going to go into gory details here (not even if you beg), just know that you can create a truly impressive effect with relatively little effort by applying the kabonger there. As always with any type of flagellation, remember to start lighter than light, build slower than slow, do an occasional "two squeezes," and reverify safe words before significantly increasing the intensity.

## *Conclusion*

Erotic flagellation offers tremendous opportunities. However, unlike bondage and administering other forms of erotic pain, it is much more of an art than a craft. Therefore, it can only be "taught" to a limited degree. The effect of a given flagellation session is unique, and extensive personal exploration, preferably on both ends of the whip, is essential to understanding this erotic art form to any meaningful degree.

ps

# Clamps

Other than whips, clamps are perhaps the most commonly used SM toys. They are applied to various places on the body, often but not always the nipples and genitals.

Clamps have many advantages. Unlike whips, they make no noise. They require no continuous effort on the dominant's part; the dominant simply places them and moves on to other matters. They provide a steady, precisely regulated amount of pain. They are inexpensive. They are usually items adapted from everyday use, so having them around the house is not particularly "incriminating."

Many different items are used as erotic clamps. Ordinary spring clothespins are the most commonly used item. Other items include various types of plastic and metal paper clips found in stationery stores, pin-substitute clothing clamps, clamps from various types of coathangers, alligator clamps, mousetraps, hemostats, tubing clamps, and even small vise grip pliers.

To prevent damage, most clamps have a some-what flat surface. Saw-toothed clamps, such as alligator clamps, cut deeper into tissue and are more likely to damage.

Clamps are a lazy dominant's best friends.

Some clamps can have their tightness adjusted. I have seen rubber bands placed either in front of the spring to make it squeeze more tightly or behind the spring to make it squeeze less tightly. I have also seen clothespins with bolts and wingnuts inserted through holes drilled on either side of the main spring so the pressure can be increased or decreased as desired. (These clamps, by the way, were painted black – a nicely sinister touch.) Many forms of "store-bought" clamps have tightness-adjusting mechanisms built into them. Clamps sometimes have a loop attached to them so they can be attached to leashes or weights.

People vary widely in the degree of tightness they find erotic. Some like tight clamps, others can take only the mildest. A wise dominant stocks

*some common types of clamps*

clamps of several different degrees of tightness. (They can store neatly in a tray designed for fishing lures.)

To begin experimenting with clamps, buy a bag of ordinary, wooden, spring-type clothespins. Take them home, strip, and try them on various parts of your body. Use only two at first, and start with your nipples. Then try your genitals, earlobes, lips, folds of skin on your neck, belly button, and the skin between your genitals and your anus (your perineum – pronounced per-eh-KNEE-um).

Masturbate or otherwise sexually arouse yourself as you do this. Take your time and, for now, don't leave them for more than about five minutes on any one area – even less if the pain starts to feel non-erotic. No heroics today.

While people vary widely in the number of clothespins they can take, most people can only handle about four clamps for half an hour or longer.

Clamps are an excellent example of the SM saying, "The more turned on somebody is, the more pain they can take." If the erotic arousal is lost, clamps start to hurt. Therefore, only apply them if the submissive feels aroused.

Important point: Avoid mixing different types of pain – such as the pain of spanking with the pain of clamps – when you play with novices or with a new partner. Mixing pain may overwhelm them, and may obscure how they react to different types of pain. You want to learn each submissive's unique reaction pattern, so only play with one type of erotic pain at a time with somebody new.

Another important point: Clamps hurt continuously, even if the dominant forgets about them. Unlike whipping or spanking, which are labor-intensive, clamps require no ongoing effort on the dominant's part to cause pain. This is true even if the dominant moves on to other matters. The clamps are still there, still hurting. Inept dominants lose track of this. Make sure you don't.

One way to stay in touch with how much ongoing pain clamps cause is to experience it yourself. Have you ever experienced having a clamp on each nipple for an hour? If not, try it before you ask somebody else to endure that. If you're not submissive, try it while you masturbate.

Another point to remember is that clamps shut off circulation to the clamped area. The skin under the pinched area is receiving little or no blood flow. Naturally, you don't want to let this continue too long. The longest you should leave a clamp on a particular place is about an hour.

One friend of mine, a novice dominant, was experimenting with clamps one night. Quite appropriately, he tried them on his own nipples so he could experience the sensation. While he was savoring it, he drifted off to sleep – and awoke when his alarm went off almost four hours later. His nipples hurt for almost a month, and he's lucky he didn't wind up with gangrene. However, he's one dominant who will never, ever forget about a clamp he left on a submissive!

**Putting them on.** Let's assume your submissive is face-up on a bed and that all prior negotiations are completed. With one hand, hold the clothespin near its free end. With the other, pinch a fold of skin and lift the skin away from the submissive's body. Gradually increase your pinch's pressure until it equals the clamp's pressure.

You should now be holding a small "tent" of skin. Pinch open the clothespin and guide it over the skin.

Tell the submissive that the clamp probably will cause a sharp pain for the first 30 seconds it's on, and then the pain will subside.

Over a period of about five to 10 seconds, gradually release pressure on the clothespin. When your hand is completely off the clothespin, gradually spread apart your pinching fingers, then slowly move your hand away. Don't bump anything, especially the clamp.

Let the submissive lie quietly for about a minute so they can get used to the sensation. Don't touch the clamp and don't distract them. You might rest your hand, without moving it, on their thigh or abdomen, but don't interfere with their adjusting to the clamp. This is an important moment for them. Don't mess it up.

I like to find out where their limits are, and then push them.

Watch their breathing. If it stays tight, the clamp might be too intense. On the other hand, if they relax and take a deep breath, you can probably continue.

Also watch their overall degree of muscle tension or relaxation. It's normal for a submissive, especially a novice, to tense in expectation of receiving pain. What's important is how they react *after* the clothespin is on. If they remain tense, they're probably not aroused. If they relax, that's a good sign.

Important point: Remove the clamp if the submissive doesn't find it erotic. If they don't relax their muscles and begin breathing normally again after about a minute, you should probably remove the clamp even if they haven't asked for that.

If they do ask you to remove it, or call "yellow," or give some other similar sign, take the clamp off at once. Afterward, don't criticize them. They may feel guilty. They also may feel angry or turned off. Be understanding.

Remember, let them get used to this at their own pace. Don't rush them. If, after about a minute, the submissive relaxes and breathes normally, proceed with the session.

Occasionally, a submissive who is used to clamps and likes them nonetheless reacts badly to one particular clamp. This clamp may be placed too close to a nerve or other structure under the skin. Sometimes moving it by only an inch or so solves the problem. If you try moving it once and it still hurts in an excessive or non-erotic way, that area just isn't ready for a clamp that day; give up and try another body part or activity.

If the submissive is completely unfamiliar with clamps, you probably should not bind them during their first exposure. They will feel more anxious, and less in control, if they are bound. This anxiety over loss of control will make it harder for them to relax and open up to the experience. The "no bondage for first times" rule is a good general rule.

Unclamped nipples almost look naked.

**Taking them off.** Another important fact about clamps: they hurt coming off. This seems especially true of clamped nipples. As blood flows back into the freshly unclamped tissue and reexpands it, pain results. Unfortunately, little can be done about this. The best you can do in most cases is warn the submissive that the spot will hurt for about 30 seconds after being unclamped, then the pain will subside.

When the submissive's sexual arousal level lessens, their ability to accept pain also drops. You want to remove the clamps accordingly. In the case of a man, this means removing the clamps a few minutes before, or shortly after, he has an orgasm. Again, the basic way to remove the clamps is gradually. Clamped tissue is hypersensitive to movement. Keep it still during unclamping.

Warn the submissive that the clamp will hurt as it comes off, no matter how gently you remove it. Let them know the pain will subside after about 30 seconds. Make sure your hands are dry enough to grip the clamp securely, and use your dominant hand. If your fingers are slippery (as they often will be if you used lubricant during the session) the clamp may slip out of your hand

and back onto just-released tissue, causing the submissive to scream. Place the thumb and forefinger of your non-dominant hand near the clamped tissue to stabilize it. Don't press on or move the tissue with your other hand. Grasp the free ends of the clamp. Again, keep it still. Taking about five seconds, pinch the ends together until the clamp is free of the tissue, then slowly move it straight up. Be careful not to move the clamp off to the side until it's completely clear of the tissue.

Important note: Once you begin to remove the clamp, continue to remove it – even if your technique becomes ragged. Don't let go and try again; that will make the pain much worse.

Clamp removal demands a delicate, sure touch. The ability to remove clamps with minimal unnecessary pain is a mark of a skilled dominant. You learn by practice. You learn even more by experiencing somebody else removing clamps from *your* body.

Caution: Unless you are deliberately trying to cause pain, *don't* rub freshly unclamped skin. This often well-meaning but ignorant gesture sharply increases the pain. Let unclamped tissue reexpand at its own rate. Try this on yourself. Put on nipple clamps and leave them in place for 15 minutes. Then remove them and immediately rub your nipples. You'll understand, and you'll remember.

I don't do it unless I know that, at some level or other, they're enjoying it.

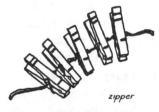

zipper

Some dominants deliberately remove all the clamps at once. This is an acceptable practice, but only with an experienced submissive – and they should be warned the first time it's done to them. For serious masochists, you can make a "zipper" by stringing several non-toothed clamps along a cord or thong, tying knots on each side of the clamp to hold its position. The clamps are placed along the skin and yanked off with a pull on the end of the cord. Try this yourself before you do it to anyone else; it's pretty intense. It's best to keep zippers off genitals and other fragile skin.

Another extreme approach is to whip the clamps off, using a riding crop or flogger. (Accuracy is extremely important here. Practice this first by placing some clamps on a towel and hanging the towel from a shower rod. Particularly if you're using a riding crop or something equally harsh, you don't want to miss the clamp.)

**What to do after the clamp is on.** Just because your submissive is wearing clamps doesn't mean you have to simply sit back and watch. One effective approach is simply to leave the clamps alone while you pay attention to other parts of their body.

Try pleasuring your submissive's genitals after clamping another part of their body. The pain of the clamps contrasts with the pleasure in their genitals to provide a powerful erotic experience. Masturbate them, perform oral sex, or – if the position permits – have intercourse. Mixing erotic pain with intense, prolonged sexual pleasure can create a deep impression in the submissive's mind.

Regarding playing with the clamps themselves, there are many things you can do. As in most other areas of SM, only do these maneuvers slowly and gradually. If either your partner or the experience is unfamiliar, avoid doing anything sharply or suddenly. You can always play harder and more intensely later. Right now, proceed gradually.

While you should only apply clamps to dry skin, once the clamps are on you can kiss and lick the tissue. If the clamps are small enough to fit into your mouth, you can suck the area.

No endorphins yet, Mistress!

You can grasp the clamp and slowly lift it away from their body. This gradually increases the pain.

You also can place your fingers over the pinching part of the clamp and increase the pinching force. You need only small pressure to increase the force greatly. Proceed gradually, on only one clamp at a time, and carefully watch your submissive's reaction.

You can twist the clamp. Only a few degrees of twisting in any direction drastically increases the erotic pain. The submissives often wince and gasp when you do this, and it can easily get too intense.

You also can shake the clamp, either by grasping it directly (be careful not to shake it loose), or by shaking the underlying part and letting the clamp snap back and forth. This shaking can vary from mild to intense, depending on the submissive's reaction.

Finally, you can attach the clamps to something. You can run rope, leather, or light chain from one clamp to the other. This allows you to pull on several clamps at the same time. You also can attach a leash to this connecting line. (Note: Even a light chain's movement can shift the clamps. This movement may change the feeling from erotic to non-erotic. Therefore, avoid using clamps connected by chain until you know that your submissive can handle such intense sensation.)

You can attach the clamps to an eyebolt above the submissive. Attach the middle of a long, thin line to the clamp, and run the two free ends through the loop. Split them, pull as tight as appropriate, separate the ends, and tie off. (This is a variant on the lark's head knot.)

You can also run the free end of the line through the eyebolt and attach a weight. Safety tip: Don't hang a weight directly over the submissive's body. If such a weight became loose, it could fall and cause injury. Always make sure the weight will not fall onto the submissive (or you). Also, be careful about applying weights to clamps if the submissive is standing. The weights could slip off and drop onto the submissive's foot, or yours.

A note about weights: Fishing sinkers work well. They come in small sizes and the load they create can be adjusted an ounce at a time. (Don't start out with a two-pound monster.) Also, they were designed to be hung. As a safety measure, I suggest you use round sinkers. Avoid the sharp-cornered, pyramid-shaped ones.

**Standing clamps.** Sometimes submissives are placed in a standing position and clamps are attached to their nipples or other parts of their body. A line is run from the clamps up to an eyebolt in the ceiling. The line is there either tied off or attached to a weight.

One advantage of this approach is that if the submissive sags or moves, the pain increases. They therefore are motivated to hold their position, and that creates "possibilities."

This can be hot and fine, unless something unexpected happens and the submissive *must* move. Let's say they faint, trip, or get bumped off balance. Many clamps, most especially these made of metal, will not readily pull off. Indeed, one design of widely used clamp, oriental textile or "clover" clamps, will dig in harder if it's pulled on. If a submissive clamped with these were to fall, major injury could result.

I therefore suggest you only attach clamps that pull off relatively easily to lines or anything similar. As with many other areas of SM, when you put a submissive in a given position, you should ask yourself: What if they faint? What if they fall? What if I have to get them out quickly? *If you don't have solid, clear answers to those questions, don't put them in that position.*

**The bed of nails.** Sometimes submissives have clamps placed on their nipples, their genitals, and other locations on the front of their body, and are then ordered to lie face-down on a bed. There they may be whipped and/or subjected to anal intercourse. (You can accomplish a "light" version of this by hugging them while the clamps are in place.) This kind of pressure against clamped tissue is extremely painful (thus the name) and even masochists can usually only tolerate it for about 30 minutes. Non-masochists can usually tolerate far less time.

Caution: This technique is a bit dangerous in that it doesn't look nearly as bad as it feels. To truly appreciate it, try it yourself.

## Clamping the Nipples

Nipples are the number-one clamp target. This is perhaps too bad. People vary widely in how they respond to clamps on their nipples. Also, this reaction is distinctly separate from their reaction to other types of erotic pain.

I know submissives who intensely enjoy, and can even reach orgasm from, getting spanked or whipped. Yet some of these same submissives can't stand even medium-strength clamps on their nipples. Other submissives like clamps on their genitals, or elsewhere on their body, yet hate clamps on their nipples. And still others like having their nipples pinched by fingers, or bitten, yet dislike clamps. Still, many, many submissives like having their nipples clamped; some enjoy it intensely. Most submissives like, or will at least accept, a moderate degree of nipple play. Others are "nipple wimps."

I thought those damn endorphins would never kick in.

Some women, especially, find that stimulating their nipples causes intense sexual arousal. They seem to have a direct line running from their nipples to their clit. Thus, unless the clamps are too tight, they find nipple clamps intensely erotic.

Note: Many a woman's nipples vary in their sensitivity with her menstrual cycle. Clamps she finds too tight at one time during her cycle may be acceptable, or even too light, a week or two later.

**Applying clamps to nipples.** A good operating principle for all SM is: introduce only one new thing at a time. Follow this principle when introducing clamps. For example, if you meet someone new who has never played SM before, and you take them home, tie them up, and put clamps on their nipples, you have introduced three new things: yourself, bondage, and clamps. This combination is likely to overwhelm your new partner, and thus increases the risk of resistance, panic, and even violence. So, unless your partner is already familiar with SM, wait a while.

How should you apply nipple clamps? In a word, gradually. First see how they react to having their nipples pinched. Don't use your fingernails; they cause sharp pain. Use the pads of your fingertip and thumb, or pinch their nipple between your thumb and the side of your index finger. (Try this on yourself.) Notice their reaction to this before you bring out the clothespins.

If the person is completely unfamiliar with the idea of nipple clamps (some people have led a sheltered life), prepare them by saying something like, "I want to place some light clamps on your nipples. They should both hurt just a little and feel good. I'll take them off if they're too intense for you, but I want you to try to handle them." You might then place the clamps on your own nipples for a minute or two, so the submissive can see them.

As an alternative approach, if you switch roles, have the new person place the clamps on you during the first time they're used.

**Where should you place the nipple clamps?** Usually behind the tip of the nipple. Placing them right on the nipple's tip causes a sharp, intense pain that few people find erotic. It usually works better to place them "deeper" on the nipple. Again, try it on yourself.

The most common way to place a clothespin on a nipple is at a right angle to the submissive's body, so the clamp is "sticking straight up into the air." To do this, first place the clamp on your own body (your own nipple, if possible, otherwise on the web of skin between your forefinger and thumb) to determine its tightness and intensity. The clamping surface should be about $1/8$ to $1/4$ inch behind the nipple's tip, and the clamp itself aligned straight up and down the body. It should not be tilted to either side.

*I love to have clamps used on me.*

If the clamps are applied sticking straight up, they might flop over, especially if they are metal clamps or if the skin under the nipples is loose. Few submissives find this type of pain erotic. One way to avoid this problem is to apply the clamps parallel to the submissive's body as opposed to perpendicular. This is an especially good way for a heterosexual, dominant man to apply nipple clamps to a woman prior to missionary-position intercourse.

To apply the clamps this way, lightly pinch the nipple's tip and raise it up, then slip the clamp under your fingertips onto the nipple. Another method is to pinch a tent of skin at the tip of the nipple (12 o'clock position) and, approaching from the 6 o'clock position, slip on the clamp.

For sexual intercourse, the clamps are usually placed straight down, straight out to the side, or someplace in between. (Left breast: 3 to 6 o'clock; right breast; 6 to 9 o'clock).

Clamps slide off wet nipples. If you wish to apply clamps, or other items, to a nipple, don't first moisten it with saliva or other lubricants.

Stroke or rub their body, give them some pleasure, before moving on with the session. Ask them how they're doing. Pleasure their genitals. After about two minutes, clamp their other nipple.

Putting one clamp on each nipple is probably as far as you should go for the first session. You can try more clamps in later sessions.

If you want to play with the clamps while they're on, try it first with one nipple, then the other, before trying it on both nipples simultaneously. The nipples may vary in sensitivity. Remember that any movement of the clamps may increase the pain they cause to a non-erotic level.

Note: even if the clamps feel good at first, they will probably start to hurt in a non-erotic way after a while. Check with a novice at 15-minute intervals to see how the clamps feel. Take the clamps off if they're getting too intense. Also, you probably should take them off after an hour even if everything seems fine. You don't want to cause lasting damage, or too much soreness the next day.

I don't have the slightest desire to hurt you. Torture you, yes. Hurt you, no.

You can lessen the pain of removal by unclamping one nipple, waiting for about one minute, then unclamping the other. A second approach is to unclamp one nipple, then have the submissive nod or otherwise indicate that they are ready to have their other nipple unclamped.

Another way to ease this moment is to stroke the submissive with your hand or some fur between the breasts as you remove the clamp. The reason for this is that the nerves in the spinal column that carry pain messages also carry touch messages, and can only carry one of the two at a time. The more of the nerves you keep busy carrying touch messages, the fewer are available to carry pain messages. (This is a simplified version of what medical folks call "the gate theory of afferent pain inhibition.")

## Clamping the Genitals

After the nipples, the genitals are the most often clamped body part. This clamping is often accompanied by bondage, whipping, and other forms of erotic "torture." It also may be accompanied by various pleasures. The combination of erotic pain and pleasure directly on the genitals is powerfully intense.

Perhaps surprisingly, genitals often tolerate clamps better than nipples do. I know many people who have difficulty tolerating even mild clamps on their nipples, yet these people can handle, and even enjoy, strong clamps on their genitals.

When clamping or unclamping the genitals of either gender, try not to catch pubic hairs in the clamps.

**Clamping the male genitals.** Clamps can be applied to five areas of a man's genitals: his scrotum, the shaft of his penis, the head of his penis, his foreskin (if he has one), and the area of skin between his scrotum and his anus – the perineum. Let's consider each area.

Of all male genital areas, the *scrotum* usually tolerates clamps best. It's usually not as sensitive as some other areas, and its loose skin is easy to clamp. Also, clamping his scrotum leaves the shaft and tip of his penis free.

You can place the clamps in a row along the line of skin running up the middle of his scrotum, or you can place one clamp directly over each testicle. (Pinch the scrotal skin, not the testicle itself). For an initial session, you probably should use only two clothespins. Some experienced, masochistic men can accept a dozen or more clamps on their scrotum.

As with clamping the nipples, you can pull on, twist, and further pinch the clamp. Again, as with nipples, do so gradually – especially at first or when playing with a new partner.

Clamps applied to the scrotum tend to shake if the penis is stimulated by masturbation, fellatio, or intercourse. This shaking increases the pain. Men vary in how they feel about that. Some love it; some don't.

About one to three clamps can be applied to the male *perineum*. Most men can tolerate clamping here.

One advantage to clamping the perineum: placing the clamps so far away from the penis allows it almost complete freedom. Sexual intercourse is often possible with clamps placed here. One disadvantage to clamping the perineum: anal play is difficult because you must be careful to avoid bumping the clamps. If he's careful, a man with a clamped perineum can still kneel. All in all, clamping a man's perineum has much to recommend it.

If he's uncircumcised, his *foreskin* offers distinct possibilities. Its sensitivity varies widely from one man to the next; I'd suggest starting with only one or two clamps and seeing how he reacts to those. Several dominants I talked to particularly cited the devious trick of pulling the foreskin up over the end of the penis and clamping it closed. They also enjoyed placing a circle of clamps arond the end of the foreskin, a trick sometimes known as the "crown of thorns."

Clamps are often placed along the underside of the *penis shaft*. The junction of the penis shaft with the scrotum is a favorite spot. A second intense spot is the junction of the shaft and head. A third spot is the junction of the top of the penis and the abdominal wall.

The skin of the penis needs to be somewhat loose in order for clamps to be applied. Therefore, this technique is not used too much in combination with cock rings and other devices that immobilize the skin over the shaft.

Clamps applied near the tip limit what else you can do to or with the penis. On the other hand, masturbation games, fellatio, and (*maybe*) intercourse are possible if the clamps are applied near the base.

The *head of the penis* is exquisitely sensitive. Many masochistic men, who enjoy having other areas of their genitals clamped, have great difficulty accepting clamps on the head of their penis. On the other hand, highly masochistic men often love having the head of their penis clamped.

You can place one large clamp directly on the head of the penis. Then you can either play with this clamp – pulling, twisting, and so forth – or leave it alone while you play elsewhere. You can also masturbate and/or lick the penis, and might be able to suck on it if you so choose.

I am erotically sophisticated.
You are kinky.
He is a pervert.

One variation is to use very small clamps, such as small, plastic clothespins (sometimes called "tormentor clamps") along the ridge of skin at the bottom of the penis tip (the corona). This can be exquisitely painful but, unlike a bigger clamp on the tip, does not block ejaculation.

One caution: Even highly masochistic men are often grateful to have penis-tip clamps removed after about 30 minutes. Many can tolerate it only for far shorter periods of time.

**Clamping the female genitals.** Clamps can be applied to her outer lips, inner lips, perineum, and clitoris.

The *outer labia* are often surprisingly tolerant of clamps. In particular, many women who can't handle clamps on their nipples can handle clamps on their outer labia without great difficulty. If the clamps aren't too long, and if she is careful, she can kneel while wearing clamps here. For a first session, one clothespin on each labia is about as far as you should go. Two on each labia are about as many as even experienced women can tolerate for any length of time.

An obvious disadvantage to clamping the female genitals is that it makes it difficult to do anything else through that forest of clamps. It's possible to masturbate her, use a vibrator (touch it to the clamps and watch her reaction), or perform cunnilingus, but sexual intercourse is all but out of the question.

One caution: Anal intercourse *may* be possible if the labia are clamped, but be careful the penis or dildo doesn't slip out and thrust against a clamp. The sharp pain that results could cause her to scream, or even faint.

You can combine clamps on the labia with items inserted into the vagina and/or anus such as ben wa balls, a butt plug, or a penis-shaped vibrator. Ropes run between her labia will hold these items in place.

The *inner labia* are both fragile and tender, and therefore are to be clamped cautiously if at all. Most women cannot tolerate clamps here for long. I suggest you stick with clamping the outer labia.

It's difficult to clamp a woman's *perineum*. It's a very small place, and you will probably find it difficult to pinch a fold of skin there. Also, clamping her perineum will interfere with both vaginal and anal play. All in all, clamping her perineum tends to be more trouble than it's worth.

Obviously, placing a clothespin on a woman's *clitoris* is highly painful. Her reaction will depend on how masochistic and how aroused she is. I have known a few highly masochistic women who reached orgasm after orgasm from this. (It is, after all, something of the ultimate in clitoral stimulation.) Most women, however, could only handle having a clamp on their clit for a few minutes. Many couldn't handle it at all.

Look at these clamps that I bought in the Philippines.

I suggest that you allow a woman one or two sessions of having clamps only on her outer labia before you consider clamping her clitoris. It's far too painful for most women to enjoy, and causes many to lose their arousal completely.

One final note: Even women who intensely enjoy having a clamp on their clitoris usually feel grateful if it's removed after half an hour or so.

Clamping her clitoris is a significant act. Do so only after proper negotiation and build-up.

## Clamping Other Parts of the Body

Almost anyplace on the body where a fold of skin can be pinched can also be clamped. Many people do not find having clamps anywhere except their nipples and/or genitals particularly erotic. However, extra clamps can add to the atmosphere and intensity of the session.

Some people like a lot of clamps, and some masochists achieve profound trance states while wearing many clamps. I have personally seen more than 100 used on a submissive at once, and I have heard of more than 1000 being used (presumably on a very large submissive).

**Other body parts.** The *earlobes* are often the third choice, after the nipples and genitals. They cause little interference and submissives usually tolerate them well for brief periods. It's interesting to perform oral sex while wearing them.

Clamping the *ear's cartilage* is very painful. A clamp placed here is significantly more painful than a clamp placed on the earlobe. Best used only with masochists. Try this on yourself.

The *eyebrows* are intense, but I feel nervous about having clamps this close to the eyes.

Obviously, it's dangerous to clamp the *nose* shut, but a clamp applied to the septum, or one to each side of the nose, can be interesting.

Having a whole lot of clamps on my skin is about the only thing that'll make me shut up during a scene.

The *lips* are a very sensitive place to which you can attach many clamps. Five can usually be applied to either the upper or lower lip. Sometimes a submissive can be "gagged" by clamping their upper and lower lips together. Obviously, if the lips are gagged this way, the mouth can't be used for much. Also, because they have a rich blood supply, lips tend to bruise. Be careful to avoid leaving "clamp hickeys."

The *tongue* offers an interesting, intense sensation. Obviously puts the mouth out of action for much else. Safety note: I have occasionally seen "tongue bondage" in which a line is attached to something clamped onto the tongue or the line is tied to the tongue itself. In one photo set I saw in an SM magazine, a young woman was placed in a standing position with her hands tied behind her back and her tongue tied to an overhead eye-bolt. Obviously, this is wildly unsafe (and therefore the type of SM imagery we should oppose). If that woman had tripped or fainted, her tongue could very easily have been ripped out. I wish SM magazines would stop printing photos like that. Such images send an inaccurate, damaging message of what SM involves.

Clamps can be easily applied to folds of skin on the submissive's *neck*. These are usually tolerated well and interfere little. It's interesting to perform oral sex with clamps attached to your neck. Keep in mind that the neck's skin is usually visible while wearing ordinary street clothing.  Be careful to avoid "clamp hickeys."

Dominants often apply clamps to folds of skin on the *chest and breasts* in addition to the clamps they apply to the submissive's nipples.  Clamps here are not exceptionally painful and are usually well-tolerated.  Sometimes these clamps are placed in a line that "marches" across the nipples – a hot sight.

*Backs, arms, stomachs* and *legs* offer a lot of "real estate" for clamps.  The scenes I've mentioned with hundreds of clamps usually include long, closely spaced rows of clothespins in these areas.  Inner thighs, underarms and lower bellies are particularly sensitive.

The *belly button* is a playful spot to clamp.  Not particularly painful; usually well-tolerated.  Many submissives can handle one or two clamps here.

A fold of skin on the *buttocks,* just beside the perineum and behind the anus, can often accept one or two clamps on each side.  The buttocks themselves accept clamps easily and are not terribly painful.

**Summary**.  Clamps offer a highly controllable, highly versatile means of exploring erotic pain.  Provided you understand their limits and dangers as well as you understand their potential, they offer a lot.

Postscript: While my New York City days are decades behind me, I'm told that "New York SM" is supposedly more rigid and builds in intensity faster than the purportedly more mellow "California SM."  While the SM New Yorkers I've met out here have denied it, I've heard that "they" have a saying in New York about "us" out here in California:  "Well, they *do* use nipple clamps out there in California, but they hang little crystals from the ends of them."

# Lubricants: Advantages, Disadvantages, and Dangers

Lubricants, creams, gels, and so forth are excellent adjuncts to SM erotic play. In addition to adding (often very considerably) to the pleasure of those involved, lubricants can be used to help prevent pregnancy, relieve vaginal dryness, and reduce the spread of sexually trans- mitted diseases. Menthol-containing lubricants cause a distinctly "hot" sensation when applied to the genitals, so some people use them for erotic play. I've discussed such lubricants in the "Erotic Torture" section.

Almost all lubricants can be grouped into one of two basic categories: oil-based and water-based. Oil- based lubricants generally stay slippery considerably longer than water-based lubricants. Unfortunately, these days they have a major, life-threatening property: oil- based lubricants rapidly dissolve latex. Therefore, any latex product that gets smeared with an oil-based lubri- cant will fall apart much sooner than it otherwise would.

**If you are in a situation where you need to use a latex condom or other latex protective device, keep oil-based lubricants away from it.**

*Come over here and do the most submissive thing you can think of.*

The single most important thing you need to know about a lubricant is whether it is water-based or oil-based. If you are not 100% sure, you would be very wise to assume that it's oil-based and treat it accordingly.

The next most important thing you need to know about a lubricant is whether or not it contains nonoxynol-9. Some people believe that only water- based lubricants contain nonoxynol-9 and, therefore, believe that if they buy a lubricant containing nonoxynol-9 they are automatically buying a water- based lubricant. This is simply not true. While most oil-based lubricants do not contain nonoxynol-9, I know of at least two different brands that do. Water-based lubricants usually plainly state that fact. Read the label carefully.

If you can, find out what percentage of nonoxynol-9 is present. Ordinary lubricants typically contain about 1% (and usually don't state the percentage on the label). Contraceptive gels tend to run 2% or a bit higher.

I have long believed that nonoxynol-9 should be used more widely than it is now. While some people are sensitive to it, most can use it with no problems, and it contributes a lot toward helping to fight unplanned pregnancy and many sexually transmitted diseases.

Water-based lubes can be used with condoms and other devices, but they tend to dry out and get "sticky" much more quickly than oil-based lubes. Therefore, smart players keep a small supply of water close by. This can either be something like a "finger bowl" or a separate bottle just for holding water. Sometimes the lubricant-containing bottle and the water-containing bottle are glued or taped together so one doesn't get quite so easily "lost." One caution: When you need to add water, add only a few drops. You can, for all practical purposes, wash the lubricant (and its benefits) away if you add too much water. Every now and then add more lubricant instead of adding more water.

Supplemental thought: Your saliva can also be used to "help loosen up" the lubricant, and contact with saliva reduces the infectivity of the AIDS virus. Welcome this extra protection, but definitely don't rely on it. Another supplemental thought: A physician told me some evidence exists that the use of any lubricant might (repeat, might) reduce the possibility of passing on a sexually transmitted disease. The thinking is that, because lubricants reduce the amount of "wear and tear" on the body parts involved, fewer breaks in the skin get created, and thus the probability of at least some forms of disease transmission is reduced. (Other bugs, of course, go right through intact skin with no problem at all.) As with the information about saliva noted above, welcome this extra protection, but absolutely do not rely on it.

A visit to your local drugstore, adult bookstore, or erotic boutique will help acquaint you with, among others, such names as Liquid Silk, Astroglide, Probe, Slippery Stuff, KY Jelly, PrePair, ForPlay, and Wet. (You should also look over their selection of condoms, contraceptive gels, spermicidal supposi-tories, and so forth.)

Your local drugstore may also have some additional, unexpected treasures. A liquefying cleanser called Albolene has enjoyed a semi-under-ground following for years as an excellent lubricant for erotic play, particularly masturbation. At some sex parties, you get a discount on your admission fee if you bring a jar – a sort of BYOA situation. One caution: Albolene is oil-based and doesn't contain nonoxynol-9, so consider carefully when to use it .

Other "non-traditional" lubricants include Johnson's Baby Magic Lotion, Crisco, coconut oil (one of my favorites), vegetable oil, and petroleum jelly. These all share Albolene's limits.

A carefully chosen lubricant can add considerable safety and pleasure to your erotic play. Make sure you clearly understand the advantages and disadvantages of each type.

# Erotic "Torture"

Yeah, I know. Even to me this chapter's title looks a little threatening. Let's define the term. I define erotic torture as any type of erotic pain given by non-flagellation means. I've already covered clamps. In this chapter I'll cover other common means of "inflicting" erotic pain.

## Using Your Hands and Mouth

Your hands are two of your most skillful and versatile "torture" instruments. Your hands can pinch, squeeze, poke, spank, pull, slap, and caress. Your fingernails can do everything from lightly stroke to deeply rake – even to the point of drawing blood and leaving scars. Your ability to give your submissive a range of sensations ranging from exquisite to agonizing by using just your hands says volumes about your authority and competence as a dominant.

If this is torture, lead me to it!

There's also your mouth. Your lips, tongue, and teeth are some of your most potent torture/pleasure instruments. Again, the range and intensity of sensations you can cause your submissive to feel by using only your mouth can be overpowering. One caution: A human bite that breaks the skin is much more likely than an ordinary wound to cause a serious infection, so avoid doing that when you bite.

Safety note: If the skin is broken anyway, immediately and vigorously clean the wound. Use soap and water followed by a disinfectant containing provodone-iodine such as Betadine. If it's a large or deep wound, immediately consult an SM-positive physician. If it's not large or deep, clean it twice a day and keep a close eye on it for a developing infection. If it gets infected, consult the physician. If you're worried about scarring, consult the physician. (Remember that mild supplements of zinc and Vitamin C will help wounds heal faster.) A human bite that breaks the skin is one of the worst types of wounds there is. Treat them with the seriousness they deserve.

The feedback you get from using your hands and mouth is invaluable. This form of play is highly intimate, and the skills you develop with this form of play will serve you well in the future. I routinely tell novice dominants: "If you want to get good at using whips, clamps, and other equipment, then first get good at using your hands and mouth."

## Hot/Cold Play

In addition to sensors for light touch, heavy touch, and pain, the skin contains sensors for heat and cold. Naturally, we perverts find ways to incorporate these sensors into our play.

**Candle wax.** Holding a burning candle over someone so the hot wax drips onto them is a classic SM technique. It's fairly popular and most people play with it somewhat. However, it does leave a messy residue of wax all over the place, and that can be bothersome.

Also, the open flame is a slight but significant fire hazard. Be careful with it, and clear your surroundings of anything easily flammable. Of course, you'll have a fire extinguisher and quick-release gear immediately available. (I know of a session involving a heavily bound submissive, a candle flame, and rubbing alcohol that ended in disaster. Both the dominant and the submissive were very seriously burned.)

Have you got any extra Ben Gay that I could use?

Major point: Candle wax cools rapidly as it falls from the flame onto the submissive's body. This allows you to regulate the wax's temperature by controlling the height of the candle above the submissive's body. As always, try it on yourself. The inside of your forearm is a good spot to check how hot something feels.

Safety note: Avoid beeswax candles, colored candles, and "utility" candles made with large amounts of plastic. These types of candles have a high melting temperature and could burn. Use ordinary white paraffin candles.

The chest, breasts, nipples, and abdomen are excellent wax targets. Avoid the neck, face, and head. Be careful around the genitals. Among other things, the wax is hard to remove from pubic hair.

**Menthol play.** *Note: The essay on menthol play is closely patterned after a similar essay I wrote for my book "Tricks: More than 125 Ways to make Good Sex Better."* Menthol, when applied to the skin, creates intense sensations. These sensations are usually felt either as heat or as "chilled heat." Menthol-containing products can be used to spice up fellatio (cough drops) or as a male masturbation lubricant (chest rubs and arthritis creams). Their labels will tell you whether or not they contain menthol.

Please note: Chest rubs and arthritis creams are oil-based, and thus should be avoided in situations that require condoms.

Chest rubs and arthritis creams are used almost exclusively to make male masturbation more intense. They are not designed, intended, or recommended for internal use, so please don't combine them with fellatio, cunnilingus, vaginal intercourse, or anal intercourse. Don't use them to lubricate a vibrator or dildo prior to insertion. I have heard of some people trying to use them for those activities, but unless they used *extremely* small quantities, such usage was more painful than they could stand. These substances can also upset the natural biological balance of such areas.

A small amount of menthol can, in some cases, be applied to the clitoris to make female masturbation more intense, but please be very careful. Remember, it's not intended for internal use, and it feels much "hotter" on mucous membranes. Ladies, I suggest you try this by yourself before involving another person.

Menthol-containing cough drops might be used during cunnilingus, but please note the warnings above very carefully.

Menthol must be used cautiously. If other forms of erotic "torture" are like spices, menthol qualifies as red hot pepper. Using a *very* small amount may spice your play up nicely. Too much, and that quantity is very easy to reach, can cause genuine pain, even agony.

> I love to be paddled really hard on a well-iced bottom.

Start slowly and with small amounts when using menthol-containing creams. It's often wise to "dilute" it with another lubricant. Never use the extra-strength brand of anything until you've used the regular strength brand successfully several times. I, by the way, once accidentally had a bad experience regarding the difference between an intensely hot, but bearable, amount of Ben Gay cream and an equal amount of Ben Gay gel. (Yeeeooowwwwccchhh!!! Owww! Owww! Owww! Mercy!! Safeword!!)

Menthol may take up to five minutes for the effects of a given "dose" to be fully felt, so take your time about adding more. One dose is usually felt for about 20 minutes, but this can vary considerably from person to person and from product to product. Menthol applied to the scrotum is usually felt sooner and feels hotter than menthol applied to the penis.

Caution: It's easy to add more, but it's very difficult to remove what you've already applied.

Another caution: If you use a menthol-containing cream to masturbate a man, a considerable amount will get on your hand as well as his cock. Because the skin of your hand is much thicker than the skin of his penis, it may take considerable time for you to feel this. "Burning Hands Syndrome" can develop an hour or more after the session. You might therefore wear latex or vinyl gloves when playing with this stuff, particularly the extra-strength brands.

Yet another caution: Be careful about combining menthol with any abrasion. Skin that has been scraped, such as by fingernails or a whipping, will be considerably less able to tolerate menthol. An amount of menthol that intact skin tolerates well can easily be too much for abraded skin to handle.

If you have a "menthol overdose," you can usually wash it off by using cold running water and lots of soap. Applying large amounts of shampoo and then washing it off works especially well. Very liberal amounts of the astringent called Witch Hazel also wash it off. (Your drugstore carries it.) You can also "cool things down" by rubbing on generous amounts of petroleum jelly (be sure you don't use a chest rub) or an oil-based cream. I haven't personally tested it, but I'm told that cold cream works well.

Don't combine menthol play with bondage until you, your partner, and the substance in question are very well acquainted. A menthol overdose is especially likely to occur the first one or two times you use it with a new partner. If they get overdosed and need to run to the shower, they'll need to be able to run there *now*. They can suffer terribly during the time it would take you to untie them.

It's not at all a bad idea to create a menthol overdose deliberately in order to test these various cool-down methods. That way, in an actual "emergency," you'll have a clearer idea of what works (and what doesn't). Understand that different people may respond better to different cooling methods.

I don't recommend using menthol with a new partner unless they (and you) are already highly experienced in its use. It's too easy for things to go wrong and perhaps harm your budding relationship. Use this only for self-play or with someone you already know well. It would be a very good idea to use a particular lubricant on yourself several times before you ask a partner to use it on you.

Because menthol "burns" for about 20 minutes after being applied (some brands burn longer), and because this feeling may be seriously unpleasant if no longer accompanied by sexual arousal, it's both wise and compassionate to wait for its sensations to fade to a very low level before bringing a man to orgasm.

Final comment: Menthol leaves a distinct, noticeable smell in the air. It's a good idea to use it only in well-ventilated areas if the lingering smell might be a problem.

As you can see, menthol usage is one of the more serious aspects of SM play. Use it properly and you can add an enormous amount of intensity and pleasure to your lovemaking. Just understand that it's not a toy. Use menthol improperly and you'll regret it.

**Toothpaste.** Some dominants use "spicy," "cinnamon," or "minty" brands of toothpaste while performing fellatio and/or masturbating their submissive to create a wonderful/agonizing sensation.

This is done by squeezing about one-quarter inch of paste or gel onto a finger. Gels will last longer and not dry out as fast. Use sparingly at first. My sources tell me that if you use too much during fellatio you'll make your eyes and nose water. (I'm also told that Close Up gel is the hottest. Crest is reportedly milder.) Apply the finger to the tip of your tongue, then apply your tongue to the penis. Concentrate on applying most of the paste or gel to the head of the penis. It will dissolve and cover the rest.

Pastes or gels can also be combined with a lubricant for masturbation games. If you want to retain "the fellatio option," remember to mix the paste or gel only with a lubricant that you feel good about putting in your mouth.

Are you sure you know how to use that thing?

**Hair blowers.** The hot jet of air produced by an ordinary hair blower is sometimes fun to play with. Aimed at the breasts or genitals, it causes an intense burning sensation with little danger of actual damage. (Of course, like anything else, it can be overdone.)

Hair blowers aren't used very much because they have some disadvantages: (1) They're noisy. (2) They tend to dry out lubricants. (3) They run on AC current, and thus pose a small but definite shock hazard. (As of this writing, I have heard of no mishaps.) Still, some people like them.

**Ice cubes.** Cheap, readily available, and unlikely to cause significant damage, ice cubes are a popular SM toy. The cube can be touched to the skin – genitals and nipples being, of course, favorite targets – or trailed along the skin. Some people drip candle wax and trail it with an ice cube; that's intense! You can also pop an ice cube into your mouth while you perform oral sex. Finally, you can insert a well-rounded ice cube into the submissive's vagina or anus. This usually gets the attention of even a jaded masochist; they emit that wonderful-sounding gasp. Don't put in too many, though. You don't want to cause frostbite.

By the way, get out the first aid book you of course have on hand and have studied thoroughly. The treatment of frostbite runs counter to many peoples' ideas about what should be done. Should you rub frostbitten tissue to help restore circulation? Look it up.

Another caution: Sudden exposure to large amounts of cold can cause a dangerous slowing of the heartbeat, and very occasionally even cardiac arrest, in some people. Build slowly when playing with ice, and be extra-cautious if the person has a history of heart disease.

Ice cubes are made of frozen water. Frozen water melts. Keep a towel handy, and be careful about slipping on a wet surface and with electrical devices.

## Conventional Sex Toys _____

*For more information and ideas on how to use conventional sex toys, please refer to my book "Sex Toy Tricks: More than 125 Ways to Accessorize Good Sex."*

It's possible to suck cock in a very dominant manner.

**Vibrators.** Vibrators can add extra spice. In addition to their standard stimulation applications, vibrators can be touched to clamps to provide an interesting sensation.

Vibrators have become very sophisticated. Now they come with simultaneous vaginal and clitoral stimulators, which can be operated at different speeds.

A rather large, wand-shaped vibrator is popular with many women. It cannot be inserted into the vagina, but is excellent for clitoral stimulation. You should have at least one vibrator.

**Ben wa balls.** Ben wa balls are two balls inserted into the vagina. As they rub against each other, they sexually stimulate the woman. Some are made of metal, some of plastic.

Ben wa balls can be some submissive women's best friends, allowing them to feel pleasure while they go about their duties of pleasing and serving their dominant. Other women get little sensation from ben wa balls (although even these women may enjoy them in combination with a vibrator).

Just make sure one doesn't fall out at an inopportune moment. Wear panties, or ropes.

**Dildoes.** These artificial penises never come too quickly or lose their erection at the wrong moment. They come in all sizes – from dainty to gigantic. Most are about the size of the average erect penis.

Many dominant women like using dildoes. They especially find something very satisfying about wearing the dildo in a harness, and fucking their submissive partner in the ass.

## Other Forms of Sensation

**Abrasion play.** Fine grade sandpaper, emery boards, nail files, exfoliating scrubbers, fingernails, and similar items can be lightly scratched across tender places on the submissive's body. Alternated with pleasure, these feelings can be intense. Abraded areas of the body become quite tender, and light, mild touches become more keenly felt.

While you have been warned to avoid combining menthol play with abrasion, one *possible* use of the combination is nipple play. Lightly abrade the submissive's nipples and apply a tiny bit of a menthol-containing cream. The effect can be intense. This technique might be a workable substitute for submissives who can't tolerate clamps on their nipples.

We're deliberately playing with the human nervous system here.

You can try this by abrading both nipples, then applying the menthol to *one* of them and see how that goes. Wait about five minutes before applying menthol to the other nipple.

Be careful with abrasion. Not too much. Otherwise even pleasant sensations will feel painful. Don't be that mean. Avoid leaving grit in the area. Try this on yourself.

**Semi-piercing.** Some people like to play with sharp, piercing sensations without actually breaking the skin. They may poke their submissive's skin with sharp-pointed toothpicks or wooden skewers. This can be an intense, painful sensation that many masochists find quite erotic.

Because the sensation can be highly localized, the nipples, clitoris, and head of the penis are favorite targets. The sensation can be administered in a series of jabs or in a single long motion. It can be done alone, or combined with pleasurable sensations. Be careful not to break the skin. A small wooden fragment could remain, creating an infection.

Another semi-piercing toy that has a lot of potential but must be used *very* carefully is a pair of egg scissors. These are used to scoop the top off soft-boiled eggs so you can eat the contents with a spoon. You can buy these in many supermarkets or variety stores. They consist of a plastic or metal ring with a scissors-like handle protruding from the side. The interior diameter of this ring is a little over an inch. When you squeeze the handles together, many triangle-like spikes move toward the interior of the ring.

This device may not be much of a "threat" to a limp cock (and it's probably best to put this on while the cock is in that state), but it can be a terror around an erect one. To liven things up even further, put two on about an inch or so apart, tighten them slightly, and twist them in opposite directions.

This can be a heavy pain toy and has the potential to cause serious injury. Use it with the respect it deserves.

A final "sharp" toy is a medical device called a Wurtenburg wheel or "neuro wheel." This consists of a metal handle with a wheel at the end, ringed with very sharp points. By rolling it across the skin like a pizza cutter, the dominant creates a series of sharp piercing sensations in a line. Depending on the sensitivity of the area and the force applied to the wheel, this ranges from tickly to agonizing. These can break skin, so start gently and build carefully.

I like to be forced to come.

**"Play piercing."** Some players enjoy placing needles (typically disposable hypodermic needles or acupuncture needles) under the skin and back out again, not to insert jewelry but simply for the sensation. While this is a form of play that has many devotees, it's too risky and requires too much skill to describe in this book. If play piercing interests you, I strongly suggest you learn how from a professional piercer, or from a workshop on the topic. (Check the "Related Practices" section of this book under "Piercing, Cutting, and Branding" for more information.) Needless to say, scrupulous hygiene, and careful attention to disposal of needles, is essential.

**Suction cups.** This may sound a bit strange at first (as if most of the rest of this book doesn't!), but many players have excellent results using the suction cups found in snake bite kits. These can work well on nipples, and can also be used on other sensitive body parts. Breast pumps are another suction device that offers interesting possibilities.

The partial vacuum inside the cups causes the tissue to expand, sometimes up to double its normal size. The possibilities offered by such "enlarged" tissue are, shall we say, interesting.

**Electricity play.** Many SM folks find the idea of playing with electricity tremendously appealing. Its long history as a technique for real-world interrogation, torture, and even execution has implanted electricity deeply into many of our fantasies. The sensations involved are unique, and very compelling for many masochists.

Many different types of electricity toys are available; they deliver sensations which range from mild shocks comparable to touching a doorknob after walking across a wool carpet, through extremely intense pain and muscle spasm. Special units designed for electricity play, with attachments for genital and anal use, are available. Other items designed for medical and other real-world uses, including violet wands, TENS units, Relaxacisors, electric train transformers, electric dog collars, and even cattle prods are also sometimes used in electricity play.

Electricity comes in two basic forms, AC (alternating current) and DC (direct current). AC is the kind that comes out of your wall sockets (assuming you live in the U.S.). Unless you have special training or expertise in electricity, I strongly recommend that you avoid playing with toys that plug into house current, including electric train transformers and Relaxacisors. (Violet wands are an exception, as I will discuss later.)

DC current usually comes from batteries. Some DC current is extremely strong – cattle prods and stun guns are examples. While it's not unheard-of to use these for SM, the sensations produced by these items are far too intense for most players (although these items may vary widely in their intensity).

Other DC toys are less intense. Specially designed electricity play units, TENS units, and electric dog collars are sometimes used for SM play, and are basically safe if you follow certain guidelines.

Keep in mind that the impulses which tell the heart when to beat are electrical in nature. Most of the guidelines for minimizing the risk of electricity play are designed to avoid "confusing" the heart's impulses. Thus, a major guideline is to be *very* careful about electricity play with people who have any history of heart disease. I'd especially avoid doing electricity play *of any type* with someone who has a cardiac pacemaker.

Another guideline is "no electricity play above the waist." This rule is useful but a bit simplistic. Among other things, it implies that play below the waist is completely safe, which it isn't. (Certainly, however, the practice of hooking one electrode to a nipple and the second electrode to the other nipple and running current between them should be mentioned only to be condemned.) Keep in mind that excessive or lengthy electricity play *anywhere* on the body can cause burns and/or bloodclots in that area; if you want to spend a long time playing with electricity, move the area of play from one body part to another, and don't go back to playing with an area that's been extensively shocked for at least a couple of days.

An electrical current passing through a muscle will cause that muscle to contract. A strong current may cause a violent spasm and result in muscle strains, sprains, and occasionally even fractures, particularly if the affected part is in bondage. Muscle spasms may also cause "post-whipping flu," which is discussed later in the "General Safety Precautions" chapter.

Electricity can cause cardiac arrest. Most people don't know that the amount of current necessary to stop the heart can be very small – less than one amp. If you play with electricity at all, you must be prepared to deal with a cardiac arrest. This means being trained in CPR, and perhaps even having advanced life support equipment handy.

Electricity does not do what you think it is doing. Electricity does what it does, and it's your job to figure out what that is. Study it well before trying it. Consult with experienced players; however, keep in mind that some such players are genuine experts, and others don't really know that much more than you do (their "expertise" often boils down to "Well, I haven't killed anybody yet").

*Slow masturbation turns a man's mind to mush. It's big fun.*

The violet wand, originally created as a hair restoration device, is an exception to many of the guidelines for electricity play. It puts out a blue-violet "spark" of electricity which is especially dramatic in a darkened room. Devotees describe its sensation as feeling like "being walked on by kittens with their claws out." Unlike conventional electrical toys, which can send a current of electricity into the body's muscles and organs, the electricity put out by a violet wand stays on the skin's surface. Thus, it is the only electricity toy which most players feel is safe for above-the-waist use. Keep it away from the eyes, and use extra caution while playing near breaks in the skin, piercings, and mucous membranes. (The regular cautions about electricity play with people who have heart disease, and especially pacemakers, apply to violet wands as well.) Be aware that prolonged use on skin may leave a slight-to-moderate sunburn-like effect. Also be aware that violet wands generate ozone, which is somewhat toxic; make sure that your play space is well ventilated.

**Blade play.** Given their long real-world history as implements of terror, torture, and even murder, it is small wonder that many SM people are sensually attuned to knifeplay. Many of us find something extremely erotic in the sight of a gleaming steel blade pressed against tender skin. Knives and other edged implements offer a tremendous spectrum of physical sensations and emotional experiences, often very powerful.

A wide variety of knives and blades come into play in SM. Knives themselves vary from foot-long bowie knives to small penknives. Knives can be kept razor-sharp, or left a bit dull for safety (there's no rule saying you have to reveal the sharpness of your blade to your submissive, though!). They can be rigid or they can fold. The blade itself may be straight or curved, serrated or plain. Knife enthusiasts may own several knives for different types of scenes.

In addition to knives, scene play may include razors (both safety and straight-edged), scissors, swords, hatchets, scalpels, and even machetes.

All blades have one thing in common: they are *scary*. Even the tamest little knife has the potential to maim or kill. I am something of a fan of knife play, particularly when I bottom, and I'll tell you that a woman sitting between your legs, smiling and toying with a sharp knife, is a real attention-getter!

Knife play is, obviously, emotionally very intense. It also carries a far higher degree of physical risk than many other kinds of SM play. I mean, come on, we're talking about a situation in which one person strips another one naked, ties them securely, and then takes out a *knife*, for heaven's sake, and begins to menace them with it. I hope it goes without saying that knife play should be very carefully negotiated, and that you should do it only with partners who you know well and trust implicitly.

*If you want to get me off, you're going to have to hurt me.*

So what kinds of things can you do with a knife or other blade? Well, let's talk first about what you're *not* going to do. You're not going to actually lacerate the skin (in other words, sutures will not be needed afterwards). You're not going to cause actual puncture wounds. You're not going to intentionally cause any kind of serious damage.

However, that still leaves lots of room for exploration with your knife. The mere sight of it on your belt can add to your authority and presence as a dominant. Simply holding it in your hand while you give your submissive orders tends to give those orders a certain extra weight. If it's a folding knife, the decisive "click" it makes as it snaps open will definitely capture your submissive's attention. If you're feeling especially fiendish, tie them up and make them watch while you sharpen it.

Simply feeling a knife's edge on their throat or genitals is a powerful erotic experience for many submissives. You can use your knife to cut off their clothes (many people who enjoy having their clothes cut off buy disposable outfits at thrift stores) or their bondage. (Also please note that a carefully chosen knife can also be a good backup for your paramedic scissors if you need to release a submissive quickly.) Using your knife to cut off a bit of their pubic hair can be hot. Many people enjoy following up a hot-wax scene by using the edge of a knife to scrape the cooled wax off the submissive's skin.

When it comes to using a knife on skin, there are four basic techniques; I call them poking, scratching, gliding and shaving. Poking is simple: simply press the tip of the knife lightly into the skin, then either release it or hold it there for a while, perhaps twisting it a bit. To scratch the skin, I recommend that you use the unsharpened back of the knife's tip. To glide, hold the blade perpendicular to the skin and gently draw the length of the blade along the skin, using no more pressure than the weight of the knife itself. To shave, place the blade at a shallow angle to the skin and perpendicular to the direction you're heading, and draw it along the skin. You can do this in a "forehand" motion that, if the knife is sharp enough, will actually shave hairs like a razor, or you can use a "backhand" motion that feels scary but sensuous. Use caution when drawing a knife over blood vessels that are clearly visible under the skin. Placing the tip of your index finger just a fraction of an inch behind the tip of the knife increases your control.

This woman is an erotic terrorist.

Scratches may not show at all at first, or may show as a white mark which may later fade to red. If you use a very sharp knife, a glide may cause little to no sensation, and yet leave an impressive line. Indeed, small droplets of blood may appear a few minutes later. Either of these kinds of play may leave a very noticeable mark, particularly if the submissive is fair-skinned or has dry skin. Such marks often last longer than you might think, and in the case of some people, especially older people, may even be permanent. (They do tend to fade with time.) So be careful not to leave them anywhere they won't be welcome; be particularly careful regarding the face, neck, and hands.

In relative order of risk: Backhand shaving feels quite sensuous, is almost risk-free, and rarely leaves marks. Poking can be fairly painful but is relatively safe, and is unlikely to mark. Scratching can feel intense and is not particularly risky, but the scratches may take quite a while to fade. Forehand shaving is not particularly painful if done properly, but an error in the angle or pressure of the blade can cut. Gliding can be physically and emotionally intense, can be risky if you put too much pressure on the blade, and is fairly likely to mark.

Some advanced practitioners enjoy doing actual cutting, often of a decorative sort. (Many lesbian SM players are particularly fond of this activity.) Most often, this is done with a disposable scalpel. Cuttings are done very shallowly, typically no deeper than a cat scratch. These cuttings usually (not always) heal without a scar. Decorative cutting is an activity best learned directly from an experienced practitioner, so I'm not going to describe it in detail here. If it interests you, you can learn more from an expert (hint: many professional piercers and tattooists are also knowledgeable about cutting, or can refer you to someone who is).

Shaving pubic or head hair can be an intense act of domination. Most people who play with shaving use electric clippers and/or a safety razor. A few highly skilled players practice with an old-fashioned straight razor until they can use it safely on skin. (The rule is "don't shave a person until you can shave a balloon without popping it.")

The main safety warning with blades of any kind is to *stay alert and focused.* A slip of the knife can cause anything from a painful cut to a serious wound. I strongly recommend avoiding blade play unless you're feeling one hundred percent alert, awake, healthy, and sober. Get very familiar with the knife you're using before you bring it near anybody else's skin; one female dominant I know, an excellent cook, likes to use her kitchen knives for SM play because she already understands their balance and sharpness so well.

What does a piercing feel like?

I recommend that if you use a folding knife like a penknife or switchblade, it should be of a type that locks into its open position. Also, be sure you can open and close it smoothly, even if your hands are slippery with sweat or lube. (Stay especially alert when you are opening and closing the knife.) If you acquire a new knife, you should probably spend some time practicing with it on inanimate objects like fruit or meat, and on your own skin, before you use it on anyone else.

Anytime you are holding your knife above your submissive, you're in a particularly high-risk situation. If the knife falls, it will fall on them. It's therefore particularly important to stay focused when using a knife in this position. Also, when you're not actually applying the knife to the submissive's skin, get in the habit of holding it point-up, blade-up, or sideways.

If you play with knives, it is essential that your first-aid kit contain wound-management materials. (See the "SM Starter Kit" chapter for details.) If a cut gapes open widely, shows muscle or bone, or is on the hand, foot or face, it should be looked at by a physician to see if it requires stitches. Keep in mind that physicians may be legally required to report knife wounds to the police, so you may want to consider exactly how much you want to tell the doctor about how the cut was acquired. (See the "General Safety Considerations" chapter for more information on this topic.)

Be aware that most states have strict rules concerning the legality of carrying knives on your person or in your car while in public. Some knives are illegal to possess at all. Check the laws in your area to find out whether you're risking arrest on felony charges of possession of a deadly weapon. ("Folk wisdom" on this point is often erroneous – check for yourself.)

## *Masturbation Games*

The only way I like having a guy eat my pussy is if I know he hates eating pussy.

Once you have your submissive helpless, sexually "tormenting" them often just simply seems like the right thing to do. That being so, I have included here, in somewhat random order, several masturbation (and other) techniques from my books "Tricks: More than 125 Ways to Make Good Sex Better" and "Tricks 2: *Another* 125 Ways to Make Good Sex Better. Those books, by the way, contain more than 100 tricks each besides the ones listed here. See the back of this book for ordering information.

### Hooker's Trick #1
Most men like to watch. Therefore, when asked to give head, many hookers position themselves so their customer can see his cock entering their mouth.

Footnote: If you feel like teasing him, position yourself so he *can't* see his cock entering your mouth.

### Brush Strokes
It's entirely true that most women like to have their genitals caressed. However, another spot very close by feels almost as good. Have her spread her legs (this works well if she's on her back) and, using your fingertips, lightly stroke the upper insides of her thighs, particularly the rear portions. This stroking can be done in a back and forth or circular motion, or you can slowly trace your way toward her vagina. You can also use your tongue effectively this way. (Rumor has it that many men also find the touch of fingertips or a tongue here pleasant.)

232

### Pin The Skin

Grasp the erect penis with your thumb and forefinger just below its tip. (If you are right-handed, this would probably work best if you used your left hand.) Keep your grasp slightly firm, and slide your hand down the shaft of the penis to its base. You should now have his penis in your hand with its skin pulled somewhat tight over it. You may see its head slightly but noticeably bulge when you pull the skin down.

Normally, when a man masturbates, gets his cock sucked, or has intercourse, this skin slides. Pinning the skin in place and then stimulating his penis produces a noticeably more intense, usually highly pleasurable, sensation. One caution: Stimulation can feel rough and unpleasant if the penis is dry, so use enough lubricant to keep things slippery, especially during masturbation.

### Tap Dancing

For this trick, the woman lies on her back with her legs comfortably spread and you lie on your side beside her, usually propped up on one elbow. Place the palm of your hand on her mons (the mound where most of her pubic hair is), and rest your fingers lightly on her vaginal lips. Rest your thumb on her opposite thigh.

Lightly but firmly press your palm onto her mons and begin to move your hand in a *tiny* circular motion. Your palm should not slide too much over her skin during this process. Instead, her skin should move underneath it. Repeat this process until you have done ten circles.

You then raise your fingers and lightly tap her vaginal lips about once a second until you have given her ten taps. Please note that these are light taps, not spanks. They shouldn't hurt.

After giving the taps, rest your hand for five to ten seconds. Then repeat the circles, then repeat the taps, then rest again, then repeat the circles...

The woman who eagerly told me about this technique swore that it drove her "absolutely bonkers."

### Climbing the Mountain

This masturbation game can drive a man absolutely nuts. It's usually done with him lying on his back. Sit or kneel either beside him or between his legs. Take his penis in one hand and gently, sensuously caress it for about ten seconds, then give it one quick up-and-down stoke. Repeat the sensuous caressing for about ten seconds – perhaps doing slow up-and-down strokes, perhaps doing other movements that feel good – and then give his penis two

233

quick up-and-down strokes. Repeat the sensual caressing, then give three quick strokes. Then more caressing, followed by four quick strokes. Then more caressing, and five strokes. You get the idea.

Continue to "climb the mountain" as long as you can. One tip: The man may reach a point where his orgasm is becoming inevitable, and slow caressing might spoil it. He is therefore allowed to say (assuming he can still coherently speak) "keep going" *one time*, after which you give him only rapid strokes until he comes. He should climax within about one minute. (If he doesn't, he gets punished.)

### Push Here to Start

After she is aroused, sit between her legs. Gently insert one finger deeply into her vagina and, when she's ready, insert a second. Then take your thumb and place it against her anus. Don't insert it. Instead, gently press there while you move your fingers. My highly reliable source tells me that, while many women are turned off by the idea of having anything inserted into their anus, they really like feeling this kind of pressure there.

Holding that position

was torture.

### Flat Top

Hold the shaft of his penis in one hand so it points almost straight away from his body. Stiffen the palm and fingers of your other (very well lubricated) hand and place your palm on the head of his penis. Lightly but firmly rub your palm back and forth, side to side, in clockwise circles, and in counter-clockwise circles. You can also tilt your hand front and rear or side to side. This technique involves a lot of stimulation directly on one of the most sensitive parts of a man's body, so make sure the stimulation doesn't get so intense that they become unpleasant for him – unless you intend that. Watching his face can give you clues.

### "Show Me How You Like It"

Let's say you are masturbating your partner and just aren't getting anywhere. Instead of continuing until both of you are exhausted and sore, get some coaching. Ask your partner to "show me how you like it" and watch their stroking pattern. The woman who taught me this trick was a bisexual sex worker who has had many, many partners of both sexes. She went on to remark, "Men are more standard; women are more individualistic."

234

### Thumb Enchanted Evening

Kneel behind your lover while she is on her hands and knees facing away from you (dog-style position). Use your thumb to pleasure the inside of her vagina while the side of your index finger caresses her ditoris.

### Make a Tent

If you're in bed and looking for a simple but effective way to spice up masturbating a penis, simply drape the sheet over it while you stroke. Just remember that you may need a clean sheet in the *very* near future.

### A Hair-Raising Trick

Grasp your lover's pubic hair in your fist so that the middle joints of yourfingersandtheheelofyourpalmrestontheirpubicmound. Then move your hand up and down, from side to side,and in cirdes. You can also tilt your hand in various directions. The intensity of this movement can be increased until you are actually rocking your partner. Caution: This "rough foreplay" trick may involve mild to moderate amounts of pain. It probably won't work on most people. I recommend you try it only on someone who is already highly aroused. Watch their face and body very carefully to see how they react. Continue only if there's no doubt that they are enjoying it.

I love being bitten.

### Fill 'er Up

Many women report that their orgasms feel more intense and satisfying if there's something in their vagina when they come. Keep this in mind when masturbating a woman or performing cunnilingus.

### Perineum Pinch

One man reports that many different women enjoy having him insert his index finger in their anus and his thumb in their vagina. These are then pinched together, thrust in and out, rocked back and forth, twisted, and so forth.

### Make A Snake

Straighten out your hands as you might do while praying and hold his penis between them. Then rub your hands back and forth, as you might do when handling cooking dough or modeling clay.

This trick has great variability. You can change – among other things – how fast you rub your hands, when you start and stop, whether or not to indude the sensitive head ofhis penis, and both what type and how much (if any) lubricant you use while doing this.

If you're feeling like being extra nice to him, take the head of his penis in your mouth while you apply this stroke to the shaft.

### Up and Down I

This is a trick for masturbating a man that requires a bit of coordination at first, but is very powerful once you get the hang of it.

If you watch a man masturbate, you'll see that he typically uses one hand to stroke his penis in an up and down motion. All well and good.

You can add some variety and spice to this by using one of your hands only for upstrokes and the other only for downstrokes. One way to learn how to do this is to have him lie on his back while you sit or kneel (whatever is comfortable) between his legs. Lightly grasp the base of his penis with your right hand and gently hold its tip with your left. (This trick usually works best when both his penis and your hands are well-lubricated.)

Stroke upwards with your right hand. Use a slow speed at first. When your right hand passes "through" the fingers of your left and off the top of his penis, grasp it with your left hand and slide down its shaft.

While your left hand is sliding down, move your right hand slightly away and back to the base of his penis. After your left hand slides down and away, repeat the upstroke with your right hand. While the upstroke is going on, your left hand returns to the head of the penis so its stroke can be repeated. Both hands move in oval-like shapes, and both move in either a clockwise or counter-clockwise direction. Of course, that direction can be reversed.

### Up and Down II

Lubricate both hands. Grab his cock with both hands at its base and hold it like you would a baseball bat. Keep your lower hand still while you slide your upper hand up and off the head of his penis. As your upper hand slides off, raise your lower hand up and off. Your upper then returns to the base and repeats the journey, and so does the lower. Vary the speed and pressure of your hands as seems right. Experiment. This sensation makes the man feel as if he were constantly withdrawing from a vagina. It can be very powerful.

A simple yet intense variant of this technique is to move your hands one over the other in a downward motion, so it feels to him like he's constantly entering a vagina. Of course, you can also do one stroke for a while, and then the other.

### Sexual Heeling

Place the heel of your hand on her vaginal area with her clitoris at the bottom center of your palm, then vibrate your hand.

### Do the Twist

The lower edge of the tip of a man's penis (the corona) is very sensitive to touch, perhaps the most sensitive part of all. Therefore, tongues, fingers, and other items can be used to good effect here.

One excellent way to make masturbation more intense and pleasurable is to give your hand a light twist as it passes over the corona in the down-to-up direction. To illustrate, make your hand into a not-too-tight fist with your thumb on top of your index finger. Hold this in front of you so your thumb is pointed straight ahead. Now turn your fist so it's facing palm-up and slide your thumb slightly toward the floor. You have just done the basic twist.

Use this twist lightly (too much pressure may spoil it) and you will dramatically improve the quality of the hand jobs you give.

### A Movable Fist

This trick is useful when masturbating or performing oral sex on your partner. Make one hand into a fist and place it just behind their genitals. The thumb side of your fist should point forward and the little finger side of your fist should point to their rear. Thrust upward against their body. The strength of this thrust can be anywhere from very light to very heavy, depending on what works for both of you. The strength can also be varied. As an extra touch, you can vibrate your fist.

I like a top with brains.

### Open Says Me

For many women, the sensation of being "opened" carries a heavy erotic charge. With her lying on her back, try holding her legs together as you run your tongue up and down the seam where her thighs meet, teasing the pubic hair and dipping your tongue in the cleft as though you were trying to reach her clit, but you can't quite. Open her legs after you feel she has suffered enough, but pinch her labia majora shut with your fingers and continue the teasing. Next, spread her majora lips with your hands while you suck the minora lips (together so you keep them shut). Then treat her to the final opening. The tension created can be exquisite and sets the stage for the first full-contact lick of her cunt being almost (note the *almost*) unbearable. Enjoy!

### A-one and A-two and A-three

Try inserting your first two fingers into her, then arch your thumb back "hitch-hiker" style, and thrust in until your thumb rests against her clitoris. You can use a variety of thrusting and twisting motions in this position. You can also vibrate your entire hand.

### The Trident

When masturbating her, try placing your thumb on her clitoris, your first three fingers in her vagina, and your little finger in her anus. Major Safety Note: Make sure your fingernails are short and smooth, especially the nail on your little finger. Test this by scraping your nails against the inside of your opposite forearm. If doing so feels sharp, rough, or jagged, file them down. In a worst case situation, a jagged nail could pierce the intestinal wall, so be careful here. She should never feel any sharp pain in her anus.

### Give Him A Wring

Grip his cock between your two (probably well-lubricated) hands. Your uppermost hand should include the top of his penis in your grip. Twist your hands together until your thumbs are pointing in the same direction, then twist your hands apart until your thumbs are pointing in parallel-but-opposite directions. Repeat this stroke, varying speed and grip strength, as appropriate.

### Close But No Cigar

If your lover has a particular spot that they like to have licked or caressed, try doing so very close to but *not quite* on that spot – except perhaps occasionally. This trick will make them take longer to reach their orgasm, but they will likely have a much stronger, more powerful orgasm when it does finally happen.

As a variant, you can do the "not quite on target" until they get close to coming, then – if you're feeling benevolent – switch to the target itself, thus earning their gratitude.

*Guess what! I had my first female ejaculation yesterday!*

### Ball Pull

While using your hand and/or mouth to pleasure his penis, encircle the top of his scrotum with the thumb and forefinger of your other hand. Squeeze this ring together until it's snug and his testicles are "trapped" below it. Slowly and lightly pull down until the skin of his scrotum is pulled tight over his testicles. Lightly pull just a little more for about five seconds while you continue to pleasure his penis. Then release the pull (keep your hand in place). Closely watch his face, breathing, and body for a reaction. Repeat, varying the strength and the length of the pull while you mix it with large amounts of pleasure.

Men will vary considerably in their reaction to this trick. Some will find it so painful as to be a turn-off and want you to stop. Others will like it and want you to continue. Some will *really* like it and want you to pull down considerably harder. (Don't get carried away. This trick, carried to extremes, could damage him.) Getting feedback from him on how long and how hard he wants the pull to be is an excellent idea.

### TesTickles

Once you have his balls "trapped" as described in "Ball Pull," you can lick, caress, and lightly scratch the tightly stretched skin over them to excellent effect.

### Pin and Win

Normally, when you lick a nipple, it moves back and forth under your tongue, and some sensation is therefore lost. To prevent this, spread your index and middle finger slightly apart and place them on either side. (Don't push down on the chest so much that you cause pain.) Once they're in place, spread them even farther apart. Your lover's nipple may noticeably bulge out as you do this. Now, with the nipple in this exposed and immobile position, apply your tongue and notice the difference.

### Before and After

During his orgasm, and for about one minute afterward, the head of a man's penis is likely to be *much* more sensitive to touch that it is at other times. Therefore, any touching there is felt much more intensely than it is felt at other times – so much so that touching it may be painful. (I know one dominant woman who would, when her submissive male reached orgasm, mercilessly rub and twiddle the head of his cock for exactly that reason.)

Some men like to have the head of their cock rubbed briskly when they come, some like to have it left alone, and some like to have it lightly stroked. Your partner can tell you which he likes. Just remember that strokes which felt wonderful to him before he reached orgasm may feel agonizing during and immediately afterward. What the two of you feel like doing with that information is for you to decide between yourselves.

### Milking It for All It's Worth

When a man comes, the sensations of orgasm mix with the sensations of semen passing through his penis. Interestingly enough, his orgasm usually doesn't pump all the semen out of his penis. Some remains behind. During masturbation or fellatio, a considerate lover can give him a tiny "extra" orgasm by pinching his cock lightly but firmly and "milking" this remaining fluid from his penis after his regular orgasm has finished.

You can even put your finger on the base of his penis and your thumb at the rear top of his scrotum and milk that section forward, then bring your hand forward and milk the penis from base to tip, producing a more complete emptying. (Be sure you don't painfully squeeze his testicles while doing this.)

Your lover can try this technique when he masturbates to find out what method feels best, then teach it to you.

This can also be done by him, and perhaps by you, during vaginal or anal intercourse. Withdraw the penis most (not all) of the way, milk it, then reinsert. Ah, bliss.

### Jilling Off

Many of the male-masturbation strokes described above can be equally well applied – with, of course, the necessary adjustments – to the clitoris.

### A Warm, Wet Touch

Our genitals remain very sensitive after we've had sex. One thing that feels great is to get a washrag moistened with warm, wet water and place it there. I once had a lover that, as I was lying there feeling somewhat exhausted, would get up, prepare the washrag, and place it on me. Oh, bliss! To this day, I have fond memories of her.

Safety note: Make sure the water is comfortably warm, but not too hot! Test it on your elbow before placing it on them.

# Humiliation

Of all SM-related subjects, humiliation is probably the most difficult to understand and agree upon. One problem is that it means different things to different people. Another problem is that the term itself causes such a strong emotional reaction that people have difficulty understanding what is involved. (This, of course, is exactly the same problem faced by SM folks.) Tremendous differences of opinion exist about what activities humiliation involves, and both the personal and interpersonal implications of those activities. Within the SM community, when one person says to another, "I'm into humiliation," the almost universal reply is, "What do you mean by that?"

What does it mean to humiliate somebody? Basically, it means to reduce them in status, usually in an embarrassing or mortifying way. As I said, opinions vary *widely* on what constitutes humiliation. Some common activities which may be considered humiliating include face-slapping, spitting, urinating or defecating on the submissive, giving the submissive an enema, ejaculating on the submissive's face or body, having the submissive lick up their own ejaculate, having the submissive play the role of an animal or an infant, forcing the submissive to wear a revealing or absurd costume, having the submissive urinate or defecate in their clothing, "forced feminization," foot worship, crawling, and groveling. There are, of course, others.

*I'd love to be made to eat out of a dog dish.*

Key point: Humiliation is mainly a state of mind. (As Eleanor Roosevelt said, "Nobody can humiliate you without your consent.") For an experience to be humiliating, the submissive must consider it humiliating. For some submissives, humiliation is a joy and a source of arousal; for others, it's an ordeal that they may or may not be willing – or able – to undergo.

For example, take the relatively commonplace order, "Kneel!" To some submissives, kneeling is an expected, even welcome, aspect of submitting. They have no problem with it and often enjoy doing this. Other submissives find this "simple" act intensely humiliating. Some submissives find wearing a collar humiliating; others consider it a privilege. I've also known submissives who happily undergo experiences that many would consider terribly humiliating, such as drinking urine.

For the dominant, there is a dangerous double edge to humiliation play. First, a dominant must carefully choose the circumstances under which they administer humiliation. Consider the relatively "minor" humiliation of ordering your submissive to kneel by your chair as you sit in it. They might feel delighted to do so if the two of you are at home in private. They would probably be a bit embarrassed (mildly humiliated), but still willing to, at an SM event – especially if other submissives were already on their knees beside their dominants' chairs. They would probably feel terribly humiliated at being told to do so at a gathering of "straight" people. If you were to order them to kneel to you in the presence of their family, they might well refuse. They might even end the relationship over it.

Consider what their straight friends or family members would think of you in such a situation. Remember this well: it can be humiliating to be revealed as someone who enjoys humiliating others.

Please piss in my mouth.

The other major danger for the dominant to keep in mind regarding humiliation scenes is their potential for violence. To be humiliated can be an intensely emotionally painful experience. Humiliation involves some of the most sensitive parts of a person's self-esteem. If you hurt this too intensely, they may attack.

Professional dominants are well aware of this potential for violence. When a man comes to them and says that he wants to be humiliated, they negotiate with him much more carefully and at greater length than they do with their other clients. They know that a humiliation client is much more likely than other submissive males to "turn" on them. Many professional dominants do not do humiliation scenes at all, and make a point of telling their customers that.

One important aspect of humiliation is the number of people involved. A submissive woman may delight in sucking her master's cock in private, yet feel terribly embarrassed about doing so at an SM party, where other people will watch her. People who want to intensify the humiliation try to increase the number of people watching.

The type of people watching is also important. This seems to apply especially to heterosexual, submissive men. Many such men are comfortable acting submissive to a woman if they are in private. Fewer are comfortable if anyone else is present, but not too uncomfortable if it's another woman, particularly a dominant woman. Some submissive men are comfortable in a group if all the women are dominant and all the men are submissive. Finally, some submissive men feel extremely uncomfortable, sometimes to the point of refusal, in acting submissive if vanilla men or, especially, dominant men, are present.

Many men find it difficult to have an erection if other men are present.

Many people feel embarrassed about urinating or defecating if somebody else is watching.

One caution: Novice dominants often feel that humiliation is mainly verbal. They feel that they should say insulting things to the submissive – the more personal, the better. This type of activity is commonly known as "verbal abuse." (I'm unhappy with that term, but it's firmly established by common usage.)

Be very careful with this. Verbal abuse can be terribly hurtful and destructive. It burns out and turns off many submissives. For example, very few women, even drop-dead-beautiful women, truly feel secure regarding their attractiveness. Insulting comments regarding their looks can therefore really hurt, sometimes to the point of ending the session. Furthermore, "endearing" terms such as "bitch," "cunt," "whore," "slut," and so forth may wound, particularly if not specifically negotiated in advance.

Insulting comments about someone's race, religion, physical appearance, sexual orientation, deformities, I.Q., earning ability, and so forth may go deeper than intended. Many men are unsure about the size, attractiveness, and ability of their cocks. Many women are unsure about their breasts.

On the other hand, some people are deeply, intensely aroused by exactly those types of verbal abuse. It gets them hot as nothing else can. Occasional references are heard about "the sweet shame" that may result.

Humiliation is often very difficult for many submissives, even intensely devoted ones, to accept. It can be harder to accept humiliation than pain, fear, or disgust. An intense whipping, or prolonged bondage, may be much more bearable. Therefore, if a submissive is willing to stretch their limits to accept a difficult humiliation, a wise dominant will let their submissive know that they are pleased and impressed by what they did.

# Dominant/Submissive Interactions

## On Being a Dominant

Courtesy. The best dominants I know are scrupulously clean in their dealings with others. Their ethics rival those of the best attorneys and physicians. For example, they are polite, friendly, and open when dealing with other dominants. (Please forgive the cliche, but some of my best friends are dominant women.) Also, they never try to dominate and, especially, never touch another person's submissive without first getting both people's consent. Finally, in much the same way as a surgeon describing an operation to a patient, they carefully describe the general features of a proposed session to a new submissive – giving that submissive ample opportunity to back out. Consent is not enough for the best dominants. They want informed consent.

> May I kneel
> at your feet?

Good dominants are noted for being open and friendly. They freely share their knowledge and skills with appropriate others. They are often helpful in organizing events and frequently serve as officers in SM clubs. Furthermore, they are not hostile to dominants of different sexual preferences. For example, many dominant gay men readily share their knowledge with dominant heterosexual women. Dominant lesbians share secrets with dominant heterosexual men. These people all recognize their own, and others', value and worth. They are not so silly as to consider their own orientation superior.

Poor-quality dominants, on the other hand, cause irritation everywhere they go. They try to dominate other dominants, cop an attitude toward strangers and non-scene people, and otherwise try to get into a one-up position. A novice submissive woman I know suddenly realized about an acquaintance, "He's not a dominant – he's a rude asshole." Furthermore, poor-quality dominants often regard submissives with disdain. They may try to give orders to, or attempt to touch (perhaps even whip), someone who has not previously agreed to submit. They may demand submissive behavior before negotiations, or even personal acquaintance, have been completed. These behaviors can provoke a strongly negative reaction, up to and including a fist in the face.

Poor-quality dominants are predatory with submissives. They attempt to dominate as many people as possible. These widely despised creatures cause anger and resentment everywhere they go and are held in contempt. They usually don't last long in the SM community.

Many of the best dominants do not appear at all dominant when you meet them in the "vanilla" world. Except for perhaps a certain unwillingness to obey a direct order as quickly as others obey it, and a lack of anxiety about making direct eye contact, they appear fairly normal. They are often among the friendliest of people. (Many heterosexual, dominant men in the SM community are notorious punsters.)

## On Being a Submissive

I haven't got a dominant bone in my body.

Again, courtesy. As a submissive, you are asking your dominant for a great deal of time, thought, and attention. Dominating someone is a *lot* of work. Be considerate. For example, while you obviously have needs, you should devote yourself to pleasing your dominant as best you can.

One way in which you can help your dominant is by being honest up front about what kinds of play interest you. If you are a masochist, with little or no interest in performing personal service, you may annoy and frustrate a dominant who expects to be served. Similarly, some submissives are interested in providing sexual service only. Others provide limited services such as domestic or office help, and some genuinely wish to serve their dominant in any way they can. Honesty about your needs and desires, to the extent that you currently know and understand them, will serve you well here. While the dominant is not obligated to ask you to do only those things that suit you, and while you should offer as many options to your dominant as you reasonably can – after all, the more ways you can make your dominant's life pleasant, the more useful you are as a submissive – you should diplomatically be as clear as you can about your limits: a frustrated and resentful submissive is no fun for any dominant.

While local customs vary, the following behaviors by a submissive are often looked at with less than total approval.

**Pushy bottoms.** First, avoid being a "pushy bottom." Don't approach a dominant and, uninvited, drop to your knees at their feet. This turns many dominants off. (It's a pet peeve of many heterosexual, dominant women regarding submissive men.) Furthermore, you may see that – in its own way – this is a nonconsensual act. A certain amount of subtle, low-key flirting is usually tolerated, but don't appoach another submissive's dominant and come on to them by kneeling or otherwise acting conspicuously submissive without that dominant's prior approval. Doing so may cause their submissive to want to have words (or worse) with you. Don't push.

**SAMs.** Second, avoid being a "SAM" (a smart-assed masochist). SAMs deliberately "misbehave" to provoke dominants into "punishing them." This can be fun within the context of a negotiated scene, but is frowned upon when engaged in nonconsensually or outside scene space. Such SAMs can be regarded as too weak to ask for what they want in an honest manner.

Some SAMs provoke real anger. This involves deliberately emotionally (sometimes even physically) hurting the dominant in order to get the desired response. Such behavior is unethical, manipulative, and stinks of nonconsensuality.

Provoking a dominant can be a genuinely bad idea. Domination, like surgery or flying an aircraft, is a highly refined skill that takes years to learn. Good dominants exercise their art, craft, and skill in a highly controlled, thoughtful manner. Deliberately disturbing their emotional balance is dangerous. Furthermore, many dominants, because they know the power they hold and its accompanying responsibilities, are slow to display anger. Yet they are fully human; when you injure them, they hurt. If things go too far the dominant, like anyone else, can erupt. An enraged, out-of-control dominant is a terrifying thing.

Dominants who are provoked to the point of losing control may feel terribly remorseful and shaken afterward. Their confidence may take months or even years to return, or may never.

Don't get seriously "SAMmy" with a dominant unless you know they can deal with that. Under the right circumstances, playing SAM can be wonderful fun. Under the wrong circumstances, it can provoke disaster.

**Resistance.** A third type of submissive behavior you should avoid until you get to know your dominant very well is resistance, especially physical resistance. Resistance on a submissive's part, particularly if the dominant doesn't know them well, can be very difficult to interpret.

For example, I was once playing late at night at a friend's house with a lady I had met at a party earlier in the evening. She was a novice but had several friends that she knew were into SM and so was at least somewhat familiar with what it involved. I had, of course, assigned her a safeword and she had agreed to use it. Our play seemed to be proceeding nicely for both of us, when she suddenly began to struggle and attempt to escape. She then, even though partially bound, kicked me hard in the face!

I didn't hit her back (I confess that I felt tempted), and I was able to pin her down on the bed without much difficulty. And so I thus found myself restraining this struggling lady, who I barely knew, and wondering what the hell to do next.

I certainly felt confused. She hadn't called her safeword, and some submissives are into "resisting" so they can be "overpowered." It's certainly not rare for a submissive lady to want to "lose a wrestling match" with a dominant man. Was that going on here?

Part of me felt like continuing, but she was glaring at me with fury – and yet her friends were in the next room and she wasn't yelling for them. What in the world was going on? Was this still play or had this become real for her?

I asked her if she wanted to be untied and she snarled back, "You're goddamn right!" Having heard that, I immediately untied her and ended the session.

In this situation, I decided to err on the side of caution. While, technically, I perhaps could have continued – she had, after all, not called her safeword – I suspected (correctly) that this woman has become so enraged that all thought of abiding by her agreement to use a safeword had simply flown from her mind. She just wanted the session ended, and right now. If I had continued the session under those circumstances, I might have been guilty of sexual assault. (I might also have gotten myself killed.)

> As a dominant, I have to control myself *much* more strictly than I control my submissive.

When I'm in the dominant role, I tell my submissives, especially new submissives, that I will let any physical resistance on their part will immediately succeed. I will also regard it as a "strong yellow" and quite possibly as grounds for immediately ending the session. Because some submissives like to be "forced," this policy sometimes spoils a session, and has cost me the occasional play partner, but it's the safest course. Trying to overcome real resistance (even if you can do so easily) in the mistaken belief that it's "play" resistance can lead to disaster. Physical resistance *must* be carefully negotiated in advance. If you, as a dominant, are in any (repeat, any) doubt, back off at once.

Dossie Easton and Catherine A. Liszt, in "The Bottoming Book: Or, How To Get Terrible Things Done To You By Wonderful People," set forth some guidelines for resistance play and other challenging playstyles which I think are excellent. If you want to explore this playstyle, I strongly recommend that you take a look at them.

**Topping from below.** A fourth type of behavior you should avoid is called "topping from below." This refers to the submissive trying to control the session while it is in progress by making excessive requests, suggestions, and complaints – especially if these have nothing to do with either person's welfare or safety. This is different from making suggestions and requests to the dominant, yet genuinely leaving it for them to decide. It's also different from asking for particular activities (or ruling out particular activities) during pre-scene negotiations.

Topping from below is frowned upon. Let them make as many decisions as you reasonably can; the submissive is there to please the dominant, not the reverse.

One note: Some people identify as "submissive sadists," who enjoy serving their partner by giving them exactly the kind of pain they want, or as "dominant masochists," who enjoy receiving exactly, and only, the kind of pain they like. This is a different matter, and can work well as long as both people agree ahead of time that this is the kind of scene they want to do.

One ethical use of topping from below is the experienced submissive respectfully making suggestions to a novice dominant. I have done this several times with novice dominant ladies, and our sessions have usually gone well. Many beginners don't have a clue about how to dominate another person in a mutually erotic way, so suggestions to the effect of would you spank me/put clamps on my nipples/have me kiss your feet are often

Do you understand that being my slave will involve a *significant* amount of suffering?

gratefully welcomed by the inexperienced dominant. If done in a respectful, considerate manner, this is a highly valid act of service on the submissive's part. (Be prepared for the moment when your trainee reaches "critical mass": when they smile and say "OK, thanks, I get it. Now we're going to do what *I* want." From that moment on, you're no longer alone with an obedient student – you're alone with a dominant.)

Novice dominants often feel terribly insecure. Being "trained" by their more experienced submissive, in a manner somewhat similar to the time-honored tradition of the experienced platoon sergeant training the new lieutenant, is a wonderful service on the submissive's part. Such dominants often go on to become outstanding. They build on their early training in ways that make their submissive proud. On the other hand, novice dominants who are abused by their submissives may never begin to reach their potential, or may even leave the SM world entirely. A stupid, tragic waste.

As a submissive, your basic job is to yield as much control as you reasonably can. Unethically retaining unnecessary control cheats both of you.

A final thought about inappropriate submissive behavior: Some dominants *like* pushy bottoms, SAMs, resisters, and/or "submissives" who try to top from below. These dominants enjoy the vying for power, the psychological (and sometimes physical) struggle for supremacy. Banter between a SAM and a dominant can be delightful, and sometimes terribly funny, to watch or participate in. Putting a pushy bottom in their place or "over-meeting" their desires can bring dark satisfaction. But in these cases the dominant must pay closer attention than they ordinarily would. Unlike the clearer, more "classic" SM, where the lines of authority are agreed upon, this no-man's-land of power play is murkier and harder to follow. The chances of having a disastrous misunderstanding are *much* greater. Be careful.

Nowadays, a woman is free to want anything except to sometimes give up her freedom.

So what *should* you do? Having just gone on at length about characteristics of a bad submissive, it behooves me to talk a bit about a few things you can do to make yourself a good submissive.

Basically, anything you can do that helps you make your dominant's life easier, more pleasant, or more arousing will increase your value as a submissive. I often recommend to submissives that they consider taking massage classes: dominants often feel depleted and burned out from having to be responsible and in control all the time, and massage is a wonderful way that they can accept nurturing sensations without breaking role.

A second thought is that you might want to consider yoga classes. The relaxation and breathing taught in yoga are very helpful in processing pain (in fact, many of the techniques taught in pain management classes like Lamaze are derived from yoga). Also, the flexibility and strength you'll acquire from yoga will stand you in good stead when it comes to taking and maintaining positions for bondage and/or sex.

## Beginning and Ending a Session

It helps to have a formal set of signals to go into and out of role. This is particularly useful when two people first start to play together. Their SM energy may "blend in" to the rest of their relationship as they get to know each other, but formal "now we're in role; now we're out of role" signals help keep things clear at first.

One example of how to do this (there are many others) is as follows: The dominant looks at the submissive and asks, "Are you ready to go into role?" If the submissive replies, "yes," the dominant may then say, "Go into role." The submissive and the dominant then look into each other's eyes while they assume their roles. When the submissive feels their role "wash over them," they lower their eyes – perhaps then saying, "Hello, Mistress."

To end the session, the process is somewhat reversed. The dominant asks the submissive, "Are you ready to come out of role?" If the submissive replies that they are, the dominant then tells them, "come out of role." The submissive then remains still until they feel the role pass away from them. (This, by the way, is often a time of quiet sadness for the submissive.) After the submissive has felt their role leave them, they raise their eyes and meet their former dominant's gaze. While, strictly speaking, not required, it is nonetheless good form for the submissive to say one final "Thank you, Mistress," or something similar.

Note: The period immediately after the session should be a time of intimacy and tenderness for both people. The submissive, especially, should understand that the dominant may feel a bit drained and depressed. (This is known as "top drop.") The dominant has, after all, broken taboos by administering a whipping or by doing similar things. The submissive should therefore try to express their gratitude and appreciation for the good things they were given (and to be skillfully erotically dominated is to receive a gift; make no mistake about it). Even if they don't say it, or even feel it themselves, the dominant is likely to need some reassurance and support. Submissives, express what appreciation you honestly can to your dominant.

> I don't want to
> be a slave.
> I want to be
> *your* slave.

## *Beginning a Submissive's Training*

Submissives need and benefit from training. There are prerequisites. First, the submissive must offer or consent to obey the dominant. Second, the dominant and the submissive must agree about when the submissive is compelled to, and when they are not compelled to, obey. This is usually done by establishing a clear beginning signal and a clear ending signal for the session. Once these matters are agreed upon, training may begin.

Negotiate such matters as limits, safewords, marks, subjects the submissive may be curious about, things they definitely don't want, and so forth well before the session begins. While a novice dominant may feel tempted to take as much control as possible as quickly as possible, a wise, experienced dominant knows that it's better to negotiate with a potential submissive while the two are still equals and not in role. They know that the submissive may not agree to as much when negotiations are conducted in this way, but the submissive *will* be more likely to honor what they did agree to, more likely to feel good about doing that, and more likely to go further next time. A wise dominant keeps "next time" in mind.

The basic nature of training is that the submissive will obey the dominant's direct orders. Such orders are commonly in the form of commands such as "kneel," "put your hands behind your back," "kiss my feet," and so forth. More detailed instruction is worked out as the training proceeds.

Don't call me 'Mistress'! You haven't yet earned the privilege of calling me 'Mistress.'

Training can be an exceptionally intense process, often deeply affecting the minds and hearts of both trainer and trainee. Even if enjoyable, too much intensity at any one time is disorienting and threatening. This may scare off even an eager submissive (or dominant). For this reason, I recommend that training be conducted in relatively short sessions, usually lasting no more than an hour or two at a time, and that only a small amount of new material be introduced in each training session. I also recommend that the dominant let a day elapse between training sessions, thus giving the submissive (and the dominant) more time to adjust to and accept the emotional effects of training. It also allows the submissive time to review, practice, and integrate the new material before they learn more.

As to the details of how you would train a submissive, that is something best worked out by time and experience. Training is about controlling the submissive. Therefore, consider what aspects of them you wish to control. A few that come immediately to mind are how they move, what positions they assume when not moving, what they say, what they wear, how they groom themselves, where they direct their vision, and how you want them to address you. One benefit from reading the works of fiction and nonfiction referred to at the end of this book is that you can learn how some others have thought about slave training. To a certain extent, such reading can save you from having to "reinvent the wheel."

One tip: Give your submissive complete, detailed orders. Many are quite willing to obey, but you need to make exactly what you want clear to them. Consider which command is better: "Lie down on the bed" or "Lie down face-up on the bed with your head towards its headboard and your wrists and ankles stretched towards the bedposts." It is, shall we say, poor form to chide or punish a submissive for failing to obey an unclear order completely.

I might begin their training by ordering them, while they are still dressed, to stand still in front of me. (At this stage, I usually preface my commands with the phrase, "I want you to...") I might say something like, "I want you to come over here and stand in front of me. Stand with your feet together and your hands at your sides. Make yourself as completely physically and mentally still as you can. You are not to speak or move except as I direct. Do you understand?"

When they respond that they do understand, I tell them that from now on, while they are in role, the last word out of their mouth when they speak to me is "Jay." (I use my name when I want to make the gentlest possible start. In a later training session, I may upgrade that to "Sir," and finally, if things go well during the early training sessions, I will upgrade it yet again to "Master.") I then ask them if they understand. Hopefully, they answer with, "Yes, Jay."

> I want to be
> the best slave
> you ever had.

Training note: When I begin my training, I pay attention to my voice. I keep it firm, calm, and business-like, much as an animal trainer would. In fact, since the publication of the first edition of this book, I've had the opportunity to train a dog – not the human kind, the canine kind. Janet and I took her to obedience classes, and I noticed many similarities between that process and the one I'm describing here. In particular, the effective combination of patience, firmness, praise, and non-abusive discipline seemed very, very familiar to me. (I kidded the trainer that she probably had the best-behaved boyfriend in town.)

I do not shout, use profanity, or insult my submissives. Calm firmness helps establish my authority. It also gives the submissive a sense of self-control on my part that helps them feel safe.

I then tell them that, upon my command, I want them to strip completely, to put their stuff on the floor in the corner, and then return to their original position. Depending on how elaborately they are dressed, I tell them they have one or two minutes to accomplish this. If they take longer, they will be punished by receiving one whip stroke for every second that they are late. I then let them see that I have a watch or other timepiece.

Safety note: I especially have the submissive remove anything that might interfere with their being bound or might be a safety hazard. Examples include wristwatches, bracelets, large rings, necklaces, and dangling earrings.

Then I give the order "strip!" I usually use that somewhat harsh term as opposed to the more genteel "disrobe" or some similar term. I want them to know that they are now under my authority.

When the submissive has returned from their usually-somewhat-frantic disrobing, I order them to kneel at my feet. I then tell them to keep their gaze slightly lowered and to the front unless they have reason to look elsewhere. They are not to look directly at my face unless I tell them, "Look at me."

At this point their clothing state, movements, speech, and gaze are under my control. This is a good beginning.

Note: Remember that a naked submissive (and a naked dominant) will feel uncomfortable unless the room is agreeably warm. Chilliness makes establishing a relaxed, erotic mood almost impossible. Keep the training area warm.

## The Four Basic Duties of a Submissive

To submit is to yield control. The basic, fundamental duty of an ethical submissive is to yield as much control as possible over what happens during the session to their dominant.

*This willing giving of power on the submissive's part, and its willing acceptance on the dominant's part, is the magic, catalytic essence of SM, and all else flows from it.*

Once the scene has been set as outlined above, and the submissive is naked and kneeling at my feet, I usually ask them, "Why are you here?" This question takes many submissives aback, especially the ones who expect me to "do" them so that they'll get off. This question is crucial because it helps clarify basic issues.

The answer I hope to hear is something like "to serve you," or "to submit to you." This type of answer shows me that they understand who is here for whom.

*The dominant is not there to please the submissive. The submissive is there to please the dominant.*

If they don't answer my question in a generally correct way, I know right then that we need more discussion about this session before going further. I have learned, through frustrating experience, that a poor answer to my question is a warning light that I definitely must not ignore. A not-close-to-the-mark answer by this person usually indicates that they are unduly selfish, or feel they are doing me a favor by playing with me, or in some other way indicates (often rather strongly) that the two of us may not be well-suited for playing together – and shouldn't. This can be frustrating, but any dominant whose desire to play with someone gets so strong that they aren't willing to walk away from a session at any time isn't really a dominant.

If their answer to "why are you here?" is generally correct (i.e., "to serve you," "to submit to you," or something similar), I then ask them, "what does that mean to you?" Again, they usually don't know quite how to answer that, and it can be fun to watch them flounder around. After I let them struggle a bit, I tell them, "Your submission has four basic components. They are as follows: to serve my needs, to obey my orders, to accept my domination, and to please my desires." I then have them repeat these back to me.

Once they have repeated those points back to me, I ask if they are willing to do those things. If they answer that they are willing, then the session really begins.

I have found that these four points cover most matters involved in a dominant/submissive relationship. Let's look at each in turn.

**"To serve your needs."** This refers to doing things that make life easier for the dominant, such as performing menial tasks (subject to the limits established during your initial negotiations). During a session, for example, if the dominant becomes thirsty then the submissive will bring them something to drink – usually offering it on their knees to the dominant. The dominant may let the slave kneel there for a while holding it out before they accept it.

Beware of the submissive who has their own collar, and it doesn't lock.

The submissive diligently tends to the dominant's needs. If the room is too cold, or the music too loud, or another whip is needed, the submissive often will be ordered to take care of those matters.

This serving of needs may continue beyond "playtime" if the two people are involved in an ongoing "lifestyle" SM relationship. Submissives may cook for their dominants, do their laundry, go grocery shopping, clean the house, and otherwise spare their dominants from having to do the menial tasks of life. Many submissives intuitively understand that one of their duties is to give their dominant as much free time as possible – to use however they wish.

Footnote: It's better if these tasks are preformed in person by the submissive. I recommend against allowing the submissive to hire someone else to mow the lawn, wash the car, or perform any other task unless their health or lack of ability prevents them from performing these duties themselves. The more personal the service, the better.

Serving may go even further. The submissive may want to give their dominant money, buy them clothes, pay their rent, and so forth. This can be wonderful, but has potential problems.

A wise dominant knows two things about being served.

First: Very little is ever given completely freely and unconditionally in this world. Most people (and submissives are certainly people, even if they sometimes want to role-play a "subhuman" status) expect something in return for what they give. In the case of a submissive, what they often want is for the dominant to continue being their dominant. A smart dominant therefore accepts little, if anything, in the way of goods or services from a submissive who does not strongly attract them. Gifts often come with unspoken, or even denied, strings attached. Wise dominants remember that. They never accept substantial gifts from a submissive unless they want to spend a lot of time with that particular submissive.

*Please don't tell me to put the collar on myself. Please, Master, you do it.*

(I know of case in which a wonderful female submissive found an elegant way to spare her new master from exactly that sort of dilemma. When she learned through other sources that he had fallen on hard times, she mailed him an anonymous letter containing cash.)

Second: Never become dependent on a submissive. There are dangers to being served. The first danger is that, as adults, we weren't really meant to be taken care of too much. If we are, we tend to become soft, lazy, and a bit spoiled. A certain amount of emotional regression is also common. Like the Romans, if the labor and struggle of others make our own lives too easy, we begin to decline.

The second danger of accepting goods, meaning any tangible thing of value, including money (this can make for a fascinating tax return) is that, again, we may become dependent. We may ethically accept items of value, even great value, from a submissive provided that we do not come to *rely* on them. Once we depend on our submissive to pay our rent, we have become *their* slaves. Wise dominants never, ever allow themselves to be placed in this position. And it *is* a distinct danger – perhaps especially for female dominants who have male submissives. Many male submissives are highly successful, even wealthy. Some are not at all above using lavish gifts to manipulate their dominant. Such manipulation can be obvious or subtle, but it is indeed there.

Still, a submissive can offer "real world" services to a dominant if it's done in a proper way – meaning as unconditionally as possible. I know one submissive man who offers his services as a carpenter. He's built many pieces of SM equipment. Also, it's been something of a joking truism in the SM community for many years that a submissive auto mechanic is not likely to be without play partners for very long.

The more a dominant's own life is in good order, the better they can properly dominate a submissive. A wise dominant conducts their affairs, including their financial affairs, in a way that allows them to be both capable of and willing to end a relationship on a moment's notice. They never allow themselves to become dependent on the goods or services offered by a manipulative "submissive."

**"To obey your orders."** Yielding control is the essence of submission. To submit is to agree to obey. The submissive needs to look deeply at how they feel about obeying this dominant's orders. If they look forward to being commanded, that's a good sign. If they do not welcome being given orders by this person, then they need to ask themselves why (and if) they want to do this.

In general, the dominant has every right to expect prompt, good-faith obedience from the submissive. Orders should be responded to quickly and willingly. If this is not so, the dominant needs to examine the situation. Is the submissive not genuinely willing to obey? Are they "misbehaving"? Are you, as a dominant, being tested to see if you are willing to enforce your orders? (This is common, especially at the beginning of a relationship.) Is the submissive trying to top from below? Is there any sign that the submissive might physically resist? It's very important that these questions be answered before you go much further.

How important being submissive is, and how much a submissive honors their relationship with their dominant, is often revealed when the submissive is ordered to do something that they don't want to do. Too many "submissives" (particularly heterosexual, submissive men) are into obeying only when activities they already like and want to do are involved.

Eventually, the dominant is probably going to want the submissive to do something that the submissive is not "into." This is a somewhat crucial moment. If the submission is genuine, and what the dominant wants is not likely to be unacceptably harmful, unsafe, or in violation of previously negotiated limits, then the submissive will genuinely try to do it with whatever grace and eagerness they can muster. A submissive who truly honors their relationship with their dominant will endure a lot if doing so will please that person. (Caution: Sometimes submissives will endure much, much more than they should. Dominants therefore need to be careful about what they want.)

The submissive who endures pain, fear, disgust, or humiliation (those words are worth remembering, by the way), or a combination of them, for absolutely no other reason than to please their dominant, has made a major statement about the importance of their relationship to that dominant – and is entitled to a moment of quiet pride. A wise dominant respects such a submissive, and asks them to endure such ordeals only if they also want such a deep, committed relationship.

One exception to the prompt obedience rule is the "captive" submissive. In this scenario, the dominant has taken the submissive "prisoner" and is holding them "against their will." This role can be a good one for novices or people who feel ambivalent about being submissive. Just make sure that you cover matters like physical resistance and "turning the tables" in your pre-session negotiations. Remember how dangerous it can be to play in these areas.

Caution: Captive scenes can be very hot. I confess that, when I take the submissive role, I like them. (Interestingly enough, I'm not too fond of them when I'm a dominant. Then I prefer more of a trainer/trainee scene.) Captive scenes are often combined wonderfully with "interrogation." They do, however, seem more vulnerable to over-escalation and too-rapid build up than other types of scenes are. Both players must stay alert for that. If you play in this area, don't let it happen. Make sure you cover that specific point in your pre-session negotiations.

*Sorry about that, Master. I'm not used to being owned this early in the morning.*

"To accept your domination." If "obey your orders" is largely about accepting what your dominant *says* to you, particularly regarding obedience, then "accept your domination" is largely about accepting what your dominant *does* to you. This can be particularly important regarding accepting pain from them. Unless specifically excluded by prior negotiations, a certain amount of pain (sometimes a considerable amount), often "comes with the job" of being erotically submissive.

Subject to pre-session negotiations and limits, your dominant has the right to touch your body in any place that they want and in any way that they want. They have the right to pinch, slap, spank, and whip you. They have the right to put clamps on your nipples, your genitals, and other parts of your body, and otherwise to give you as much, or as little, pain (and, if *they* wish it, pleasure) as they wish. They have the right to tie you up or otherwise restrain you. They have the right to steer you where they want you to go by pushing you, pulling you, turning you, leading you on a leash, and so forth. You should be clear about these points before you submit.

Once the session has begun, your dominant does not have to justify to you on your terms why they want to give you pain. The fact that they want to give it to you is usually all you need to know. Your job as a submissive is to accept it as best you can. The more you can develop your ability to accommodate your dominant's desires in a healthy manner, the better a submissive you will be.

**"To please your desires."** This is the flip side of "to serve your needs." It's also often more pleasant. A need is something that must be met or the person will experience distress. For example, a dominant may feel thirsty, so kneeling at their feet and offering them a glass of something to drink helps meet that need.

On the other hand, nobody "needs" a massage, to have their toenails painted, to listen to pleasing music, or to receive skillfully administered oral sex. Pleasing desires can be the fun part of submission.

It's much easier for me to go from being a top to being a bottom during a session than to go from being a bottom to being a top.

Such pleasing often involves SM activities. If you wish to know why your dominant wants to tie you up, whip you, and otherwise "torture" you, understand that you should be ready to hear an answer to the effect of "For absolutely no other reason than because it pleases me to do so." If this is not a good enough reason for you, then you have some thinking to do about why you are being erotically submissive to this person.

Another point to keep in mind about the importance of pleasing your dominant's desires is the matter of physical sensation imbalance. The rewards of being erotically submissive can be both psychological and physical. The rewards of being a dominant are often "only" psychological. In terms of raw physical sensation, an SM encounter is often many, many times more intense and rewarding for the submissive than for the dominant. After such a session, this imbalance often leaves a dominant, especially a novice dominant, with a vague sense of somehow having been cheated.

Such a confused dominant may be unable to understand this vague sense of having been ripped off. After all, they were in total control of the session. The submissive diligently obeyed them and did everything they were told to do. Why does the dominant have a vague sense of loss? Why does it feel like something is missing?

The answer is often found in the matter of physical sensation. The submissive usually received loads of it. The dominant, on the other hand, often set the session up so that they received little or none. A wise dominant therefore asks themselves before or at the beginning of a session what they want in terms of physical sensation from this submissive. Do they want oral sex? Intercourse? A massage? A foot rub? (Many submissives increase their desirability by becoming skillful at giving massages and foot rubs. They often read books, watch videos, and take classes in how to perform these acts.)

Some dominants want little or no touching from their submissives. Others want a lot. All benefit from considering before playing with a particular submissive how much touching, and of what type, they want from them – and then examining their feelings afterward to see how they feel about the decision they made.

## The Collar

Of all pieces of SM equipment, the one with the deepest psychological implications is probably the collar. The collar is an instrument of ownership and control. Therefore, even if the submissive is otherwise completely free, wearing a collar may have intense effects on them. Permitting another person to collar you can be a deeply significant act.

*I only dominate men, and only submit to women.*

The collar is the primary emblem of submissiveness. Dominants essentially never wear them; submissives often do. Some magazines, in an attempt to create an SM-like atmosphere, put collars on their "dominant" women – thus revealing their ignorance.

I once saw a collar on a dominant woman at an SM party. When I asked her about it, she seemed a bit flustered. She then insisted that it was a "dominant collar" because it had no D-rings or other attachment points on it. I grinned and kept quiet. She certainly didn't convince me, and I doubt she convinced herself. The next time I saw her at a party, she wore no collar. I didn't say anything to her about it, but I did smile.

I can just hear some of my more dominant readers yelling, "A dominant can wear any damn thing they want!" Technically, that is, of course, entirely true. Still, the collar is an emblem of submission.

Most SM collars are made of leather; a few are made of metal. Some players use improvised "hasty" collars made of rope or similar binding material wrapped and knotted around the submissive's neck, but most use actual collars.

Inexpensive collars can be purchased at pet shops and variety stores. Trying them on your submissive while still in the store can be great fun if you're into freaking out the other customers and the staff. Be careful, though. Don't go too far.

Collars have also become popular item in stores catering to punk, goth, and other alternative culture fans. Finally, SM stores and mail-order catalogs sell collars.

I firmly believe that a collar should have one essential characteristic: *it should lock.* Non-locking collars that can be removed by the submissive at a whim do not, to my way of thinking, qualify as real slave collars. Some people disagree with me on this point. That's all right. They can go on being wrong if they wish. I'll just point out that, based on experience, I've had a personal motto for several years: "Beware of the submissive whose collar doesn't lock."

Also, remember what I said about how the entire chemistry of the session is altered, usually for the worse, if the submissive believes they can escape from their bondage any time they wish? A non-locking collar is much the same. Being locked into a collar, even if it's one you could cut off, can be a very intense experience.

My Master
is a wimp!

(I know of one submissive woman, by the way, who symbolized ending her relationship with her master by destroying her collar.)

I think it's best when only the dominant places the collar around the submissive's neck, and only the dominant removes it. While some dominants, as a point of control, order their submissives to collar and uncollar themselves (and they are within their rights to order this), it usually seems to "feel righter" if the dominant collars and uncollars the submissive.

A collar should be slightly loose – generally loose enough for the dominant to grab in their fist. A too-tight collar is difficult to wear for any length of time. Among other problems of wearing a too-tight collar, it can limit the submissive's ability to perform oral sex, especially fellatio – and we can't have that.

A submissive can sleep in their collar. It can be a powerful experience to be allowed to sleep with your dominant in their bed, drifting off to sleep while you caress the collar they locked around your neck. The dreams can be incredible.

The collar should be of strong, durable material. The submissive must not feel it is made of such flimsy material that they can simply break it off. I once saw a submissive woman who, when locked into a collar for the first time, grabbed its lock and tried with all her (considerable) strength to break it. A long, all-out pull made it creak a bit, but left it intact. Thus she knew herself collared. This sent her into a deeply submissive state.

I recommend that a dominant have a relatively plain training collar. (Or perhaps two, for when special company drops in.) This can be an inexpensive dog collar, and used during "basic training." If the submissive satisfactorily completes such training, and the two decide to enter an ongoing relationship, the dominant might then present the submissive with a more expensive, perhaps custom fitted, collar. This may be given at a special ceremony, perhaps with guests invited.

While some people can wear a collar lightly, others are deeply moved by it. To kneel at another person's feet while naked, feeling and smelling the leather they locked around your neck, can be deeply moving. Sometimes submissives "dissolve" into their role. On the other hand, being collared may cause feelings of resistance or anger to surface, or the submissive may feel overwhelmed by shame or fear. If the submissive becomes too emotionally unstable to continue the session, one way of helping them to regain their balance is to remove the collar.

*The more I top, the better bottom I am, and the more I bottom, the better top I am.*

Be careful about attaching the submissive's collar to anything over their heads, such as an eye-bolt. If they were to faint, fall, or trip, you could have a life-threatening situation on your hands. The collar is usually left free-standing, although a hand-held leash can be attached.

With a little thought about where you're going and who you might encounter, the collar can be worn in public. Doing so can lead to people starting interesting conversations with you, and perhaps allow you to meet kindred spirits.

Finally, submissives may grow deeply attached to their collar, and to the state of mind that it represents. It is not at all rare for submissives to not want to be uncollared. Some will even genuinely beg the dominant to leave the collar on.

## Basic Position Training

Training fundamentals include teaching the submissive to assume different positions upon command. Fortunately, certain positions of the body, arms, and legs frequently recur, and so "shorthand" commands can be taught, thus simplifying matters.

It takes considerable time, attention, and care to train a submissive. A dominant should do this only when they expect to get something worthwhile in return, such as the ongoing, devoted obedience of a pleasing submissive. (Submissives should understand that it's a privilege to be trained by a skilled dominant, and feel appropriately grateful.)

The basic body positions, and the commands associated with them, are described below. The following commands are one (and, please note, only one) example of how such training might proceed. They may be used as described, or modified to satisfy a particular dominant.

A wise dominant will spend considerable time in these positions before ordering a submissive to assume them. The dominant can do this on their own, in private, so they need not fear that their "purity" has been compromised. The value of the empathy and insights that result from such experience far outweigh its discomfort.

Note: Submissives should acknowledge their commands, usually by saying, "Yes, Master," "Yes, Mistress," or some similar term, as they obey.

I hate it when you make me stop being submissive.

**Keeping things in perspective.** In general, the submissive should not be physically above the dominant, unless avoiding this would be excessively inconvenient. For example, if the dominant is sitting in a chair and the submissive approaches it, they should not stand close to the chair, towering over their dominant. Rather, they should bend down as the approach and kneel by the chair. When they leave, they reverse this process. With training and practice, the submissive can learn to do this beautifully and smoothly.

The submissive should also generally avoid crawling over the top of their dominant while the two of them are lying down together, such as when in bed, unless doing so is necessary to serve.

**Command: "Kneel!"** This is the basic command. Essentially every dominant orders their submissive to kneel to them.

A good basic kneeling position can be adopted from the martial arts. In the basic position, the submissive kneels with their buttocks resting on their heels; their knees are two fist-widths apart. Their back is straight and their pelvis tilted slightly forward. Their head is held erect except for the very top of the spine, which is bowed slightly forward. The submissive's gaze is slightly downcast – about 30 degrees below the midline – and straight ahead. Their hands are placed palm-down on the top-middle of the thighs. The insides of their big toes are lightly touching. Their fingers and thumb are lightly pressed together (this is called "focusing"), and the fingertips directed straight down their leg toward their kneecaps. Their elbows are held close to the sides, but not rigidly squeezed against them.

The entire position is relaxed, yet poised. Nothing is rigidly tense, yet the submissive is alert, focused, and ready.

The submissive may also be ordered into this position by the command "On your knees!"; or the command "Kneel down!"; or by snapping the fingers; or by a hand signal such as pointing the finger toward the place where you want them to kneel.

This is the basic submissive position, similar to the "attention" position of military close-order drill. Both the dominant and the submissive will make sure the submissive becomes expert at assuming it.

**Command: Adjust right!** Unfortunately, the "kneel" position often interferes with circulation to the lower legs. Many submissives feel their toes, feet, and calves begin to tingle, then go numb, after a relatively short time – sometimes only a few minutes.

Numbness should be avoided, so many dominants allow their submissives to adjust their position slightly if necessary to relieve that. Usually the submissive may adjust on an as-needed basis, without requesting permission to move, provided moving does not interfere with the submissive's duties.

Note: I train my submissives to tell me immediately whenever a part of their body begins to feel numb. This notification must be given early, preferably when the submissive first notices it.

To assume the "adjust right" position, the submissive places their right hand directly on the ground about 18 inches to the side. The fingers and thumb remain lightly pressed together and pointed straight ahead. The elbow is straight, but not rigidly locked.

The submissive then gracefully shifts their body so their right buttock rests on the ground. Shifting into this position should relieve numbness or tingling in the submissive's legs within five minutes. When the submissive's legs again feel normal, they should return to the "kneel" position.

"Adjust left" is simply the mirror-image of the "adjust right" position, moved into and out of in the same way, for the same reasons.

The submissive should understand that the "adjust" positions are provided for their benefit. Being allowed to assume them is a privilege granted out of the dominant's graciousness and concern. A good submissive appreciates that, and assumes them neither longer nor more often than necessary.

I usually let my submissives choose freely between the "adjust-right" and "adjust-left" positions.

Note: The human body was not designed to kneel for long lengths of time. The submissive's skin is compressed between their bones and the floor. If both surfaces are hard, then considerable pain, in addition to the other problems associated with kneeling, results. Therefore, a considerate dominant avoids ordering their submissive to kneel on a hard surface, such as linoleum, hardwood, or concrete, for any significant length of time. A soft, clean carpet often makes an excellent training surface.

**Command: "Kneel up!"** In this position, the submissive is "standing" on their knees. The knees remain two fist-widths apart and the big toes still lightly touch. The fingers and thumb still lightly press together in the front-center of the thigh, but they rise slightly as the submissive moves from the "kneel" position. Their back remains straight and their eyes remain slightly lowered and straight ahead.

This is a useful position to order your submissive to assume when you wish to collar or bind them. It also will probably, if you are standing directly in front of them, place their mouth at about the same height as your genitals.

A submissive whose hands are tied behind their back, or otherwise restrained, often finds it difficult or impossible to move from "kneel" into "adjust left" or "adjust right" and back again. Some can learn this with practice, but others – because of their build – find such moving impossible. They will fall in a dangerous way if they try. One alternative in dealing with this problem is for the dominant to "spot" the submissive as they move, stabilizing them and catching them if they begin to lose their balance.

Note: Some bound submissives can maintain an "adjust" position on their own once the dominant helps them into it; others cannot. Also, some submissives need help moving from "kneel" into "adjust" but can move back into "kneel" on their own; others cannot.

On the other hand, most submissives, even with their hands tied, can move easily between "kneel" and "kneel up" without needing help. A compassionate dominant allows their submissive to move between these positions as needed.

Note: Submissives vary in how long they can maintain any kneeling position. A fit, healthy submissive may be able to spend hours on their knees

*The greater the demands in my outside life, the likelier I am to feel submissive sexually.*

without problems. On the other hand, a submissive with a bad back, bad knees, or some other problem may only be able to kneel for minutes at a time. A few cannot kneel at all.

**Command: "Sit!"** In this position, the submissive sits cross-legged on the floor. Their hands rest palm down on their knees, and their back is in the usual straight, erect position.

"Sit" is moved into from "kneel" by sliding into "adjust," then bringing the opposite leg around to the cross-legged position. Like "adjust," some bound submissives can move into and out of this position without assistance; some cannot.

This position may relieve lower-leg numbness and tingling; however, it also may cause it to appear after a while in some submissives. Many submissives can hold this position without developing numbness for quite some time.

**Command: "Kneel forward!"** To assume this position from "kneel," the submissive places their right hand palm-down on the ground about a foot in front of their knees. The thumb is spread away from the hand at about a 60 degree angle. The fingers are lightly pressed together. The left hand is then brought down to match the right hand. The thumbs touch each other and the index fingers touch. The submissive's hands now form a triangle directly in front of their body. The wrists are straight, bent neither outward nor inward. The submissive bows their head and places the top of their forehead in the triangle.

*Having a slave is like having a lover, a child, and an employee all rolled into one.*

Note: Many submissives can press their foreheads to the ground in this position with their hands bound behind them. Some may need help in doing so or they could "crash land" and hurt themselves.

This is a very submissive, penitent position. It exposes the submissive's back, buttocks, anus, and genitals. This position may be used to administer "punishment" whippings or spankings. (Be careful when spanking a submissive male who is in this position. His testicles will be *very* exposed. You don't want to strike them – at least not by accident.) This position is excellent for the submissive to assume when apologizing to the dominant – as they so often must.

Safety note about "kneel forward": This position may place significant strain on the submissive's neck, especially if they are ordered to assume it while their hands are bound behind their back. I know of one submissive who developed a painful neck sprain that lasted for months after enduring it for a long time during a harsh session. Be alert to neck problems. Change the position immediately if significant neck pain develops. No "submissive heroics" regarding enduring pain to please the dominant in this matter.

Command: "Kneel back!" To assume this position from "kneel," the submissive spreads their ankles apart until they are slightly wider than their hips. They then lower their buttocks to the ground and lean back until as much of their body as possible is resting on the ground. (Technically, the submissive is not kneeling at all; rather, they are lying face-up.) Their hands go palm-down by their calves, fingers and thumb pressed lightly together.

This position offers excellent access to the submissive's breasts and genitals. Some dominants who are particularly fond of genital and nipple torture order their submissives to assume this position. The dominant may then bind the submissive's wrists to their ankles. The advantages of this position include that the dominant can use their hands and their mouth. (If they choose to touch their submissive's body with their mouth. Some do; some don't. It's a matter of what the *dominant* wishes.) The submissive's mouth is somewhat available.

I don't want anyone washing my Mistress's dishes but me.

One disadvantage of this position is limited access to the submissive's anus. Another disadvantage is that sexual intercourse is likely to be difficult or impossible.

Safety note: This position may place a *substantial* strain on the submissive's body, especially the lower back, the fronts of the thighs, and the knees. Submissives who are no longer as young, light, or flexible as they used to be may suffer serious injury if they are ordered to assume or maintain this position in the face of difficulty. (Yoga classes or other stretching exercises can help.) Many submissives will be unable to assume this position at all. They also may be *very* seriously injured if the strain of the position is worsened, as it might be if the dominant sat on them. Be careful.

I know two ways to make this position easier and safer to assume. The first involves placing a thick, wide pad – such as a sofa pillow or a folded blanket – under the submissive. This pad should run from under their buttocks to the top of their head.

A second method of relieving the strain of this position is to modify it by having the submissive lie on their back and pull their feet up toward their buttocks, perhaps grabbing their ankles with their hands. (Their wrists may be tied to their ankles.) This position, although technically not a kneeling position at all, preserves most of the position's good points while relieving much of the strain on the submissive's back.

This position is a very vulnerable, helpless one. It is worth exploring, but be careful. More than any of the other positions, the strain caused by assuming and holding it exposes the submissive to injury.

**Command: "Stand!"** In this position, the submissive rises to a standing position. Their spine is erect and their shoulders back. Their gaze is slightly lowered. Their hands are held by their side with the palm-sides of their thumbs and the tips of their fingers slightly pressed against the sides of their thighs. Their feet are comfortably together, spaced neither noticeably widely nor narrowly.

To prevent fainting, the submissive should be cautioned not to stand with their knees locked. To help prevent fainting, and for the aesthetic effect, the submissive may be ordered to keep one heel always slightly lifted off the floor, changing heels as needed.

When the submissive rises from their knees to a standing position, they should do so gracefully, preferably rising from both knees at once. If they cannot rise from both knees at once, they should place one foot in front of them (preferably the right foot) and rise. If they cannot drop to both knees at once, they should place their left knee down first.

*Please, Master, don't let me get away with that.*

**Command: "Supine!"** In this position, the submissive lies face-up. Their hands rest naturally by their sides, palm down, with fingers and thumb lightly pressed together. Their heels lightly touch. Their gaze is straight up and does not wander.

**Command: "Prone!"** In this position, the submissive lies face down. The tops of their feet rest against the floor. Their heels and toes lightly touch. Their hands rest palm up with the fingers and thumb together. Their thumbs lightly touch their sides. The entire backs of the fingers rest against the surface the submissive is lying on. The tip of the submissive's chin rests on the floor. (This head position may put an uncomfortable strain on the submissive's neck, so I allow the submissive to turn their head to either side as needed.)

## Arm positions

There is often a need for the submissive to place their arms in certain positions, often to offer them for binding.

**Command: "Arms up!"** In this position, the submissive places their arms directly over their head in line with their ears. For example, if the submissive were told "arms up" while they were standing, their arms would point toward the ceiling. On the other hand, if they were ordered "arms up" while supine or prone on a bed, their arms would reach toward the head of the bed, not straight up into the air.

The upper arms are usually about two inches away from their ears, not pressed tightly against them. The palms are usually facing directly ahead but may, if the dominant instructs, be placed facing toward each other. The fingers and thumb are together.

**Command: "Arms out!"** In this position, the arms are held up and away from the side of the body at a 45 degree angle. The palms face forward, fingers together.

**Command: "Arms level!"** The arms are held straight out to the side, palms forward, fingers together.

**Command: "Arms down!"** If the submissive is standing, on their stomach, or on their back, their arms are placed against the sides of their thighs, palm side of the thumb and fingertips touching. If the submissive is in any other position, their hands return to their standard place for that position – for example, in "kneel" the hands would return to the front center of the thigh.

**Command: "Arms forward!"** The submissive extends their arms straight out in front of their body at shoulder level. The hands are about a foot apart and the palms pointed toward each other. Alternatively, as the dominant instructs, the palms may be pointed either up or down.

**Command: "Arms back!"** This command is classically used to order the submissive to place their hands behind their back for binding. The submissive brings their hands behind their back and places the backs of their hands against their lower back or upper buttocks, whichever is more natural. Their palms face straight to the rear, fingers together. The dominant then moves the submissive's hands into the desired position and binds them.

**Command: "Arms behind!"** The submissive places their hands behind their neck, with the fingers of their left hand resting upon the back of their right hand.

## Leg Positions

**Command: "Legs out!"** The submissive spreads their legs until each is at a 45 degree angle to the midline, thus forming a 90 degree angle at their crotch.

Command: "Legs in!" The legs are brought back to the midline and positioned as in the "supine" or "prone" command.

Command: "Legs back!" The submissive bends their knees until their feet are bent close to their buttocks.

Command: "Legs down!" The legs are unbent and again laid flat.

## Combinations

Some positions frequently recur, and the commands associated with them can be combined and streamlined. For example, the combination of "legs out" and "arms out" (the classic "spread-eagle" position) can be combined into "double out" or "spread-eagle." This can be combined with a body position command into: "Stand, double-out" or "Supine, spread-eagle."

The "arms back" and "legs back" position, so popular for bondage, can be combined into "double back" and used with a body position: "Prone, double back."

I can't wait to kneel to you again.

The submissive should be required early in their training to memorize these positions and the commands associated with them. The dominant should test the submissive on their knowledge, being very understanding, forgiving, and gently correcting with the first training session, and progressively less so from then on.

The submissive should move from position to position with a quick but smooth, obedient grace. They should not jerk or snap from position to position unless that is what their dominant desires.

The dominant should pay close attention to the details of how the submissive assumes these positions. Unfocused fingers, and toes not touching in the "kneel" position, are particularly common errors.

The teaching and learning of physical obedience to commands is a cornerstone in the foundation of a submissive's training. A wise dominant makes sure this is done solidly.

## Speech Training

In general, the submissive should begin and/or end everything they say with a respectful term. To give one example, if a dominant woman were to ask a submissive man what time it is, he might reply, "Mistress, it's 3:15 p.m., Mistress."

The submissive should usually speak only when directly spoken to, or after being given permission to speak. They can request permission by slightly raising their hand, or by giving some similar signal.

There are exceptions to the "begin and end everything you say with Mistress" rule. Exceptions include the terms "Hello, Mistress," "Goodbye, Mistress," "Yes, Mistress," "No, Mistress," and "Thank you, Mistress."

When a submissive is given a command, they should acknowledge it. For example, when commanded "arms back," the submissive male would reply "Yes, Mistress" as he put his hands behind his back.

If the submissive male wanted to ask something of his Mistress, the correct form of address (after first, of course, being granted permission to speak) would be, "Mistress, please..., Mistress?" For example, let's say a submissive male wanted to remove his watch. He would first raise his hand. If she were then to say, "You may speak," he would first reply, "Thank you, Mistress." (This expresses his gratitude at being allowed to speak at all while in his Mistress's presence.) He would then say, "Mistress, please may I remove my watch, Mistress?" If she were to reply, "You may," he would answer, "Thank you, Mistress," and remove his watch. He would then return as quickly as possible to his original position.

> I saw the most wonderful whipping being given last night.

If a submissive needs to attend to personal care, such as to go to the bathroom or get a drink of water, the proper question is, "Mistress, please may I be briefly excused, Mistress?" (A brief excuse normally lasts no longer than five minutes.)

Note: Unless instructed otherwise, a submissive need not request permission to speak before replying to a question or direct order from the dominant.

Some submissives just simply don't understand the simple order, "Begin and end everything you say with 'Mistress'." For example, give them this test. Say to them, "Slave." (To which they should reply, "Yes, Mistress?") "Say Mistress three times."

The correct response, of course, is, "Yes, Mistress. Mistress, Mistress, Mistress, Mistress, Mistress." I have had some submissives struggle with this for over half an hour. It became hysterically funny after a while – the SM equivalent of "Who's on first?"

Note: As part of a submissive's training they should be taught to lick, kiss, and suck anything that is held to their mouth, such as a whip, penis, or nipple. Many submissives know this instinctively.

Note: As part of their training, the submissive should be ordered to recite their rules of speech (and their other rules).

Note: The rules of speech do not apply to calling safewords, although it's a nice touch if the submissive includes them. On the other hand, not including "Mistress" or "Sir" with the safeword shows that the degree of upset is greater.

**Restriction of the personal pronoun "I."** Some dominants do not allow their submissives to refer to themselves as "I" or to use the words "me" or "my" in speech. They are, instead, required to speak of "your slave," "this slave," "slave Bruce," or simply "slave." Example: "Mistress, your slave's left hand is beginning to feel numb, Mistress." It is also sometimes required that slaves refer to themselves in writing using only the lower case, and that they capitalize all references to their dominant.

These rules of speech often seem cumbersome at first, but they are rather easily learned and come naturally after a while. A submissive who has learned how to speak precisely and correctly reflects well on both themselves and their dominant.

## Slave Duties

Historically, the purpose of slaves was to work for their dominants. Slaves were valuable primarily as a source of labor.

Today, slaves continue to work for their dominants. Many people enjoy the submissive role, especially what I call "passive submission," where all they have to do is lie back and absorb all the "goodies" their dominant gives them. "Active submission," on the other hand, involves the submissive doing things for or to the dominant. Giving the dominant a massage or performing oral sex on them are examples of active submission.

In an ongoing SM relationship, it is typical for slaves to serve their dominants. This is especially true concerning the more menial tasks of life. Good submissives clean up after a session. They also may cook for their dominant, clean their house, do their laundry, go shopping for them, and otherwise perform the routine tasks of life for their dominants.

A classic ploy used to unmask an insincere submissive (usually a heterosexual male) is, when he says, "Mistress, I'll do anything you want, Mistress," to ask him, "Great! Will you wash my windows?" A sincere submissive will live up to his promise. He will also wash your car, and anything else dirty.

Some professional mistresses allow their poorer submissives to perform tasks in exchange for a session. Naturally, the submissive must do quite a bit of work, and do it well, to be rewarded.

I want to take a minute to talk about the special relationship between a submissive and the SM gear used on them. Some dominants don't like the submissives to touch the gear. Others want the submissives involved with its care and maintenance. For example, the dominant and the submissive could go shopping together for the rope and other equipment that will be used on the submissive. (I've done this myself a few times, and these excursions can be both great fun and highly memorable.)

Afterward, the submissive could then take the rope home, wash it, cut it, mark it, and whip-stitch the ends, then present the finished rope to the dominant.

Sometimes the dominant and submissive work together to set up and install the equipment. I have even been to "eyebolt installation parties."

I also believe it's a good idea for the submissive to be assigned the duty of repacking the gear and straightening the room after a session. (This, by the way, seems to best be done as soon as reasonable right after the session, while the erotic energy still lingers. Clean-up done "the morning after" can often be a cold and dreary duty.) They should also be in charge of properly cleaning the toys.

In general, I regard the care, maintenance, and storage of the SM gear as the submissive's duty and the dominant's responsibility.

> When my dad died, I found bondage photos in with his stuff, and I felt really sad that he'd had to keep that side of him hidden all his life.

**Serving.** When ordered to fetch something, a submissive may bring it to their dominant, drop to their knees, kiss the object, and gracefully hold it out to the dominant. The submissive will keep it held out until the dominant takes it. This may not be for a little while.

## Punishment

The question obviously arises of what the dominant should do when the submissive does something displeasing.

First, the submissive should understand that there is only one fundamental offense: displeasing the dominant. The submissive is there to please the dominant. Failing to do so, or, worse, actively displeasing the dominant, is grounds for punishment.

Second, the submissive should understand that the dominant is the sole judge as to whether or not the submissive has been pleasing or displeasing. There is no appeal.

In considering punishment for being displeasing, the dominant should closely consider the issue of *intent*. In general, a good-faith error on the submissive's part should be dealt with relatively lightly. Intentional misconduct, on the other hand, is *much* more serious.

Remember this key point of training: a dominant should absolutely never punish, discipline, or in any way reprimand a submissive for raising a safety issue in good faith. This would include calling a safeword. On the contrary, they should always praise and otherwise reinforce this behavior.

About the punishment itself, there are several considerations. First and most important, I firmly believe that a dominant should *never* slap, spank, paddle, bind, confine, or otherwise perform any common SM act on a submissive as punishment. We are trying to create positive, erotic connections with these activities. Let's reserve them for that area of the relationship alone, and not cloud the connections. I also firmly believe that a dominant should *never* slap, punch, kick, or otherwise touch a submissive in anger.

*Mistress, I wasn't asking if I could urinate, I was asking if I could go to the bathroom to do it.*

When a submissive acts in a displeasing way, the first thing the dominant should do is immediately stop what's going on. They might then ask the submissive, "What was your error?" The submissive should then consider the matter until they discover their error. It is important for the submissive's training that they discover their error on their own. The dominant should not point it out to the submissive unless they fail to see it for themselves.

Once they know their mistake, they should apologize for it in terms as specific as possible. For example, they might fall to the "kneel forward" position and say, "Mistress, I'm sorry that I accidentally spilled a few drops of coffee on your boots, Mistress."

The matter of how to punish a submissive or masochist is somewhat tricky. Punishment often involves pain, and many of these people enjoy pain. Indeed, some manipulative masochists deliberately provoke their dominants so they can be "punished." So, again, I strongly recommend that a dominant *never* use pain as a punishment.

Keep in mind that learning they have failed to please their dominant is the only punishment a good submissive is likely ever to need. All that is necessary is to point out how to please, and the submissive will self-correct. Further action is usually not necessary.

In general, the punishment of choice is *withdrawal*. For a very minor offense, the submissive might be told to do something on the order of "go stand in the corner." For a greater offense, they should be told to put their clothes on and leave. Another form of punishment is to remove their bondage or their collar. Do not call them names or yell insults. Do not throw things. Leave.

For a serious offense, the dominant should call "red," get dressed, and either leave the house or order the submissive to leave, for exactly one hour. (This is highly similar to the "time out" taught in domestic violence prevention programs.) If the dominant is leaving, they should tell the submissive that they will return in exactly one hour and that the two of them can discuss what happened then.

Then leave.

*Perhaps* it is all right for the dominant to physically punish the submissive for misconduct if the *submissive* raises the issue (and does so entirely on their own). Some submissives need punishment as part of the healing process (and others absolutely do *not*).

The submissive may later be given the chance to atone for displeasing the dominant by performing an atonement task. I suggest that the task cause at least three times as much pleasure as the offense caused displeasure. It is important that the submissive *personally* perform this atonement task. For example, it would be acceptable for the submissive to fix and serve the dominant a meal, but it would *not* be acceptable for the submissive to pay for a meal, even a very expensive one, in a restaurant – particularly if the submissive is wealthy. The submissive personally committed the offense; the submissive must personally perform the atonement task.

I love you, Master.

Any physical items that were damaged or broken by the submissive should be repaired or replaced. Again, it is not enough to offer money – particularly if the submissive is wealthy. The submissive should personally go to the trouble of replacing the items, plus perform service.

Good atonement tasks often include menial, physical chores such as cleaning the bathroom, doing the shopping, or washing the car. If the submissive already does these things, some similar task must be found. Naturally, this task must be done excellently.

After the task is completed to the dominant's satisfaction, the submissive should present themselves, perhaps on their knees, to their dominant and ask for forgiveness. If the dominant honestly feels forgiveness in their heart, they should forgive the submissive.

A dominant unwilling or unable to forgive should not assign an atonement task.

**Should the dominant ever apologize to the submissive?** Absolutely, yes. While the dominant has the right, under carefully agreed-upon conditions, to expect the submissive to endure pain and hardship, the dominant has no right to expect the submissive to accept unduly harsh or abusive treatment.

Dominants are human beings, and they have a human being's complete share of faults. If a dominant messes up, I believe they should immediately and openly admit this. They should offer the same amount of atonement they would expect from a submissive.

In conclusion, I want to say that both parties should try to resolve disputes and preserve the relationship. Summary ending of a relationship can be devastating. We are becoming more sensitive to the issues of physical abuse and verbal abuse. We must now become aware of another form – something that might be called *abandonment abuse*. Permanently ending a relationship, particularly without warning and/or explanation, can traumatize a submissive (or a dominant) for a very long time.

# SM Relationships

In our rapidly shifting culture, we are seeing an increasing desire among freely consenting adults for new forms of committed relationships. We see it in the struggle for same-sex marriage. We see it in the growing desire for multiple-partner relationships. And, more to the point of this book, we are seeing an increasing desire for relationships based in SM dynamics.

The prevailing trend over the last several decades has been toward establishing equality between partners within committed relationships. What we are now seeing, to the shock of many, are increasing numbers of adults who have already established their equality, and who are choosing without apparent coercion or duress to enter into or restructure relationships to include a consensual *inequality* of power. These are usually called either master/slave or mistress/slave relationships. Relationships styled after parent-child roles – daddy/boy and the like – are also common, particularly among gay men and lesbians.

I hate it when my collar is taken off.

This is a profound act of social pioneering. After all, equality has been held as the gold standard for relationships for so long that it's all but inconceivable to many people that a relationship which recognizes another standard could be healthy, stable, and happy for all concerned. And yet, there seems to be a large and growing number of couples in this country who are in consensually unequal SM relationships.

This inequality may take various forms, and be subject to various limits. It may be an erotic power transfer only; it may involve day-to-day decisionmaking; it may require that one partner commit to serving the other one's needs on an ongoing basis; it may even involve one partner taking full responsibility for handling the couple's money and similar "real-world" interactions. Couples who seek SM relationships are exploring these options, and more.

Thus we see the emergence of a third type of primary partner: not only the boyfriend or the husband, but also the master or the slave; not only the girlfriend or the wife, but also the mistress or the slave. At this time, our society has absolutely no mechanism to recognize these relationships or to give them legal standing. Many people think that society should *not* give these relationships recognition or standing; indeed, they feel that such relationships should be vigorously opposed. Somewhat astonishingly, a growing number of apparently mentally healthy, stable adults are beginning to believe otherwise, and they are acting on these beliefs. Whatever are we going to do?

That two autonomous, equal adults could responsibly choose to enter into an ongoing, unequal relationship raises many highly valid questions. In particular, the questions of how to protect the submissive partner against abuse, exploitation, or abandonment by the dominant partner are very real and very far from being completely answered. A large amount of experimentation is under way in this area; couples are discovering what does and doesn't work for them, and sharing their results with interested, supportive others.

While I probably won't live long enough to see it, I would like for there someday to be some form of legal recognition and standing for these relationships.

> It's an interesting
> feeling to know
> that your girlfriend
> and your slave
> are getting
> together for lunch.

### "24/7" Relationships

From time to time, people decide that they want to enter an ongoing SM relationship in which they will spend most or all of their time in role. These are sometimes described as "24/7" relationships, meaning the people are in role 24 hours a day, seven days a week. I want to take a moment to discuss the broader aspects of such a relationship and its similarities to, and differences from, a more conventional relationship.

There are a few characteristics found in almost all these relationships.
1. Both parties recognize that such a relationship exists.
2. Both parties agree to put time and effort into maintaining that relationship.
3. The SM energy always goes in only one direction. That is, one person is always dominant and the other is always submissive. (That means that only one person controls what is going on. It is entirely valid, for example, for the dominant to order their submissive to tie them up and torture them. The behavior is not the issue. The issue is who is controlling what happens.)

It helps keep both dominant and submissive clear about who is supposed to do what, when, where, and how if a written agreement is made regarding the arrangement. Such agreements are sometimes called "slave contracts" and can range from brief and general to lengthy and detailed. Signing such a contract is sometimes done as part of a ceremony, with guests invited.

**Ethics.** I want to discuss the ethics of establishing such a relationship. I have read "field manuals" on interrogation and/or techniques. These manuals disturb me quite a bit. The first thing that disturbs me is that they describe nonconsensually inflicted torture techniques. Many of these methods would cause permanent, severe damage in an agonizing way. Obviously, they have no place whatsoever in what we do during SM erotic play. Second, they describe methods of breaking down resistance by sleep deprivation and other methods.

I firmly believe it is absolutely unethical for someone to try to "brainwash" another person into accepting a submissive role. If somebody does not have a natural inclination and interest in this direction, I oppose attempts to establish them. I'm also certain that such attempts will fail. As soon as the pressure is let up, the "submissive" will begin to revert to normal. The "dominant" must therefore keep up an ongoing effort to maintain the relationship, thus imprisoning themselves as much as the submissive. All of this is *much* more trouble than it's worth.

Knee!!

Accordingly, an ethical dominant gives their submissive every chance to refuse to go further, and does nothing to make the submissive unfairly dependent on them. (This has many facets, too many and too diverse to go into at length here, but I will say that *financial* independence is often a good place to start. A submissive should have their own bank account, and a source of income adequate to support them.)

If a person does not seem erotically submissive, a wise dominant will not waste time and effort futilely trying to make them so. Instead, they will move on and find another person who is erotically submissive. If they go about this in a reasonably intelligent manner, such a search will not take all that long.

**Can inequality and intimacy co-exist?** All human beings have a built-in need for contact with their peers. People in positions of power or control over others understand well that "it's lonely at the top." Factory managers like to talk to other factory managers, infantry company commanders like to talk to other infantry company commanders, mothers like to talk to other mothers, and so forth.

While it's satisfying to talk to "workplace peers," it's also satisfying to talk to intimate peers. A husband and a wife, or other committed romantic partners, are presumably such intimate peers. However, if two people have structured their relationship so that on a very fundamental level they are *not* peers, how can they obtain peer intimacy?

The commonest solution to this problem is for the couple to evolve a pattern of behavior in which they are in role some of the time, and relating as intimate peers at other times. The main difference between a 24/7 relationship and a more conventional dominant-submissive relationship usually seems to be the fluidity with which the partners move in and out of role: often, a simple change of demeanor or tone of voice on the dominant's part signals that they have just "picked up the reins" and are now relating, not as a peer, but as an owner, and the submissive must comply.

However, some people's desire to be dominant or submissive all the time is so strong that this arrangement does not satisfy them. In my experience, a desire this strong is very unusual, particularly among mentally healthy people. Few people can maintain a dominant or submissive role all the time. These are consciously assumed roles, much like those assumed by actors, and require effort to maintain. After a while, maintaining that effort may become tiring, even exhausting. Continued too far, it leads to burnout. This is true even if both parties consent and find the roles highly enjoyable. The two of you may go into role for prolonged periods of time, but ultimately most people feel the need to come out of those roles and relate on more equal, intimate terms.

Most people want and need personal intimacy. This intimacy *must* be between two equals, without roles or conditions. Furthermore, this intimacy must be freely and willingly given. You cannot demand intimacy or manipulate another person into giving it to you and have it remain satisfying to receive. You cannot demand this anymore than you can demand to be loved, and it is this loving intimacy between equals that is the essence and lifeblood of most romantic relationships.

No highly structured dominant/submissive relationship, and no exotic sexual activity, can ever replace or substitute for a mutually loving, intimate relationship. Some lucky people are both SM-compatible and personally compatible. They are very fortunate indeed.

**Non-traditional partnerships.** If you and your partner are in a 24/7 relationship, or even if you are simply in a relationship that, for one reason or another, does not include legal marriage, you need to give some serious thought to what will happen if one of you dies or is incapacitated.

I recently attended a memorial service for an acquaintance of mine who had been in a 24/7, owner/slave relationship with a lovely and very submissive lady. There was a dramatic moment when the woman stood up and introduced herself to the other guests, including her deceased owner's mother and co-workers, as his slave. (I believe this announcement was a surprise to very few people.)

There is no legal standing for such a relationship. Therefore, she had no claim on his estate. While her friends in the SM community stepped forward to make sure that she would be taken care of, she was just plain lucky in this regard. Many people do not have anything like this level of support if their non-traditional partner dies.

Janet and I took a long look at this matter a while ago. We wanted to give our relationship a little more substance, and so we had a "ceremony of commitment." While it was a wonderful ceremony, it had no legal standing and did not change the status of our relationship. After a little investigating, we found out that there were some steps we could take, short of getting married. We learned that there were three basic things that we could do.

1. We could each have a will drawn up.
2. We could each have drawn up what's called (in California, anyway) a "durable power of attorney for health care" that would designate a specific person, and a back-up person, to make decisions regarding our health care if we could not. (Janet gets to pull the plug on me.)
3. We could each have drawn up what's called (again, in California) a "general durable power of attorney" that would designate a given person, and a back-up person, to make decisions regarding our finances and business affairs. Such a person could sign checks on our bank accounts and so forth.

Have you ever been whipped while you were getting your cock sucked?

After checking various sources for such documents, including forms sold in office supply stores and forms suggested by an attorney, we were particularly impressed by the information and forms in the Nolo Press book called "The Legal Guide for Gay and Lesbian Couples." Everything was clear and easy to understand, and the forms were far more complete than the ones from the attorney or the office supply stores. (By the way, Nolo Press puts out a whole line of self-help law books; see the Bibliography for contact information.)

At an "SM and the Law" panel that was put on by three attorneys at a leather conference I attended, all three recommended that, in addition to the documents recommended above, you prepare a "hospital visitation list" specifying which people you want to be allowed to visit you in the hospital (and also which people you *don't* want to be allowed to visit you). I'd personally suggest that you have such a list notarized.

I have seen a number of "living wills" that specify which procedures someone does or does not want to have performed on them in the case of a condition that leaves them unable to speak competently for themselves. The only problem I have with the ones I've seen is that these are often put forth as "no heroic measures" documents when, in fact, many of the procedures described as "heroic" in the document, such as defibrillation and tube feeding, are in fact quite routine and ordinary. I strongly suggest that, if you sign such a living will, you first go over it in some detail with a medically informed person. Your personal physician would, of course, be a priority in this respect. However, if they don't have the time to explain each procedure to the extent you need to have it explained, you might also seek out another health professional. The stakes here are high, so it's crucial to have a clear understanding of what you're agreeing to have done, or not done, to you. Again, please make sure your personal physician, and others close to you, understand what you do and don't want done, and that these are *informed* decisions on your part.

Finally, there's the matter of organ donation to consider, and to discuss with those close to you.

I should point out that requirements vary regarding what it takes to make a will, a durable power of attorney for health care, a general durable power of attorney, and the other documents legally valid, and that these requirements also vary from state to state. It would, of course, be an excellent idea to check with an attorney *knowledgeable in these specific matters* (many just whip out their "boiler-plate" forms, and the forms I saw left me distinctly unimpressed).

These documents should be kept in a place where they can be accessed with little difficulty in the event of an emergency. Therefore, someplace like a safe deposit box may not be a good choice.

# SM Organizations

There are many good reasons to participate in a community of like-minded SM people. Most importantly, you can obtain context and perspective – a framework in which to place the new knowledge you're acquiring. You can also learn new techniques, talk over issues that might be bothering you, share your triumphs and heartbreaks, protect yourself and others against possibly dangerous play partners, pool your resources for purchasing and donations, learn about available resources and events, and maybe even meet the dominant, submissive, or switch of your dreams – not to mention having a lot of fun.

Some of you reading this are already members of one or more SM communities, and can attest to the many rewards (and occasional frustrations) that are part of participating. But, because this is an introductory book, I will assume that the reader is not already part of such a community. So I want to talk a bit in this chapter about how to find your local SM community if it already exists, and what to do if it doesn't.

*I've been thinking a lot about bottoming to you.*

## *Finding Your Local Community*

Let's assume that you've done some thinking about SM, and some exploring either on your own or with your regular partner, and you now feel ready to contact your local community. How do you go about finding it?

Maybe you already know someone who is in contact with it. For example, if you have visited a professional dominant, she might know how to contact the local community. If you don't already know someone, here's a good approach for finding your local community.

Step one: Check your phone book. I would suggest that you start with your telephone book. Open up to the yellow pages and look under the following categories:
   (A) Lingerie dealers, retail. This should give you the names, addresses, and phone numbers of your local erotic boutiques. Pay special attention to the stores that also sell videos, literature, playtoys, and adult items.

(B) Leather apparel, retail. This should give you the names, addresses, and phone numbers of stores that sell leather gear. Some of these stores may have an obvious SM-type slant.

(C) Books: Check this section for the names of avant-garde and/or nontraditional bookstores, gay and lesbian bookstores, and adult bookstores. It's also worth noting that some mainstream bookstores may have worthwhile books in their "health" or "sexuality" sections.

(D) Video tapes and disks, sales and rentals: This will also give you the addresses of places that sell books and magazines as well as videos.

**Step two: visit local stores.** Once you've spent some time gleaning what information you can from your phone book, it's time to do a little cruising around your town. Visit as many of these stores as you can. Walk in. Look around. See what's there. Look to see if they have a community bulletin board that may contain interesting and relevant announcements. You might ask the staff is they know of any local men-only, women-only, or mixed-gender SM organizations. (It wouldn't hurt to do this as you're making a small purchase.)

I like to be tied to a chair so that I can look out at a busy street. Everybody is free to move around but me.

**Step three: check your local publications.** Check out your local coffee shops, libraries, bookstores, and newsstands for free or low-cost periodicals that cover events in your area. Check particularly for the more "alternative" and gay/lesbian periodicals. They frequently contain basic contact information regarding local SM organizations, and often contain SM personal ads as well.

**Step four: check national periodicals and guide-books.** Several national periodicals contain listings of local SM groups. Such publications include Sandmutopian Guardian, Leather Journal, Boudoir Noir, and Prometheus. Books to check out include "The Black Book," "The Bob Damron Guide," and "Places of Interest to Women."

**Step five: check the Internet.** Announcements of "open to the public" meetings of SM groups more than occasionally appear on the Internet. Check out the alt.sex.bondage, alt.sex.femdom, and alt.sex.spanking newsgroups. Be particularly alert for announcements of "munches" in your area. If you don't see anything listed there, you might consider posting a polite query asking about any SM-related organizations or groups in your area.

**Step six: check related groups.** Many types of people tend to gravitate toward SM, and if you can learn where such people hang out, you may find some SM people, or people open to experimenting, among them. One such category of people are folks with a combination of high intelligence and an active fantasy life. Many such folks are found in science fiction fandom (many science fiction conventions, or "cons," have the occasional play party going on behind the scenes), gaming groups, Mensa, and the Society for Creative Anachronism. (One well-traveled dominant lady I know says that when she finds herself in a strange city, all she has to do to find play partners quickly is to find the local SCA chapter.)

Another category is people who have a spiritual connection with human sexuality, such as tantra practitioners (check out the magazine "Tantra" and the alt.magick.tantra newsgroup) and pagans (look for the magazines "Green Egg" and "Shaman's Drum," or in the alt.pagan.magick and alt.magick.sex newsgroups). Internet and World Wide Web keyword searches on all of these topics can be useful.

Finally, many people who are into one form of alternative sexuality are into others as well; the folks you find at groups focusing on bisexuality, polyamory, transgenderism, and other such interests may often be into SM or open to experimentation.

Keep in mind, however, that "like attracts like." If you don't know your Asimov from a Heinlein in the ground, and you show up at a science fiction convention looking for play partners, you'll (rightfully) be given a cold shoulder. Similarly, heterosexuals cruising bisexuality events looking for SM partners will be shunned if not banned outright. Still, if any of these ideas correspond to any of your personal interests, they may represent a place to look for kindred spirits.

I've been his slave for about a year.

Making contact. By now, you should have at least a few leads. (If you don't have any leads, it's possible that no local organization exists in your area. That means that you may have to travel to an organization in a nearby, bigger city. It also means that you might want to look into the possibility of starting an organization on your own.)

Let's say that you have a lead or two. What do you do now? The first thing you do, and this is very important, is follow the contact instructions to the letter. These groups tend to get a *lot* of inquiries, so they don't look favorably on those who don't follow instructions properly – and often refuse to have any further contact with them.

Follow the instructions to the letter. If it says to call a certain phone number only between certain times, call only during those times. If it says to send a self-addressed, stamped envelope to a certain address, make certain that your letter contains a properly stamped and addressed return envelope. If it says to meet at a certain time at a certain place, be there at the right time.

One caution: A legitimate organization will need very little information from you at first – usually only a phone number, mailing address, or e-mail address, and maybe a first name. Be suspicious of any requests for further information, particularly requests for information of a personal or sexual nature. While such events are rare, every now and then someone will falsely claim to be starting or running an SM club.

**Etiquette.** Certain standards of behavior have evolved over many years of SM parties to ensure the maximum comfort and safety of the guests. These are some of the most common points of good manners in that community. Be sure to ask what the "local customs" are.

1. Courtesy always. As a rule, the higher a person's status in this community, the nicer and more courteous they are. People, especially dominants, who "cop an attitude" are likely to become laughingstocks. For example, you do not have to address anybody as "Master" or "Mistress" unless you want to and doing so is all right with them. Nobody has the right to expect you to act submissive (or dominant) to them unless you have previously agreed to do that.

2. Be very careful about who and what you touch. Other than the ordinary handshakes associated with routine courtesy, it's wrong for you to touch another person or their property, or for them to touch you or your property, without first getting permission. Remember the point of handshake etiquette that a gentleman never extends his hand to a lady, but rather always waits for her to extend her hand, if that's what she feels like doing.

   Also, the times being what they are, affectionate hugging is much more common in social situations than it used to be, and this custom can be wonderful. Just don't be aggressive or intrusive about it, particularly if you're a man who likes hugging women. Additionally, people who enjoy being hugged may hate it (and you!) if the hug includes picking them up off the ground. I have seen some moron males do this as a way of running a nonconsensual power trip on dominant women, and it's a great way to make an instant, bitter enemy. When hugging, never lift anybody off the ground without first getting their permission.

3. Respect roles, choices and orientations. It's not "better" to be dominant than submissive. It's not "better" to be a heavy, frequent player than a light, infrequent player. It's most certainly not "better" to be heterosexual than gay, lesbian, or bisexual. (It's also not better to be gay than heterosexual.)

4. Respect people's privacy. In particular, avoid all but the least intrusive questions about where people live or what kind of work they do. It's fine if they volunteer such information, but don't probe.

5. Phone numbers and home addresses are particularly sensitive information. It's very rude to ask a third person for the phone number of someone you're interested in seeing again. Either offer your number to the person you're interested in or ask the third person if they're willing (and able) to pass your number on to the person who interests you.

6. Keep answering machine messages discreet. Unless you are leaving a message on an answering machine specifically set up to take SM-type messages, choose your words carefully. Spouses, kids, roommates, and others not in the scene may hear them. Therefore, references to "the party" and "the meeting" are highly preferable to more graphic terms.

7. Watch play from a respectful distance. If you see people playing together, as you might at a party, watch from a discreet distance. They shouldn't be able to notice your presence or your comments, particularly any negative comments. (If you have questions or concerns about what they're doing, ask the dungeon monitor or partygiver.) Also, it's usually best to wait about approaching either player to ask questions or otherwise talk until the scene is over.

   Subpoint #1: Never join a "scene in progress" unless you first get the dominant's permission (and don't be surprised if the dominant discusses it with the submissive before deciding.)

   Subpoint #2: Once you are done using a piece of equipment, such as a whipping post or doctor's examination table, clear off of it so others can use it. Of course you will leave it in spotlessly clean condition.

   Subpoint #3: Routine social conversation should be done well away from play areas. Talk about everyday matters shouldn't be audible to someone involved in a session.

8. Be willing to take "no" for an answer. Clubs understand that a certain amount of cruising takes place. However, if you meet someone you want to have more contact with, but they don't have a similar desire, don't press your case beyond a mild degree. Instead, move on to someone else. The sooner you move on after hearing a "no," the sooner you'll hear a "yes."

9. Play by the rules. Show up at the proper time, with the proper admission fee (preferably cash), and with the proper attitude for that particular event. Don't show up single at a "couples only" event unless

I'm really into being bitten.

287

you've had that approved in advance. Find out the ground rules for that particular event and stay within them. (Don't argue about the ground rules or try to change them at the event itself. Save your concerns for later.)

10. If you RSVP, then show up. Many people who put on events buy food and other supplies based on the number of people who say that they will attend. If you RSVP and then don't show up, the person putting on the event is stuck with the extra supplies, and un-fond memories of you. If you can't "de-RSVP" by the deadline, then at least offer to pay to cover the cost of your materials. (Some clubs now have an "RSVP no-show fee" that you have to pay before you can be admitted to their next event.)

11. Beware of gossip. In particular, try never to say something bad about somebody not present that you haven't already said to their face. Your remarks get back to the person being talked about more often than you might think, and can lead to serious bitterness and interpersonal difficulties. Malicious gossip can be terribly destructive; spreading it usually says more about the spreader than it does about the subject of the gossip. People with reputations for engaging in gossip are not generally held in high regard.

12. As you spend time around some of the more "open to the public" organizations, you may hear about more private, by-invitation-only events, particularly play parties. You may even learn who is putting on these events. Although you may *really* want to attend, it's important to wait to be invited. In particular, don't approach the partygiver directly to ask if you can come. If they wanted to invite you, they would have done so. (You might try engaging them in general conversation, but, whatever you do, don't *you* be the one to raise "the" subject.) As an alternative, if you know somebody well who is already on the private invitation list, ask them if they would be willing to bring you as their guest or to recommend you. Most partygivers have a pretty good idea of who is compatible with their events; they may be keeping an eye on you already to see if you and their events might be a good match.

13. Remember the 13th Commandment. "Thou shalt not cause administrative hassles for persons putting on SM events." Keep this in mind and the number of events at which you're welcome will grow.

### *When There Is No Local Community*

As part of researching this book, I got out an almanac and checked out the 100 largest cities in the U.S. I compared that list to my own list of regional SM clubs. I was very surprised to note that there were quite a few good-sized cities that, to my knowledge, have no organized SM community – not to mention the smaller cities, suburbs, and rural areas where no such thing exists for many hundreds of miles.

On the other hand, there may be one or more organizations near you – yet they may not be a good match for you. The most common reason for this is that they may not match your sexual orientation: they may be oriented toward heterosexuals while you are gay or lesbian, or vice versa. Less commonly, the people there may be into a playstyle that you don't enjoy, or may not be a good match for your age or lifestyle. On the other hand, people who seem on the surface like a mismatch may surprise you with how friendly and accessible they are; SM crosses many boundaries.

If there's no community that's a good match for you in your vicinity, you have three options: live with it, move, or start your own organization. Many people have done the first two (a surprisingly large number of people have moved to a large city specifically to be closer to an SM community), but for some, the third will be the best option.

I don't know how many events I've attended in the last two-plus decades, but it's probably getting close to a thousand. I've also put on well over 100 SM events, including socials, programs, and parties. Finally, I've started two SM organizations, and been a charter member and, later, director of a third. (I've since greatly scaled back how active I am in putting on events.) Here are some of the approaches that have worked for me, and for others I know.

I think I may be a masochist!

The decision to start an SM group is a big one. Setting it up and running it will require a *significant* amount of your time and energy, and will almost certainly involve at least some loss of privacy for you. If you're not willing to deal with these issues – if you're very busy, or if you're in a situation where a breach of confidentiality could cost you your job, security clearance, marriage, or kids – you're probably not a good candidate to start a club; let someone else be the trailblazer.

But let's say you are in a position to start an organization. You've got a little time on your hands, being "outed" would not totally destroy your life, and, most important, you *really* want to be a part of an SM community. Now is the time to sit down with a pad and pencil, and do some thinking. Before you recruit your first member, you're going to have to make some very fundamental decisions.

The most important thing a group leader can have is a clear vision of what they want the group to become. If they have this clear vision, nearly all important decisions almost make themselves. If they lack this clear vision, the club will lack a sense of direction, and numerous troubles will emerge. With this understanding, let's explore some matters that will help clarify your vision of how you want your organization to be. Consider the classic journalist's questions: who, what, when, where, why, and how.

- **Who?** Who will run your organization? Will it be an individual (e.g., you), a couple (probably you and your partner), or a committee (you and some friends)? In my experience, most organizations, at least in the beginning, are spearheaded by the vision and drive of one person. Although others may coalesce around that person to help with the grunt-work of running things, the initial pioneering work has a way of coming down to one dedicated individual.

- **What?** What will your organization be called? (I suggest you choose a name that is not obviously SM-oriented, particularly if you're trying to maintain a low profile. Many of the large national clubs, including The Eulenspiegel Society, Society of Janus, Chicagoland Discussion Group, and Threshold have chosen this option.)

> I've learned that when a guy says "Mistress, I'll do anything you want," what he means is "Mistress, I want to eat your pussy."

  Will your organization be for men only, for women only, for couples, for bisexuals, for heterosexuals – or will it be pansexual, i.e., for all genders and orientations? (Note: if you're going to have restrictions regarding gender, you may eventually need to establish definitions for "man" and "woman." In particular, your group will have to decide how to regard pre-operative and post-operative transsexuals.)

  What kind of people will your organization attract? While you may not want to turn away people who are older, younger, richer, poorer, "wilder" or "tamer" than you, keep in mind this basic reality: like attracts like. Many of your subsequent decisions, including your recruitment strategy, will depend on the answer to this question.

  What will be the minimum age for attendance at your organization? (For most organizations, the answer to this question is either 18 or 21.)

- **Where?** How wide a region will your organization include? And where will it meet – in a private home, in rented space, in public space like a park, in a restaurant or bar, on a college campus?

- **When?** How frequently will your organization meet? At what time of day? Will you meet on the same day each time, or will you rotate days?

- **Why?** What will be the purpose of your organization? Will it be a commercial enterprise or a noncommercial organization?

  What kind of events will your organization have? Will it have purely "talk-only" socials (probably the safest type of events to give), will it have programs and workshops, will it have parties?

Will your organization be for all styles of SM play, or will you focus on one style only? (There are organizations exclusively for male-top/female-bottom play and organizations for female-top/male-bottom play. There are also organizations for specialized playstyles such as spanking, fisting, fetishism, age play, and water sports.)

How? How will your meetings be conducted? Who will have authority to do what? (Many SM organizations have foundered on this particular rock, so be careful to set things up explicitly from the beginning.) It usually works well to have one ultimate "captain of the ship" who has final decision-making authority on virtually all points. This individual is also often known as "s/he who takes the blame" and/or as "that arrogant shithead."

Once you've made these decisions, you have yet another decision to make: you'll need to decide exactly how high a profile you want your new organization to have. If your organization is a commercial enterprise, if you live in a relatively liberal urban area, and/or if you're already pretty much "out" as an SM person, you may want to maintain a fairly high profile. On the other hand, if you live in a conservative area, if you don't have a lot of experience in running organizations, or if you have a lot to lose by being "outed," I'd suggest you opt for starting out in a low-profile manner.

I'll turn you into a sadist yet.

The high-profile option. If you choose this route, you will probably advertise your new organization pretty widely, and do relatively little screening of members or attendees. It's worth keeping in mind that the more open to the public your organization is, the greater effort you will have to make to keep things physically and emotionally safe for your members. This is doubly true if alcohol is served at any of your events. (I've attended SM events that were so large, and where attendance was so unscreened, that the organizers went so far as to hire armed guards.)

Advertising options include ads in your local newspaper(s). The local daily will reach a wider audience, but if your region has one or more of the free "lifestyle" tabloids which usually come out weekly or biweekly, and which feature (usually liberal) political commentary, restaurant and theater reviews, and personal ads, those are often a very good place to reach likely people. The Internet, any regional adult papers that cover your area, and your local adult computer bulletin boards are also excellent venues for high-profile publicity about your new organization.

You might consider printing up flyers announcing the formation of your organization, describing its structure and intent, and inviting people to join you.

These flyers can be posted on bulletin boards in leather stores, coffee houses, bookstores (especially gay/lesbian and alternative bookstores), lingerie shops and erotic boutiques, and clubs and bars which cater to the type of people you're trying to attract.

It's worth keeping in mind that just because *you're* willing to maintain a high profile doesn't mean your potential members are. Many people cannot afford to be publicly associated with any kind of SM group. Have your meetings in a place where people can come and go discreetly, without having to walk through a door labeled "Mistress Bitch's Dungeon." And be sure to emphasize to all attendees that they are to keep the identities of their compatriots, and the activities of the organization, confidential. (Breaching the rules of confidentiality is grounds for expulsion from many SM organizations.)

**The low-profile option.** This can be a little trickier, but is the more widely used approach, and the one I'd recommend. As I write this, a good friend of mine is starting a noncommercial SM club in a small city in a very conservative part of the country. She is running a small risk to herself by doing this (she is, among other things, a parent). Her deeper concern, though, is the confidentiality and safety of her members; it's far from out of the question that attendees could be subject to harassment or even attack by frat boys, rednecks, religious conservatives, doctrinaire "feminists," or police officers.

So for her, and for anybody who wants their organization to maintain a low profile, the strategy is quite different. In some more populated parts of the country, one option might be to accept new members by referral only. If you can't do that, it's particularly important to build a reasonably high barrier between yourself and people who are interested but unscreened, and to screen potential attendees carefully.

In making the following advice, I'm going to assume that you intend to start a small, discreet, noncommercial SM club, and that you live in an area where many people would be hostile to that idea. I'm therefore going to describe how to take an extremely cautious, conservative approach to creating your organization. If the area you live in is not so hostile, you can "ease up" as you feel appropriate.

**Initial recruiting.** Keep in mind what I call the 90-9-1 rule: of every 100 people you encounter in building your organization, 90 of them will be basically stable and sincere, nine will be genuinely interested in SM but too unstable to work out well in the organization, and one will be malicious, outright crazy, and/or dangerous. Your job is to screen in the 90 people (at a manageable rate) while screening out the nine and assiduously avoiding the one – not always an easy task.

If I were starting a low-profile organization (which I have done), the very first thing I'd do would be to get a P.O. box. Then I'd get a voice mail number, and possibly an anonymous e-mail address with a friendly carrier. (It's important to note that, while all three of these venues are confidentiality-conscious, there's no such thing as perfect privacy. Once again, if you really can't afford to be outed, you probably shouldn't be starting an organization.) While you're doing this, write up a single-sheet informational handout about what kind of organization you're trying to start. This doesn't have to be fancy; a neatly typed and photocopied information sheet will work fine.

A good next step might be to place a small, discreet ad in the classified section of your local paper. If you have a local adult newspaper, you *might* want to consider an ad there as well. How you word this ad may depend on the policies of that particular paper, and you may have to do a little wordsmithing before you get the wording to a point where they're willing to accept it. (If they won't accept any form of wording, find a different paper.) The phrase "erotic power exchange" is fairly well understood and isn't too threatening. Some papers may be willing to accept a phrase like "bondage and related practices." One friend of mine ran an ad seeking people "to discuss the works of Pauline Reage, Pat Califia, Anne Rice, and Jay Wiseman" (blush).

If you live within hailing distance of a city that does have an SM club, a very good bet would be to place an ad in that club's newsletter, looking for people in your area. After all, guess where *they're* looking for *you?*

Tell people to respond to the ad by sending a self-addressed stamped envelope to your mailbox, by leaving a message at your voice mail number, and/or by sending you an e-mail message. If they send a SASE, respond with the informational handout, and a note directing them to call the voice mail leaving their phone number if they're interested. If they e-mail you, you can send back the text of the informational handout, and direct them to send back a phone number if they'd like to be contacted. It's a very good idea to ask them to tell you what time of day is good to reach them, and whether or not it's OK to leave messages on their answering machine or voice mail.

Let me know when you're about to take that clamp off my clit.

In these times of caller ID and "star-69" technologies, I strongly recommend that you call them from a pay phone, or have a second separate phone line installed for this task – just keep in mind that it may ring a lot. Tell them a bit about your organization and let them know that you're thinking of having an informal get-together in a couple of months. During this call, it's important to appear as solid, responsible, and ethical as you can (remember, they're subject to the 90-9-1 rule too – how do they know what kind of a nut *you* might be?). Don't press them for a great deal of information; usually a first name and phone number is plenty. Also, don't ask questions like "Are you a cop?" Such questions can be considered "consciousness of guilt," and you're not doing anything wrong. Also, it's very well established that police officers conducting an investigation can deny that they are police officers.

If they seem basically OK – and *trust your instincts* on this – you can set up a time to meet them in a public place like a restaurant or coffee house. If your potential members have presented themselves to you as a couple, both members of the couple must show up for this meeting. If possible, it's best that single men get screened by men and that single women get screened by women; opposite-sex couples can be screened by either gender or by a couple. (And behave yourself – propositioning the candidates is *very* bad form.)

How will you recognize them, or they recognize you? (The one who makes themselves "recognizable" is at greater risk; you'll have to decide which of you that should be.) It often works for the recognizable party to carry a significant newspaper, book, or similar item; if they arrive first, they can leave it in a visible spot on their table.

Spend half an hour to an hour with them, partly to learn a bit more about their interests, but more importantly to get their "vibe." A bit of discreet questioning about their interests and level of experience is OK, but there is no need for either side to go into or to request graphic details. At the end of the meeting, tell them you'll be in touch with them if the group does indeed become a reality. If you feel they'll be an asset to your group, you should get in touch with them a couple of weeks before your first meeting.

Could you scratch my nose, please?

**Gender balance.** If your organization has a significant heterosexual component, you are very likely, sooner or later, to come up against a problem: you will almost certainly receive much more interest from single men than from single women. This, unfortunately, is a problem that can worsen rapidly. If there are many more men at an event than there are women, the men may well become increasingly competitive and predatory, scaring away the few women who *did* attend. Horror stories abound: I've attended several SM events with a 5:1 male/female ratio, and one – nominally pansexual – which got so bad that eventually it was attended *only* by single heterosexual men.

This unfortunate situation requires you to make some tough decisions. Some organizations solve it by admitting couples only; a few admit only committed couples. A less extreme solution may be to put the single guys on "standby," telling them that they can join as soon as a single lady joins to balance them out.

Certainly, it's a very good idea to recruit women for your organization. Women are likelier to attend an organization where they feel that they will be physically safe, protected from overly predatory approaches, and treated with respect and honesty. There *are* lots of women with SM fantasies around you, I assure you. If you make your group a safe place for them to come and talk, they will appear. (Note:

Having too many women isn't a good idea, either. I remember one event I put on for which I'd been assiduously recruiting women. I realized I might have gone a bit overboard when I saw no fewer than four lovely ladies sitting to one side of the room, looking for all the world like wallflowers at a high school prom. Not the kind of outcome I like.)

**Social meetings.** Once you've got enough people to put together a small get-together – eight to 10 is about the minimum to reach "critical mass," and be sure to allow for some people to chicken out – it's time to schedule your first "talk-only" club meeting!

It's a good idea to keep this first meeting very simple and informal. My preference would be to have it in a public location such as a restaurant (try for a large enough restaurant that your gathering won't garner undue attention, or a restaurant that has a private room you can use). Bars are a possibility if you don't mind dealing with a bit of cigarette smoke, but watch out for people drinking too much. Discreet sections of public parks can also be nice, if weather permits. Be a little cautious about having this first meeting in a private home, although if someone involved is willing to open their home to strangers this is certainly a possibility.

It's not a good idea to charge admission for this meeting; among other things, doing so may increase your chances of violating some local ordinance, may increase your liability in the event of a mishap, and may also create some difficulty for you when you decide how to deal with reporting this income. (If you do charge, I suggest that you keep your fees low and that you keep things on a cash-only basis.) Let people bring their own refreshments, or pot-luck dishes to share.

This isn't social chat, we're negotiating.

What should you do at the meeting? Simply let people chat and get acquainted. Aside from making a few brief welcoming remarks in the beginning, I wouldn't try to run things much. I strongly recommend that you not try to schedule any kind of demos, play, or nudity for this first get-together.

This is as far as many groups go – informal get-togethers in restaurants or in members' homes – and it works quite successfully for them. (Regularly scheduled restaurant get-togethers, called "munches," are a frequent social event for Internet-oriented SM folks. Such events are announced on the alt.sex.bondage, alt.sex.femdom, and alt.sex.spanking newsgroups.) A purely social group like this is already a huge step toward helping people overcome fear and isolation, and toward learning and growing as SM players. You can share information, trade books and tips, and possibly carpool to workshops and parties given by larger organizations.

**Programs.** So, say you and/or your group decide that you'd like the organization to become more formal and perform more functions. What happens next?

The next step that most organizations take is toward giving some sort of programs. These can be interactive programs, like round-table discussions on a predetermined topic or games like Truth or Dare. Or they can be educational programs, such as workshops or demos put on by a speaker who has special expertise in a particular topic.

If you're going to have programs, particularly if they include demos, you've grown beyond the restaurant stage. (I know of one group which got permanently banned from a restaurant when their demonstrations went too far.) At this point, you will either have to rent space – which involves some sort of contributions from members, and thus opens up some financial issues – or meet in a member's home. If you decide to take the latter course, it may be a good idea to rotate the meetings from one home to another. Also, be sure to emphasize to the attendees that they must arrive dressed in discreet outer clothing, park properly, and avoid discussing SM-related topics until they are indoors.

I love Velcro cuffs – they're so easy to put on and so fast to take off.

The total time of your get-together should allow for some socializing at the beginning and end of the event, as well as time for the program itself. Keep in mind that minds can't outlast fannies: after about 75 minutes, attention will be wandering and bladders will be filling, and your attendees will start taking breaks whether you tell them to or not. Also, set up a time for announcements at the start of the meeting, and maybe a time to allow attendees to briefly introduce themselves to the group.

It's important that one particular person be in ultimate charge of the event. This person should have very broad authority, including the right to tell people to leave if necessary. The person in charge of the event may or may not be the overall director of the organization.

The timing of your event might break down as follows:

| | |
|---|---|
| 30 minutes | Doors open & social period |
| 10-20 minutes | Announcements |
| | Introduction of speaker (and, perhaps, attendees) |
| 45-75 minutes | Program, Part 1 |
| 10-20 minutes | Break |
| 45-75 minutes | Program, Part 2 |
| 20-30 minutes | Social period & cleanup |

Thus, the minimum time for a successful program is about 160 minutes (two hours and 40 minutes).

Educational programs might be on such topics as bondage, whipping, spanking, play piercing, owner/slave dynamics, safer sex, male or female genital torture, "ask the doctor," body modifications, electricity play, and temperature play. There are dozens more.

Interactive programs can include moderated discussions on topics of particular concern to your members, or games.

Other functions. What are some of the other functions your organization can perform? To name just a few:

- compile and maintain a resource list
- publish a newsletter and/or events calendar for your region
- recruit new potential members ("recruiting outreach")
- send speakers to human sexuality classes, mental health professionals, and law enforcement agencies ("educational outreach")
- sponsor specialized discussion groups
- provide play space
- give parties
- hold "top & bottom auctions"
- maintain a lending library
- hold commitment ceremonies and memorial services
- hold fund-raisers and make donations to related charities (battered women's shelters, Amnesty International, ACLU, AIDS charities). Note: Some organizations will not accept donations from an SM group, so you may have to make your donations anonymously or through an individual member.
- pool resources to purchase leather, rope, safer sex supplies, and so on in bulk
- provide a silent alarm service
- make referrals to SM-friendly physicians, therapists, attorneys, and other professionals
- watch for unfair representations of SM in the media, and sponsor letter-writing campaigns ("media watch")
- publish personal ads
- hold flea markets for new and used toys, literature, and equipment
- publish and compile an annual membership questionnaire

If you think creatively, you can probably come up with others. (SM scholarship funds? Hmmm....)

## Parties

Why on earth would anybody want to do SM at a *party*, for heaven's sake?

That may be a tough question to answer, unless you've actually attended an SM party. It can be hard to put into words the wonderful synergy of doing a scene when you're surrounded by the sounds and sights of other scenes all around you, and when you're bathing in the eager gaze of supportive onlookers. For someone who has a bit of an exhibitionistic streak, playing at parties can be the ultimate high.

But even if you're not into that kind of showing off, parties offer some unique benefits. First of all, there's simply the pleasure of attending a party where you can schmooze, gossip, cruise, be yourself, and just generally hang out. (I rarely play at parties, and yet I really enjoy attending them.) Many people like to do their first scene with a new partner in the relative safety of a party environment. Parties give people the opportunity to watch different playstyles and to learn new techniques. You can also sometimes get an idea of what an individual's skills and style are like, thus helping you decide whether or not to approach them for play.

**Deciding to put on a party.** Putting on a party is a *lot* of work and responsibility. Although it gets somewhat easier with time and practice, even hardened partygivers experience moments of stress, exhaustion, and panic.

Still, let's say you've decided your organization is ready to put on its first party. Let's consider some of the decisions you need to make before you send out your first invitation.

I was really getting off on topping you.

- When will you give your party? In general, people in most areas seem to prefer to party on Saturday night. If your area has a lot of SM or sexuality organizations, you may find that all the Saturday nights are already taken (it's generally a good idea to avoid scheduling your party to conflict with another group's party). In that case, you might consider a Friday night, a Sunday afternoon/early evening, or possibly even a weeknight. Any of these options may have a negative impact on the number of people who will be able to attend. If you *must* give a party or other event on the same night that someone else is giving one, it's very important that you contact them ahead of time and explain your situation. Let them know that you're not intentionally scheduling a conflict with them. Some sort of compromise, such as combining guest lists, might be a possibility. Show proper consideration regarding these matters. The bad feelings created by such conflicts can last for a long time. When will your party start and end? Customs on this point vary according to what region of the country you're in, and the age of your party group. In general, younger groups, gay and lesbian groups, and groups back East seem willing to party later into the night. We old hetero hippies need our sleep, so many of the parties I attend start as early as 7 p.m. and wrap up by 1 a.m. Typically, parties have a time when the doors open, a time when the doors close and nobody else is admitted, sometimes a brief period for announcements and/or orientation, and a time when the party ends. The cleanup crew may be asked to hang around for half an hour or so after the formal ending of the party.

- Who will be in charge of your party? (This may or may not be the person who is in charge of the overall group. It also may or may not be the person who owns the space in which the party is held.) It's very important that your party organization have clear agreement about the lines of authority during the party.
- Who will be invited to your party? Who will be allowed to bring guests, how many, and under what circumstances?
- Where will your party be held? Most small organizations start by holding parties in the private homes of the members. I've found that the minimum requirement for a comfortable party is a house with at least two bedrooms and, if possible, two bathrooms. It's far from unheard of for SM people to convert their basements into dungeons, and a house with one of these can make an excellent party environment – people can eat and schmooze upstairs and play downstairs. Later, you may wish to rent space in a scene-friendly nightclub, loft, warehouse conversion, professional domination studio, or other similar environment.
- What kind of party will it be? Will it be for women only? Men only? Mixed genders? If the genders are mixed, will it be exclusively male-top, female-top, or "anything goes"? Will the focus be on a particular type of play, such as spanking, fisting, or age play? Will there be a special event such as an auction? Will there be a theme? Will there be a dress code?

I love getting hog-tied.

**Who will do what?** It takes more people than you might think to put on a successful party. The "cast of characters" at most parties includes the partygiver, the space owner, a doorkeeper, a cashier, one or more food people, a music person, one or more dungeon monitors, and a cleanup crew. Typically, these people receive free admission to the party in exchange for volunteering.

So what do all of them do?

The *partygiver* has the ultimate authority and the ultimate responsibility for the party. If any of the other helpers fall through or flake out, the partygiver must arrange a substitute for the derelict person (or do it themselves). If there is a conflict among helpers, or among attendees, the partygiver must resolve it.

The *space owner* is the person who owns, rents, or manages the space where the party is held. When there is a difference between the rules laid down by the space owner and the rules of the party organization, it is customary to default to the more conservative rule (in other words, if the party group allows hot wax play but the space owner doesn't, there will be no wax play at that party). The partygiver and the space owner must reach agreement before the party about who will be liable for damages, and to what monetary extent. They should agree on how to handle matters if the space owner has a problem with the behavior of any party attendee. It is customary for the partygiver to give the space owner a certain number of complimentary admissions to the party.

The *doorkeeper* is responsible for letting people into the party and for checking them against the reservation list. Since the doorkeeper usually doesn't feel like spending the entire night opening and closing the door, most parties have a pre-established door-closing time.

The *cashier* takes admission fees, makes change, hands out rule sheets, and collects signed waiver forms. At smaller parties, the doorkeeper and cashier may be the same person.

The *food prep team* makes sure there is plenty of food to eat. It's a very good idea to serve high-protein snacks to stave off low blood sugar among players. Many people also enjoy sweets when they play; chocolate is a particular favorite. Most importantly, make sure there are *lots* of non-alcoholic beverages, including fresh water – many people sweat heavily while playing, and you don't want anybody fainting from dehydration. It's considerate to offer vegetarian snacks as well. Unless you're giving an extremely fancy party, cold foods will usually suffice. The food prep team should also make sure that the supply of food and beverages is kept refreshed through the course of the party. (Note: in some cases, particularly if the party is small, the partygiver may choose to have attendees bring pot-luck food. This can work out fine, as long as you enforce the rules and make some effort to be sure that a variety of dishes is provided – a long table full of strawberries looks lovely but probably won't fill the stomachs of a houseful of exhausted perverts.)

The *music person* makes sure that appropriate music is played throughout the evening, at a volume that is comfortable for the players. What constitutes "appropriate music" depends on the preferences of your group; some groups prefer rock or techno with a driving beat, while others prefer trance-inducing New Age music, and still others like something classical. The music person may be responsible for setting up the sound system as well. In some cases, the dungeon monitor may double as music person.

The *dungeon monitors* are responsible for making sure that the party rules are followed. They are available for answering questions, diplomatically suggesting safer ways to do scenes that don't look adequately safe, and making sure the onlookers behave themselves in a courteous and non-intrusive manner. They may help out by bringing items like water or condoms to aid in a scene. They are also the first line of defense in case of an emergency – a medical emergency such as illness or injury, an environmental emergency such as a power outage or fire, or a behavioral emergency such as a freakout or flashback. Usually, each dungeon monitor works a shift of one and a half to two hours. You probably should have one dungeon monitor for about each 40 people in attendance.

The *cleanup crew* are the real heroes of the evening. When everybody else is exhausted, endorphined out, and ready to go home, they spring into action and restore the space to pristine condition. (*Big* hint: if you want to ingratiate yourself with a partygiver, volunteer for the cleanup crew.)

Equipment. As a general rule, attendees at a party bring their own toys (rope, restraints, whips, clamps, etc.) If they have special preferences regarding lubes, condoms, and so on, they should bring these items, too.

The partygiver and/or space owner usually provides some large items of bondage equipment, if possible. At some parties, this may be minimal (it's amazing the fun you can have on a plain old bed). Others offer roomsful of enticing racks, posts, crosses, horses, cages and other equipment. A partygiver will often find it worthwhile to invest in some pieces of equipment that can be broken down and carried from one party location to another, a strategy which is especially useful if you give parties in private homes.

Can we do a scene that involves lots of bondage and clamps?

Also, the partygiver and/or space owner should provide emergency equipment. A space where parties are held should be equipped with blackout lights, six-volt lanterns, fire extinguishers and a first aid kit. (It's a nice touch to include common over-the-counter medications such as aspirin, ibuprofen, decongestants, and antacids in this kit.) There should be some sort of sound system available, even if it's only a portable tape player.

The partygiver, or sometimes the space owner, is usually also responsible for providing safer sex supplies. These should, at a minimum, include lubricated and unlubricated condoms, latex gloves in all sizes, non-latex gloves for people with allergies, lubricants with and without nonoxynol-9, some dental dams or plastic wrap, and cleanser and paper towels that people can use to clean up their play areas after they're done. If you allow bloodletting at your parties, you should have and maintain a properly marked sharps container, and you should make sure it's properly disposed of after the party. (Drugstores in some parts of the country will give you empty sharps containers and accept filled ones for disposal.) It's also a nice touch to put out zip-lock plastic bags that attendees can use to store and carry dirty toys.

Food equipment such as paper plates, cups, flatware, napkins, and platters may be provided by the food people, by the partygiver or by the space owner.

Each dungeon monitor should be equipped, while on duty, with a small flashlight, a pair of paramedic scissors, a pair of gloves, and some sort of easily recognizable insignia such as a badge or armband. The partygiver ordinarily provides these.

**Setting the rules.** Your party group will have to reach agreement regarding what rules you intend to enforce. It's a good idea to have your rules established *before* you start inviting people – in fact, I'd suggest that you consider including a copy of the rules with the party invitation. A would-be attendee discovering a deal-breaking rule at the door is frustrating and disappointing for all concerned.

Above all, do not make rules that you're not willing to enforce. Nothing harms a party-giver's credibility faster than a lot of people visibly breaking the rules.

If you make a rule, enforce it without exception – even if the rule-breaker is your best buddy. (Note: It's not unknown for a certain type of attendee to attempt to test the mettle of a party host by bending or breaking the rules. When this happens, act promptly; the sooner you approach them, the easier it will be to resolve the problem amicably. Be prepared to be polite but firm.)

Some of your rules will simply be to make your own life easier. For example, I've found that it's a good idea to charge people a small additional fee for showing up after the doors have closed (unless they notified the partygiver first), for RSVPing after the deadline, or for RSVPing and then not showing up. Other rules will have to do with etiquette and courteous behavior.

*Bring me something to cause you pain and something to cause you pleasure.*

Still other rules have to do with SM activities. Here are some of the issues that various party groups have chosen to restrict, or not to restrict.

| | |
|---|---|
| penetrative sex | firearms |
| unprotected sex | loud screams |
| drugs and alcohol | suspension |
| bloodletting | inverted suspension |
| open flame | gags |
| suffocation and strangulation | disturbing scenes (for example, Nazi play |
| "consensual nonconsent" | or rape scenes) |
| open flame | scat and piss scenes |
| hot wax play | branding |

For a sample set of party rules, as well as descriptions of a Truth or Dare game and a tops & bottoms auction, see Appendix I in the back of this book.

## *More Formal Organizational Structures*

As your organization grows, the complexity and amount of work involved grow along with it. The amount of money passing through it may become uncomfortably large; responsibility may need to be shared; space owners may be getting nervous about liability issues.

Moreover, a "boss" never lasts forever. The person who's been running things will eventually become exhausted, and wish to step down. It may be time for the membership to hold an election, a crucial point in the organization's growth. Elections need to be thought through well in advance – particularly who is eligible to vote. (I have seen at least one organization fail because of a lack of consensus on this matter.)

Also, the form of the organization may need to come under periodic review. You may wish to stay loose and informal, or to become more formally organized. Some SM clubs have even gone so far as to become legally recognized nonprofit corporations.

If you decide to go the "fully legit" route, you might wish to look into incorporating as a church – an organizational vehicle with a great deal to recommend it. In addition to the benefits of other nonprofit corporations, churches have special status. What is said between a church leader and a member of the congregation may be considered privileged information, an important point regarding confidentiality. Also, spiritual advisors have greater latitude than others in visiting people who have been imprisoned or hospitalized. Thirdly, government agencies may be a bit less eager to intrude into a church's activities then those of other organizations (that "separation of church and state" business is still taken fairly seriously in this country).

On being an SM club officer. Being an officer in an SM club can be a great deal of fun, and includes a certain amount of prestige and status. However, you will quickly find that the job also comes with substantial responsibilities.

When you become an officer, you have been placed in a position of trust. It is now your duty to serve the interests of the club and its members, rather than your personal agenda. Also, now that you're one of the "first among equals," people are looking to you for an example of how to behave. Thus, it's crucial that you conduct your club dealings fairly to all concerned. That means you have to treat your worst enemy as fairly as you treat your best friend. If you feel that you cannot treat every member of your club with adequate fairness and objectivity, spare everybody a lot of grief and leave the officership to someone who can.

# General Safety Considerations

**Musings on safety.** The overall subject of safety is one that gets considerable attention in the SM world. Participating in SM involves both obvious and not-so-obvious risks to our physical well-being, our emotional well-being, and the well-being of our relationships. That being so, I'd like to take a minute to talk about safety in general.

A dictionary I have handy defines "safe" as follows: Not apt or able to cause or incur danger, harm, or evil; free from danger, injury, or hazard. "Safety" is defined as freedom from danger, risk, or injury. "Risk" is defined as the possibility of suffering harm or loss; danger.

It can be tricky to talk about safety and risk in the context of SM. Many players go through a long and glorious career doing SM, without ever experiencing a serious injury or other problem. Others, often through no fault of their own, encounter several.

I was putting out enough endorphins to sedate a cancer ward.

There is no such thing as a risk-free life. Even a person sitting quietly in their living room watching TV is at some degree of risk. That being so, a person participating in SM, no matter how cautiously and responsibly, is obviously at a much higher degree of risk. There is no such thing as risk-free SM.

On the other hand, I've seen the fact that all SM contains at least some risk used by people to try to justify highly reckless and dangerous practices. I call this the "hey, everything is risky" fallacy. Of *course* everything is risky – *but not to the same degree.*

It may be more useful to think of safety and risk in the context of statistics. Instead of trying to figure out what *your* chances of encountering a problem may be, imagine yourself as part of a group of 1,000 perverts, all doing the same scene. Five hundred of you try the scene using Technique A, and the other 500 try Technique B. In the first group, one person gets hurt; in the second group, 25 people are hurt. Thus, we say Technique B is riskier, or less safe, than Technique A.

**SM and risk.** SM is the riskiest form of sex. Even under ideal conditions, with all reasonable precautions taken, danger sometimes appears. For example, an earthquake might strike. A bound, blindfolded, or otherwise hampered submissive is vulnerable. (Such vulnerability is part of SM's attractiveness for many players.)

Some critics say SM is too dangerous to do at all. I disagree. Responsible SM play is not unacceptably risky. The critics may say *any* risk taken for the "mere" purpose of feeling pleasure (especially – horrors! horrors! – *sexual* pleasure) isn't worth it. Again, I disagree. People frequently take risks to feel pleasure. All sporting events, for example, involve risk. Amusement park rides, circuses, and many other pleasurable events are risky. Driving to the movies is risky.

Serious injuries rarely occur during SM play. Many fewer than seem to occur, for example, in a similar-sized group of people playing softball, practicing martial arts, or enjoying touch football – let alone jogging! Ignorance and sloppiness cause many more injuries than abuse causes. (One of my main purposes in writing this book is to reduce the number of injuries caused by such ignorance and sloppiness.) If you follow basic safety guidelines, you probably will never face any serious injury, medical emergency, or psychological crisis.

Still, as in any other part of life, emergencies sometimes occur. They may be completely unrelated to the SM play. For example, people with heart disease, epilepsy, high blood pressure, and other medical conditions sometimes develop problems during a session.

If you decide to play, especially in the submissive role, do so only after carefully considering the risks and benefits. If you avoid high-risk activities, such as choking or playing with electricity, then ordinary safety measures should suffice. Let's review those.

First, you should not study safety issues without a frame of reference. Every aspect of SM has its safety considerations.

Second, your number-one safety measure is to play *only* with people you know well and with whom you are on good terms. Playing with a stranger, with someone you are not on good terms with, or with someone stoned, upset, tired, or drunk *drastically* increases the risk.

Third, set up safewords, discuss health matters, define limits, and otherwise fully negotiate the session *before* beginning it. *Rushed or sloppy pre-session negotiations are probably the most common cause of a bad session.* (See the negotiation section in "Basic Basics.")

Many SM players state that they feel limited by what they perceive as excessive concern regarding safety issues. (Indeed, the first edition of this book was criticized for its "OSHA-like" approach to SM.) While these people have a point, I would like to mention another perspective: safety as enabler. When I am about to play, particularly when I am about to do a session that I know will be more intense than I normally do, and double-particularly if I am intending to be in the submissive role, I find it very reassuring to know that all reasonable safety precautions have been taken. If I know that the environment has been made as safe as it can be under the circumstances, and if I know that my dominant is both trained and equipped to take care of me if something goes badly wrong (which it occasionally does), I relax and am much more likely to "go for it" than I otherwise would. I find I can relax and concentrate on what's going on, rather than worry myself with "what-if" concerns. Thus, proper attention to safety concerns actually enables my play, rather than restricting it.

## *What About Leaving Marks?*

This is a problem area. Spanking, whipping, clamping, pinching, and other practices can all leave bruises, welts, and other marks. You've heard of a pain threshold. There is also something you can think of as a "bruise threshold." Some people can take outrageously intense floggings and barely show a welt the next day. Others can have marks that last for weeks left by only a very light whipping.

It is a bottom's prerogative to admire their marks.

Unfortunately, it's often difficult to determine how much force will leave a mark until you've already gone far enough to create one. If marking the submissive would cause a problem, you're in trouble.

There's also the pesky matter that sometimes marks don't appear for up to a day after the session. This can lead to a rather intense "morning after." I once, at an SM party, used a new, narrow-tipped, riding crop on my lady. (My regular riding crop has a tip nearly three times broader.) We had a great time, and her skin looked clear afterward, but when we woke up the next day she looked like her skin had been painted in some unusual type of camouflage. It bore many, many large, colorful bruises that lasted for well over a week. She felt fine about the situation, and even thought it was a bit funny. I, on the other hand, felt distinctly like a heel – thus adding even more to her amusement. We were both just flat-out lucky in this situation.

It's very important to discuss leaving marks during pre-session negotiations. If marks are absolutely not acceptable, your play needs to be significantly altered.

If you are playing with a new submissive who cannot be marked, you might start by asking them if they bruise easily. Most people have some idea. What SM play have they done in the past that did or didn't leave marks? What other types of activities?

Look at their skin. Light, pale skin will show bruises more readily than darker skin will show them. Older people will bruise more easily than younger people. Women seem to bruise more easily than men, especially when near their period. There is some anecdotal evidence that people who feel tense or nervous bruise more easily than relaxed people.

Find out if the submissive is taking any anti-clotting drugs. Such drugs can dramatically increase the amount of bruising caused by play. *Aspirin* is such a drug, by the way. (Indeed, I've even heard of some submissives taking aspirin two to three hours before a session because they wanted marks on them afterward – the little perverts.) Does the submissive have any blood or blood vessel diseases – including diabetes?

If marks must definitely be avoided, much of your play is limited. Keep the following principles in mind.

Go ahead.
Do it.
It's all right.
Whip me.

1.  The narrower the flagellation instrument, the more likely it is to mark (and, by the way, the quieter it is). To give an extreme example, an almost-silent coat hanger is much more likely to mark than a broad, flat, noisy paddle.

2.  The more times you strike a particular area, the more likely you are to mark it – particularly if you strike that area with a series of strokes.

3.  The "harder" the tissue underneath the skin, the more likely a stroke there is to mark. The upper thighs, for example, with their underlying muscles, are more likely to mark than the buttocks.

4.  Bondage should use broad, flat restraining methods such as leather cuffs as opposed to hard, narrow restraints such as handcuffs.

5.  Play that has a low probability of leaving marks includes sensory deprivation (this intensifies what sensations the submissive does feel), extensive and/or uncomfortable bondage, hot/cold play, anal play, electricity, and verbal games. For more hints, see the "Related Practices" section of this book.

6. As a "don't mark me" submissive, you might want to avoid playing with a blindfold. Wearing a blindfold could prevent your seeing that marks are starting to appear. You also might ask that mirrors be placed so that you can see the body area the dominant is playing with.

7. Tightly bound body parts bruise *much* more readily than unbound body parts. Keep this in mind when striking or clamping bound breasts, genitals, and so forth. (And remember that a cock ring is, in its own way, a form of bondage.)

8. If a bruise does start to appear, immediately elevating the area and applying a cold pack directly to the involved tissue will reduce but probably not entirely eliminate the amount of bruising. (Don't apply ice directly to skin, and leave it on for only about 15 minutes at a time. You don't want to cause frostbite.)

As a footnote, I've heard that taking an antihistamine two to three hours before a session may reduce the amount of bruising. This sounds rational to me, but I haven't tried it myself and it's not a practice in wide use within the community, so don't consider this highly reliable information.

I've also had it reported to me (but haven't yet had a chance to confirm) that ultrasound treatment can make bruises go away quickly. Other people speak highly of oral or topical arnica (available in health food stores) or bruise plasters (available at oriental herbalists) as ways to help heal bruises fast.

> After I've had a really heavy whipping I always feel strong, powerful, and centered.

Remember that a hot shower, sauna, hot tub, or similar exposure can bring non-visible bruises and other marks "to the surface" up to several days after a session. On the other hand, taking a cold shower shortly after a session may help prevent marks from appearing.

Creams that cover bruises and other marks such as port wine stain (think of Gorbachev's forehead) can be bought at drugstores and department stores. One popular brand is called Dermablend. I recommend that you pick some up *before* you need it.

The general rule when playing in a "no marks" situation is: If you're not sure whether or not a given activity will leave marks, don't do it.

**"Post-whipping flu."** Myoglobin is an oxygen-transporting protein that exists in muscle cells. When muscle cells are damaged, they may rupture

309

and release myoglobin into the body's circulatory system. While the body can usually handle small amounts of myoglobin without much difficulty, larger amounts in the blood can damage the kidneys.

A submissive who has done a heavy scene, particularly if they've been playing with enough impact to leave deep bruises or enough electricity to cause muscle spasm, may feel a little out of sorts the next day, sort of as though they had a mild case of the flu. This phenomenon is due in part to the release of myoglobin into their bloodstream. Flushing the myoglobin out of their system may help them feel better. It's therefore very important for them to drink a lot of fluids for the next day or two to help the kidneys with this process. (If their urine is noticeably dark, they should probably see a physician.) Some people also like to take some extra vitamins – particularly Vitamin C, Vitamin A and zinc – to aid in healing.

## SM During Pregnancy

OK, so she's pregnant. Does this mean you have to give up SM for the next nine months?

Probably not – but you may have to alter, modify, or even temporarily give up some forms of play. Her body, biochemistry, self-image, and emotions are going through dramatic and sometimes rapid changes; accommodating them will require communication, sensitivity, and flexibility.

I like feeling trapped.

Obviously, she should receive professional prenatal care as early in the pregnancy as possible. (Physicians are aware that 17 percent of pregnant women are victims of domestic violence during their pregnancy, so now may not be the best time to show up at the doctor's office with a collection of welts and bruises.)

The most important thing to keep in mind is that she *will* change while she is pregnant – physically, hormonally, and emotionally. Exactly how she will change cannot be predicted, so it's important to stay in touch with the here and now. Some examples are:

**Physical changes.** Toward the end of the pregnancy, she will find it increasingly difficult to lie on her stomach, and lying on her back will compromise blood flow to the baby. She may also find all-fours positions difficult.

She may have more frequent episodes of dizziness or nausea. Be careful with gags.

Her breasts will increase in size and become more sensitive. Later in the pregnancy, she may also start to secrete colostrum from her nipples, particularly if they are being stimulated. Heavy impact play to the breasts is probably not a good idea.

Changes in her balance may make it difficult for her to stand for long periods of time, particularly in bondage. She may also find prolonged standing painful to her back and legs. She may want to avoid wearing very high heels.

She may suffer from hemorrhoids, so be careful about inserting anything into her anus.

The connective tissue in her joints is loosening, making her more flexible. However, it may not be a good idea to take advantage of this flexibility; keep bondage relatively comfortable.

She will have to urinate frequently. If you like to play with bondage, now is a good time to invest a couple of bucks in a small portable urinal.

**Emotional changes.** She is in the process of adjusting her self-image to accommodate the idea of being a mother. She is also dealing with extreme fluctuations in mood-affecting hormones.

Some women report that they feel sensations more intensely during pregnancy, so they may not be able to handle levels of pain that they would have been able to manage before.

It's also common for pregnant women to feel emotions more intensely. Most mothers I talked to while researching this section stated that they avoided negative, stressful scenes (and people) while they were pregnant. One made a point of avoiding heavy fear play. (Many people believe that the maturing infant is aware of its mother's emotions during pregnancy.)

**Sexual changes.** Her sexuality may change very distinctly during pregnancy. Her libido may increase or decrease, or both at different times. Her interest in SM may also increase or decrease, or it may change. (One woman I talked to went from being a sweet submissive to being a hellish sadist during pregnancy.) It's also worth keeping in mind that her sexual and SM interests may change *after* the arrival of the baby. She may not be interested in sex or SM play at all for a period of weeks or months – especially receiving pain! She may be too exhausted to feel like doing much of anything. I have known a few women who permanently lost *all* interest in SM once they made the transition from "hot babe" to "mom."

**Important cautions.** Obviously, delivering blows to the abdominal area of a pregnant woman is a really, really, really bad idea. Less obviously, blowing air into the vagina during cunnilingus or other activities, particularly later in her pregnancy, has a small but real chance of causing an air embolism.

If she has experienced any bleeding, pain, or fluid leakage from her vagina, I would definitely avoid any sort of vaginal penetration. Paramedics are cautioned never to do a vaginal examination on a woman who has third-trimester bleeding. Doing so can provoke a fatal hemorrhage.

Vaginal fisting during pregnancy is a very controversial topic. Some women have reported no problems with it, and possibly even some benefits in terms of helping to ease the birth process. I'd say that if you're accustomed to being fisted, you can probably proceed safely, at least for the first two trimesters. I wouldn't explore this activity for the first time during pregnancy, though.

**A possible benefit.** Childbirth education classes such as Lamaze or Bradley teach pain processing skills that will stand you in good stead throughout the rest of your life as a pervert. I have on several occasions seen Janet go into the conscious relaxation and breathing exercises she learned in Lamaze during an intense scene. One male dominant/female submissive couple I know took great and perverse pleasure in hearing their husband-coached childbirth teacher instruct the women to "yield to their husbands and accept the pain."

When we're alone, I want you to kneel by the side of my chair while we watch TV.

In summary, the only thing that will stay the same during pregnancy is constant change. Don't concentrate on the way things were yesterday or last month, concentrate on the way they are *now*. This is not a good time for pushing limits or setting records; it's a great time for increased intimacy and giving her nurturing support in whatever way works for the two of you.

## Common Causes of SM Disasters

The following are frequent causes of SM sessions "going bad."
1. Playing with strangers, especially someone not "in the scene."
2. Playing with someone toward whom you feel anger, fear, or other negative emotions.
3. Playing without safewords, even if experienced.
4. Playing for reasons other than erotic pleasure or personal growth (for example, from a sense of anger or revenge, or as a substitute for therapy).
5. Playing while intoxicated, ill, or tired.
6. Negotiating inadequately before you begin.
7. Leaving a bound submissive alone.

8.  Blindfolding and/or gagging a submissive you haven't previously played with several times.
9.  Disregarding safewords or implying, even jokingly, that you might disregard them.
10. Using worn-out equipment.
11. Engaging in unfamiliar activities without adequate prior education.
12. Escalating the session's intensity too quickly.
13. Playing with someone other than your steady partner without a silent alarm in operation.
14. Administering unrelenting, increasing pain to a submissive not ready for that.
15. Physical resistance during SM play, unless *very* carefully negotiated beforehand.

## *First Aid and CPR Training*

All SM players should know first aid and CPR. The Red Cross offers an excellent basic class called Standard First Aid. The class lasts about seven hours. You should repeat this class every year. Everybody, both dominant and submissive, should take this class. Sometimes SM club members go to the Red Cross and take the class as a group. At least one SM club has all of its officers take the class annually. Some clubs have "in-house" instructors.

Please don't untie my hands.

I've been an instructor for many years, and teach several "all-perv" Standard First Aid classes each year. They're great fun! (I also teach the more advanced First Responder course to an all-perv group about once a year.) Also, about once a year, I hear that one of my former students got into a situation where they really needed what they learned in class.

Note: Other companies also teach good quality first aid/CPR classes. Check your local yellow pages under "First Aid Instruction."

Nothing about SM is so dangerous as to increase the need for such training. Learning first aid and CPR is a basic act of responsibility, nothing more. It is *not* something SM players have a uniquely high need to know. (But, like everyone else, they do need to know it).

Attention submissives: I would feel doubtful about bottoming to anyone who didn't have, at a minimum, current first aid and CPR cards. How will they care for me if something goes seriously wrong? It's entirely proper to

313

ask to see your dominant's certificates before playing with them. If they can't produce current cards, I'd consider refusing to play.

Major point: If you haven't taken first aid and CPR training within the last twelve months, you cannot call yourself a responsible dominant. (I was challenged on this point when I published the first edition of this book, but since then, some of my challengers have had experiences which changed their point of view.)

## First Aid Supplies

Only five common conditions kill before help arrives: an obstructed airway, stopped breathing, cardiac arrest, severe bleeding, and a severe allergic reaction. You need no special equipment to manage the first three, but you'll need dressings and bandages to control bleeding. You could improvise with towels or similar material, but as a responsible player you should have the actual supplies handy. You'll also need an over-the-counter epinephrine inhaler (Primatene, Bronkaid) and diephen-hydramine tablets (Nytol, Sominex) to cope with a severe allergic reaction. (These are stopgap measures only. If you know that you have severe allergies, contact your physician to obtain an Epi-Pen or Ana-Kit.)

The way to get me to be really submissive is to blindfold me.

For your home, I suggest you keep the following supplies in a portable box, such as a plastic toolbox, in your bathroom.

**"In-house" supplies:**
- A small flashlight (I recommend a white Life-Lite by Garrity)
- Ten 4x4 gauze pads
- Two rolls of three-inch bandage
- One roll of one-inch tape
- Two triangular bandages
- One pair of paramedic scissors
- Two pairs of vinyl or latex gloves
- Five foil-wrapped alcohol wipes
- A bottle or packets of a broad-spectrum disinfectant containing provodone-iodine. Betadine is the most widely known brand.

Besides the above, keep the following supplies in your toy bag.
- A small flashlight (I really like the LifeLite as a toybag flashlight)
- Five 4x4 gauze pads

- One roll of three-inch bandage
- One triangular bandage
- One pair of paramedic scissors
- Two pairs of vinyl or latex gloves
- Five alcohol wipes
- A tube of provodone-iodine disinfectant

Note: You can find a white, bright yellow, or similar colored flashlight much more easily in the dark than you can find a black or dark-colored flashlight.

Key point: In an emergency, you'll want these supplies *in the room with you.*

These supplies are cheap, simple to use, and take up little room. There is no excuse for not having them available. (Hey submissives! It's also not out of line to ask to see the dominant's safety equipment.)

*paramedic scissors*

The paramedic scissors popular with rescue squads are excellent. They are particularly useful if, for some reason, you need to get the submissive free from their bondage *right now.* These bandage-type scissors are curved with blunt tips and large, plastic handles. They rapidly and safely cut clothing, leather, rope, and similar material. You can buy these scissors for about $10.00 at most medical supply stores. (Please note: many stores that sell SM gear also sell paramedic scissors.)

She hates being spanked, and she'll take a really heavy spanking for me.

If you can't find them locally, call one of the medical supply companies listed below and ask for a catalog. Quantity discounts are available, so some SM clubs buy in bulk. As always, it's wise to comparison shop.

Armstrong (800) 323-4220
Dyna-Med (800) 854-2706
Gall's (800) 477-7766 (puts out good police/fire/EMS catalog)
Life Assist (800) 824-6016
Moore (800) 678-8678 (several catalogs: ask for Medical and EMS)

## Common SM Emergencies

Five conditions account for most SM-related emergencies. These are, in rough order of frequency, loss of emotional balance, falls, fainting, electrical power failure, and fire. You can remember them by the "Five-F" memory device: "freakouts, falls, fainting, failure, and fire."

**Loss of emotional balance ("freakouts").** Loss of emotional balance (freaking out) due to sensory or emotional overload is the most common SM emergency. This is usually due to failure to follow basic safety procedures. (But not always. Sometimes SM play unexpectedly touches an unknown emotional hot spot. Repressed memories sometimes get triggered, phobias get tweaked, and so forth.)

Submissives experience most freakouts, but dominants may also experience them. For example, a novice dominant who has just finished giving their first heavy whipping (even if the submissive loved receiving it) may not be able to deal with learning that they are someone capable of doing that.

SM's intensity is one of its main attractions for many people. This intensity excites, but it also stresses the bodies and minds of the players. Sometimes that stress is more than a player can stand.

A subtle but very effective way to prevent emotional upsets is to stop the session if you emotionally "lose touch" with your partner. Dialogue, even if it's only having the submissive nod "yes" at certain points, or other non-verbal communication, helps keep you connected with each other. Remember, always keep SM play interactive.

Submissives can help maintain their emotional balance by using a safeword when they realize they are becoming seriously scared or otherwise emotionally unstable.

Most players who lose their emotional balance will recover it within a few minutes. Be supportive but not intrusive. Follow their lead about whether they want to talk, be untied, and so forth. Listen sympathetically. Touch them only if they want you to touch them. Don't argue with them, and try not to be too defensive or blaming. Remember, they probably will regain their emotional balance within a few minutes. Let that process happen on its own. Assist it, but don't think that you can control it.

Afterward, the player may feel embarrassed or ashamed about losing their balance. Reassure them that it happens to everyone now and then (which it does). Let them decide whether or not to continue the session.

If they are having emotional aftershocks for more than a week after the session, consider referring them to an SM-positive psychotherapist. Refer them even sooner if they need that.

**Falls.** Most serious SM-related injuries I've heard about involved a fall. A strap breaks, an overhead eyebolt pulls loose, or something similar happens, and the victim – usually the submissive – falls. Many falls involve a submissive bring ordered to stand with their hands tied behind their back and their ankles tied together. Obviously, in this unstable position, they can't use their arms to stabilize themselves or to catch themselves if they fall.

I heard of a woman who was seated on a chair with her hands tied behind her and her ankles bound together. She was not, however, tied to the chair. Feeling "rebellious," she decided to escape by hopping away. She fell, bashing her face against a doorframe as she did. The accident left a permanent scar on her face.

Submissives wearing high heels face a strong risk of falling if made to stand with their ankles tied together. Even with untied legs and bare feet, a submissive whose hands are tied behind them faces some falling risk (although some submissives become remarkably skillful at moving while bound). *Climbing or descending stairs is particularly risky.*

A submissive with tied ankles risks falling if made to stand, so wise dominants often tie the submissive's feet last and untie their feet first – thus the saying "feet last, feet first." Corollary: Submissives with bound-together knees, as opposed to bound-together ankles, are often more stable when standing, and can usually walk somewhat.

That clamp on my right nipple felt really intense.

The dominant must stay near the submissive to catch them if they start to fall. This is called "spotting." Also, it's unsafe to shove or pull when moving a submissive whose legs are bound. Unless they're resisting, *let the bound player set the pace.*

Blindfolded submissives are also at increased risk for falling – again, especially on stairs. I once saw a dominant woman (a professional who should have known better) leading a submissive man down a twisting, narrow stairway. She had blindfolded him, tied his hands behind his back, and was leading him by a leash tied to his balls. The only safe thing she did was stand in front of him, and I doubt she did that intentionally. (She, very foolishly, had her back to him.)

Bound submissives should be spotted if they are ordered to move, especially if they are blindfolded and "double especially" if stairs are involved. When guiding a submissive on level ground, stand slightly behind and to their side. Guide them by grasping their elbow or upper arm. When moving the submissive up or down stairs, stand *below* them and facing them. Doing so will help you steady them if they start to fall. (And guard your own balance!)

Avoid sharp, strong pulls and pushes when guiding a submissive. Unless they're deliberately delaying, let them set the pace. If you want a clear idea of how to do this, have someone tie your hands behind your back and blindfold you, then move you around – especially up and down some stairs. This experience teaches lessons you will remember for a long time.

**Fainting.** Submissives occasionally lose consciousness during a session. This can be frightening, but is usually not too serious. The most common cause is too much pain. Other causes include intense emotion and medical conditions such as epilepsy.

The most important points in treating someone who has lost consciousness are to protect them from harm and to assure an open airway. You can usually open their airway by tipping their head back. Immediately remove any gag, hood, or other equipment covering their mouth. An unconscious submissive can vomit. If they vomit into a gagged mouth, they will inhale the vomit. This can kill within minutes.

After making sure their airway is open, check for breathing and a pulse. The most reliable pulse point is in their neck just beside their adam's apple – try finding your pulse there.

(It's a good idea to find the pulse in your submissive's neck – especially the first time you play with them. Among other things, the rate and force of the pulse can give you valuable information about their emotions. As eastern healers know, you can learn a lot about a person by feeling their pulse. Also, this touching helps create intimacy between you and the submissive.)

If the victim has a pulse and is breathing, they probably will wake up within a few minutes. If they are not breathing or have no pulse, immediately lay them on their back, begin resuscitation as needed, and call an ambulance. (A first aid class will teach you the details of this.)

Many people believe the most important point in caring for an unconscious submissive is to untie them immediately. *This is not true.* The most important points are keeping them from harm, safeguarding their airway, and checking their pulse and breathing. Untying them, if necessary, comes after that.

Most faintings I've heard about involved the submissive being given pain while standing. Submissives standing with their hands over their heads are even higher risk. Submissives rarely faint while receiving pain, even heavy pain, if first made to lie on their back or stomach.

If your submissive faints while tied with their hands over their head, your first concerns are their airway, breathing, and pulse. Your next concern is usually that they are hanging "dead weight" from the restraints around their wrists. Obviously, this could cause serious injury.

Unfortunately, many dominants don't plan for this possibility. Never tie a submissive into a position that would require their help in releasing them. If you aren't strong enough to release and safely lower their unconscious body, tie them in another position or have another method of lowering them available. Remember, a good dominant asks themselves, "What will I do if they fall? What will I do if they faint?" If they don't have solid answers to those questions, they change the activity.

**What if the dominant faints?** The possibility that the dominant may be the one who faints (or falls, or is otherwise injured) must be considered. Once, during a very hot, humid summer afternoon, I was enjoying being tied up and energetically whipped by a petite, mischievous dominant lady. Things were going along nicely until she began to get pale and sweaty. I looked over my shoulder and saw her leaning up against the playroom wall. She was dizzy, nauseated, and barely able to stand. We both agreed that ending the session and getting some liquid into her was a truly excellent idea.

This incident was easily handled, but it left me wondering what *would* have happened if she had passed out while I was tied up. In this case, we were in an apartment complex, I wasn't tied *to* anything, and I wasn't gagged, so the prospects weren't all that terrible, but we were both somewhat lucky. Had we been more isolated, or had she continued even though she wasn't feeling well, things could have turned out very differently. If you play in any sort of isolated location, both of you need to make sure that you have a workable, realistic plan regarding how to deal with the dominant's suddenly becoming unconscious.

**Sudden loss of electrical power ("failure").** An electrical failure occasionally disrupts a scene. The main hazard of this is the sudden, unexpected darkness. Wise dominants equip their play rooms with back-up lighting systems that start automatically if the power fails. You can buy basic, adequate emergency lights in hardware stores, general merchandise stores, department stores, and similar places for about $15 to $20 per unit. One per playroom is usually enough (but test this in your play area). I've tested various blackout lights, and the one I like best, and buy for personal friends, is the Brinkman Model 827-0395-0. It's the brightest and longest-lasting power failure light I can find.

**Fire.** While rare, fires sometimes occur during a session, and being tied up in the presence of an out-of-control fire is one of the most terrifying things I can imagine. (A recent post on alt.sex.bondage described a situation in which a woman tied a man to a bed and told him that she was going out for a while. When he asked, "What if there's a fire?" she responded sweetly, "But there won't be." A few moments later, they looked out the window and saw a brush fire rapidly approaching their house!)

Fires may be related or completely unrelated to the SM activity. SM-related fire hazards include burning candles, flammable liquids such as rubbing alcohol, poorly wired electrical devices, and clutter.

If you play with open flame, such as a candle, be certain you know whether items in the area are flammable. Alcohol-containing liquids (and their vapors!) are especially hazardous around flame. A few years ago we had an outright disaster in the community involving a bound submissive, rubbing alcohol vapor, and a candle flame. Nobody was killed, but both people were very seriously burned.

Besides following general precautions, put a fire extinguisher in an immediately available place, perhaps on the wall outside the playroom. Some experts recommend mounting fire extinguishers near exits. The minimum size I recommend for this extinguisher is a UL rating of 3A:40BC. (I used to recommend the smaller 1A:10BC extinguisher, but I have since learned of too many cases in which these extinguishers were inadequate.) Rating labels are found on the extinguishers. Smoke detectors should be placed as needed.

These items of equipment might sound excessive and too much trouble, but they are necessary. It's easy to keep a first aid kit, a blackout light, and an extinguisher on hand and yet completely preserve your play area's erotic atmosphere.

Most SM players never face any serious emergency, but they know the risks involved. The knowledge and equipment needed to prevent and deal with SM-related emergencies is easy to use and inexpensive to acquire. Responsible players do so gladly.

## *Safety Checklist*

The following checklist will help you make sure you have at least a minimally reasonable amount of the proper emergency equipment on hand.
- Certificate from a first aid/CPR class issued less than one year ago.
- One small, light-colored flashlight (with batteries checked) either carried on your person or in a known place in your toybag and reachable in the dark within five seconds. This flashlight should be of a shape that does not roll easily if placed on flat, level ground.
- One pair of plastic-handled (light color) "paramedic scissors" either carried on your person on in a known place in your toybag and reachable in the dark within five seconds.
- One small first aid kit in your toybag with contents as described above.

- One larger first aid kit on the premises with contents as described above.
- A reliable means of summoning professional help in an emergency. This usually means a telephone. In isolated areas, it could mean a two-way radio.
- Condoms; latex, vinyl, or plastic gloves; lubricant containing nonoxynol-9; spermicidal suppositories; disinfectant solutions; and other safer sex/birth control supplies stored in an immediately available place.
- At least one properly charged "blackout light" per average-sized bedroom that will come on automatically if the electricity goes out.
- At least one emergency flashlight *in addition* to the blackout light. Minimum size: two D-cell batteries. Recommended size: 6-Volt lantern, preferably with extra-bright bulb.
- At least one 3A:40BC dry chemical fire extinguisher stored on the same floor as the playroom or bedroom. One additional extinguisher of at least the same size stored by each exit to the home.
- Mirrors placed near (and, especially, above) a bound person are made of mylar or other non-breakable material.
- Suspension equipment of a type that can safely lower and release an unconscious submissive.
- A reliable means, such as a silent alarm, cordless phone, or panic button, for the submissive to summon help while bound or confined if the dominant becomes unconscious.

While not safety equipment *per se*, the following items are often useful to have in a playroom: thermometer for measuring room temperature, clock (need not be visible to the submissive), urinal with cap that secures into place, something non-alcoholic to drink in a squeeze-bottle with a built-in straw.

# SM and Safer Sex

The following are a few of the most widely agreed-upon, basic precautions against catching or transmitting the AIDS virus and other sexually transmitted diseases. Keep in mind that I'm not an expert on this topic, that opinions and recommendations vary, and that new facts are discovered often. For example, there are increasingly frequent reports of new strains of AIDS virus that are far more transmissible via vaginal intercourse than previous strains. Therefore, try not to use this book as your only source of information. (And remember that many "expert" sources of information are inaccurate, incomplete, out of date, and/or and biased.)

The HIV virus lives in infectious concentrations in blood, semen, and possibly vaginal fluid. Contact with these fluids – especially on a mucous membrane or open wound – is potentially infectious.

It appears the most common method of sexually transmitting HIV is active-to-passive anal intercourse without a condom. Apparently, anal intercourse creates small wounds inside the rectum. HIV-infected semen enters the victim's bloodstream through those wounds. Evidence suggests the virus also may be absorbed directly across the intestine even if no break in the membrane exists.

After I've been whipped, my skin is so sensitized that the slightest touch just drives me nuts.

Vaginal intercourse is also risky. Evidence suggests that oral sex is safer, but not entirely risk-free. Masturbating your partner, in the absence of any open wounds and/or with the use of a hand gloved in latex or vinyl (lubricated, please), is apparently fairly safe. (One way to check your hands for wounds is to wipe them with rubbing alcohol and pay close attention to any stinging.)

I think one of the most important precautions you should take regarding HIV is to determine whether you or your proposed partner has been exposed to HIV. Many people think the disease can lie dormant for years with no sign. This is not true. The disease itself may or may not lie dormant, but most infected people develop antibodies within two months. Have one antibody test, then another six months later, and, to be absolutely sure, a third test six months later. If all three are negative, and you have done nothing unsafe meanwhile, you are almost certainly not infected.

If your partner is also antibody-negative, and has done nothing dangerous in the last few months, then the two of you can probably do anything you want (regarding the HIV virus) as long as neither of you does anything risky outside the relationship.

If I were entering a new relationship, I would want both of us to have our blood tested before we did anything high-risk – certainly before we had any type of unprotected intercourse. (Janet and I had such a "new relationship" test.) Many clinics perform the test free and anonymously.

If, as is often the case, it's not possible to be certain of either person's antibody status, (and remember that many, many people will lie if doing so will get you to have sex with them) you *must* assume they're infected and proceed accordingly. This means wearing a condom *and* taking other precautions.

I very strongly question whether using only a condom provides adequate protection. Condoms often break or slip off, and during the "heat of the moment" neither party may realize that has happened.

(Both of these events have happened to me on several occasions, and I'm completely certain that I had put on the condom in the manner recommended by AIDS-prevention experts. Nowadays, when I'm in a condom-requiring situation, I check every few minutes to make sure everything's all right. I also, partially because doing such checking is a real drag, get into considerably fewer condom-requiring situations.)

The more sensitive the condom, and many brands highlight precisely this aspect of their product, the more likely unnoticed-condom-failure occurrences become.

*The person on the inside of the ropes lives in a different world than the person on the outside of the ropes.*

Water-soluble lubricants, unlike oil-based lubricants, cause no deterioration of latex. Many experts recommend using water-soluble lubricants that contain nonoxynol-9. (Nonoxynol-9 tastes slightly soapy to some people, however, so some people who give head don't like using it during oral sex.)

The simplest precaution regarding SM toys is to have equipment for use on only one person. This is particularly important for any equipment that might break the skin or is used for insertion.

Other precautions include:

1. Not using possibly contaminated equipment, such as whips, on a second person until that equipment has been thoroughly disinfected. Exactly how to do this is not yet widely agreed upon,

but common recommendations include washing the toy with warm water and soap, then wiping it thoroughly with a provodone-iodine solution such as Betadine and letting it dry. After it's dry, wipe off the Betadine with rubbing alcohol. Note: Leather will probably have to be reconditioned after such treatment. Second note: Betadine may stain certain items. Third note: A product called Z-Best, with an active ingredient called Cychohexyl-One, is currently being advertised as a leather and metal cleaner. I haven't tried it myself yet, but it might be worth looking into.

Such cleaning agents are often used with a fingernail brush or something similar to help make sure all the "nooks and crannies" on braided whips and other "complicated" items are reached.

Caution: If you buy an expensive whip or another piece of high-priced leather equipment, be sure to ask the vendor how to disinfect it. Some disinfectants can be murder on leather. Double-check what you're told with a second reliable source.

2. Covering dildoes and vibrators with condoms before inserting them. The standard practice after using an item for insertion is to remove the condom, thoroughly clean the item with a substance known to kill the AIDS virus such as Hibiclens, Betadine, rubbing alcohol (70% solution), or hydrogen peroxide (3% solution). If the item is immersible, it should then be soaked in a solution of nine parts water to one part chlorine bleach for at least 20 minutes, then rinsed and allowed to dry at least overnight. It can also be disinfected by soaking it in a glutaraldehyde solution (Wavicide, Banicide, or Cidex) for ten minutes, or sterilized by soaking it for ten hours. Please note that drying itself kills many viruses. The item is then covered with a fresh condom before using it for insertion again.

*Sometimes I don't want to have a choice.*

3. Thoroughly cleaning items that might have become contaminated before using them on someone else. This would especially include anything used in or around the anus, genitals, and mouth, such as ropes, leather straps, gags, etc. For immediate use after a session, and even during the session, diaper wipes that contain

nonoxynol-9 are popular. A paper towel dipped in alcohol can also be used.

4. Wearing latex or vinyl gloves. Wear gloves when doing anything that might involve exposure to possibly infectious blood, semen, or vaginal fluids. Many people consider latex gloves to have a better "feel" than vinyl gloves have. On the other hand, an increasing number of people are allergic to latex, and vinyl gloves can be a boon to them.

5. Immediately treat a freshly contaminated wound. If possibly infectious fluid gets onto a wound, clean it at once. Use alcohol, provodone-iodine, or hydrogen peroxide if *immediately* available. (Now do you understand why I recommend that you have your safety equipment in the room with you?) If such disinfectants aren't handy, go into the bathroom and wash the wound with soap and water.

Saliva has been proven to inhibit the infectivity of the HIV virus in a very substantial way. If nothing else is immediately available, then it's quite rational to spit on the wound! The important point is to begin cleaning the wound immediately.

*We could fix up this closet as a place to keep me confined.*

After cleaning the wound, apply an HIV-killing solution or cream. The ones containing provodone-iodine are excellent.

6. Immunizations are now available against Hepatitis A and Hepatitis B. These are particularly recommended for those who do anal play with multiple partners. I strongly recommend that you look into them.

## What To Do If a Condom Fails

OK, guy, while having vaginal or anal intercourse you look down and you see that the condom you were wearing has broken and you are now wearing a small latex ring around the base of your cock. Or maybe you look down and discover that the condom is gone. (You were thinking that this particular brand caused very little loss of sensation.) Perhaps you have already come. What do you do now?

STOP! Then, first of all, if they don't already know, you gotta tell them. Try not to sound too alarmed (they may regard what has happened as a big deal, or they may not), but let them know what happened.

OK, you told them.  Now what?  If you're worried about getting a sexually transmitted disease, go into the bathroom and wash your genitals several times with generous amounts of soap and water, then empty your bladder (and maybe drink fluids so you can flush out your urethra some more). One nurse who worked in a VD clinic told me that washing and urinating after sex would reduce a man's chances of getting gonorrhea by 50%. (She had no information about whether it reduced his chances of getting other diseases.) Another nurse, who also works in a VD clinic, told me that she spends a lot of her time treating "that unlucky 50%" of men who had tried doing this and it didn't work.

If you weren't already using a lubricant containing nonoxynol-9, but have some handy, consider applying a liberal amount to your genitals and the surrounding areas.  Let it sit there for five to ten minutes before washing it off.  Nonoxynol-9 can kill the bugs that cause AIDS, herpes, syphilis, gonorrhea, and many other diseases, so giving it a chance to help makes sense to me.

This could be overkill, but after you shower, consider applying an antiseptic (Betadine, or a generic version of it, would be a good choice) as a final touch.

What about your partner?  The receptive partner is in a riskier situation.  Trying to wash out your semen (and whatever it contains) may drive some of it further up into their body.  Therefore, consider immediately inserting two spermicidal suppositories into the vagina or rectum.  This will place a considerable amount of nonoxynol-9 or octoxynol-9 into the orifice without driving whatever's already in there further in (as the pressure caused by using a syringe full of contraceptive foam might).

When SM energy and creativity blend, there's just no telling what will happen.

Once the suppositories have had a chance to work (15 minutes?), then they can wash off, and out.  Opinions differ as to whether or not a douche or enema is a good idea.  While you're waiting, nonoxynol-9 can be applied to their external genital region, and washed off later, to help zap any bugs or sperm lurking there.

Again, this may be overkill, but I'll point out that it's possible to douche with a dilute Betadine-type solution.  Also, antiseptic creams can be applied to the external genital/anal region.

If you feel you need immediate advice, call your doctor or clinic.  If it's late at night (when these events tend to happen), consider calling a hospital emergency room.  They won't consider such a call out of line.

In the morning, it's crucial (repeat, crucial) that you call your regular doctor, a local VD clinic, or family planning center for advice.  They may want you to come in, either that day or within a day or two, for an examination. Among other things, if you're worried about getting pregnant they can arrange for you to get a "morning after" pill.

Perhaps the most important point of this essay is to point out, once again, that a condom by itself is just not complete protection. I suggest you consider limiting higher-risk activities, particularly anal or vaginal intercourse, to monogamous or fluid-bonded relationships.

# A Novice Woman's Quick Reference Guide to Erotically Dominating a Submissive Man

The most common type of person interested in SM seems to be the heterosexual, submissive male. These men often know "straight" women who feel willing to try erotic domination, but have little idea of how to proceed. Therefore the "single most probable" type of SM play seems likely to be heterosexual, female-dominant type – possibly involving a novice dominant woman and a somewhat more experienced submissive man. I have therefore written this section for such a woman, and will address my remarks directly to her. I hope that others, with different interests, will also find these instructions useful.

All men are slaves to their cocks.

Hello and welcome. If you are reading this, I'll assume that you are a woman who has been asked by a man to dominate him erotically. You are willing to try, but aren't certain how to proceed. This section provides quick, basic instruction. Admittedly, it's a bit "recipe-like," but it should serve quite well as a blueprint for a first, basic encounter. One major tip: Please read this entire section before beginning the session. (I suggest reading it at least twice.)

Please use as much, or as little, of the advice given below as works for you. Also, feel free to "improvise" if doing that feels right, but please be very conservative about doing so during a first session. In many respects, it's more important that a first session between two people not end badly than that it end really, really well.

I'll assume that you would feel comfortable about being somewhat sexual with the man involved, at least to the extent of having him perform cunnilingus on you and/or you masturbating him to orgasm.

Additionally, I'll assume that the man you're playing with has already read this material , has no objection to anything suggested below (he should

329

tell you before the two of you begin if he does), feels comfortable about being under your direction, and is at least somewhat familiar with SM.

If any of the above assumptions do not apply in your case, please come to clear agreement about what works for both of you *before* beginning.

Caution: The two of you should do this only if neither of you is noticeably intoxicated, tired, or emotionally upset.

If you do not know each other well, you might call a friend and let them know who you are with, what you are doing (you don't need to be *too* explicit) and that you will call them later. Tell them to make sure you are all right if you don't check in when you said you would.

Before you begin, agree with him about the length of the session, physical and emotional limits, safe words, degree and type of any sexual interaction, and other necessary matters. If you are unfamiliar with any terms, have him explain them. You also might read the "Basic SM in One Page" section of this book.

His body should be clean. If he is so stupid as to present himself with unbrushed teeth, bad breath, or unshaven beard stubble, he must correct these matters before you allow him the privilege of being erotically dominated by you. His clothing must also be clean, as must be any surroundings he provides.

**The Mistress always wins.**

1.    To begin, sit on the edge of a bed. Order him to strip and to kneel at your feet.

2.    Order him to call you "Mistress" or some similar term such as "My Lady" or "Ma'am." He is not to call you by your name (except, perhaps, as a safe word). He is to remain silent unless he is answering a question or you have given him permission to speak (which he requests by slightly raising one hand). When you give him an order, he should reply with "Yes, Mistress" or some similar term as he obeys. It's probably all right to call him "slave" during this session, but save "heavier" terms for the future.

3.    Order him to keep his eyes down. He is not to look at your face unless you give your permission or order him to do so.

4.    Collar him. He is yours. It is important to put a symbol of your ownership on him. This collar should preferably lock, and he should not have access to a key. If you don't have a standard collar, improvise one.

5. Tie him up. Tie his hands behind his back unless you want them elsewhere. (Save more extensive bondage for later sessions.) Only experienced, trusted, submissive males are allowed any significant degree of physical freedom.

6. Bind his genitals. Unless you are using his genitals in a way that requires their freedom, bind them. Wind rope between his genitals and his body and between his penis and scrotum, or make him do this before you tie his wrists. Genital bondage should be attention-getting tight but not so tight as to cause damage.

7. Spank him. It is important for both of you that he learn to accept pain from you and that you learn to accept giving it. Spank him in a firm, yet controlled, manner. Verify that he (and you) remember the safewords before you begin. Start with your hand. Switch to a paddle if that makes things easier for you. Tell him that you're going to give him a series of five swats, and that he is to nod his head when he's ready to receive each series of five. Start with five very light swats. If those go well, make the next five slightly stronger.

I'm a middle-class, middle-aged, suburban pervert lady.

One hundred or so swats, even if you both feel you could go further, is about as many as you should give for this first spanking. You can always give him more swats later in the session if you want.

8. His mouth is yours. A dominant woman makes good use of a submissive male's mouth. Her boots, feet, nipples, and vagina often receive extended attention. A dominant woman should feel completely within her rights to make use of the submissive male's mouth. (Many of them love doing this anyway.) Also, she should feel under no obligation to reciprocate. (Although, of course, she may – if doing so pleases *her*.)

It's a good idea to have him start with your boots and/or feet. Save other parts of your body for later in the session, when his good behavior has earned him the privilege of touching them with his mouth.

9. Maintain a slight but noticeable level of "background pain" as you train him. Mild clamps are often good for this, especially when applied to his nipples or scrotum. Caution: Don't mix two types

of pain, such as spanking with clamps, unless you are sure he can handle that.

10. Penetrate him. Every male benefits from learning how penetration feels. A wise dominant woman will consider making good use of gloved fingers and/or a condom-covered dildo or butt plug. Remember to use lots of lubricant. (If this step, or any of the others, seems a bit too much for a first session, save it for future sessions.)

11. Reward him for good behavior. If he's been very good, and if the idea pleases you, permit him to touch your breasts and/or genitals with his mouth. This may continue for as little or as long as you want.

12. Delay his orgasm. Do not let him come too quickly. This is both a devilish and a considerate action on your part. It's devilish because the submissive male often wants, more than anything else, to have an orgasm. Simply delaying this will string out his frustration and make the experience more intense. It is considerate because a man's sexual desire, and his desire to submit, often evaporates after he has had an orgasm. Nipple clamps that felt erotic now simply hurt. Bondage that felt deliciously trapping now feels restrictive and uncomfortable.

   A wise dominant woman, then, makes full use of her submissive before she allows him an orgasm. She may also decide to remove his bondage and/or clamps before she allows him to come.

13. Afterward. An hour or so after the session, or perhaps the next day, spend "straight time" talking about how the session went for both of you. Discuss what worked and what didn't, and what you might do differently if the two of you play together again.

These guidelines should help you have a satisfying first session. Any additional sessions, when you are more familiar with both your partner and SM techniques, can involve more intense and/or more varied activity. One of SM's truisms is that a perfect ending for a first session is one where afterwards both people feel that they could have gone further.

# Constructing an SM Starter Set

SM play usually requires equipment. Such gear can range from the ordinary and cheap to the exotic and expensive. Let's go over some items.

## *Let's Start With Your Mind*

The knowledge and skills you bring to a session are important. Your underlying attitude and outlook are more so. SM begins in the mind. Hopefully you will feel clear, alert, and focused – a state of "relaxed tension" similar to what you might feel just before participating in a contest involving something both you and your competitors are good at. It's likely that you'll feel a very strong sense of erotic anticipation. Perhaps you'll also feel a powerful attraction blended with just a bit of fear.

If you're a dominant, you may feel yourself "powering up" and centering as you prepare for the session. If you're a submissive, you may feel a warm wave of relaxation, happiness, eagerness, and/or gratitude sweep over you as you prepare to surrender. In either case, you should definitely feel good about the person you are about to do this with.

> The first toy I ever used was a hairbrush, and it still has a special place in my heart.

Strong caution: If you aren't energized, alert, in a good mood, and pleased about who your partner is, you probably shouldn't play just then.

If your mind is not in tune with SM energy, then expensive fetish clothing and elaborate equipment will be of little use. On the other hand, if your mind is in tune with this energy it will show, and even ordinary items can become powerful pieces of SM gear.

Your eyes and facial expressions will almost undoubtedly reveal your mental state to somebody who can read them. (That's one major reason not to blindfold a new partner.) Remember my saying: "If you want to know what they're into, watch their eyes. They can't fake the eyes." They can try, but they'll always stumble sooner or later – and it's usually sooner rather than later.

### Now Let's Consider Your Body

Remember: "If you want to get good at using equipment, first get good at using your hands." Please remember that, as a dominant, you can create a heavy, intense session using nothing but your hands. Your hands are incredibly versatile instruments. The palm of the hand, fingers, and fingernails each have their own potentials, as does the entire hand itself.

Here are 20 things you can do to your submissive's body with your hands:

| | | | |
|---|---|---|---|
| 1. | Caress | 11. | Restrain |
| 2. | Drum | 12. | Rub |
| 3. | Flick | 13. | Scratch |
| 4. | Insert | 14. | Shake |
| 5. | Knead | 15. | Slap |
| 6. | Massage | 16. | Spank |
| 7. | Pinch with fingers | 17. | Squeeze |
| 8. | Pinch with fingernails | 18. | Tickle |
| 9. | Pluck pubic hair | 19. | Vibrate |
| 10. | Pull hair | 20. | Masturbate |

If that's not enough, here are ten things you can do with your mouth:

| | | | |
|---|---|---|---|
| 1. | Bite | 6. | Kiss |
| 2. | Blow | 7. | Lick |
| 3. | Engulf | 8. | Tongue flick |
| 4. | Hickey | 9. | Moisten |
| 5. | Hum | 10. | Suck |

As you can see, the combination of your mouth and your hands makes a powerful, versatile, erotic "toolkit."

(More specific, detailed information about how to use your hands and mouth, including masturbation "tortures," see the Erotic Torture chapter of this book. You also might want to take a look at my books in the "Tricks: More than 125 Ways to Make Good Sex Better" series.)

### A Basic SM Starter Kit

Now as to what equipment you might use for "semi-formal" SM play. Let's look around the ordinary apartment. The following ten items could be regarded as an "SM starter kit." They are found in most households, inexpensive, "deniable," require minimal clean-up, and usually work well together.

| | Item | Use |
|---|---|---|
| 1. | Plastic wrap | Bondage |
| 2. | Adhesive or duct tape | Bondage |
| 3. | Rope | Bondage |

| | | |
|---|---|---|
| 4. | Clothespins | Erotic torture |
| 5. | Menthol-containing rubs | Erotic torture |
| 6. | Ice cubes | Erotic torture |
| 7. | Leather belt (see note #1) | Flagellation |
| 8. | Leather bootlaces | Flagellation/genital bondage |
| 9. | Pillow cases | Flagellation/bondage (hood) |
| 10. | Hairbrush (see note #2) | Spanking/erotic torture |

Note #1: A belt used for flagellation would probably be at least one inch wide and relatively flexible. It should not have any sharp edges or corners on the part that strikes the submissive's skin. Using any metal parts of a belt to whip a submissive is a genuinely bad idea.

Note #2: A "spanking" hairbrush would have a sturdy handle and a rectangular or oval back. As with a belt, it would have no sharp edges or corners on the part that strikes the submissive's skin. In addition to using the back of the hairbrush for spanking, the bristles themselves can be used to excellent effect on various tender (or tenderized) parts of the submissive's body.

Note #3: See the "Flagellation" chapter for instructions on how to use a bootlace to make a basic flogger.

Having my inner thighs pinched is really hard for me.

In addition to the above, the following are some of the items you could incorporate into your SM play.

### Mood/Atmosphere Items
Candles
Heat (relaxed nudity requires warmth)
Incense
Lighting
Music (helps create mood, shut out outside distractions, ensure "sound privacy.") For more information, see the section titled "Setting the Scene" in the "Basic Basics" chapter.

### Everyday Items You Can Use as Toys
Candles (plain white paraffin)
Coathangers (unpainted)
Elastic bandages
Emery boards
Enema bag
Egg scissors
Feather duster
Feathers

Fur
Gauze bandages (at least four inches wide)
Hand-held hair dryer
Metal paper-fastening clamps
Nail file
Nylon stockings (may bind – do not use for bondage that may be pulled against)
Paddles – ping pong, paddle ball, sporting, etc.
Rubber ball
Rulers
Sashes from bathrobes and other items of clothing
Scarves  (knots pulled really tight can be hard to loosen)

Shoelaces

_____

Skewers (use for semi-piercing and/or scratching, but don't break skin)
Snake bite kit suction cups (use on nipples)
Spatula
Toothbrush
Toothpaste or gel

How come none
of my submissives
are ever ticklish?

Triangular bandages (very good for bondage, blindfolds, and gags)
Tweezers
Vegetable oil
Wooden spoons
And, of course, regular sex toys such as vibrators, dildoes, ben wa balls, anal beads, and so forth.

_____

When using any of the above items, remember that items with sharp edges or corners should not be used for flagellation.  Remember to start lighter than light and build slower than slow.  Remember to get feedback.

**Safety Items**
Condoms
Contraceptive jelly (3% nonoxynol-9)
Dental dams
Flashlight
Fire extinguisher
First aid kit
Hydrogen peroxide (3%)
Latex, vinyl, or plastic gloves

Spermicidal suppositories
Paramedic scissors
Provodone-iodine solution
Rubbing alcohol (70%)
Water-soluble lubricant containing nonoxynol-9

Note: Remember that a male urinal with a cap that fastens in place can be very useful if the session involves highly immobilizing bondage.

**Items to Avoid**

The following household items are too dangerous to play with until you have received expert instruction in their safe, effective use. Serious, even fatal, injury could result from attempting to use these during SM play without proper training.

Candles other than white, paraffin candles
Clothing irons
Curling irons
Electrical shock devices of any kind
Formal weapons such as firearms, swords, and tear-gas canisters
Fireplace equipment such as a poker
Hot rollers
Open flame other than a candle (watch out for vapors!)
Sewing needles for piercing (use only equipment designed for going through skin)

There are undoubtedly other unacceptably dangerous items that I forgot to list. When in doubt, stay with the play items listed previously in this section or actual SM gear you bought in a store.

My toy bag got stolen out of my car once. On the police report, I said it contained 'crafts supplies', 'massage tools', and 'equestrian equipment.'

## *Buying "Formal" SM Gear*

The time is likely to come when you will want to purchase "real" SM supplies. This can be fun and exciting, but I recommend that you pay attention to where you buy what. Intelligent consumerism is just as important here as it is in any other part of life. Price, quality, and safe construction can vary tremendously in this field.

*Remember the number one rule of consumerism: Comparison shop.* Some prices are reasonable, but more than a few are absolutely exorbitant. Please also remember that it's possible for a very expensive item to be a wonderful value and for a very cheap item to be a total ripoff.

Stores that sell items which can be used in SM play include supermarkets, drugstores, variety stores, hardware stores, horseback riding supply stores, medical supply stores, office supply stores, farm equipment stores, police supply stores, adult bookstores, erotic boutiques and, of course, actual SM supply stores. (See my book "Supermarket Tricks: More Than 125 Ways to Improvise Good Sex" for ideas.)

I have found that riding supply stores usually offer excellent buys on riding crops. (I selected mine from a large bucket of them in such a store. The young lady clerk looked on as I inspected the various crops at some length – I had a date with a heavy masochist later that week – and I could see her suspicion growing into certainty.)

Office supply stores often carry an extraordinary variety of clamps at quite reasonable prices. Police supply stores carry handcuffs, but may look at you with a certain scrutiny if you want to buy leg irons. (Remember to stick with well-known brands such as Peerless or Smith & Wesson when buying such items.) Medical supply stores often carry paramedic scissors, Kerlix gauze, triangular bandages, and other fun items. (Gauze and bandages do not need to be sterile for our purposes, and "clean" materials are *much* less expensive.)

"Really formal" SM gear such as collars for humans, a flogger, or leather restraints are best bought at adult bookstores, erotic boutiques, and SM supply stores. (Truth be told, it might be better for all concerned if you bought your handcuffs and such here as well.) Remember to comparison shop, and be alert for things like whips with sharp edges and corners. Many of the poorer quality stores will gleefully sell you such dangerous trash, but make up for it by charging you a truly astronomical price.

Don't feel reluctant to ask questions at an "erotic" store. The staff at the better ones should be happy to spend a reasonable amount of time explaining the construction and workmanship of various items. One request: Please don't take up large amounts of their time unless you truly intend to make a significant purchase during that visit.

Footnote: I've occasionally been subtly and/or not-so-subtly insulted or otherwise been made to feel less than welcome by sales clerks at a few stores because my underlying gender or sexual orientation was different from theirs. If you don't feel genuinely welcome, don't give them so much as a dime. Go somewhere else, and call or write the store's owner to tell them why.

Also remember that many stores do mail order business. They'll send you a catalog for a few bucks and an I'm-over-21 statement. They may also be able to answer questions over the phone. (Just remember to keep your call business-like. They're alert for phone freaks.)

# SM Sayings

1. You almost never get into serious trouble by going too slowly.
2. SM is something you do with someone, not something you do to someone.
3. If it's going to go bad, it usually goes bad in isolation.
4. Introduce only one new thing at a time, preferably only one new thing during a session.
5. If you want to know what they're into, watch their eyes. They can't fake the eyes.
6. Harder is not necessarily better. Faster is not necessarily better. More often is not necessarily better. More elaborate is not necessarily better. More expensive is not necessarily better.
7. Beware the trap of over-eagerness.
8. Think with your head.
9. How someone will react to erotic bondage is one thing. How they will react to erotic submission is a second, separate reaction. How they will react to erotic pain is a third.
10. Experience it yourself before you do it to someone else.
11. If you want to know what you're into, take a close look at what you're fantasizing about just before you come while masturbating.
12. A good place for a first session to end is one where both people feel they could have gone further than they did.
13. It's much more important that a first session not end badly than that it end really, really well.
14. The first session with a new partner is the one most likely to go wrong.
15. There are three aspects to an SM activity: The activity itself (what is done), the technique (how it's done), and the person doing it. You can like, or not like, each separate component.
16. The main characteristic of a top-quality dominant is trustworthiness.

---

Submissives tend to spend a lot of time with genitals in their mouths.

---

17. There's nothing "only" about being a bottom, particularly about being a good bottom.

18. Start lighter than light. Build slower than slow.

19. SM can play with primordial fears such as helplessness in the face of something more powerful.

20. The submissive may become pure id.

21. Never break through armor unless you're fairly certain that you can deal with what's on the other side.

22. If you're going to open them up, you're obligated to close them down. This may take some time.

23. The more aroused somebody is, the more pain they can take.

24. The more the bottom can relax mentally and physically, the further they can go.

25. Submissiveness and masochism are two very different things. While a degree of one often accompanies a degree of the other, some submissives aren't at all masochistic, and some masochists aren't at all submissive.

26. Learning SM is like learning how to have sex all over again.

I live but to serve.

27. When two people are alone together, and one of them is naked and tied up, and the other is standing over them holding whips and other torture implements, this is *not* the time to have a serious mismatch of expectations.

28. If you don't have a current CPR card, you cannot call yourself a responsible dominant.

29. Never tie a submissive into a position that would require their cooperation in releasing them.

30. If you want to get good at using equipment, first get good at using your hands.

# Related Practices

Many local resources can be found by carefully checking your phone book and by visiting the library to check the phone books of nearby cities, particularly the large ones. Local newspapers and magazines, particularly the free or low-cost ones that come out on a weekly or less frequent basis, often carry valuable listings. These periodicals are often found at bookstores, post offices, bus stations, train depots, and major boarding points for commuter mass-transit lines. Look them over carefully. Many alternative sexuality clubs and other resources advertise in adult papers and other periodicals with a gay, lesbian, or erotic slant. Also, check out Appendix II, "SM and the Internet," for tips on using cyberspace.

Important notice: When writing to any organization listed below, it's very wise to include a business-size, self-addressed, stamped envelope.

Another important notice: This book is updated frequently. If you know of other resources for this section, or if you have special knowledge of any of these resources, please let me know so I can include that information in future editions.

## *Age Play*

It's not uncommon for players to assume the personas of people significantly younger than they really are when they play. Roles such as teacher/student and babysitter/naughty child are common.

Age play can be fun but also dangerous. A professional dominant who specializes in this form of play once remarked that many people could emotionally regress to about the age of six without running into problems, but "going younger" could be emotionally risky.

One psychotherapist who is highly knowledgeable about this area is
William A. Henkin, Ph.D.
1801 Bush St., #111
San Francisco, CA 94109
(415) 923-1150

Infantilism is an extreme form of age play in which people regress all the way back to infancy. Some infantilism fans even buy custom-made cribs, bottles, and other "baby" equipment. The most prominent referral in this area is the following (somewhat colorfully named) organization.

Diaper Pail Friends
38 Miller Ave. #127
Mill Valley, CA 94941

## *Anal Play*

The anus, perhaps especially in a submissive man, seems to cry out for attention. To control this extremely personal, private part of the submissive's body is to control the submissive in a powerful way.

Yet only the educated should engage in anal play. Soreness, infections, and even occasional deaths have resulted from uninformed activities.

Anal play can involve inserting fingers, dildoes, vibrators, vibrating eggs, anal beads, and even an entire hand (see the section on Fisting in this chapter).

Basic suggestions:

1.      Proceed very, very slowly, especially at first.

Never shove anything in quickly. Never use force. The dominant should let the submissive tell them what they need in this situation. Anal penetration can easily be traumatic unless those involved closely communicate.

One excellent approach is to let the submissive set the pace. Place the item lightly on their anus and let them "back onto it." Let the submissive tell you if the item's angle or pressure need changing. The submissive can back onto the item until their sphincter is ever-so-slightly stretched, then be still and allow that muscle to relax. This should happen in about 30 seconds. The relaxed sphincter will dilate a little bit, and the process can then be repeated.

You see the important role patience plays. Given time, the sphincter may relax enough to accept surprisingly large objects. A penis-sized dildo or, of course, an actual penis can often be accepted this way. With time, practice, and patience, the submissive can often accommodate even larger items.

2.      Wear latex, vinyl, or plastic gloves.

Gloves help keep things clean and greatly reduce the chance of an infection being transmitted in either direction.

Note: It is particularly important to wear gloves if an open sore exists on the dominant's hands or the submissive's rectum. Very small open sores on the hands may be hard to detect. One good way to detect them is to swab your hands with rubbing alcohol to see in any spot begins to sting. Another method is to put your hands into a bowl of vinegar or hydrogen peroxide. Again, sore spots will sting.

Subnote: Rubbing alcohol is flammable, so don't use it near open flame – and watch out for vapors!

3.      Be careful with your fingernails.

The submissive's rectum is exquisitely sensitive. The submissive easily feels the contour of anything inserted and immediately notices even tiny spots that are sharp, hard, or rough.

If you so much as graze their rectum with your fingernails, they may feel sharp, definitely unerotic pain. This applies even to closely trimmed, filed, polished fingernails covered by gloves. One way to help reduce the odds of this occurring is to aim your fingernails away from the rectum's wall and toward its "centerline" as you slowly enter. (Some dominants, particularly dominant women, deliberately keep their nails short on their "fisting hand.")

Note: One time-honored method of testing your fingernails is to scrape them along your forearm or along the tricep-side of your upper arm. If you feel any sharp, hard, or rough spots, the submissive certainly will.

Subnote: You could demonstrate your hand's fitness by doing a "test scrape" on your partner's arm. Likewise, you could check the fitness of a hand whose use is proposed on you by this method.

4.      Use *lots* of lubricant.

You almost cannot use too much lubricant during anal play. One major point regarding its use is to apply additional lubricant *before* you feel more is needed and before your submissive asks for more. If you wait until they ask for more lubricant, you've probably waited too long. Remember that submissives, unless trained otherwise, often delay asking for something they need. They don't want to risk displeasing their dominant by asking for something they need, so they (unwisely) tough it out.

The rectum's lining "sheds" easily. It only lasts so long even if copious amounts of lubricant are used, then it begins to unpleasantly "burn" if touched. In my experience, the most common cause of needing to end an anal play session before both parties wish to end it is that the rectum begins to burn. Applying lubricant very frequently helps prevent this.

Safety note: Remember that oil-based lubricants rapidly break down condoms, latex gloves, and similar items. (The new polyurethane condoms, and vinyl and plastic gloves, are oil-proof.) If you are in a situation that requires latex condoms, gloves, and similar materials, make sure you use a water-based lubricant. If you are not absolutely sure that a lubricant is water-based (the container should clearly state that) then presume it's oil-based and act accordingly.

5.      Experience it yourself.

As is true with almost every other aspect of SM play, you can learn a lot by having a skillful, experienced player do these things to you.

6.      Consider giving the submissive a cleansing enema before an anal play session.

See the section on "Enemas" in this chapter for more information.

One highly regarded book on anal play is:

"Anal Pleasure and Health" (Second Edition)
by Jack Morin
Published by Yes Press
This book contains many safer-sex precautions.

## Bisexuality

Bisexual Resource Center
P.O. Box 639
Cambridge, MA   02140
(617) 338-9595
Publishes a "Bisexual Resource Guide" of more than 1500 bisexual groups worldwide for $10.95.  Also, scan the Internet for bisexuality resources.

## Breath Control

Some people play with choking, suffocation, and other forms of "breath control." The first symptom of oxygen deprivation is often euphoria; also, the idea of this degree of control can be compelling (one submissive woman gasped with delight when she considered that her master might "control the very air I breathe"). Unfortunately, my research shows that this activity is an *extremely* dangerous type of erotic behavior.

Since this is a fairly unusual activity, I'm not going to take up a lot of space here discussing the medical risks of breath control. If you're considering playing with this, I urge you to read Appendix III, "A Monograph on Breath Control Play."

## Circumcision

NOCIRC
P.O. Box 2512
San Anselmo, CA 94960
An anti-circumcision organization.

## Corsetry

For people who enjoy wearing corsets, and people who enjoy people who enjoy wearing corsets. Also, check out alt.sex.fetish.fashion on the Internet.

B.R Creations
P.O. Box 4201
Mountain View, CA 94040
Ask about their "Corset Newsletter."

## Enemas

A cleansing enema removes feces. This often makes the anal play session more esthetically pleasing. (Those who prefer more "earthy" anal play may skip this measure.) Also, giving a submissive an enema – and therefore controlling this highly personal part of their body – is distinctly dominant. Furthermore, accepting an enema often sends the submissive deep into their submissive headspace. All in all, an enema prior to further anal play has much to recommend it

A few basics: The nervous system is divided into two basic parts: the central nervous system and the peripheral nervous system. The central nervous system (CNS) consists of the brain and spinal cord. The peripheral nervous system consists of the nerves that branch off them. These branching nerves have three major subdivisions: the sensory, the motor, and (here's where it starts to get kinky) the autonomic [pronounced auto-NOM ick].

The autonomic is divided into two subparts: the sympathetic and the parasympathetic. The sympathetic nervous system handles the "flight or fight" aspect of the nervous system. It mainly uses epinephrine (adrenalin) and norepinephrine (levophed).

The parasympathetic nervous system covers the "rest and relaxation" aspects of the nervous system. It mainly uses acetylcholine. This aspect of the nervous system comes into play during such activities as salivation, crying, urination, erection, and, more to the point, defecation.

A small amount of parasympathetic outflow can cause a feeling of relaxation and contentment. (Thus giving rise to the saying "a good shit is better than a bad fuck.") More moderate outflow can cause feelings of drowsiness, even up to a slighly hypnotic, suggestable, submissive state. This is the state often played with by people who use enemas in an erotic and/or SM sort of way.

Large amounts of parasympathetic outflow can slow and weaken the heartbeat; in some cases, it can even stop it altogether. Intense straining during a bowel movement can cause such a large outflow – as can compression of the neck, which is what makes strangulation play so dangerous – and it's not rare for people with weak hearts to be discovered sitting on a toilet in cardiac arrest. (I've heard a rumor that Elvis was found in this position.) It's also the reason why patients in cardiac care units are sometimes put on laxatives.

If I wanted to give someone an enema, I would particularly ask about any history of heart disease and any history of colon disease. If my partner had any history of either, I would procede very cautiously. (Actually, I probably wouldn't proceed at all.)

There are many different types of enemas, including cleansing, retention, and high colonic. Textbooks written for home health aides and nursing assistants often give excellent, step-by-step instruction on how to administer a standard cleansing enema. (They also include tips on things like how to apply restraints.) The intensity of an enema depends upon factors such as the pressure with which the liquid flows in, the temperature, and the quantity. (Thus giving rise to the "3H" saying: high, hot, and a hell of a lot. None of which I'd recommend for a first enema.) I'd probably start with only very slight elevation of the bag, ordinary tap water (no soap) of baby-bath-water temperature (elbow test it) and no more than 500 c.c. of fluid. I'd place the recipient lying on their left side. From experience, I've learned that it's a good idea to give the enema in a location relatively close to the toilet and without bondage. They may need to get to the toilet *fast*.

The major purpose of the large intestine, other than storage, is to absorb fluids. Therefore, anything potentially toxic, such as alcohol or caffeine, should be given very cautiously – if at all. Administering alcohol by enema can be fatal. The practice kills a fair number of otherwise healthy people each year. Among other things, it's a fairly common cause of deaths that occur during fraternity initiations. One little-known danger is the extremely cold enema. Ice-water enemas can cause massive parasympathetic outflow and thus induce cardiac arrest.

It's best to administer the fluid slowly. The recipient frequently develops cramps during the enema, and the flow should be stopped until the cramp passes – which it usually does within a minute or so.

Some people play games with how long the recipient must retain the enema. Again, with a beginner to this practice or with a new partner, I suggest the time be brief.

I've enjoyed what enema play I've done. An enema can certainly send some people into a deeply submissive head space, and it's usually fairly safe if you follow precautions. For more information, you might check out the books described above. Also, chiropractors generally receive more enema training than M.D.'s receive – particularly in the more advanced practices. There's a newsgroup called alt.sex.enemas that you might also want to check out.

Enema play demands specialized knowledge and equipment. Do not attempt this without adequate prior instruction. Try to be taught by someone experienced in this area. Be careful, though; some people into enema play have dangerous misconceptions.

For further information, try your local erotic boutique or SM toy store. Also check local health food stores and read both medical and nursing books on the subject. The sections on cleansing enemas are most relevant. Also, Greenery Press may be publishing a book on this topic sometime in 1997.

## Fetishism

Not all SM people are fetishists, and not all fetishists are SM people – but there is definitely a large overlap.

Common fetishes in the SM community include, of course, leather and rubber. Many people fetishize garments such as corsets, boots, and high-heeled shoes, or behaviors such as smoking. There are blood fetishists, urine fetishists, and scat fetishists; foot fetishists and ass fetishists; people who have a fetish for hairy bodies and people who have a fetish for naked bodies. People also sometimes refer to a strong preference for a specific SM activity such as spanking or piercing as a fetish.

There are a couple of common misconceptions about fetishism. First, people tend to believe that fetishism is both rare and sick. Arguably, however, almost everybody has at least some fetishes. Anytime you put on an item of clothing or pick up a toy, or see a potential partner doing so, and begin to feel turned on by it, you're experiencing at least a bit of fetishism.

Also, it's commonly believed that the fetishist prefers their fetish object to the exclusion of more conventional sexual activities. In my experience, fetishism at this level is almost unknown. The fetishist typically considers their fetish to be "the frosting on the cake." They are perfectly capable of having and enjoying conventional sex, it's just more fun if they can indulge their fetish at the same time.

Several fetishes, notably transvestism, age play, and corsetry, are so common among SM people that I've dealt with them in their own sections of this chapter.

## Fisting

The word "fisting" is a bit of a misnomer. It refers to the practice of inserting the entire hand into the anus or the vagina, but many people (including the author of a recent vanilla sex manual) are misled by the term into thinking that one balls up a fist and rams it into the orifice in question. In actuality, fisting is – particularly among novices – an *extremely* gentle and gradual practice, which may take many months to accomplish successfully. It rarely if ever includes sticking a balled fist into anything. (More typically, the hand is introduced gradually in a "swan's head" shape, as though you were making a shadow picture of a bird on the wall. Once the hand is fully in, it naturally tends to curl into a loose fist.)

Fisting is one of the practices which the vanilla world regards with the greatest horror; many people have a very hard time believing that something the size of a hand could be introduced into a vagina or anus without causing major damage.

To the contrary, many people can be successfully fisted, if they and their partners have the desire and patience to do so. Some people are such accomplished fisting recipients that they can accept two hands at once, although this is rare.

Properly done fisting does not harm the tissues involved. It does not make the vagina or the anus "looser" for their other functions. It can also be a deeply, profoundly intimate and erotic experience for the fister and the fistee alike.

A highly regarded book on anal fisting is:
"Trust: The Handbook"
by Bert Herrman
Alamo Square Press
P.O. Box 14543
San Francisco, CA 94114
Send a SASE and a signed, I'm-over-21 statement when you write.

In late 1996 or early 1997, Greenery Press will also publish:
"A Hand In the Bush: The Fine Art of Vaginal Fisting"
by Deborah Addington
Write to them for more information.

## Gay and Lesbian Resources

See Appendix II, "Sex and the Internet," for information on how to use the Internet to locate other gay and lesbian resources.

National Gay Yellow Pages
Box 292, Village Station
New York, NY 10014

The Bob Damron Guidebook
The Damron Company
P.O. Box 422458
San Francisco, CA 94142-2458
(415) 255-0404

Places of Interest to Women: A Guide to Women's Travel
Ferrari Publications, Inc.
P.O. Box 37887
Phoenix, AZ 85069
(602) 863-2408

## Non-Monogamous Relationships (Polyamory)

There are three basic forms of non-monogamous play.

1. 'Swinging," which usually consists of a male/female couple meeting similar couples or attending couples-only sexually oriented parties.

Many mainstream Americans swing. In fact, so many otherwise-conventional people are into swinging that its sometimes called "the Republican vice." Single women are often welcome in the swinging world, but single men face very sharp restrictions. Most clubs won't allow single men in at all.

Bisexual women are fairly common in the swinging community. Bisexual men are relatively rare – and often shunned.

North American Swing Club Association (NASCA) puts out a publication called "International Directory of Swing Clubs and Publications." Their address is:

NASCA
P.O. Box 7128
Buena Park, CA 90622
(714) 821-9953

2. An "open relationship" in which the two people have agreed between themselves as to when and how they will play outside their relationship. (My lady and I have such an agreement.)

3. Multiple partner relationships in which three or more people have a sense of relationship identity similar to that a couple might have. Sexual fidelity within the group, often called "polyfidelity,' is a common but not universal practice in these relationships. "Poly" group members are often somewhat "new age."

Two excellent resources for learning more about this type of relationship and finding out what resources are in your area are:

IntiNet Resource Center
P.O. Box 150474
San Rafael, CA 94915

PEP
Box 6306
Captain Cook, Hawaii 96704-6306

To find out about the many things these good folks offer, please send them a self-addressed, stamped envelope, an I'm-over-21 statement, and mention that you heard of them through this book.

In late 1996, Greenery Press will publish a book called "The Ethical Slut," by "Bottoming Book" and "Topping Book" authors Dossie Easton and Catherine A. Liszt. It promises to be an important addition to the literature on the subject.

## Piercing, Cutting, and Branding

These subjects are part of a larger practice generally known as "body modification." The entire subject of body modification can be very rich and deep. Its applications range from the playful to the profoundly spiritual. Many of the practices involved are distinctly dangerous, but can be made acceptably safe with proper equipment and instruction. I've provided the major references for such equipment and instruction in this section. Serious, permanent injuries (even fatalities) could result from attempting these procedures without first obtaining such equipment and instruction.

*Piercing* refers to making a hole through flesh. Piercings may be either temporary (designed to last only for the duration of the session), or permanent. The nipples and genitals are the most commonly pierced body parts. Many people have their nipples permanently pierced and wear rings through the holes.

Many submissives have themselves pierced as a way of demonstrating their devotion to their dominant. In such cases, the piercings are often done in a ceremonial manner, with guests present. A party usually follows.

While an experienced piercer attends, sets up, and supervises, the actual penetration of the flesh is sometimes done by the dominant. In other cases, the dominant allows the piercer to do the piercing.

*Cutting* (sometimes known as scarification) involves making partial-thickness cuts in the submissive's skin, usually in a decorative pattern. These cuts go only through the upper surface of the skin, typically no deeper than a cat scratch. The results often resemble tattoos, particularly if tattoo ink is rubbed into the cut. Obviously, cutting is a highly specialized art.

*Branding* is what you think it is: the deliberate creation of a pattern or design on the skin by burning with hot metal. As with cutting and piercing, this should only be done by properly trained, properly equipped practitioners.

The following highly respected magazines contain information and referrals on body modification procedures.

Body Play and Modern Primitives Quarterly
c/o Insight Books
P.O. Box 2575
Menlo Park, CA 94026-2575
(415) 324-0543

This magazine covers piercing, scarification, branding, and other related practices. Sample issue is $12.00 and I'm-over-21 statement.

Piercing Fans International Quarterly
c/o Gauntlet Mail Order
2215-R Market Street, #801
(800) RINGS 2 U

A sample copy of PFIQ, plus their catalog, is $15.00 plus tax if ordered from New York or California. (Call if you have any questions about this.) Be sure to, as always, include a signed I'm-over-21 statement.

## Prostitute Support Groups

(Mailing addresses only. For sex workers. No would-be customers need write!)

Coyote
2269 Chestnut St, # 452
San Francisco, CA 94123

Coyote – Los Angeles
1626 N. Wilcox Ave., # 580
Hollywood, CA 90028

Prostitutes of New York (PONY)
25 West 45th St., # 1401
New York, NY 10036

Hooking is Real Employment (HIRE)
P.O. Box 98386
Atlanta, GA 39359

Prostitutes Anonymous
11225 Magnolia Blvd., # 181
North Hollywood, CA 91601
This group is for those who want to leave the sex industry or for those who want help afterward.

## Tantric Sex

Tantra – The Magazine
P.O. Box 79
Torreon, NM 87061-0079
(505) 271-3155
This is a glossy, quarterly magazine that contains numerous articles and essays on tantra and somewhat related practices such as Quodoushka and Healing Tao. It includes contact information on most of the major teachers in this country.

## Transvestism and Transsexuality

More and more people are experimenting with wearing the clothes of the opposite sex (or opposite gender, as it's more correctly called). Also, more and more people are wondering if their biological sex matches their psychological sex. People exploring these issues can, just like SM folks, often use support and peer companionship. Some of the major resources are listed below. These can put you in touch with many more.

American Educational Gender Information Service (AEGIS)
P.O. Box 33724
Decatur, GA 30033
Publishes Chrysalis Quarterly magazine.

Cross Talk
P.O. Box 944
Woodland Hills, CA 91365
Publishes monthly newsletter. Sample $2.00 and I'm-over-21 statement.

ETVC
P.O. Box 426486
San Francisco, CA 94142-6486
(510) 549-2665
Bay Area support and social organization. Can make referrals to resources in other parts of the country.

Gender Identity Center Newsletter
3715 West 32nd. Ave.
Denver, CO 80211

International Foundation for Gender Education (I.F.G.E.)
P.O. Box 367
Wayland, MA 01778
(617) 894-8340
This organization publishes the "TV/TS Tapestry Journal." A 150+ page magazine containing articles, references, and other resources. Sample copy $12.00.

FTM
5337 College Ave., # 142
Oakland, CA 94618
Information, referrals, and peer support for female-to-male cross-dressers and transsexuals. Quarterly newsletter.

San Francisco Gender Information
P.O. Box 423602
San Francisco, CA 94142
Extensive data-base listings for $3.00.

# Finding Help with Problems

## *Where and How to Find Local Resources*

Probably the most important advice I can give you regarding finding help for the problems listed below, and other problems, is to grab your phone book and start looking. Many communities have local resources to deal with such problems. Check the first few pages and look over the telephone book's table of contents. Look up these and related topics in both the white and yellow pages. Check your phone book for an index.

If this doesn't help much, go to your local library and look through the phone books of nearby communities, particularly those of nearby big cities.

Local newspapers and magazines, particular free or low cost ones that come out on a weekly or less frequent basis, often carry valuable listings. Look them over carefully.

Please note that this book is updated frequently. If you know of other useful resources, or if you have feedback on these resources, please let me know so I can include that information in future editions.

## *Abuse/Battering/Neglect*

National Domestic Violence Hotline  (800) 799-SAFE
National Child Abuse Hotline  (800) 422-4453
Parents Anonymous  (800) 421-0353

## *AIDS*

National AIDS Hotline (800) 342-AIDS
National STD Hotline  (800) 227-8922

## *Birth Control/Abortion*

Check your local yellow pages under "Birth Control Information Centers." Note: Some anti-abortion agencies have been accused of being less than totally honest about that fact in their advertising. If a given resource doesn't explicitly say that it offers abortion, please consider that it may have a very strong interest into talking you into taking a particular course of action.

## Censorship

American Civil Liberties Union
132 West 43rd. St.
New York, New York 10036

Californians Against Censorship Together (Cal-ACT)
2550 Shattuck Ave., # 51
Berkeley, CA 94704
(510) 548-3695
(Please include SASE with information inquiry.)

National Coalition Against Censorship
132 West 43rd. Street
New York, New York  10036
(212) 944-9899

People for the American Way
2000 M. Street N.W., Suite 400
Washington, DC  20036
(202) 467-4999

## Death During Sex  *(Warning: I go on a bit of a tirade here.)*

People, especially older men, die during sex far more often than is commonly believed.  One reason for this reporting gap is that their partners are often too embarrassed to tell what was going on when the death occurred.

Studies have shown that the person in the community who faces the highest risk of sudden cardiac arrest is a man over the age of 50, and the person most likely to be with him when it happens is his wife.  If your boyfriend or husband is over 50, I strongly recommend that you schedule such training.

Studies have also shown that the second highest risk group for a sudden cardiopulmonary emergency is, to simplify matters, anyone wearing diapers. A saying often heard in CPR classes is "Someone is more likely to need emergency life support during the first one to two years of their life than they are in the next 48 years combined." If you help take care of young children, schedule a class that teaches infant and child CPR. (The technique is considerably different that the technique used on adults.)

By the way, I recommend that a pregnant woman, and those who will be helping to care for her baby, take a class during the first three months of her pregnancy that includes infant and child CPR. Repeat the class within three months after the baby is born.

354

You can look in the yellow pages under "First Aid Instruction" to find out where classes are offered. The American Red Cross, American Heart Association, some hospitals and emergency service agencies, and private firms all offer classes.

One final note: I worked on ambulance for eight years and have been a first aid and CPR instructor for over a dozen years. I've seen and worked with many other instructors. Frankly, entirely too many of them did extremely poor quality work. If you take a CPR class, try hard to get a good instructor. I suggest someone who has a minimum of one year of full-time experience in pre-hospital emergency care. A paramedic might be a good first choice. (Although people who are good at providing emergency care are not necessarily good at teaching others how to do so.)

All else being equal, I would prefer someone with experience in pre-hospital emergency care to someone with in-hospital experience. Hospitals, even busy, inner-city emergency rooms, are protected ivory towers when compared to the streets.

In any event, try to find someone who has considerable experience. It's entirely reasonable to ask your proposed instructor how often they have performed these skills "in real life." A person who has seen many, many heart attacks and strokes can teach you things that the inexperienced simply cannot. A person who has done CPR dozens, maybe even hundreds, of times will have priceless tips and insights to share.

If you get a good instructor (and that's different from an instructor that you like or one who takes it easy on you) learn all you can. If you get a bad one, and they're common, complain to their boss and (note this next part well) *take another class from a different instructor*. Anybody who thinks they can learn life-or-death skills from an incompetent instructor is asking for disaster.

## Herpes

Herpes Resource Center (HRC)
P.O. Box 13827
Research Triangle Park, North Carolina 27709

These folks offer wonderful information for those coping with any aspect of herpes. Among other things, they sponsor a nationwide network of excellent support groups. If somebody I cared about had herpes, I would make certain that they were fully informed about what these folks offer.

National STD Hotline (800) 227-8922

## Incest

Incest Survivors Anonymous
P.O. Box 5613
Long Beach, CA 90805-0613
(310) 428-5599

Survivors of Incest Anonymous
P.O. Box 21817
Baltimore, Maryland 21222
(410) 433-2365

Both groups sponsor meetings all over the country. They will also help you start a group in your area if one does not already exist. (Starting a group is not all that difficult.) Incest is one of the most under-reported forms of abuse in this country.

## Old Age

Sex Over Forty Newsletter
PHE, Inc.
P.O. Box 1600
Chapel Hill, North Carolina 27515
As people age, their needs and their bodies change. This newsletter is one of the most informative and useful sources of information on the topic.

## Rape

As soon as you safely can, call 911, a rape treatment center, or a similar resource. Check your phone book under Rape, Battering, and Sexual Abuse Aid. It's very, very important from a medical, emotional, and legal point of view to seek help as soon as possible after the assault.

Know that an attempted rape can be almost as damaging, and take as long to recover from, as a completed rape. If you can safely do so, have the authorities come to the scene so they can look for valuable evidence. Try not to shower, douche, brush your teeth, or change clothes until you've been examined.

If you need support or don't feel your case is being handled properly, by all means contact a rape crisis center for more help.

## Sex Therapy

You don't necessarily need a formally trained sex therapist to help you cope with sexual problems. Many therapists with broader training do excellent work in this field.

That being said, I want to mention that the organizations listed below help train and set policies for sex therapists. I would imagine that someone representing themselves specifically as a sex therapist would have extensive contact with at least one of them.

Sex therapy is not an exact science. In particular, such issues as the use of surrogates are highly controversial. You should understand that the organizations listed below are far from in total agreement on every issue. AASECT is considered the more conservative.

Society for the Scientific Study of Sex (SSSS)
P.O. Box 208
Mount Vernon, Iowa, 52314

American Association of Sex Educators, Counselors, and Therapists
    (AASECT)
435 Michigan Ave., Suite 1717
Chicago, Illinois 60611

## *Sex and Love Addiction*

These are 12-step groups designed to help people achieve "sexual sobriety" by using the principles of Alcoholics Anonymous. They have chapters in many parts of the country. If one doesn't exist in your area, they will help you start one. (Don't be at all surprised if your initial outreach efforts draw more people than you expected.)

Sexaholics Anonymous
P.O. Box 300
Simi Valley, CA 93062

Sex and Love Addicts Anonymous
P.O. Box 119
New Town Branch
Boston, MA 02258

## *Suicidal/Homicidal Feelings*

Almost every local community has telephone crisis hotlines. Again, check your telephone book – particularly the first few pages.

## *Additional Resource Information*

San Francisco Sex Information, at (415) 989-7374, offers referrals and a sympathetic ear. They most definitely do not, however, offer phone sex.

# References and Resources

Note: This book is updated frequently. If you're aware of references not listed here, or of changes in contact information for these resources, please let me know so I can include them in future editions.

Another note: To quote Dorothy, "People come and go so quickly here!" SM resources go in and out of business, and move around, at a dizzying rate. I've done my best to include current information here, but names, phone numbers, and addresses may have changed by the time you read this.

## Gateway Resources

These resources can open doors to a vast number of people, clubs, publications and ideas: hence, I call them "gateways."

Black Book
P.O. Box 31155
San Francisco, CA   94131
(415) 431-0171
An international compendium of resources for various sexual minorities, particularly leatherfolk. I *highly* recommend this book.

Kink-Aware Professionals
c/o Race Bannon
584 Castro Street #518
San Francisco, CA 94114-2500
e-mail: race@bannon.com, http://www.bannon.com/~race/kap
Race Bannon, author of "Learning the Ropes," has compiled a nationwide listing of therapists, physicians and other professionals who have understanding and sympathy for sexual minorities. You can look at the list on his web site, or send him a business-sized SASE with two regular stamps on it.

## Academic Books

An Initial Study of Nonclinical Practitioners of Sexual Sadomasochism
by Janet P. Miale
The Professional School of Psychological Studies
San Diego, CA

<u>Sexual Behavior in the Human Female</u>
by Kinsey, Pomeroy, and Martin

<u>Masochism: A Jungian View</u>
by Lyn Cowan
Spring Publications

<u>Masochism and the Self</u>
by Roy Baumeister
Erlbaum Publishers

## Academic Articles

Moser, C. Sadomasochism. <u>Journal of Social Work and Human Sexuality</u>, Vol. 7(1), 1988, 43-56.

Moser, C. and Levitt, E. An exploratory-descriptive study of a sadomasochistically-oriented sample. <u>The Journal of Sex Research</u>, Vol. 23, No. 3, August 1987, 322-389.

Weinberg, M.S., Williams, C.J., and Moser, C. The social constituents of sadomasochism. <u>Social Problems</u>, Vol. 31, No. 4, April 1984, 379-389.

Breslow, N. Evans, L. and Langley, J. (1985). Comparisons among heterosexual, bisexual, and homosexual male sadomasochists. <u>Journal of Homosexuality</u>, <u>13</u>, (1), 83-107.

Spengler, A. (1977). Manifest sadomasochism of males: Results of an empirical study. <u>Archives of Sexual Behavior</u>, <u>6</u>, 441-456.

Gebhard, P. (1976). Fetishism and sadomasochism. In M. Weinberg (Ed.), <u>Sex Research</u>. New York: Oxford University Press, 1976.

## SM and Related Subject Books – Nonfiction

*Note: Obviously, I think highly of the books available from my publisher, Greenery Press. Their books are listed on the last page.*

<u>The Complete Guide to Safer Sex</u>, *edited by the Institute for Advanced Study of Human Sexuality*
Barricade Books, Fort Lee, NJ

<u>The Condom Educator's Guide</u>
Daniel Bao & Beowulf Thorne
Condom Resource Center, Oakland, CA

<u>Different Loving: An Exploration of the World of Sexual Dominance and Submission</u>, *by Brame, Brame and Jacobs*
Villard Books, New York

Exhibitionism for the Shy, *by Carol Queen*
Down There Press, San Francisco

Gay and Lesbian Couple's Guide
Nolo Press, Berkeley, California
(Nolo Press also publishes many other legal self-help books, which I highly recommend.)

Consensual Sadomasochism: How to Talk About It and How to Do It Safely, *by William A. Henkin, Ph.D. and Sybil Holiday*
Daedalus Publishing Co., San Francisco

Learning the Ropes, *by Race Bannon*
Daedalus Publishing Co., San Francisco

Leatherfolk, *edited by Mark Thompson*
Alyson Publications, Boston

Leathersex, *by Joseph Bean*
Daedalus Publishing Co., San Francisco

The Leatherman's Handbook, *by Larry Townsend*
available from the author at P.O. Box 302, Beverly Hills, CA  90213

The Lesbian S/M Safety Manual, *edited by Pat Califia*
Alyson Publications, Boston

The Loving Dominant, *by John Warren*
Masquerade Books, New York

My Private Life: Real Experiences of a Dominant Woman, *by Mistress Nan*
Daedalus Publishing Co., San Francisco

On the Safe Edge: A Manual for S/M Play, *by Trevor Jaques*
WholeSM Publishing, Toronto
(A useful book, but a fair amount of its content is disturbingly similar to previously published material – including some of mine.)

Safe, Sane, Consensual – And Fun, *by John Warren*
Diversified Services, Boston

Screw the Roses, Send Me the Thorns, *by Philip Miller & Molly Devon*
Mystic Rose Books, Fairfield, CT

Sensuous Magic, *by Pat Califia*
Masquerade Books, New York

SM: A Player's Handbook, *by Lady Tanith*
Self-published; available fromQSM, San Francisco

A Tangled Web, *by Lady Tanith*
Self-published; available from QSM, San Francisco

Ties That Bind: The SM/Leather/Fetish Erotic Style – Issues, Commentaries and Advice, *by Guy Baldwin*
Daedalus Publishing, San Francisco

## *SM and Related Subject Books – Not Recommended*

Kink: The Hidden Sex Lives of Americans, *Susan Crain Bakos*
St. Martin's Press

The Q Letters, *by "Sir" John*
Prometheus Books, New York

Welts: Female Domination in an American Marriage, *by Gloria and Dave Wallace*
Artemis Publishing

## *SM and Related Subject Books – Fiction*

I don't necessarily want to include every work that has somebody getting tied up and/ or whipped in it, but the following books have something of a following in the SM world.

The "Beauty" trilogy, *by A.N. Roquelaure*
Dutton Books, New York

Exit to Eden, *by Anne Rampling*
Arbor House

The "Gor" science fiction novels, *by John Norman*
Published by Daw Books
(Every "Gor" novel comes complete with soapbox.)

The Image, *by Jean DeBerg*
Grove Press
(I've met Jean. She's a fascinating lady.)

The Love of a Master, *John Preston*
Alyson Publications, Boston

Leatherwomen, *edited by Laura Antoniou*
Masquerade Books, New York

Macho Sluts, Doc and Fluff, Melting Point, *by Pat Califia*
Masquerade Books, New York

The "Marketplace" trilogy, *by Sara Adamson*
Masquerade Books, New York

9½ Weeks, *by Elizabeth McNeil*
Dutton, New York
(Rings fairly true, but I think they made up the ending.)

The Story of O, *by Pauline Reage*
Grove Press

Telepaths Don't Need Safewords, *by Cecelia Tan*
Circlet Press, Boston

The Warrior Within, *by Sharon Green*
Published by Daw Books

## *Periodicals*

*Note!:* Include I'm-over-21 statement when contacting anybody listed below (or any other resource in this book).

Bad Attitude *(lesbian)*
P.O. Box 390110
Cambridge, MA 02139

Body Play and Modern Primitives Quarterly *(piercing, cutting, branding focus)*
P.O. Box 2575
Menlo Park, CA 94026
(415) 324-0543
Sample issue $12.00

Black Sheets *(pansexual)*
P.O. Box 31155
San Francisco, CA 94131
(415) 431-0171

Boudoir Noir *(pansexual)*
Box 5, Station F
Toronto, ON M4Y 2L4
CANADA
(416) 591-2387

CuirUnderground *(pansexual)*
3288 21st St. #19
San Francisco, CA 94110

Drummer *(gay male)*
P.O. Box 410390
San Francisco, CA   94141-0390
(415) 252-1195

EIDOS *(pansexual – civil liberties focus)*
P.O. Box 96
Boston, MA 02137
(617) 262-0096
Current issue $10.00

Kinky People, Places and Things *(heterosexual)*
P.O. Box 16188
Seattle, WA   98116

Leather Journal *(primarily gay male)*
published by Cedar Publishing Co.
7985 Santa Monica Blvd., # 109-368
West Hollywood, CA 90046
(213) 656-5073
Sample Copy $6.00

Piercing Fans International Quarterly *(pansexual)*
c/o Gauntlet Mail Order
2215-R Market St. #801
San Francisco, CA  94114
(800) RINGS 2 U

Prometheus *(Eulenspiegel Society newsletter; pansexual)*
P.O. Box 2783
New York, NY   10163-2783
TES@dorsai.com

Sandmutopian Guardian *(pansexual)*
The Utopian Network
P.O. Box 1146
New York, NY   10156
(516) 482-1711

## BBS's (Computer Bulletin Board Services)

SM and sexuality-oriented BBSs exist in many parts of the country.  Current listings may be found in the periodicals Prometheus, Sandmutopian Guardian, Boudoir Noir, and Leather Journal.

# *Videos*

**Fiction – Mainstream**

The Story of O
The Punishment of Anne
Venus in Furs

**Fiction – Adult**

Diary of a Dominant Woman, volumes 1-3
Bad Kitty Productions
San Francisco, CA

Painful Mistake
Blowfish Productions
San Francisco, CA

Pain Suite, Journey into Pain
Bud Russell Productions

Blush Entertainment has produced a number of lesbian videos that contain mild to moderate SM scenes. Two in particular are Hungry Hearts and Clips.

**Educational**

Blood Sisters: Leather, Dykes and Sadomasochism
Michelle Handelman

Learning the Ropes (a series of SM how-to videos)
Ona Zee Productions
Culver City, CA

Safe, Sane, Consensual SM – A Documentary
B&D Video Production and Distribution Co.
San Francisco

Welcome to SM
Oranj Productions
San Francisco
(I appear briefly in this one.)

# *SM Workshops*

The House of Differences
elizabeth@differences.com
(Note: Differences also puts on several other types of events.)

QSM
P.O. Box 880154
San Francisco, CA   94188
(415) 550-7776

SKIN (Seattle Kink Information Network)
Crossroads Learning Center, Seattle, WA
(206) 368-0384

Taurel Enterprises
250 W. 57th St. #260
New York City, NY   10107
(Mention this book, please.)

## SM Clubs

I cannot recommend strongly enough that those who are interested in SM, or those whose lovers are interested in SM, contact a local group for proper orientation, instruction, and support.

Groups form and disband frequently, and some groups prefer to maintain a low profile. The following are some of the largest and best-known, and may be able to refer you to a club closer to your location and/or interests. If your club would like to be listed in future editions of this book, please contact me with your address and other pertinent information.

Note: Friends of mine who travel the country report that they have had good results by stopping at "alternative-type" leather stores and simply asking if any local clubs exist. Gay and lesbian bookstores, adult bookstores, and the local newspapers they carry, are often also helpful.

Current listings on national and international clubs may be found in Prometheus, Boudoir Noir, and Leather Journal.

### National Club (chapters in many cities)

National Leather Association *(pansexual but primarily gay & lesbian)*
3439 North East Sandy Blvd., #155
Portland, OR   97232
(614) 470-2093

### Pansexual Clubs

Alternative Erotic Lifestyles (AEL)
P.O. Box 80676
Albuquerque, NM   87198
(505) 345-6484

Arizona Power Exchange (APEX)
P.O. Box 67532
Phoenix AZ 85082-7532

Black Rose
P.O. Box 11161
Arlington, VA 22210-1161
(202) 686-5880

Chicagoland Discussion Group
3023 N. Clark St. #806
Chicago, IL 60657-5205
(312) 281-1097

Club X
P.O. Box 3092
San Diego, CA 92163
(619) 685-5149

C. O. P. E.
1015 S. Gaylord St. #200
Denver, CO 80209

Group With No Name
P.O. Box 18301
Austin, TX 78760-9998

LBW
3140-WB W Tilghman #1 39
Allentown, PA 18104
LBW1femdom@aol.com

O P C (Omaha Players' Club)
P.O. Box 34463
Omaha, NE 68134-0463

PEP New Brunswick
PO Box 812
Morrisville, PA 19067
(908) 281-8689

PEP Philadelphia
P.O. Box 812
Morrisville, PA 19067
(215) 552-8155

The Phoenix Society
1131 S. Clinton St.
Baltimore, MD 21224
(410) 385-3331

Rose City Discussion Club
P.O. Box 1370
Clackamas, OR 97015
(503) 650-7052

SAAFE
BOX 42014 Postal Outlet
Calgary, Alberta, T2J 7A6
CANADA

Sacramento Leather Association
P.O. Box 5789
Sacramento, CA 95817

Service of Mankind Church
P.O. Box 1335
El Cerrito, CA 94530
(510) 232-1369

Society of Janus
P.O. Box 426794
San Francisco, CA 94142
(415) 985-7117

Threshold
2554 Lincoln Blvd Suite 1004
Marina Del Rey CA 90291
(818) 782-1160

United Leatherfolk of CT
P.O. Box 281172
East Hartford, CT 06128-1172

Vancouver Leather Alliance
P 0 Box 2253
Vancouver, BC V6B 3W2
CANADA

*Important note: Most of the clubs listed above are open and friendly toward people of all genders and sexual orientations. However, if you prefer men-only, women-only, or gay- and lesbian-oriented clubs, please contact the National Leather Association (see p. 365) to see if they have a chapter near you, or get in touch with one of the following:*

## Men's Groups

Chicago Hellfire Club
P.O. Box 5426
Chicago, IL 60680

Fifteen Association
P.O. Box 421302
San Francisco, CA 94142

GMSMA
332 Bleeker St. #023
New York, NY 10014
(212) 727-9878

## Women's Groups

Briar Rose
P.O. Box 163143
Columbus, OH 43216

Female Trouble
P.O. Box 2284
Philadelphia, PA 19103

Lesbian Sex Mafia
P.O. Box 993
Murray Hill Station
New York, NY 10156

Outcasts
P.O. Box 31266
San Francisco, CA 94131

## Clubs on College Campuses

*Several of these clubs are struggling for official recognition from their campuses. Please support them if you can.*

Conversio Virium
Ferris Booth Hall, Columbia University, NY
conversio@columbia.edu

SM Aces
Bard College, Annandale-on-Hudson, NY
ja522@bard.edu

Society for Human Sexuality
University of Washington, Seattle, WA
sfpse@u.washington.edu

# Glossary

## *Words*

**Age play:** Role-playing the persona of someone substantially younger (or sometimes older) than your actual age.

**Alpha Dilemma:** The problem faced by someone who is normally dominant (particularly in a vanilla kind of way) regarding where and how they can safely express their submissive side. Can be particularly difficult for women.

**Animal games:** A form of role-playing in which one person pretends to be some kind of animal – often a dog or horse.

**Assertive fantasies:** A "code phrase" sometimes found in personal ads to indicate dominant interests.

**Best/worst/most memorable:** A structured method of reviewing a session to determine its most prominent features. Often combined with "on a scale of one to ten, how good, bad, or memorable was it?"

**Blue:** A safeword often used to indicate "Please, no more of *that* particular activity."

**Body-fluid monogamy (also "body-fluid bonding"):** A safer-sex practice in which an HIV-negative, non-monogamous couple agrees to practice safer sex when playing with other partners.

**Bondage:** Physical materials applied to a submissive to restrain their ability to move and/or to otherwise restrict them. Also, the act of placing the submissive in such materials.

**Bottom:** A slang term for a submissive and/or masochist. Many people use the word "bottom" to mean specifically someone who enjoys being given various sensations, as opposed to a "submissive," who enjoys being controlled.

**Bottom's disease:** A habit of taking a submissive attitude toward others without justification or negotiation. Generally considered undesirable and a bit clueless. See Top's Disease.

**Bottom space:** The psychological "head space" or attitude of being submissive.

**Boy:** A submissive (often, but not always, male) who relates to their dominant in a child-to-parent mode. More common among gay men and lesbians.

**Brat:** A submissive who enjoys rebelling in a childlike way against their dominant. Brats are fairly common in the spanking scene.

**Brown showers:** The act of one person defecating on another in an erotic context.

**Burning Hands Syndrome:** An unintended burning sensation of the hands that sometimes results after play using menthol-containing creams without wearing protective gloves.

**Caning:** Using a relatively long, thin, flexible rod to whip someone. The rod is usually made of supple, varnished rattan, although some canes are made of manmade materials like fiberglass. Caning is often more damaging than a novice might expect. Novices should be careful.

**Cat:** Cat-o-nine tails. A multi-tailed whip in which the tails are braided.

**Cinch loop:** A bondage technique in which coils of rope, or other bondage material, are wound between wrists after they have already been encircled by other bondage material. Cinch loops can closely regulate tightness.

**Clean:** Has no sexually transmitted diseases.

**Cock and ball torture:** SM concerned with giving strong sensations to the male genitals.

**Consensual:** An activity done with the consent of adults competent to give that consent. One of the central features of SM play.

**Counting games:** Rituals engaged in during whipping, or during other forms of flagellation, in which the submissive is required to keep count of the number of strokes delivered, often thanking the dominant after each one and asking for more. Example: "That's five, Mistress. Thank you, Mistress. Mistress, please may I have another, Mistress?"

**Crop:** Riding crop.

**Crossdresser:** One who dresses in the clothing of the other gender. Male to female or female to male.

**Cunt torture:** SM that involves giving strong sensations to the female genitals. (Note: using the word "cunt" for female genitals is not as taboo in SM culture as it is in most parts of the straight world.)

**Cutting:** An SM activity in which very shallow decorative cuts are placed on the skin, usually with a sterile scalpel. Requires considerable knowledge to do safely.

**Daddy:** A dominant (usually, but not always, male) who has a submissive "boy" or "girl," and who relates to that submissive in a parent/child mode. More common among gay men and lesbians, but gaining currency among heterosexuals and bisexuals as well.

**Deal-breaker:** A point on which players are so far out of agreement as to prevent their playing together. Frustrating, and better discovered earlier in negotiations than later.

**Discipline:** Training by a dominant in how they wish their submissive to behave. Also, the punishment and correction administered by the dominant when the submissive fails to act in the proper manner.

**Do-me queen:** A submissive who is more interested in what the dominant can do for and to them than in what they can do for the dominant.

**Dominant:** One who enjoys assuming control. One who decides what happens and when. A dominant may or may not be sadistic.

**Dominatrix:** A female dominant.

**Dom:** A male dominant.

**Domme:** A female dominant.

**Erotic power exchange:** A somewhat genteel term for SM.

**"Feet last, feet first":** A safety slogan used during bondage. People standing with their feet tied together are in an unstable position. This is therefore minimized during SM play.

**Feminization:** An activity that involves dressing the submissive in female attire and requiring traditionally female behavior. May also be played as "forced feminization," in which the submissive is "forced" to dress or act like a woman. Feminization may be perceived by the submissive as humiliating or as a privilege.

**Fetishism:** Sexual responsiveness to items, body parts, or behaviors that are not innately sexual. Most people are at least to some degree fetishistic.

**Fisting:** The practice of inserting the entire hand into the vagina or anus. This practice takes time, training, and special equipment

**Flagellation:** The general act of one person striking another, usually in an erotic context. Includes spanking, paddling, and whipping.

**Flogger:** A multi-tailed whip in which the tails are long, flat strips of leather or a similarly flexible material.

**Forbidden Zone:** The abdominal area containing the kidneys, liver, spleen, and other organs vulnerable to serious, even life-threatening, damage from a whipping. Runs all the way around the body and from the hip crests to the xiphoid process. (The angle felt at the front of the rib cage.)

**Force-me queen:** A submissive who gets off on being "forced" to do something. "Force" play must be carefully negotiated in advance.

**Gender play:** Play in which one or both partners assume the role of a sex other than their usual one.

**Girl:** A submissive (usually, but not always, female) who relates to their dominant in a child-to-parent mode. More common among gay men and lesbians.

**Goddess worship:** A worshipping of divine, feminine images and of women as manifestations of "the Goddess."

**Going under:** Entering a submissive "head space." Assuming a submissive attitude. See "bottom space."

**Golden shower:** The act of one person urinating on another as an erotic activity.

**Gorean:** Male dominant/female submissive interests as portrayed by the "Gor" novels by John Norman. Sometimes used as a "code word" in personal ads.

**Go under:** A slang term meaning to assume the submissive role. Example: "I'd gladly go under for her."

**Heavy:** A somewhat imprecise slang term meaning extreme. Example, "I'm not into heavy pain." Note well: what is heavy to one player may not be heavy to another.

**Humiliation:** Activities which cause the submissive to feel shame, embarrassment, or degradation. Varies widely from person to person. Possibly psychologically explosive.

**I'll call out. You call in:** A safety slogan used to verify phone numbers and location when playing with a new partner.

**Infantilism:** An extreme form of age play in which one person assumes the role of an infant. May bring needs unmet while young to the surface. Should, therefore, be done by those prepared to deal with that.

**In role:** Assuming a dominant or submissive attitude during SM play. "Please excuse me but I can't socialize right now, Sir. I'm in role."

**In a scene:** Engaging in SM play. "I can't talk on the phone right now. Susan and I are in a scene."

**In the scene:** In the SM community. "Guess what? My new boss is in the scene."

**Isolation Syndrome:** The emotional distress, sometimes severe, from believing that you are the only person in the world interested in SM.

**Kamikaze:** A submissive who deliberately seeks out possibly dangerous practices or partners. This type of person is not particularly respected within the SM community.

**Key word:** An alternative term for a safeword.

**Malicious warning:** Deliberately lying to potential play partners that someone is an unsafe player. Best countered by asking the individual in question to provide their own references, and telling them who is spreading "warnings." Spreading "malicious warnings" is strong grounds for expulsion from an SM club.

**Masochismo:** Pride felt by a submissive or masochist regarding how much pain or other heavy play they can take. Can be competitive. Some masochists collect the paddles, canes, and other devices that have been broken on their body during play. (Have five broken on you and you're an "ace bottom.")

**Masochist:** Loosely defined within the SM community as a person who specifically enjoys receiving pain. It is quite possible for a person to be masochistic without being submissive, and to be submissive without being masochistic.

**Master:** A term for a male dominant. Often used as a term of address, such as "Master Tom." It is often considered somewhat rude to address a man by this term without being first given permission to do so. (Note: dominants do not usually address each other by such titles.)

**Master/slave relationship:** An ongoing SM relationship in which the slave is submissive to a male dominant.

**Mistress:** A term for a female dominant. The use of this term often follows certain customs. See "Master" above.

**Mistress/slave Relationship:** An ongoing SM relationship in which the slave is submissive to a female dominant.

**Mommy:** A dominant (usually although not always female) who relates to submissives in a maternal role.

**Monday Morning Rebound Syndrome:** Feelings of remorse, disgust, fear, and so forth that sometimes emerge hours or days after a person willingly, and often lustily, takes part in SM play.

**Mummification:** Immobilizing bondage, usually done by wrapping the submissive in many coils of materials uch as plastic wrap, or by placing the submissive in a body bag designed for this purpose.

**Munch:** A gathering of SM people, usually in a restaurant, for the purpose of socialization and chat. An Internet term, although it is spreading into general use.

**Neck snap:** The involuntary, reflexive act of a submissive snapping back their head and neck after being struck a strong blow on their back or buttocks. Can cause serious injury unless prevented or minimized.

**Negotiate:** To discuss (and hopefully agree) on the details of what will and will not be done during a specific SM session.

**9¹/₂ Weeks:** A "code phrase" sometimes found in personal ads used to indicate an interest in SM, particularly male-dominant/female-submissive SM. Refers to the book by the same name.

**Nipple torture:** Singling out the nipples for particular attention; usually with clamps, fingernails, teeth, and other fun items.

**Nod:** A nodding of the head by the submissive. Usually used to indicate that they are willing to receive the next whip stroke or other "bit" of pain.

**Nonconsensual:** Anything done by one person to another without their agreement.

**Novice:** A person just beginning to learn about and explore SM. Often treated with special kindness and attention by the more experienced members of the community.

**"Now":** A verbal signal used by a submissive to indicate that they are ready to receive the next whip stroke or other "bit" of pain.

**One to ten:** A way for the submissive to indicate the intensity of the whipstroke or other pain that they are ready to receive. "I did a one-to-ten with him when he bottomed to me last night."

**Orange:** A safeword sometimes used to indicate "I'm getting close to my limits," or sometimes "Let's rest for a while."

**Paddling:** The striking of the submissive, usually on the buttocks, with a flat, rigid instrument such as a hairbrush or paddle.

**Pain slut:** A slang term for a masochist. Often used by masochists to describe themselves.

**Persona:** A role assumed for the purpose of exploring an aspect of oneself. "I was in my child persona for that scene."

**Pervert:** An SM person. Often used as a term of affectionate recognition within the SM community.

**Poignant sensations:** A term used by the Marquis de Sade to describe pain. Gave rise to numerous jokes within the SM community along the lines of, "Well, of course I'm not into pain, but I really love receiving poignant sensations."

**Play:** To engage in SM. Example: "I played with him at a party last week." Also a term referring to particular activity, i.e. nipple play.

**Play piercing:** An SM activity which involves inserting sterile hypodermic or acupuncture needles below the skin, not for the insertion of jewelry but simply for the sensation. Requires considerable knowledge to do safely.

**Playroom:** A room especially set up for SM play. Often equipped with eyebolts, slings, whipping posts, blackout lights, mirrors, sound systems, special lighting, and so forth.

**Pushing limits:** SM play designed to take the submissive right up to the edge of what they can stand, and then coax them into going "just a little bit further."

**Red:** A safeword indicating "Stop completely and immediately." The calling of this word usually is a signal that ends the session entirely. Calling "red" is a serious matter, and is not to be done lightly.

**Restraints:** Bondage devices, usually made of leather.

**Rimming:** A slang term for analingus.

**Roissy:** A personal ad "code word" referring to SM, particularly male-dominant/female submissive SM. Refers to the town mentioned in "The Story of O."

**Sadist:** As loosely defined with the SM community, a person who specifically enjoys administering pain. A person may be dominant without being sadistic. It's also possible to be sadistic without being dominant.

**Sadomasochism:** A rather vague term referring generally to fantasies and experiences regarding the introduction of domination, submission, bondage, sadism, masochism, humiliation, and related activities into erotic play.

**Safeword:** A specific word or other signal used, by prior agreement, to indicate that things are "really" becoming too intense for the person. Usually used by the submissive, but may also be used by the dominant. "Safeword" itself is sometimes used at SM parties to signal a desire for outside intervention.

**Scene:** A slang term for an SM encounter. Example, "I had a really hot scene with him the other night." A synonym for "session."

**Session:** A slang term for an SM encounter. Example: "I shall always remember my first session with Mistress Alice." A synonym for "scene."

**Scat:** A slang term for feces (shit).

**Silent alarm:** A danger signal that requires no effort to activate. For example, if an "I'm all right" phone call is *not* made by a certain time, the "silent alarm partner" is to assume their friend is in very serious trouble.

**Silent alarm partner:** The person who "backs up" the person meeting with a new partner.

**SM-positive:** Regarding consensual SM play as a good form of sexuality. Example: "My new physician is SM positive."

**SM virgin:** Somebody inexperienced and/or naive about SM.

**Slave:** A person who has an on-going, structured relationship with a dominant. One who assumes the submissive role, often in a highly developed and committed way to a particular person. Calling someone "my slave" generally indicates a relatively sophisticated, ongoing relationship between the two of you.

**Spanking:** Striking the buttocks, usually with a bare, or sometimes gloved, hand. Striking the buttocks with an object such as a board specially made for the purpose is more often called "paddling."

**Straight:** From this perspective, usually refers to someone uninterested or unknowledgeable about SM.

**Submissive:** One who yields control. One who obeys orders and may permit themselves to be bound or "tortured" if doing so pleases their dominant.

**Suspension:** A style of bondage in which the submissive's body is held off the ground by the bondage. Requires considerable knowledge to do safely.

**Switch:** One who switches roles. One who enjoys both the dominant and submissive aspects of SM. (Also, occasionally, a slim tree branch used for flagellation.)

**The "Oh My Gods":** The period of intense emotional reactions that a novice typically goes through during their first year or so in the community. The expressions on their faces can be fun to watch.

**Tit torture:** See "nipple torture." Also sometimes refers to erotic torture of the entire breast area.

**Top:** A slang term for a dominant and/or sadist.

**Top's Disease:** An unwarranted attitude of superiority taken by a dominant. Believing that bottoms are somehow inferior and treating them so in either obvious or subtle ways. Usually a sign of insecurity or ignorance. Dominants who suffer from Top's Disease often (surprise, surprise) complain about how hard it is to find people willing to play with them. A mirror image of this syndrome is called Bottom's Disease.

**Top drop:** Feelings of guilt, depression, and so forth that sometimes come up for a dominant after SM play. The dominant may or may not be aware of these feelings.

**Topping from below:** Attempting to control the session while ostensibly in the submissive (non-controlling) role. A type of behavior generally frowned upon.

**Top space:** A dominant attitude or "head space."

**Torture:** Somewhat loosely defined. Generally refers to erotic pain administered by means other than flagellation.

**Toy:** A device used for SM or sex.

**Two Squeezes:** A "squeeze signal" between players used to non-verbally signal that "I'm all right."

**Vanilla:** Non-SM. Conventional sex is often referred to as vanilla sex.

**Verbal abuse:** A form of erotic play that involves calling the submissive names, insulting them, and so forth. Must be done with caution.

**Water sports:** Sexual activity involving urine and/or enemas.

**What if they faint? What if they fall?:** Two questions a dominant keeps in mind when dealing with a bound submissive.

**Whipping:** Erotic pain administered by the use of relatively flexible instruments to strike the submissive's body. Commonly used whipping instruments include the flogger, cat-o-nine-tails, riding crop, and cane.

**Worship:** To adore the personage of the dominant. Often combined with performing some service to the dominant's body such as massaging, kissing, or licking their feet, painting their toenails, massaging their body, bathing them, or brushing their hair. Explicitly sexual activity, such as performing oral sex on the dominant, may or may not be a part of such play.

**Wrapping:** The unintentional delivering of a whip stroke in a manner that causes the tips to land on the side of the body rather than the front or back. Wrapping often leaves marks and is often a sign of a lack of skill on the dominant's part.

**Wurtenburg wheel:** A medical implement, used in the real world for neurological testing, which is popular among SM players. A small spiked wheel on the end of a handle. Sometimes called a "neuro wheel."

**Yellow:** A safeword often used to indicate "lighten up" or "let's stop or slow down for a while."

**Yes/No/Maybe:** A negotiation strategy in which participants list all possible activities, then each participant codes each activity with a Y for "yes, I'd like to do that," M for "I might like to try that under certain circumstances," and N for "I don't want to do that at this time."

**Yielding fantasies:** A personal ad "code phrase" referring to fantasies of being submissive.

**Zipper:** A pain device made by stringing several clothespins or other non-toothed clamps along a cord, so that the clamps can be yanked off the skin rapidly.

## *Abbreviations*

**BD, B&D, B/D:** Abbreviations for "bondage and discipline." No clear or widely agreed upon dividing line exists between S&M and B&D.

**BDSM:** A fairly recent term, coined on the Internet, which is gaining in currency as a combination of B&D, D&S, and S/M.

**CBT:** Cock and Ball Torture. See definition above.

**D&S:** Dominance & submission. Sometimes used as an umbrella term for what in this book is called SM; other times is used to refer specifically to play in which one partner takes control of another's behavior.

**DUBS:** Dominant's-Utility-Belt-Syndrome. Characterizes the super-hero like appearance many dominants have due to all the equipment that hangs from their belts.

**Femdom:** SM play that is female-dominant in theme.

**Five-F:** Common SM emergencies: freakouts, falls, fainting, failure (electrical power failure), and fire.

**SAM:** A "smart-assed masochist." A masochist who deliberately angers, insults, or otherwise provokes a dominant into "punishing" them. SAM play is considered OK only when done in a negotiated and consensual way; otherwise, it is not held in high regard in the SM community.

**SM:** Sadomasochism.

**S&M:** Sadism and Masochism, also Sadomasochism.

**TPE:** Net-speak for "Total Power Exchange." A relationship in which the dominant holds complete power and control over the submissive. For most people, more an ideal than a real-world possibility.

**WIITWD:** An Internet abbreviation for "what it is that we do." Coined in an attempt to sidestep disagreements about the meaning of terms like B&D, D&S and SM.

**YKINOK:** Your Kink Is Not OK. A not-very-friendly Internet term for the belief that a playstyle which is consensual and fundamentally safe is somehow just "too much."

**YMMV:** An Internet acronym for "your mileage may vary." Indicates that the writer's experience may not hold true for the reader.

# Appendix I
# Sample Event Rules

### *Sample Rules for a Party Given by "The Club"* _____

Welcome! Please read tonight's rules carefully. Your questions, comments, and recommendations for future changes are welcomed by the Party Director. If, after reading these rules, you feel that you cannot agree to them, please leave the party. Your money will be refunded. If you stay more than 20 minutes after being shown these rules, you have agreed to abide by them.

1. Ask before touching.
   Do not touch another person's body, clothing, or equipment without their specific permission.

2. Everybody here is equal and entitled to courteous treatment.
   A. A person is permitted to act dominant, or submissive, to you only after you have agreed to that.
   B. An offer to play is not an insult. If you must decline an offer to play, please do so as politely as possible.

3. Respect the privacy of scenes in progress.
   A. Watch from a non-intrusive distance.
   B. Do not interrupt a scene in progress for routine questions or conversation.
   C. Join a scene in progress only with the dominant's permission. It is usually preferable to wait to be asked.
   D. Do not make negative comments about a scene in such a way that the players can hear.
   E. If you have safety questions or other concerns about a scene in progress, please communicate them immediately to the Dungeon Monitor (preferably) or to the Party Director. Do not try to handle the situation yourself.

4. Keep social conversation in the social areas.
    A. Please hold ordinary conversations in the social areas. When in the play area, please keep your voices low.

B. Please do not sit on or near play equipment unless you're using it or about to use it.

5. Keep your SM play safe.
    A. Play involving any sort of suffocation, strangulation, or firearm (or other projectile weapon) is strictly prohibited.
    B. Electricity play, piercing, cutting, and so forth may be done only by experienced, properly equipped, players and only after receiving the advance permission of the Dungeon Monitor.
    C. Needle points protruding from skin must be blunted with tape, cork, or similar material if the pierced person is moving about the party.
    D. Bondage may not impair circulation, feeling, or balance. Mouth stuffing must be attached to the gag.
    E. Watch your backswing! Make sure the area beside, behind, and above you stays clear.
    F. Anyone who has been bound to an fixed object, such as a chair or post, must be kept under close, constant watch by a specified person who stays within "lunge distance" (typically no more than 20 feet) of the bound person.
    G. In order to prevent an injury-causing fall, a person whose hands have been bound behind them or secured by their sides, and/or a person whose legs are restrained in any way, must be escorted by a "spotter" while they move from place to place. This spotter must remain within arm's reach.

6. Think carefully about sexual behavior.
    A. The Club recommends but does not require that physical barriers be used during sexual activity. However, please think very carefully about with whom and how you will be sexual. Remember the risks involved! Condoms, gloves, and other safer-sex supplies (for party use only, please) are available at no cost.
    B. All body fluids must be contained within the scene. (No blood spraying from the ends of whips!) Thoroughly clean up any blood, semen, and so forth immediately after you play. Cleaning supplies are readily available.
    C. Please do not use a piece of equipment that might have one person's fluids on it on another person. Please do not leave soiled equipment where another person might sit or step on it.

7. Respect people's privacy.
    A. Some guests must remain deeply "in the closet" about where they live, their real names, their profession, what company they work for, and so forth. Please refrain from asking direct questions about these areas. It's fine if they volunteer information, but don't probe.
    B. Disclosing another person's name, address, phone number, or other personal information without their specific consent is extremely serious misconduct.
    C. Photographing, taping, or otherwise making any record is generally discouraged and may be done only after obtaining consent of the Party Director and the people involved.

8. No pestering!
    A. If your second offer to play with a particular person is declined, please don't make a third offer at this particular party.
    B. If someone says to you, "Please leave me alone," that is considered a "social safeword." Do not initiate further conversation with them or hover near them for the rest of the event.
    C. Single women at the event are not necessarily there as dates or partners for the single men.

9. Pay attention to special announcements.
    A short announcement after the doors close will cover party rules, house rules, announcements, and so forth. All guests must attend.

10. No violence, threats, or challenges.
    Starting a fight, over-reacting to provocation, threatening another person in any way, or challenging them to fight either at the event or "outside," is extremely serious misconduct.

11. The Party Director is in overall charge.
    His decisions are binding for the duration of the event. Failure to obey the party rules or otherwise disturbing the event may result in being told to leave the party. In such a case, no refund will be made. Refusing to leave the party promptly after being told to leave by the Party Director may result in the police being called. The Club reserves the right to suspend and/or remove apparent violators from its mailing list and to notify other SM clubs and related entities of any apparent misconduct.

12. Safewords, etc.
    A. "Safeword" itself is a "Mayday!" emergency signal indicating that the person calling it wants outside help and/or intervention from the Dungeon Monitor, Party Director, and their assistants in ending a scene or otherwise needs urgent assistance.

B. "Two thumps" is the non-verbal equivalent of calling "safeword."
C. "Two squeezes" can be used by the Dungeon Monitor to check on someone's well-being.
D. Depending on available facilities, people may be able to play in private. However, doors may not be locked to prevent entry. After obtaining permission from the Party Director, a "do not disturb" sign may be put up for up to one hour. The Dungeon Monitor and the Party Director may enter any "do not disturb" area as often as they feel necessary to check on the participants' well-being. The use of gags, hoods, and other speech-restricting devices during "in private" play is prohibited.

13. Help us keep a low profile.
    A. Please avoid blood-curdling screams, high-pitched shrieks, and other sounds that might alarm people outside the party.
    B. Verbal play must not be so loud that it disturbs other scenes.
    C. Please arrive at the party door wearing relatively normal outer clothing.

14. You are responsible for the behavior of your guests.
    A. Each person who has been directly invited may bring guests if approved in advance by the Party Director. All guests must have passed their 21st birthday.
    B. If you bring guests, you are responsible for making sure they know what kind of a party this is, what the rules are, and that they can emotionally handle being at such an event. You are responsible for their behavior.

15. Drugs, alcohol and tobacco.
    A. Intoxication of any kind that leads to unsafe or objectionable behavior will not be tolerated.
    B. The Club does not serve alcohol. Guest may bring beer or wine (only). No hard liquor or illegal drugs are allowed.
    C. All smoking is to be done outside or in designated areas.

16. You attend at your own risk.
    Attendees understand and agree that participating in or being around SM activity and other forms of erotic play is always distinctly risky and agree to assume all risks. With the exception of intentional, malicious misconduct or extremely gross negligence on the part of those most directly and specifically involved, nobody associated with hosting or attending a The Club event is at all responsible or liable for any sort of loss, harm, or other damages.

17. These parties are (only) for the private, personal enjoyment of the attendees.
   If you believe someone may be attending for any other reason, please inform the Party Director.

18. Please help keep the space clean.
   Please properly dispose of your plates, cups, and so forth. Clean up completely after your scenes.

19. Please share the special equipment.
   So that others may enjoy using them too, please limit your usage of special large items of equipment such as slings, posts, and so forth to no more than one hour unless given prior permission by the Party Director.

20. Dress code.
   The Club has no special dress code per se, but advises attendees that fetish-type clothing is certainly welcome and admired.

21. Special rules for single-energy parties.
   At one-gender-dominant parties, we ask that a person of the dominant gender be in direct, immediate control of any scene in progress. A person of the dominant gender may bottom to another person of the dominant gender. A person of the submissive gender may top another person of the submissive gender only if a member of the dominant gender is in immediate control of the scene. We ask that people of the submissive gender not top members of the dominant gender.

## Sample Rules for a "Truth or Dare" Game

1. Spectators, wimps that they are, may be asked to go elsewhere for the duration of the game. Players only!

2. An Umpire is chosen by majority vote. This Umpire is issued "the Wuss paddle." (Loud whack. Little pain.)

3. The Umpire picks a person to start the round.

4. That person looks at another person and asks "truth or dare?"

5. The questioned person may respond with "truth," "dare," or "your choice."

6. If "truth" is chosen, the person must answer a "fair" question truthfully. (Cracking a joke will not be considered an adequate answer.) Questions may be probing and pointed but, because the point of the game is to have fun, may not be harsh, mean-spirited, or violate serious "real world"

confidentiality matters. Answers should take less than two minutes. (No filibustering!) If the Umpire rules that the question is unfair, the asked person may either request another question or that the Umpire award them a "pass."

7. If "dare" is chosen, the person must perform the requested action. A "fair" dare must be something that can be done then and there, and take less than two minutes. Dares may not be physically dangerous. Dares involving explicit sexual contact, including self-play, may be declined without penalty (or, of course, accepted). Dares involving nudity are fair. Dares involving additional people may be done only with their consent. If the Umpire rules that the dare is unfair, the asked person may either request another dare or that the Umpire award them a "pass."

8. If the Umpire determines that the person has inadequately responded to a fair question or a fair dare, that person has revealed that they are a *Wuss*. They must then turn their back to the group, expose their bare buttocks, and accept three swats, administered by the Umpire, from "the Wuss paddle."

9. After the asked person has successfully completed their "truth or dare," or been awarded a "pass," or "wussed out," it is then their turn to ask "truth or dare" of someone else. This must be someone in the circle who has not yet been asked that question. (Don't forget the person who started the round.) The Umpire may either decline to answer a "truth or dare" or may appoint a "Deputy Umpire" to manage the game during their turn. A round is over when all (except possibly the Umpire) have been asked "truth or dare."

10. At the end of the round, if people wish, a new Umpire can be chosen and another round started.

## Sample Rules for a Tops & Bottoms Auction _____

1. Each attendee will be handed an envelope of play money upon admission. Each attendee will receive an equal amount.

2. *[for fund-raising events]* Additional play money will be available for purchase throughout the evening. $5,000 in play money can be purchased for $5.

3. If you would like to be auctioned off, please fill out an Auctioneer's Information Form. You may choose to be auctioned as a top, a bottom, or a switch. If you prefer to be purchased by men only or women only,

please indicate that on the form. Also, please indicate any particular limits or desires, or any special service that you are "selling."

The form includes space for a brief "marketing statement." The Auctioneer will be sure to include this statement when he auctions you off. Be creative!

4. Purchasers are buying the "first right of negotiation" with the people they purchase. Having bought someone does not entitle you to exceed their limits, or to do anything beyond what you negotiate with them. Both parties are encouraged to be cooperative and flexible.

5. Any play that is purchased or negotiated may take place here at the event, or at another time and place, at both parties' discretion.

6. If you are bought, you receive the money spent on you. You can spend that money on purchases of your own lataer in the evening.

7. Trading, bartering, coalition-building, and other underhanded practices are encouraged. Several people may pool their money for a purchase, and share the results of that purchase as they and their acquisition deem fit.

# Appendix II: SM and the Internet

One of the greatest changes that has occurred since "SM 101" was first published has been the explosive growth of the Internet.

This international network of computers has revolutionized the nature of how information moves through society, and its influence is pervasive. Tens of millions of people are "on-line," and each day sees thousands more joining them.

The Internet offers numerous possibilities. The major benefit for most people seems to be the ability to send and receive electronic mail, called e-mail, quickly and at very little cost.

Another major benefit is the ability to participate in discussion forums called newsgroups, where people post messages relating to various topics. To get an idea of how quickly the Internet is growing, consider that when I went on-line in May of 1994 there were about 5000 newsgroups devoted to various topics. As I write this in September of 1997, there are over 21,000 newsgroups.

(I had been thinking more and more about getting on the Internet for some time, but two events at the 1993 World Science Fiction convention pushed me over the edge. 1. Another SM publisher told me that she was processing at least half a dozen requests for her e-mail catalog per day, and 2. a very attractive lady that I was having a wonderful conversation with gave me her card so that we could stay in touch – and the only contact information on it was her e-mail address.)

A third benefit is the ability to put up what's called a "web page" that describes yourself, your interests, your company or other matters. If you want to get lots of SM information quickly, use your web browser to search on the phrase "BDSM."

A fourth benefit is the ability to engage in "chat" with other people who are also logged on at the same time. This can take place in "chat rooms" that exist inside the confines of large Internet service providers such as America Online or Compuserve, or out on the Internet as a whole on what's called Internet Relay Chat or IRC for short.

Other Internet technologies that may be of use to you are FTP (File Transfer Protocol), which enables you to post and obtain large files and pieces of software, and telnet, which can hook you up to any of the adult computer bulletin board services (BBSs) around the nation that have telnet capability.

Given their tendency to be highly intelligent and adventuresome, it should come as no surprise to learn that a very large number of SM poeple are on the Internet. Indeed, I know of at least four party groups that only send out invitations over the Internet. If you don't have an e-mail address, you literally can't be directly invited.

The newsgroups are a special interest of mine. The most popular one is called soc.subculture.bondage-bdsm (an offshoot of a group called alt.sesx.bondage, which became so overrun with unwanted ads that it nearly ceased to function). Newsgroups called alt.sex.femdom and soc.sexuality.spanking also exist. If you're looking for a kinky partner, check out alt.bondage.personals and alt.spanking.personals to see what they offer. Do a search on the word "personal" to find literally dozens of other newsgroups devoted to personal ads of various types.

Many other sexuality related newsgroups exist. Try searching on the words "gay," "lesbian," "bi," and "bisex" if those are interests of yours. Leave the comma out. Also try a search on the term "motss," which stands for members of the same sex.

One thing to keep in mind is that e-mail does not come with the expecta-tion of privacy that regular mail has. Your e-mail may bounce to several different sites before it reaches the sender. That being so, think twice before putting anything in e-mail that you wouldn't want anybody besides the sender to see.

The business of being an Internet Service Provider (ISP) has become very hotly competitive. Be sure to shop around and compare rates and policies. Be especially leery of ISPs that charge per-hour charges. As of this writing, good, basic service can be purchased for about $15 to $30 per month in the Bay Area, with unlimited access time. Also, some ISPs are very comfortable when it comes to adult material, while others are much more resistant.

One interesting aspect of the Internet, particularly its interactive venues such as chat rooms and IRC, it that it's possible to engage in "cyberplay" SM. Indeed, there are many people who have done hundreds of hours of cyberplay SM but have almost no real-life experience. It's easy to assume that since cyberplay isn't "real," you don't have to negotiate. In fact, though, cyberplay has most of the same emotional (if not physical) risks as face-to-face play; negotiate it as carefully. Cyberplay can also involve real-world danger – I heard of one woman whose "cyber-master" commanded her to chain herself to a park bench, with the key in a block of ice beside her.

One aspect of this is to keep in mind that you can never be entirely sure of who is sitting on the other terminal. Unless you've met them, you can't tell if the other person is male or female, or how old they really are, or anything else about them. Even if you have met them before, you don't *really* know who is sitting at that other keyboard. It could be someone else using that person's account. Also, it's relatively easy to keep permanent logs of cyberSM sessions – logs that could embarrass you later.

Finally, there is a code of on-line courtesy called "netiquette." Because of the relatively anonymous and impersonal nature of this medium, entirely too many people feel that it's OK to act like jerks. Keep in mind that (even though it's not readily apparent) there is another thinking, feeling human being at the other terminal, and behave accordingly.

You've heard of a gateway resource? (A phrase I coined which is seeing wider usage). The Internet is the gateway of all gateways.

# Appendix III

# A Monograph on Breath Control Play

*Excerpted from an article posted to alt.sex.bondage in August, 1996, entitled "The Medical Realities of Breath Control Play."*

For some time now, I have felt that the practices of suffocation and/or strangulation done in an erotic context (generically known as breath control play; more properly known as asphyxiophilia) were in fact far more dangerous than they are generally perceived to be. As a person with years of medical education and experience, I know of no way whatsoever that either suffocation or strangulation can be done in a way that does not intrinsically put the recipient at risk of cardiac arrest. (There are also numerous additional risks; more on them later.)

Furthermore, and my *biggest* concern, I know of no reliable way to determine when such a cardiac arrest has become imminent. Often the first detectable sign that an arrest is approaching is the arrest itself. Furthermore, if the recipient does arrest, the probability of resuscitating them, even with optimal CPR, is distinctly small. Thus the recipient is dead and their partner, if any, is in a very perilous legal situation. (The authorities could consider such deaths first-degree murders until proven otherwise, with the burden of such proof being on the defendant).

There are also the real and major concerns of the surviving partner's own life-long remorse about having caused such a death, and the trauma to the friends and family members of both parties.

Some breath control fans say that what they do is acceptably safe because they do not take what they do up to the point of unconsciousness. I find this statement a bit worrisome for two reasons: (1) You can't really know when a person is about to go unconscious until they actually do so, thus it's extremely difficult to know where the actual point of unconsciousness is until you actually reach it. (2) More importantly, unconsciousness is a symptom, not a condition in and of itself. It can have underlying causes ranging from simple fainting to cardiac arrest, and which of these will cause the unconsciousness cannot be known in advance.

I have discussed my concerns regarding breath control with well over a dozen SM-positive physicians, and with numerous other SM-positive health professionals, and all share my concerns. We have discussed how breath control might be done in a way that is not life-threatening, and come up blank. We have discussed how the risk might be significantly reduced, and come up blank. We have discussed how it might be determined that an arrest is imminent, and come up blank. Indeed, so far not one (repeat, not one) single physician, nurse, paramedic, chiropractor, physiologist, or other person with substantial training in how a human body works has been willing to step forth and teach a form of breath control play that they are willing to assert is acceptably safe– i.e., does not put the recipient at imminent risk of dying. I believe this fact makes a major statement.

Other "edge play" topics such as suspension bondage, electricity play, cutting, piercing, branding, enemas, water sports, and scat play can and have been taught with reasonable safety, but not breath control play. Indeed, it seems that the more somebody knows about how a human body works, the more likely they are to caution people about how dangerous breath control is, and about how little can be done to reduce the degree of risk.

In many ways, oxygen is to the human body, and particularly to the heart and brain, what oil is to a car's engine. Indeed, there's a medical adage that goes "hypoxia (becoming dangerously low on oxygen) not only stops the motor, but also wrecks the engine." Therefore, asking how one can play safely with breath control is very similar to asking how one can drive a car safely while draining it of oil. Some people tell the "mechanics" something like, "Well, I'm going to drain my car of oil anyway, and I'm not going to keep track of how low the oil level is getting while I'm driving my car, so tell me how to do this with as much safety as possible." They then get frustrated when the mechanics scratch their heads and say that they don't know. They may even label such mechanics as "anti-education."

A bit about my background may help explain my concerns. During my ambulance days, I responded to at least one call involving the death of a young teenage boy who died from autoerotic strangulation, and to several other calls where this was suspected but could not be confirmed. (Family members often "sanitize" such scenes before calling 911.) Additionally, I personally know two members of my local SM community who went to prison after their partners died during breath control play.

The primary danger of suffocation play is that it is not a condition that gets worse over time (regarding the heart, anyway; it does get worse over time regarding the brain). Rather, what happens is that the more the play is prolonged, the greater the odds that a cardiac arrest will occur. Sometimes even one minute of suffocation can cause this; sometimes even less.

Quick pathophysiology lesson #1: When the heart gets low on oxygen, it starts to fire off "extra" pacemaker sites. These usually appear in the ventricles and are thus called premature ventricular contractions – PVCs for short. If a PVC happens to fire off during the electrical repolarization phase of cardiac contraction (the dreaded "PVC on T" phenomenon, also sometimes called "R on T") it can kick the heart over into ventricular fibrillation – a form of cardiac arrest. The lower the heart gets on oxygen, the more PVCs it generates, and the more vulnerable to their effect it becomes, thus hypoxia increases both the probability of a PVC-on-T occurring and of its causing a cardiac arrest. When this will happen to a particular person in a particular session is simply not predictable. This is exactly where most of the medical people I have discussed this topic with "hit the wall."

Virtually all medical folks know that PVCs are both life-threatening and hard to detect unless the patient is hooked to a cardiac monitor. When medical folks discuss breath control play, the question quickly becomes: How can you know when they start throwing PVCs? The answer is: You basically can't.

Quick pathophysiology lesson #2: When breathing is restricted, the body cannot eliminate carbon dioxide as it should, and the amount of carbon dioxide in the blood increases. Carbon dioxide ($CO_2$) and water ($H_2O$) exist in equilibrium with what's called carbonic acid ($H_2CO_3$) in a reaction catalyzed by an enzyme called carbonic anhydrase. Thus: $CO_2 + H_2O$ <carbonic anhydrase> $H_2CO_3$. A molecule of carbonic acid dissociates on its own into a molecule of what's called bicarbonate ($HCO_3-$) and an (acidic) hydrogen ion. ($H+$). Thus: $H_2CO_3$ <> $HCO_3-$ and $H+$. The overall pattern is: $H_2O + CO_2$ <> $H_2CO_3$ <> $HCO_3- + H+$ Therefore, if breathing is restricted, $CO_2$ builds up and the reaction shifts to the right in an attempt to balance things out, ultimately making the blood more acidic and thus decreasing its pH. This is called respiratory acidosis. (If the patient hyperventilates, they "blow off $CO_2$" and the reaction shifts to the left, thus increasing the pH. This is called respiratory alkalosis, and has its own dangers.)

Quick pathophysiology lesson #3: Again, if breathing is restricted, not only does carbon dioxide have a hard time getting out, but oxygen also has a hard time getting in. A molecule of glucose breaks down within the cell into two molecules of an acid called pyruvate, thus creating a small amount of ATP for the body to use as energy. Under normal circumstances, pyruvate quickly combines with oxygen to produce a much larger amount of ATP. However, if there's not enough oxygen to properly metabolize the acidic pyruvate, it builds up and produces one form of what's called a metabolic acidosis. As you can see, either a build-up in the blood of carbon dioxide or a decrease in the blood of oxygen will cause the pH of the blood to fall. If both occur at the same time, as they do in cases of suffocation, the pH of the blood will plummet to life-threatening levels within a very few minutes. The pH of normal human blood is in the 7.35 to 7.45 range (slightly alkaline). A pH falling to 6.9 (or raising to 7.8) is "incompatible with life." Past experience, either with others or with that same person, is not particularly useful. Carefully watching their level of consciousness, skin color, and pulse rate is of only limited value. Even hooking the bottom up to both a pulse oximeter and a cardiac monitor (assuming you had either piece of equipment, and they're not cheap) would be of only limited additional value. While an experienced clinician can sometimes detect PVCs by feeling the patient's pulse, in reality the only reliable way to detect them is to hook the patient up to a cardiac monitor. The problem is that each PVC is potentially lethal, particularly if the heart is low on oxygen. Even if you "ease up" on the bottom immediately, there's no telling when the PVCs will stop. They could stop almost at once, or they could continue for hours.

In addition to the primary danger of cardiac arrest, there is good evidence to document that there is a very real risk of cumulative brain damage if the practice is repeated often enough. In particular, laboratory studies of repeated brief interruption of blood flow to the brains of animals and studies of people with what's called "sleep apnea syndrome" (in which they stop breathing for up to two minutes while sleeping) document that cumulative brain damage does occur in such cases. There are many documented additional dangers. These include, but are *not* limited to: rupture of the windpipe, fracture of the larynx, damage to the blood vessels in the neck, dislodging a fatty plaque in a neck artery which then travels to the brain and causes a stroke, damage to the cervical spine, seizures, airway obstruction by the tongue, and aspiration of vomitus. Additionally, there are documented cases in which the recipient appeared to fully recover but was found dead several hours later. The American Psychiatric Association estimates a death rate of one person per year per million of population – thus about 250 deaths last year in the U.S. Law enforcement estimates go as much as four times higher.

Most such deaths occur during solo play, however there are many documented cases of deaths that occurred during play with a partner. It should be noted that the presence of a partner does nothing to limit the primary danger, and does little or nothing to limit most of the secondary dangers.

Some people teach that choking can be safely done if pressure on the windpipe is avoided. Their belief is that pressing on the arteries leading to the brain while avoiding pressure on the windpipe can safely cause unconsciousness. The reality, unfortunately, is that pressing on the carotid arteries, *exactly* as they recommend, presses on baroreceptors known as the carotid sinus bodies. These bodies then cause vasodilation in the brain; thus, there is not enough blood to perfuse the brain and the recipient loses consciousness. However, that's not the whole story.

Unfortunately, a message is also sent to the main pacemaker of the heart, via the vagus nerve, to decrease the rate and force of the heartbeat. Most of the time, under strong vagal influence, the rate and force of the heartbeat decreases by one third. However, every now and then, the rate and force decreases to zero and the bottom "flatlines" into asystole – another, and more difficult to cope with, form of cardiac arrest. There is no way to tell whether or not this will happen in any particular instance, or how quickly. There are many documented cases of as little as five seconds of choking causing a vagal-outflow-induced cardiac arrest.

For the reason cited above, many police departments have now either entirely banned the use of choke holds or have reclassified them as a form of deadly force. Indeed, a local CHP officer recently had a $250,000 judgment brought against him after a nonviolent suspect died while being choked by him.

Finally, as a CPR instructor myself, I want to caution that knowing CPR does little to make the risk of death from breath control play significantly smaller. While CPR can and should be done, understand that the probability of success is likely to be less than 10%.

I'm not going to state that breath control is something that nobody should ever do under any circumstances. I have no problem with informed, freely consenting people taking any degree of risk they wish. I am going to state that there is a great deal of ignorance regarding what actually happens to a body when it's suffocated or strangled, and that the actual degree of risk associated with these practices is far greater than most people believe. I have noticed that, when people are educated regarding the severity and unpredictability of the risks, fewer and fewer choose to play in this area, and those who do continue tend to play less often. I also notice that, because of its severe and unpredictable risks, more and more SM partygivers are banning any form of breath control play at their events.

If you'd like to look into this matter further, here are some references to get you started: "Medical Physiology" by Guyton; "Emergency Care in the Streets" by Caroline; "The Pathologic Basis of Disease" by Robbins; "Textbook of Advanced Cardiac Life Support" by American Heart Association; "Forensic Pathology" by DeMaio and Demaio; "Autoerotic Fatalities" by Hazelwood; Journal of Forensic Sciences. People with questions or comments can contact me at jaybob@crl.com or write to me at P.O. Box 1261, Berkeley, CA 94701.

## BDSM/KINK

**The Artisan's Book of Fetishcraft** *(fall 2013)*
John Huxley                                   $27.95

**At Her Feet: Powering Your Femdom Relationship**
TammyJo Eckhart and Fox                       $14.95

**... But I Know What You Want: 25 Sex Tales for the Different**
James Williams                                $13.95

**The Compleat Spanker**
Lady Green                                    $12.95

**Conquer Me: girl-to-girl wisdom about fulfilling your submissive desires**
Kacie Cunningham                              $13.95

**Erotic Tickling**
Michael Moran                                 $13.95

**Family Jewels: A Guide to Male Genital Play and Torment**
Hardy Haberman                                $12.95

**Flogging**
Joseph Bean                                   $12.95

**The Human Pony: A Guide for Owners, Trainers and Admirers**
Rebecca Wilcox                                $27.95

**Intimate Invasions: The Ins and Outs of Erotic Enema Play**
M.R. Strict                                   $13.95

**Jay Wiseman's Erotic Bondage Handbook**
Jay Wiseman                                   $16.95

**The Kinky Girl's Guide to Dating**
Luna Grey                                     $16.95

**The (New and Improved) Loving Dominant**
John Warren                                   $16.95

**The Mistress Manual: A Good Girl's Guide to Female Dominance**
Mistress Lorelei                              $16.95

**The New Bottoming Book**
**The New Topping Book**
Dossie Easton & Janet W. Hardy          $14.95 ea.

**Play Piercing**
Deborah Addington                             $13.95

**Radical Ecstasy: SM Journeys to Transcendence**
Dossie Easton & Janet W. Hardy                $16.95

**The Seductive Art of Japanese Bondage**
Midori, photographs by Craig Morey            $27.95

**The Sexually Dominant Woman: A Workbook for Nervous Beginners**
Lady Green                                    $11.95

## GENERAL SEXUALITY

**A Hand In the Bush: The Fine Art of Vaginal Fisting**
Deborah Addington                             $13.95

**The Jealousy Workbook: Exercises and Insights for Managing Open Relationships** *(fall 2013)*
Kathy Labriola                                $19.95

**Love In Abundance: A Counselor's Advice on Open Relationships**
Kathy Labriola                                $15.95

**Phone Sex: Oral Skills and Aural Thrills**
Miranda Austin                                $15.95

**Sex Disasters... And How to Survive Them**
C. Moser, Ph.D., M.D. & Janet W. Hardy   $16.95

**Tricks... To Please a Man**
**Tricks... To Please a Woman**
both by Jay Wiseman                      $13.95 ea.

**When Someone You Love Is Kinky**
Dossie Easton & Catherine A. Liszt            $15.95

## TOYBAG GUIDES:
**A Workshop In A Book**                  $9.95 each

**Age Play,** by Bridgett "Lee" Harrington

**Basic Rope Bondage,** by Jay Wiseman

**Canes and Caning,** by Janet W. Hardy

**Chastity Play,** by Miss Simone *(spring 2014)*

**Clips and Clamps,** by Jack Rinella

**Dungeon Emergencies & Supplies,** by Jay Wiseman

**Erotic Knifeplay,** by Miranda Austin & Sam Atwood

**Foot and Shoe Worship,** by Midori

**High-Tech Toys,** by John Warren

**Hot Wax and Temperature Play,** by Spectrum

**Medical Play,** by Tempest

**Playing With Taboo,** by Mollena Williams

---

*Greenery Press books are available from your favorite on-line or brick-and-mortar bookstore or erotic boutique, or direct from The Stockroom, www.stockroom.com, 1-800-755-TOYS.*
*These and other Greenery Press books are also available in ebook format from all major ebook retailers.*